This book was developed by STEVEN PENSINGER, Inc.

THE McGRAW-HILL COLLEGE HANDBOOK

1 2 3 4 5 6 7 8 9 0 FGR FGR 9 5 4 3 2 1 0

ISBN 0-07-040416-X

This book was set in New Baskerville by Progressive Typographers, Inc.
The editors were Steve Pensinger and Jeannine Ciliotta;
the designer was Jo Jones;
the production supervisor was Janelle S. Travers.
The cover was designed by Joseph Gillians.
Arcata Graphics/Fairfield was printer and binder.

Library of Congress Cataloging-in-Publication Data

Marius, Richard.
    The McGraw-Hill college handbook/Richard Marius, Harvey S. Wiener.
        p.   cm.
    Includes index.
    ISBN 0-07-040416-X
    1. English language — Grammar —1950-   2. English language —
Rhetoric.   I. Wiener, Harvey S.   II. Title
PE1112.M33   1991
808′.042— dc20   90-13381

W9-ARM-253

The
McGraw-Hill

COLLEGE
HANDBOOK

THIRD EDITION

Richard Marius
Harvard University

Harvey S. Wiener
The City University of New York

McGRAW-HILL, INC.

New York   St. Louis   San Francisco   Auckland   Bogo
Caracas   Hamburg   Lisbon   London   Madrid
Mexico   Milan   Montreal   New Delhi
Paris   San Juan   São Paulo
Singapore   Sydney
Tokyo   Toronto

ABOUT
THE AUTHORS

Richard Marius has been the Director of Expository Writing at Harvard since 1978, in charge of a required freshman course that all Harvard students must take. His program includes a large writing center and inter-disciplinary work in writing across the undergraduate curriculum. He teaches a popular advanced writing course, and in 1990 the student government at Harvard gave him the Levenson Award for outstanding teaching by a member of the senior faculty.

He was born on a farm in Tennessee and worked on a small county newspaper for five years while he was finishing high school and taking a degree in journalism at the University of Tennessee, Knoxville. Later he took the M.A. and the Ph.D. at Yale. He is the author of two biographies, *Luther* in 1974 and *Thomas More* in 1984. *Thomas More* was a finalist in the nonfiction category for the American Book Award. He has published two novels, *The Coming of Rain* in 1969 and *Bound for the Promised Land* in 1976. His third will appear in 1991. He writes a regular book review column for *Harvard Magazine,* and his articles have appeared in publications as diverse as *Esquire* and the medieval journal *Traditio.*

He has published many articles about the teaching of writing, and he has written or coauthored three writing textbooks. Since 1986 he has directed a two-week "Governor's Academy for Writing" in summers for Tennessee teachers from kindergarten through twelfth grade to help them teach writing more effectively. By 1990 over 1200 teachers had attended the Academy, and Tennessee's governor has made him a Tennessee Colonel for his efforts on their behalf.

Harvey S. Wiener, professor of English at LaGuardia Community College, is now University Dean for Academic Affairs of the City University of New York, where he coordinates new program review on the seventeen campuses of CUNY. As Director of the Instructional Resource Center, he

iii

oversees publications and seminars to advance the teaching of reading and writing. He also is adjunct professor of Adult and Higher Education at Columbia Teachers College. He was founding president of the Council of Writing Program Administrators.

He is the author of many books on reading and writing for college students and their teachers, including *The Writing Room* (Oxford, 1981). His book for parents, *Any Child Can Write*, was a Book-of-the-Month Club alternate. A revised edition appeared in 1990. He has written two other books for parents, *Talk With Your Child* (1988) and *Any Child Can Read Better* (1990). He has written for network television and was trained in Columbia Broadcasting System's daytime television Writer Development Project. He is a member of the Standing Committee on Assessment of the National Council of Teachers of English and he was chair of the Teaching of Writing Division of the Modern Language Association (1987).

Born in Brooklyn, he has worked in public education for thirty years. He has taught writing and literature at every level of education from elementary school to graduate school. A Phi Beta Kappa graduate from Brooklyn College, he holds a Ph.D. in Renaissance literature from Fordham University. He has won grants from the National Endowment for the Humanities, the Fund for Improvement of Postsecondary Education, the Exxon Education Foundation, and the Ford Foundation.

CONTENTS

PART THREE
USING WORDS EFFECTIVELY

BOOK TWO
USAGE RULES AND OPTIONS

PART FOUR
**UNDERSTANDING GRAMMAR AND WRITING CORRECT
SENTENCES**

**BOOK THREE
SPECIAL WRITING TASKS**

**PART SEVEN
WRITING A RESEARCH PAPER**

PART EIGHT
OTHER WRITING TASKS

PREFACE

To the Teacher

The *McGraw-Hill College Handbook* assumes that students must write regularly and revise continually if they are to become good writers. We show students how to revise and how to think about their writing so that they become their own best critics. We have practiced this, our own philosophy, in preparing the third edition of the *McGraw-Hill College Handbook*. In the first and second editions, we worked hard at providing clear explanations of both the process and the product of writing. How do writers write? What can they do to make their work clear, logical, and (we hope the word is not out of date) elegant? We considered these issues always with the students in mind, always with the desire to convey to students the results of our study in language in a way that was friendly without being condescending, clear without being shallow, and accurate without being pedantic. The testimony of the several hundred teachers and thousands of students who have used this book throughout the United States and Canada has been that we succeeded.

Once again, we focus as much on process as we do on product. Too often handbooks have focused on showing students a correct writing product without telling them how to produce one. In our chapters on the writing process, we have given a realistic account of how writers write by providing drafts of a typical freshman student's paper and showing the changes made by the writer on the way to a final draft. Students who follow our trail through the process will arrive at a piece of work that will make them proud of their effort and their accomplishment.

We expect this book to be used in freshman composition classes and in other courses in writing offered by English departments. We value literature, and we draw many examples from it. But we also think that students should learn to write well in courses across the entire curriculum. Therefore we have assumed throughout that students can be helped by our book in whatever courses they take. We provide examples from writing about history, psychology, economics, physics, biology, business, engineering, and sports (to name just a few areas of many) to illustrate our conviction that good writing is valuable in any discipline.

We have looked for a comfortable middle ground between the extreme positions about rules for writing. We have tried to be neither too rigid nor too flexible in our presentations and interpretation of the rules. We start with the simple assumption that students do not learn to write by memorizing the rules. They learn to write by discovering that they have something to say and by learning then that there are ways of saying it clearly and effectively.

There are rules, but we make a distinction between those that can be broken now and then, and those that cannot. We do not scream in agony at the sight of a split infinitive, but we think writers are confusing if they tack a plural verb onto a singular subject. We think some sentences can end perfectly well with a preposition, but we don't think good writers can use double negatives. Our philosophy is that writing is guided by principles rather than rules, and we have tried to state those principles clearly and to illustrate them by the work of good contemporary authors.

In This Edition

In our effort to be comprehensive, we discovered that we had made the second edition very long. In developing the third edition, we have tried to remember what Shakespeare said, that brevity is the soul of wit. Our goal for this revision has been to be even sharper and more efficient than we were in the earlier editions and to provide examples, explanations, and exercises that will be helpful both to the students who must struggle to write anything and to those who are good writers already when they come to college.

We have made several important changes in this edition: We have streamlined discussions and updated examples and exercises to keep our work lively and relevant to students' needs. The design has been redone to make the book even more attractive and practical to use. We have revised every chapter so that concepts are clearly stated and well illustrated.

We have thoroughly revised our presentation of the writing process and improved the section on research papers dramatically. We condensed the chapters on writing research papers, but we still provide ample information to help students see what research is and to help them go about it efficiently. We show both the APA style of referencing and MLA style common since 1984.

Reviewers and users of the two previous editions of *The McGraw-Hill College Handbook* commented warmly on its stylistic excellence. We have worked hard in this revision to hold to the standard we have set for ourselves. Here and there we have sprinkled wit that is never condescending. We think we have produced a handbook that can be read with pleasure and used with profit. We think we have written a book for these times, and yet a book that respects and uses the strengths of tradition.

Supplements

We have provided a package of aids that teachers will find helpful throughout the course, and supplements that students will find useful in enhancing their work.

For teachers, the aids consist of:

An **Instructor's Manual, Diagnostic Tests,** and **Additional Exercises** that contain teaching tips, answers to exercises, and additional testing materials for the classroom teacher. For these we thank Santi Buscemi of Middlesex County College.

For students, the supplements include:

The McGraw-Hill College Workbook, which includes exercises that may be assigned by the teacher, prepared by John Bean of Seattle University. **The McGraw-Hill On-Line Handbook,** a computer disk that can be stored in memory and accessed to answer students' questions about grammar and usage.

Acknowledgments

We are grateful to the many people who helped us with this book in both its first and second editions. Teaching English composition is probably the most difficult job in any university. Perhaps it is the very difficulty of our profession that makes its members feel so strongly the mutual obligations and respect that bind us all together. We have been the beneficiaries of helpful opinions from many teachers in the field who have reviewed this book at its various stages, and we could not have done our work without their searching commentaries and their generous encouragement.

Because so much of the structure and personality of the two previous editions persists throughout this revision, we would like once again to thank and acknowledge all those who helped with their reviews of this and of the many drafts of the previous editions: Jay Balderson, Western Illinois University; Raymond Brebach, Drexel University; Richard H. Bulloch, Northeastern University; Santi Buscemi, Middlesex County College; David Chapman, Texas Tech University; John Chard, Gloucester County College; Joseph J. Comprone, Michigan Technological University; Virgil Cook, Virginia Polytechnic Institute; Harry H. Crosby, Boston University; Janet Eber, County College of Morris; Robert M. Esch, University of Texas at El Paso; Peter Farley, Adelphi University; James A. Freeman, University of Massachusetts at Amherst; Dennis R. Gabriel, Cuyahoga Community College; Pablo Gonzales, Los Medanos College; Frank Hubbard, Marquette University; Maurice Hunt, Baylor University; Lee A. Jacobus, University of Connecticut, Storrs; Ben Jennings, Virginia Highlands Community College; Larry Kelly, Widener University; Russ Larson, Eastern Michigan University; Peter D. Lindblom, Miami-Dade Community College; Joe Lostracco, Austin Community College; William MacPherson, Essex County College; Sheila J. McDonald, C. W. Post Center, LIU; Donald A. McQuade, University of California, Berkeley; Robert Meeker, Bloomsburg University; Doris Miller, U. S. Air Force Academy; Pat Murray, DePaul University; Sharon Niederman, Metropolitan State, Denver; Rosemary O'Donoghue, Western New England College; Jack B. Oruch, University of Kansas, Lawrence; Margaret Panos, Southeastern Massachusetts University; Compton Rees, University of Connecticut; Karen Reid, Midwestern State University; Kathleen W. Ritch, Santa Fe Community College, Gainesville; Annette T. Rottenberg, University of Massachusetts at Amherst; Donald C. Stewart, Kansas State University, Manhattan; John Stratton, University of Arkansas, Little Rock; Margaret A. Strom, Eastern Maine Technical Institute; Sebastian J. Vasta, Camden Community College; Bryant Wyatt, Virginia State University.

John C. Bean, Seattle University; Kathleen Bell, Old Dominion University; Mark Coleman, Potsdam College; Larry Corse, Clayton State College; Joe Glaser, Western Kentucky University; Rosalie Hewitt, Northern Illinois University; Pat C. Hoy II, Harvard University; Beverly Huttinger, Broward Community College; Larry P. Kent, William Rainey Harper College; Patricia Maida, University of DC; David A. Martin, University of Wisconsin, Milwaukee; Joseph McLaren, Mercy College; Albert H. Nicolai, Jr., Middlesex County College; Della H. Paul, Valencia Community College; Donnetta Heitschmidt Suchon, Daytona Beach Community College; Carroll L. Wilson, Somerset County College.

We want to say too how much we have always enjoyed working together on this book. We have had the exciting pleasure of thinking through our long experience as deeply engaged classroom teachers of writing and the difficult delight of thinking through our glorious English language in its rich and lively American version. We have worked far into the night more times than we can possibly count in producing the three editions of this book. We have not been content to study other textbooks and to rephrase their advice; we have gone directly to the English prose that we both love to see how it works and to express our finding in the spirit of discovery and excitement that stands behind all true scholarship.

We have picked up many debts through the years. Dozens of people at McGraw-Hill have helped, sometimes giving us excellent technical advice, and sometimes making evenings ring with laughter over the dinner table after long, long hours of difficult work.

For this edition we are especially grateful to C. Steven Pensinger, who cheerfully and energetically took this project under his general editorial wing. Jeannine Ciliotta served as the developmental editor, spending hours with us on the telephone, working out an infinity of details. Developmental editors should have a special place in heaven, reserved for those patient and responsible shepherds who manage to keep their sheep from running off in twelve different directions at once. In such a heaven, Jeannine would be a saint.

Both our families have put up with our silences as we have withdrawn to our computers and our desks to write new prose and to prune back old. Our wives receive our loving gratitude not only for their presence but for the enthusiasm they managed to muster when we felt compelled to read to them some nugget of prose that we found especially fine. They managed to say once again that they liked it, too. Above all, they seemed to like us no matter how preoccupied we were with our work.

Perhaps most remarkable, we have worked closely with each other now for more than a decade through three editions with a mutual respect and affection that endure.

Richard Marius

Harvey S. Wiener

TO THE STUDENT

The best way to use this book is to keep it handy as a reference. Pick it up every day and browse through it at random. When your teacher assigns a section, read it carefully and do the exercises to fix its principles in your mind. By all means read Chapters 1 through 4 before you begin to write your first paper.

The index and the plan of the text outlined inside the back covers will help you locate information that deals with your special problems and interests. The correction symbols and the directory of special features on the inside front cover will help you find special sections quickly.

The ability to write well can give you both pleasure and power. You owe it to yourself to discover the joy of writing, the excitement of expressing your ideas, your feelings, your thoughts, your discoveries, your opinions about everything from daily events to the demands of a promising future. As you learn to write well, you will also discover that people are more likely to respect and accept your opinions because you express them in writing that engages and persuades your readers.

Some textbooks seem to promise that they can make writing easy. They are wrong. Good writing always takes hard work, and all writers are sometimes discouraged. Effective writers go back to work after their discouragement and try again. We hope that *The McGraw-Hill College Handbook* can make writing less difficult and can give you guidance and pleasure along the way.

PART ONE
WRITING ESSAYS AND PARAGRAPHS

PART TWO
WRITING CLEAR AND EFFECTIVE SENTENCES

PART THREE
USING WORDS EFFECTIVELY

BOOK ONE

THE WRITING PROCESS

PART
ONE

WRITING ESSAYS AND PARAGRAPHS

CHAPTER

1

PLANNING
A PAPER

Most writing teachers require a paper within the first class session or two. To help you do that early assignment, the first part of this handbook describes the various steps to take from the moment you decide to write something until the time you finish your final draft. Called the **writing process,** these steps involve thinking about a topic, gathering notes, making outlines, deciding on an introduction and a conclusion, and preparing all the drafts that writers produce on their way to a final version. It may involve writing trial sentences or paragraphs that you may want to insert later on in the paper. Of course, writers develop their topics in a variety of ways, so you don't want to think of the writing process as a rigid, defined sequence of activities. Nevertheless, from the time you consider writing something until you actually produce a final manuscript, you do certain things. Sometimes you can skip one thing or another, but most often you must do them all. A finished piece of writing is the product of a developmental process that includes many steps. The first of these steps is a form of preparation called **prewriting.**

1a
Using Prewriting Techniques

The following suggestions for prewriting are presented in no particular sequence. You can use them in any order you find convenient to develop and shape your essay.

Thinking About Your Subject

Good writing begins with clear thinking. Although this point may seem obvious, many students start writing an essay before they have thought about it. As you consider a subject, take your feelings and impulses seriously. You like some things about a subject; you dislike others. Why? Once you start thinking hard about why you have the feelings you do, you may have an idea for a paper.

You should think about your audience. Who will read your paper? What do your readers know already about your topic? What can you tell your readers that they don't know? What thoughts do you have about a subject that your readers may not have had themselves? What do you want your readers to think about you as a writer and a person?

Think about your subject, and try to keep those thoughts as honest as you can. Honesty in judgment is the first step toward producing a good and original paper once you have decided on your general topic.

Learning About Your Topic

Good writing flows out of knowledge. You must know about a topic to write about it well.

Good writers study their subjects. They spend time in libraries. They read popular magazines as well as serious books. They talk to experts. They try out ideas on friends. They think about their subject when they watch television or films; often they will see something that will make them understand their subject in a fresh way. They recall past experiences. They make comparisons.

No matter how familiar you may be with a subject, you can see it better if you talk to another person who is also acquainted with it or with a subject akin to the one you are writing about. Not least among the benefits of talking to someone else is the clarity you may get in your own mind from hearing yourself discuss the subject. Talking about a subject is a good way to know what you are thinking, to discover those areas where you don't have enough information, where you must study some more. Talking about your topic is also an excellent way to narrow it down to something manageable. Your teacher may divide your writing class into small groups so that you can talk to others in the group about what you are doing and listen to them tell you what they are doing.

Listing: Jotting Down Ideas

As soon as you can, start jotting down things you may want to write about in your paper. Moving a hand across a page seems to move the brain. The more you write, the more inspiration you get. Carry your list around with you. Let it grow over several days as your thoughts develop and become more specific — one or two sentences or phrases scribbled in the morning, another few dashed off as you return from class, perhaps something jotted down in class itself.

Here's a sample:

Country Life

living on a farm and hearing the silence at night
My father had a job as teacher in the high school in the consolidated school.
He loved farming.
He had been brought up on a farm and determined to farm, even if it did not make him any money.
We raised our food. Most of it, at least.
beauty of nature
But nature is hard, too.
snakes and birds
killing pigs
the country church
Why did the preacher's wife leave him?
the time I broke the egg in my pocket when I was four or five
the cat I shot in the foot
My father's two personalities: school principal and farmer
his names for everything
He taught us the names of birds, of trees, of plants, and of animals.
how proud he was when Peggy learned to be a good mechanic
working together
his death; the drunk driver
We moved away.

This list records many fragmentary ideas about country life by a student brought up on a farm and trying to work out a subject for the first paper he will do in his writing class. As he thinks about his subject, he realizes that what he has been thinking about most is the influence of his father on him while he was growing up. Now he makes another list.

Subject: My Father's Legacy

My father left me no money.
He left me a lot of pleasures.
his own pleasure about farming
You can have so much pleasure by enjoying the things you do every day.
He was not a daring man.

He tried the farm out, and he liked it, and that's where he stayed.
I can't even say he tried the farm out; that was all he ever knew.

his fascination with small things

Tell the story of how he kept me from disturbing the woodcock. The
mother woodcock on her nest. I didn't see her. He suddenly put his
hand on my arm. We were walking through that little sliver of woods
that separates the pasture from the hay field, and he saw her before I
did and put his hand on my arm and made me stop talking.

Tell something about the community?

He had such a good time with the young people.

But he was tough in school.

the names of things

poison sumac; poison ivy; red maples; red oaks; white oaks; white
pines; loblolly pines. Larks, thrashers, all those birds. King snakes.
Copperheads. Corn snakes.

"Don't kill anything unless it's dangerous to you or you're going to eat
it."

He died in the accident, hit head-on by a drunk driver.

The driver was a senior in the high school.

He'd been to a party where people were drinking hard liquor.

He cried and cried when he found out what he had done.

The writer has defined a limited topic and sees ways of limiting and
defining the topic even more. Notice that the list contains a question. The
writer will try to answer it, to discover whether the subject adds anything
significant to his story. Successive revisions of the list will eliminate some
points, expand others, and add some that are not now on it. Writing the
list prepares you for writing the paper itself.

You can use the same process in composing a paper from texts. As
you read a short story, an essay, or some other text that you must analyze
in a paper, you can jot down ideas about it. When you are going to write
about any text, it's always a good idea to read it through quickly before you
take any notes. But when you go back through and read it again, you can
start writing down some thoughts about it. Jotting down such thoughts
will stimulate your mind to think other thoughts.

Asking the Journalist's Questions

To stimulate ideas, writers frequently ask themselves questions about a
subject. Some questions appear in the two preliminary outlines above.
One good way of organizing questions is to think of the five *w's* of journalism. Reporters are taught to ask *who, what, when, where,* and *why.*

To use the journalistic questions, write your subject at the top of the page. Then, with ample space for your answers, write down as questions *who, what, where, when,* and *why.* You may want to add the question *how.*

You might proceed in the following way:

Who was my father?

Who am I because of him?

Who are the people most different from me because of the farm?

Who were some of the most important people in my father's life?

What did my father like about the farm?

What made him become a schoolteacher?

What did we do on the farm?

What did he teach us?

When did my father and mother buy the farm?

When did I realize that my father loved the farm more than he loved his teaching?

Why did my mother fall in love with him?

Why did she consent to live on the farm?

Where did my father grow up?

Where did my father teach?

Where did he learn everything he knew about nature?

As you ask as many versions of these questions as possible, you start uncovering material that will fit well with your paper. You cannot answer all the questions you raise; you will not want to answer them all because the answers to some of them will not contribute to your paper. But raising a great many questions will help you scan your subject, seeing things in it that may make your writing interesting.

Freewriting: Writing Nonstop for a Stated Time Period

Filling up a page with your writing may help overcome some of the nervousness that often grips people when they sit down to write. Practice **freewriting:** Make yourself spin sentences out ten minutes at a time. Do not get up in that time. Do not stop writing. Do not try to preserve any order. You can leap around all over the place in a writing exercise like this. The ideas will flow. You can gather them up later into coherent forms. The student writing about his memories of his father produced the following nonstop writing. He did not pause to consider whether he was organizing things well, spelling all the words correctly, or getting all the grammar right.

I was scared to death when I got to the college and saw all these people who knew things I didn't know and who looked at me like I was a refugee from a zoo when I said, yes, I really did grow up on a farm, although my father was a high school teacher. When you consider what schoolteachers make, I guess you'd have to say that my father was an odd one — using school teaching to make money enough to let him stay on the farm. He loved tractors, and he loved putting hay in the barn and fixing things and turning up the soil, and I loved it, too. Well, I loved most of it. I hated the cows and milking and the tedium of having to be there morning and night at the same time, and cows are dangerous, too. We never could go anywhere because we had to milk the cows, and we couldn't or my father wouldn't trust anybody to milk the cows for him, although my mother said she thought he was just making an excuse not to have to go anywhere. I think my father loved the farm because it gave him something to do all the time; it occupied his mind. And it kept all of us together. He had been in a close family. We were all a close family. We worked side by side in the fields, and we were a team. There was work that had to be done, and if we didn't do the work, it wouldn't get done, and we'd all suffer. We all had to work together to make it, and there was a lot of satisfaction in that, a lot of pleasure. He took so much pleasure in teaching us things. The names of birds, the names of plants, the names of animals, the names of snakes. "Never kill anything unless it's dangerous or you plan to eat it," he said. A good motto for living in nature. He wouldn't let us kill the king snakes in the corncrib because they ate the rats that ate the corn. I'd rather have the rats myself. But we let the king snakes alone. They kept the copperheads away, too.

These sentences are a long way from a finished essay. But the ideas are beginning to flow. The writer is beginning to get his thoughts in order.

Clustering: Drawing a Subject Tree

The subject tree allows you to jot down ideas in a rough organization, with your general subject as the trunk from which more specific ideas branch off. As you can see, the accompanying subject tree produces a number of ideas that can be developed into a paper. Making up a subject tree helps you identify potential topics in relation to a general subject. The subject tree breaks knowledge down into manageable chunks, and you can then put those chunks together in a paper. It's just a device for **clustering**, tying together various related ideas.

Subject Tree

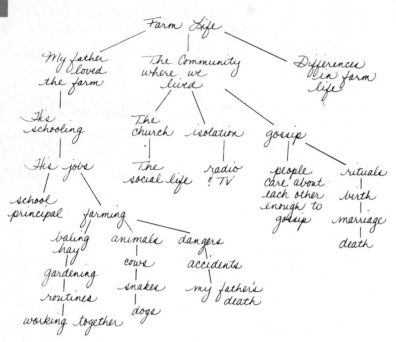

Researching Your Subject

For many topics, reference books, other texts, and magazine articles will suggest ideas you have not thought of yourself. Several hours of browsing in the library and taking notes give many writers just the materials they need to develop a specific topic with confidence. You may also wish to interview people who know about your topic. Many interesting papers do not depend on libraries. Writing a personal experience paper, for example, may not require you to work in the library. But other topics will always be much better if you do some general reading about them. Researching a subject always broadens your understanding and provides important details you can draw on later.

■ **Exercise 1.1** Use some of the prewriting techniques explained on the previous pages to explore one or more of these general subjects:

1. exploration in space
2. drugs and athletes
3. alcohol abuse
4. violence in the movies
5. gun control
6. advertising of tobacco and alcohol
7. exercise
8. religion and morals
9. gender roles for children
10. feminism and parenthood
11. teaching in high school

1b
Limiting the Subject

When you must choose your own subject, you may immediately decide what you want to write about. But most writers arrive at their topics by a slow, uneven process. You may want to write about religion and morals. Thousands of books have been written on that subject. You must boil it down to an essay you can manage in five or six pages. You want your essay to be interesting, to grab attention. If you write in general about religion and morals, you will probably not interest anyone. But suppose you write about the differences among Christians, Muslims, and Jews with respect to drinking alcohol? Suppose you write about the problems of separation between church and state in this country, taking an issue such as prayer in the public schools or federal aid to church-supported schools or the teaching of religion in the public schools? Find out what various religious groups have said on these subjects and you may have the basis for a fine paper.

Sharpening your subject to make it more interesting may take much thought. You may find it easier to develop a specific topic if you take a series of steps to limit it progressively.

Even topics in the column "Still less broad" may be narrowed further. Only you can decide how much to limit your own topics for papers. That decision depends on the physical demands of the task—minimum or

1c plan

✓ CHECKLIST: LIMITING A TOPIC

Too broad	Still too broad	Less broad	Still less broad
exercise	good exercises	jogging	the effects of jogging on the heart and blood pressure
	bad exercises	manic jogging	the damage excessive jogging does to the knees and feet
farm life	my sixteen years on a farm	my father's place in my memories of farm life	the major ways my life on the farm makes me different from city friends
	nature	farmers and nature	nature as beauty and as destructive force in farm life

maximum length, for example — and how much time you have to write. Once you do limit a topic, your ideas about it will expand. Record those ideas as they come to you, and add them to your prewriting materials.

■ **Exercise 1.2**   Using the checklist above as a model, limit, in a series of steps, any five topics in Exercise 1.1.

1c
Planning Your Approach to the Topic

There are four long-established rhetorical categories, or "modes" of writing and speaking — description, narration, exposition, and argumentation. Most writing involves a combination of these modes. You rarely find a description that does not involve narration, a narration that does not have some description in it, or an exposition or argument that does not include the other two. Many papers may include all four. But it helps to know the different modes so you can think about what you are doing as you write and so you can decide which mode ought to predominate in your paper.

☐ **Description** provides a visual image of a scene, an object, or a person.

☐ **Narration** tells a story, usually in chronological sequence.

☐ **Exposition** explains.

☐ **Argument** usually maintains a point of view against other, opposite points of view.

Much college writing is expository because college papers usually explain texts, statistics, observations, or whatever. The line between an expository paper and an argumentative paper may be thin. You may explain your interpretation of a short story, for example, to prove that someone else's interpretation is incorrect. Then your exposition drifts over into argument.

The checklist shows how a writer might develop the same general subject along four distinct lines once a specific purpose is established.

You can see how easy it is to move from one mode to another. You can also see that the final purpose of your paper will lead you to emphasize one of these modes above all the others. If your purpose is to present a convincing argument, you may want to keep description and narration to a minimum. If you want to write a straight news story about an accident, you may not want to make any arguments at all: you will tell what happened; you will write a narrative. If you are explaining the various steps doctors take in treating an accident victim, you may find that telling the story of an actual accident is a distraction.

✓ CHECKLIST: DEVELOPING THE TOPIC

Mode	Purpose
Description	To present a picture of our house and our community in the foothills of the Great Smoky Mountains
Narration	To describe how my family happened to live there and to tell some of the stories that illustrate what sort of man my father was and how he influenced my life
Exposition	To explain some of the attitudes my father had and what effect they had on his life
Argument	To persuade readers that living on the farm with my family was valuable, even in a world where farming is a declining way of life

1c

plan

■ **Exercise 1.3**   Choose one of the topics you have thought of for a paper and jot down some thoughts about the modes you would use to develop it. Answer these questions, perhaps by devoting a short paragraph to each: What would you describe in this paper? What would you narrate? What would you explain? What would you argue?

CHAPTER

2

DEVELOPING
A PAPER

As you develop a paper further, you will do several things to shape it and to give it a clear focus. There is no special order to this process, but there are parts of it that you must consider. You are still using prewriting techniques at this stage of your work.

2a
Considering the Audience

Who will read your writing? Avoid thinking of your audience only as the teacher who will evaluate your paper. Write to appeal to others—your friends, the other members of the class, or other people you know. Try to write to engage the attention of people you admire.

In many respects, you create your audience as you write. If you write sensibly, interestingly, clearly, and with occasional flashes of wit, you will draw the sort of audience that does most of the reading in America. If you write with passionate emotion and uncompromising anger toward everyone who disagrees with you, your audience will be a small group of people whose emotions rule their way of looking at the world. These people do not read to be persuaded of a point of view because they have made up their minds already. If you write in a dull, plodding effort to fill pages and to avoid taking risks, you will get a dull, plodding audience of a few people who will read your prose because they have nothing better to do at the moment. Or you will get an audience of one: your teacher, who is paid to read your writing no matter how dull it is.

You should always think of writing within a discourse community. A **discourse community** is a group with certain interests, knowledge, and expectations and with certain conventional ways of communicating with each other. We usually belong to several discourse communities. Baseball fans make up a discourse community; they talk and write about the game in familiar ways, and they understand each other even though people outside the community may not know what they are talking about. Every baseball fan would understand this sentence:

> Mickey Mantle switch-hit for the Yankees for eighteen seasons, compiling a .298 lifetime batting average and an astonishing slugging average of .557.

For someone outside the baseball fan's discourse community, such a statement is gibberish. But consider this statement from the discourse community that includes biologists:

> Endocytosis of liposomes occurs in a limited class of cells: those that are phagocytic, or able to ingest foreign particles. When phagocytic cells take up liposomes, the cells move the spheres into subcellular organelles known as lysosomes, where the liposomal membranes are thought to be degraded.

> —Marc J. Ostro

To a biologist, these sentences convey clear thoughts; to people outside the discourse community made up of biologists, they are gibberish — just like the baseball fan's language to the nonfan. Historians, specialists in literature, economists, philosophers, astronomers, model-railroad enthusiasts, pilots, engineers, salespeople, stockbrokers, dentists, surgeons, and thousands of other groups have their own discourse communities, within which certain expectations control the way members communicate with each other.

You don't have to define *switch-hitter* to a baseball fan. You don't have to define *liposomes* to a biologist. But you would have to define both these terms to readers outside these two discourse communities.

You determine your audience in part by how much you think you have to explain. Are you writing for people who already know about your subject? Or are you writing for those who might be interested only if you can relate your subject to something in their own experience, which does not happen to include much knowledge about your subject?

In a college writing class, you will usually assume that your audience includes the other members of the class. What do they know about your subject? What do you have to tell them if they are to make sense of what you are saying? If everybody in the class has read *King Lear*, you don't have to summarize the plot; if nobody has read it, a short summary will be in order.

Part of the expectations of any discourse community involve style or tone. For any community, you should write as though you respect the reader and respect the subject that presumably interests you both. Readers familiar with conventional ways of approaching knowledge rebel at reading a style radically different from the conventional style of that discourse community.

In thinking about your audience, keep the journalistic questions in mind. Whenever you introduce a new character or a new piece of information, ask yourself if your readers know who the character is, what is happening, why it is happening, where it is happening, and when it is happening.

■ **Exercise 2.1** Suppose you wanted to write an essay about the positive effects of careful diet on long-range health. Explain how each audience below would influence the content, style, and language of your essay.

1. Overweight business executives
2. Nutritionists who plan hospital meals
3. A class of third-graders
4. One-time coronary patients
5. Teenage women

2b
Choosing Supporting Evidence

When you make assertions, provide some evidence to back them up. You may have strong opinions, but few readers accept opinions just because a writer believes them passionately. You must present details that others can accept as evidence. If your teacher writes "Be specific" in the margin of a paper, she is probably asking you for some details that support some assertion you have made.

If you say, "Faulkner sometimes seems to get lost in his prose and to lose readers, too," quote a text from Faulkner to support your assertion. You may say, "Dickens lamented the plight of the poor in nineteenth-century England, but he seemed to have no solution except the hope that some good rich people would be generous." If you make such an assertion, give some examples from Dickens's novels to support it. If you say, "James Baldwin puzzled over the Swiss villagers who had never seen a black as much as they puzzled over him," back your statement up with something from Baldwin's essay "A Stranger in the Village."

✓ CHECKLIST: KINDS OF EVIDENCE

Source of evidence	Kind of evidence
Personal experience and observation	Concrete sensory details. Describe specific actions, colors, sights, sounds, smells, and tastes to recreate an experience for a reader.
	Dialogues and indirect quotations. By reproducing the words people say, you can enliven a scene.
	Tell stories of events you have witnessed that make you believe something.
Authorities: books, periodicals, TV, radio, films, interviews	Quotations, paraphrases, summaries. Support your points by quoting the words of authorities or by restating their ideas in your own words.
Statistics and cases	Use data (often from charts, graphs, and tables) to lend force to your assertions.
Inferences	Draw conclusions that seem to come from the evidence, though they may not be explicit in the evidence itself.

Considering Various Kinds of Evidence

A paper filled with assertions and lacking details that constitute evidence is nearly always a bad paper. Evidence varies. You may use one kind of evidence for one paper, another kind for a different essay.

Using Inferences Carefully

In both your observations and your use of data, you will have the chance to infer. When we **infer,** we try to make sense of our observations by reasoning about them on the basis of experience or what we often call *common sense.* We awake in the morning and see snow on the ground; when we went to bed last night, the sky was clear and there was no snow anywhere in sight. So on seeing the snow, we infer that it fell during the night even though we did not see it happen. **Inference** is the way the mind operates to tell us what happened even when we did not see it happening.

Fitting Various Kinds of Supporting Evidence Together

These various kinds of details that form evidence do not exclude one another. A paper rooted in statistical or quoted evidence also benefits from the concrete sensory details that engage readers. A newspaper story recently told us that government debt in the United States was approaching $1 trillion. It illustrated $1 trillion by saying that that was enough money to give every ant in the United States a dollar bill. Or that if you put a trillion dollar bills end to end, they would reach the star Alpha Centauri, which is over four light-years from earth. By converting numbers into something we can visualize, we make the meaning of the numbers more vivid.

When you consider your chosen topic and the audience you have in mind, think about the kinds of evidence that will best suit your purpose. Ask yourself how you will gather the details to create the evidence you need. For most papers, you will find questions like these helpful:

1. What experiences in my own life will help me make this topic interesting?
2. What have I read recently in books, newspapers, or magazines — or what can I read before I write — that will help me support my topic?
3. What have I heard on the radio or observed on television or in the movies that will help me support my topic?
4. What have I learned in recent conversations with friends, parents, relatives, teachers, and associates that will help me support my topic?
5. What do people in my audience know about my topic? What will interest them? What will bore them? What may even surprise them?

■ **Exercise 2.2**　Return to the topics you limited in Exercise 1.2 (or limit some new topics of your own choosing). For each topic, state your reason for writing about it, describe your intended audience, and suggest some probable sources of the kinds of evidence and details that you could use to develop the topic.

2c
Writing a Thesis Statement

Define your main idea, or **thesis** — the essential thing you want to say about your subject — before you plan and write your paper. As you write and revise, you may change your mind about your thesis. Writers often start a paper and discover that their original thesis is not exactly what they want to say. Then they formulate a new thesis. That is all part of the writing process, and you should accept the proddings of your own mind to change your thesis when those proddings become insistent.

All the same, you will save yourself much time, and you will write much more to the point, if you formulate a main idea before you begin your first draft. You may change it slightly or transform it into something altogether different later on. But you may very well keep the same main idea from first to last draft. Having a thesis focuses the mind and helps you control the sentences and paragraphs that make up your composition.

Once you have narrowed the focus of your topic, construct a thesis statement. A **thesis statement** may be one sentence. Or it may be a couple of sentences or even a short paragraph that tells your readers what they are going to be reading, what tone you are going to use in your piece. It also tells readers why they should read what you have written. It lets them know what to expect and lets them decide whether they want to go on with your work. It usually describes your position on the subject as well. The following limited topics at the left led writers to produce the thesis statements at the right.

Limited topic	Possible thesis statement
surprise endings in fiction	The good surprise ending, as in William Faulkner's short story "A Rose for Emily," makes us feel that we should have expected it, for in subtle ways the writer prepares us for it throughout the story.
the effects of jogging on the body	Despite its many advantages, jogging can cause serious injuries to the feet, the knees, and the back.
passenger trains in the United States	Passenger trains can do great service in American transportation if Americans will only realize that transportation is too important to be supported only by the people who travel.
school architecture in my high school	The architects of our high school at home thought they would save on fuel by having many classrooms without windows, but the result was disaster.
my growing up on a fairly isolated farm	I spent the first sixteen years of my life on a farm in Tennessee, and my father gave me some of my most vivid memories.

■ **Exercise 2.3** Write a broad phrase that covers the subject of the paper you will write. Then write a thesis statement to focus the paper.

2d
Organizing Ideas

As you write your thesis statement, you will probably think of more ideas related to your topic and ways to expand ideas you have already recorded. Do not hesitate to add these new ideas to your prewriting papers. You may start with one thesis statement and, as you begin to write a draft, discover that your thesis —what you really want to write about—is changing.

Next, examine all your prewriting materials and put together related thoughts. You can do this in many ways: cutting and pasting, drawing lines and arrows from one point to a related one, or identifying ideas that belong together with a letter or a symbol in the margin. Some writers look at their lists or jottings produced in prewriting and recopy them into groups of connected thoughts.

As you read your materials, look for some principle to guide you in clustering ideas. For instance, which points on one page depend on points you have made on other pages? If you tie together related ideas before you write, you can improve your chances for producing a clear and logical paper.

Arranging Your Information

As you group your ideas, think about ways of organizing them. Of course there are many possible ways of arranging the thoughts you have grouped together. At this stage, however, most writers find it helpful to consider the following common methods for arranging information in an essay:

Chronological arrangement

A **chronological arrangement** relates events as they happen in time, from the first event to the last.

Spatial arrangement

If you select a **spatial arrangement,** you choose a logical starting point and then move through space systematically. If you were told to describe a painting in a local art gallery or in an art book, for example, you might look at the central focus of the painting and then move outward to the edges of the canvas.

Movement from general to specific or from specific to general

You may see a relation between a general point and some specific points that would support it. To group these related points together, you can move from a general statement to specific details **(deductive arrangement)** or you can start with the details and make your general statement at the end **(inductive arrangement).** The writer about surprise endings in fiction could begin with the general statement that surprise endings in stories are best when we see that they were inevitable.

Arrangement by order of importance

You may decide to present your points by **order of importance.** Some points will seem less important than others in supporting an idea. You may make an argument in the opening paragraph of your paper, then support it by points that climb from the less important to the more important. A student writing about the need for passenger trains could argue first that passenger trains are a graceful and convenient way to travel, then that railroads offer a way to keep cities from choking with automobile fumes, and finally that a good passenger railroad system provides a sense of community for people who cannot afford air transport and yet want to travel comfortably and with dignity.

The writer has to decide which ideas are more important than others. Writers may make a variety of choices—just as they make a variety of arguments.

Creating a Rough Outline

When you put your ideas in sequence, you create a **rough outline** to expand and develop. A rough outline is an informal, private convenience for the writer, and it follows no prescribed format. You should always jot down a rough outline before you start to write a draft. It will help you see the shape and direction of your paper and help you decide what you have to say and how you will go about saying it. It will raise helpful questions about limitations.

From prewriting material, one writer prepared this rough outline for a composition:

✓ **CHECKLIST:** A ROUGH OUTLINE

Tentative thesis statement: My father's love for his family farm in Tennessee made him a special person and created the legacy that he gave to his children.

Introduction: Tell about my childhood farm home in Tennessee and my father's place on the farm until he was killed in a car accident.

1. **First steps**
   Earliest memories: Who was in our family; what sort of life we had; where we lived; why we lived there.

2. **What farm life was like.** The routines of farm life; my father's love of nature, of planting things, of seeing it all as a great experience. Why did he like the farm so much? It was a relief from his job as a school principal. Did he like being a school principal? I never knew.

3. **What we did in the community** — church, parties, funerals, etc. Different from the city, where you don't know your neighbor next door. Our life in the church. Church every Sunday.

4. The advantages of farm life over city life — healthier, safer, more secure.

5. The disadvantages — isolation, no real vacations.

6. Why everything changed. My father was killed in a car wreck. We had to leave the farm.

7. **Conclusion:** How things are now with the farm and with me.

You can also write up a fully developed formal outline (discussed in 36b). But a rough outline will usually suffice. As you develop the first draft of your paper, you may change your rough outline to include some new ideas. But even if you do not follow your original outline exactly, it can provide a first check on unity and coherence. A paper has **unity** if all the ideas support the thesis. A paper has **coherence** when each thought flows logically into the next, allowing readers to follow the connections from one point to the next.

Checking the Rough Outline

Checking his rough outline, this writer saw that he should develop his paper within a broad chronological framework. He planned now to begin by describing his earliest childhood on the farm and then come forward to the time when he left the farm and moved to the city. But he realized that within that broad framework, he did not have to be strictly chronological. He could be selective in the order in which he told various stories while still following a general chronological sequence. So the dominant modes in his paper would be narration and description.

This writer saw some difficulties in his outline. When he wrote it, he was still toying with the idea of defending farm life and of arguing that it was better than city life. But now as he looked at the outline, he began to wonder if that argument was necessary. He decided that his paper might lose coherence if he tried to argue that one was better than the other. Maybe it would be sufficient to tell his story without any argument at all. He would think about this issue as he wrote.

A rough outline can save you time later on. Sometimes you may do several drafts of such an outline—just as you will do several drafts of a paper. Each draft allows you to think more about your subject before you commit yourself to writing. A strong organizational effort at the beginning will save you much time in the writing process and give you confidence that you do have something worthwhile to say.

■ **Exercise 2.4**   Make a rough outline of a subject you are thinking of writing about. Write a tentative thesis statement. Then write a series of statements that support that thesis. Exchange outlines with another student in your class. Ask that student to read your outline just as you read the outline that he or she has prepared. Discuss the following questions:

1. Is the thesis clear enough and limited enough to provide for a good paper?
2. Does every heading in your outline support the thesis statement?
3. Can you write interestingly about the subject of the paper in the time you have before the assignment is due?
4. Does your outline provide for a satisfying conclusion?

CHAPTER

3

WRITING AND
REVISING
A PAPER

This chapter will take you through a sample writing process that will involve producing drafts of a paper. Follow it carefully to see how the writer of this draft can help you understand what you are doing in drafting your own composition.

3a
Preparing the First Draft

With the results of your prewriting and your rough (or formal) outline at hand, you can start writing. Don't try to make it perfect. Don't worry too much about errors of fact, questionable spellings, or awkward constructions. Write your first draft as fast as you can. At this stage, you should concentrate on producing a flow of ideas. When you have a draft in front of you, you can change it, correct the misspellings, smooth out the rough places, and shape the whole into a pleasing design.

Don't worry about a title now. If you think of one, fine. If not, develop your title later. Here is the first draft of the essay by a student named Tim about his early life on a farm in Tennessee. For this assignment early in the term, the instructor asked students to write on this topic: "What experience more than any other has shaped you as a person?" The comments in the margins were made by a student who read Tim's draft in class.

**3a
rev**

My Father's Farm

Our farm was about thirty
miles from Knoxville in a county
called Bourbon that is very
beautiful. Or at least it was
beautiful when I was growing up
there in the 1970s, although
now it has changed a lot, and
it is not so beautiful any more.
Anyway, I was born there and
grew up there until I was a
<u>sophmore</u> in high school and my
father got killed in a car
wreck, and we had to move.

I want to write about my
father, I want you to know him
as I knew him. He was born on
the farm, and he never did want
to leave it, although he went
to college and majored in
education and became a school
teacher. My father's Uncle
Edward hated the farm and went
off to school and never
returned. ''Bob was crazy about
the place,'' Uncle Edward said.
''I never could see it
myself.'' I wondered if my
father just didn't have enough
confidence to leave the farm.
Uncle Edward became a lawyer.
Very successful. My father never

*Do you need to
tell us all this in
your first
paragraph?*

spelling?

*Is this a run-on
sentence?*

*Maybe you really
want to write about
your father in this
piece.*

was successful. Maybe he wouldn't take a risk.

But he was good to us. He didn't want much out of life. And yet he wanted everything out of life--satisfaction, love, some object for his work.

You can't make a living by farming alone, and my father wanted to do something to keep the cash flow going, as they say, but to let him live where he wanted to live. And that was the farm. He got a job teaching, but pretty soon he got to be the principal of the high school. Anyway, he went off to college in Virginia. Because that's where his father wanted him to go, since his father had a big thing about Virginia, thinking all the people there were aristocrats or something, but he never was happy any place else but the farm, and he majored in education because he had his heart set on coming back and he didn't know what he could do except teach.

You sound too informal here. I think you can compress.

My mother didn't feel so hot about living on the farm, I don't think she ever got used

Don't you think this is too informal?

to it. She was from Richmond, and they met in college, and I guess they loved each other because they got married and she came back to live on the farm with him after college.

I was the oldest, and I had a brother and a sister younger than me. We all learned to do all the farm work. My sister learned to drive the tractor when she was six years old, and by the time she was eight, she could drive while we put up hay. We had two tractors. With the big one my father would pull the baler through the field, dropping off the bound up bales. <u>Me and my brother picked</u> the hay bales up after my father <u>run</u> the baler through the field, and we put them on the wagon that was pulled behind the tractor, and my sister drove, and people thought it was wonderful to see an eight-year-old girl driving that tractor like she'd been doing it all her life. Well, she had been doing it a big part of her life.

I like this part.

Subject? My brother and I?

Did you leave out a helping verb?

Our community was very close, everybody knew everybody else. People were helpful, and when you were in trouble, you could depend on a lot of help. When I was very small, too young to drive the tractor, my father got sick. I don't know what kind of sickness it was, but he was in bed for a long time. But some of the nieghbors came and did our plowing for us, and they didn't charge anything. It was just the way you did in my nieghborhood.

My father always wore a suit to his job at the high school. When he put on his suit in the morning. He became like a different person. I think he hated his suit. He always said wool scrached his skin. He wore cotton on the place. Blue jeans. Long cotton underwear in winter time. But he wore a suit to school. He stood up straight and got quiet when he put on his suit and seemed to think about everything he was going to say before he said anything. We rode to school with him. I

3a
rev

These are interesting details, but do they go with the paper? Are you writing about the farm or the community?

Spelling?

Spelling?

Fragments?

Check spelling here.

Aren't these sentence fragments? Do you want to use them for emphasis?

mean my brother, my sister and me. He didn't have much to say to us then. You know how it is; he had to think about everything he had to do during the day, all the teachers he had to supervise and all those students, and he didn't want to talk. He was always so talkative, but you know how it is when you've you a big job a head of you, you've got to think about it, and I don't think my father ever much liked being a school principal. People liked him, but he didn't like bossing people. He never said, but that's just my opinion. We called his school work ''suit work.'' We thought it was funny.

We came home on the school bus because he always worked late. There were always papers to fill out and letters to write and reports. School principals make a lot of reports, but who reads them? My father wrote reports and got everything in on time, and then at five o'clock or so he came home. As soon as he came home, he changed his clothes, he put on blue jeans or <u>kakis</u> and an old <u>flanell</u> shirt, and he was out to the garden or to the barn or somewhere. And he got to work.

Spelling?
Spelling?

And everything about him changed then he was like another person. He was relaxed and calm and happy, and he'd talk to us about the different kinds of trees on the place and the different kinds of birds and different kinds of cows and chickens and all that. They're even different kinds of grass. That's something you don't suspect about a farm. It seems so simple. But really it's very complicated. You have to know a lot of names, my father knew them all. He knew the loblolly pine and the Virginia pine and the white pine. He knew the red maple and the silver maple and the mountain maple. He knew poison ivy and poison oak and taught us how to know them and avoid them and how to tell the difference between the poison sumac that grew in a marshy

I really like this. But could you pull it together?

Run on sentence?

This is a comma splice.

I like the names of things

place along the creek in the
lower field and the smooth sumac
that grew in the woods.

He loved wild flowers. Things
that looked like weeds to me to
him were beautiful, and he
could hold a <u>dandilion</u> in his   *Spelling?*
hand and marvel over it like it
was a star that had fallen down
to earth. Sometimes we walked
back up in the mountains, and
he'd carry a little notebook in
his shirt pocket, and he'd
write down the names of all the
flowers he saw. It was like a
contest with him. To see how
many flowers he could see in a
day. When the honeysuckle was
blooming, he'd pull off some of
the little blossoms and show us
how to suck the <u>necter</u> out of   *Spelling?*
them.

And the birds. He loved to
look at birds. Once we were
walking through a field, and he
stopped me all of a sudden by   *Don't cut this.*
just lying a hand on my arm,
and he pointed, and I couldn't
see anything, but then real
slow I saw a bird the color of
leaves sitting on a nest. ''It's
a woodcock,'' he said real

<u>quite</u>. And he made me walk
around so we wouldn't disturb
her.

Spelling?

It was fun working with him.
He loved to be out in the open
and to have us with him, and
when we got through doing
something--getting in the hay,
for example--he'd talk about
how much fun it was to work
together. It was fun. Hard work
but fun. He loved to plant
things and to watch them grow
up. And he loved to harvest
things. He said we were his
finest crop, and he couldn't
wait to see what we'd turn out
to be.

Maybe you could compress this.

We didn't think we were
specially happy or unhappy. We
just lived from day to day, and
some days we were happy, and
some days we were so tired that
we thought we were unhappy. But
I guess in the end you'd have
to say we were definitely
happy.

But then in my <u>sophmore</u> year
in high school my father was
killed in a car wreck. A drunk
driver hit him one night when
he was coming home after a

Spelling

school board meeting. My father had a bag of corn seed on the back seat of the car when he was killed. I guess his last thoughts were about planting something.

This is good.

My mother thought that we should move back to Richmond. She had family there, she had lived on the farm only because my father wanted to live there. We sold the place for a pretty penny. Knoxville was spreading out. Lots of people were commuting. A lot of people were selling off land for divisions. And so we did, too. My mother got a good job in Richmond. So everything turned out all right.

Comma splice?

This last summer I went back. My father has a brother in Knoxville who works for TVA, and I went to spend a couple of weeks with him, and he drove me back down to the old homeplace. Everything was changed. Our house had been bulldozed away. Streets had been laid out. There were alot of houses built and others going up. We had a driveway running down from the house to the highway, and at

the bottom next to the highway
we had a couple of big maple
trees. They are gone, and in
their place is a couple of brick
pillars with a sign on them. It
says ''Happy Valley
Subdivision.'' I was really
unhappy when I looked at that.
I realized how happy we had all
been on the farm and how it was
all gone, and it never will
come back again.

I like these details. But is the ending to this paper strong enough? It seems to trail off.

3b
rev

Notice that Tim concentrated on recording his thoughts and did not worry about correctness. Obviously many errors appear in these pages. Many ideas in this draft are rambling and unclear and far from their final shape. There are problems with language and with form. Here and there the tone is too informal. Some sentences are confused. Some thoughts are repeated unnecessarily.

■ **Exercise 3.1** Rewrite Tim's paper. Write in the first person as if these events happened to you. Try to put yourself in his place and live these events in your mind. You may reorganize the draft in any way you want. Try to cut out the unnecessary details. Make the language a little more formal without making it stiff. Then compare your draft with Tim's second draft on pages 38–47.

3b
Revising the Draft

After you complete the first draft of a paper, take a long break. Put some time and distance between you and your paper to clear your mind.

When you return to your draft, be prepared to reread it carefully several times and to make changes in content, word choice, and sentence structure. As you revise, you will cut some things out and add others. You will change some words, substituting more precise language for generalities. You may want to shift sentences from one place to another or shorten or combine them. If you have a title already, look at it carefully and revise it, if necessary. It should suit your thesis and should engage the reader's attention. The checklist below focuses on key elements to consider.

Revised drafts can get messy. Whenever your draft gets too messy to read easily, rewrite it as a new draft. If you are using a computer, you can mark up your printed copy, make all the changes on the computer, and run off a new and clean printed copy. Writing habits and skills vary, but most writers need to do at least two drafts. Professional writers and good student writers nearly always do more.

When you have produced a readable draft, show it to someone whose opinion you trust. Don't ask that person, "What do you think of my paper?" The person will almost always say, "I like it." Ask, rather, "What do you think I am trying to say?" As your friend tells you what he or she

---

✓ CHECKLIST: REVISING

A. Revising ideas
   1. Is the thesis clear? (*2c*)
   2. Does the paper speak consistently to an audience? (*2a*)
   3. Are there enough details to support your major points? (*2b*)
   4. Does the paper show unity? Do all the ideas relate clearly to each other? (*2d*)
   5. Is the paper coherent? Do ideas flow logically and smoothly from one to the other? (*2d*)
   6. Are ideas stated in precise language? (*4c, 10c, Chapter 14*) Should any words be replaced by more accurate or appropriate ones?
   7. Does each sentence state its information clearly? Is there sentence variety to hold the reader's interest? When read aloud, do the sentences sound right to the ear? (*Chapter 8*)
   8. Are there any unnecessary words that can be eliminated? (*12a*)

B. Revising for essay structure
   1. Does the introduction capture and hold the reader's interest?
   2. Does the conclusion complete the ideas established and supported in the paper? (*4d*)
   3. Does the title engage the reader's attention?

C. Revising for correctness
   1. Sentence completeness
      a. Are periods and other end marks used to set off complete statements? (*15a*)
      b. Are there any run-on sentences that should be separated by end marks or combined with connecting words and suitable punctuation? (*15e*)
      c. Are there any sentence fragments that you can correct by joining

thinks you are trying to say, you may discover that you have not made your purposes clear. Once you and your friendly reader have agreed that the most important issue is what you are trying to say in the paper, you can then discuss some better ways to achieve your purpose. You may want to go in a new direction altogether. Or you may want to straighten out a few confusing places in the paper as you have written it.

Make things as clear as you can. Many sentences will require radical changes to make your ideas easier to understand. Start by fixing the problems you marked in your first draft. Then answer any questions readers may have raised as they talked with you about your paper. Thereafter, you should check every draft slowly and thoughtfully for errors. Mark your sentence boundaries clearly with periods or other end marks. Look for troublesome verbs, vague pronoun references, and misspelled words.

✓ **CHECKLIST:** REVISING (continued)

them to other sentences, by adding subjects, or verbs, or both? (*16a*)

2. Sentence logic
   a. Are parallel ideas expressed in parallel forms? (*Chapter 7*)
   b. Have you corrected all the needless shifts in tone or point of view? (*Chapter 22*)
   c. Do modifiers stand near enough to the words they describe to avoid ambiguity?
   d. Are the references to pronouns clear? (*Chapter 21*)
   e. Do subordinate sections relate correctly to main clauses? (*7b*)
3. Verbs
   a. Do subjects and verbs agree? (*Chapter 17*)
   b. Are verb tenses correctly formed and consistent? (*18a–c*)
   c. Have you corrected all unnecessary shifts in tense, mood, voice, number, or emphasis? (*Chapter 22*)
4. Punctuation and mechanics
   a. Are punctuation marks clearly and firmly written? Do end marks, commas, colons, and semicolons serve the meanings of sentences? Are apostrophes placed to show possession or contraction? (*Chapters 23–28*)
   b. Are quotation marks used in pairs to set off someone's exact words? (*27a*)
   c. Do italics, numbers, and symbols follow conventional uses? (*Chapters 31, 32*)
   d. Do capital letters follow the conventions of American English? (*Chapter 30*) Is the title of the theme correctly capitalized and punctuated?
   e. Have troublesome words been checked in a dictionary for accurate spelling? (*20c*)

The writer of the first draft (pages 26–35) reconsidered his work carefully. He found some errors in grammar and spelling and some confusion in diction. But he realized that correcting these errors was not the major task he faced. He had to shape the thoughts in his first draft into a coherent essay. That took some careful revising.

He also had to think about his audience. Who would read this paper? How could he make the paper appeal to people who did not know his father and who had no sense of farm life? How could he sustain interest to the end? What was the main problem or issue that he wanted to introduce early in the essay so he could get people to read on to see how it all ended?

He went back to his rough outline and studied it and compared it with his piece of freewriting. This process gave him a little better sense of what he wanted to say and how he wanted to shape his essay.

He worked through his first draft carefully, willing to make drastic revisions. Here is what finally emerged. (Comments are the teacher's.)

```
''If your father had been as
interested in business as he
was in birds, he might have
left you a legacy.'' That was
the growling comment of my
grandfather, my mother's father,
last year when I went back to
see the farm where I grew up in
Tennessee. My grandfather had
not wanted his daughter to marry
my father; and once they were
married he did not want her to
go off to live on a farm.
    We lived on the farm because
my father never wanted to leave
the place where he had grown
up. His father barely made a
living off the farm, and my
father knew he would have to
have outside income to make
ends meet if he stayed on the
```

Good beginning. You set some tension at the start.

place. So he got a scholarship
to a college in Virginia,
supplemented the scholarship
with a part-time job as a
janitor in a college building,
majored in education and became
a school teacher.

3b
rev

Good sentence. Nice use of verbs.

He and my mother met in an
English class. They were
required to read each other's
papers before handing them in to
the teacher. He wrote a paper
about birds, she was surprised
that a man would be interested
in such things. And that was
how it started.

CS 17

Her parents--especially her
father--objected to the marriage
from the first. Her father told
her that my father would never
make any money. They did not
want her to live on a farm far
from home. They never came to
visit as long as we lived
there.

How sad!

Mother loved the city with
its broad streets, its people,
and its things to do. She
studied to be an architect, and
she wanted to live in a city
where architects could find
work. I don't think she was
happy on the farm. Perhaps she

3b

rev

was not happy with my father.
Once when she was angry at him,
my mom said, ''You don't have
any ambition.'' She apologized
again and again for saying that,
but it may have been true.
Still, she never complained
much except when she had to
fight off the cockroaches that
came in from the woods or when
she ran into snakes in her
flower garden or when the roof
leaked because the house was so
old and my father was to busy   *us*
to fix it.

   My father eventually became
principal of the high school in
nearby Bourbonville. But his
real passion was the farm and
the natural world that thrived
there.

   He sang when he drove a
tractor, and at a distance we
could hear his tenor voice
rising above and carrying beyond
the puttering sound of the
gasoline engine. He gardened,
<u>sometimes working late by the
light of the moon when it was
full</u>. Sometimes he made a pot of   *Nice free modifier.*
coffee when he got up around
sunrise, and he walked out to

his garden with a coffee cup
and looked at the growing things
like a king admiring his
kingdom.

I was the oldest child. My
brother Edward was two years
younger than I, and my sister
Peggy was two years younger
than Edward. My father taught
Peggy how to drive a tractor
when she was 6 years old. By the
time she was 8, she could drive   N (see 33b)
while we put up hay. We had two
tractors. With the big one my
father would pull the baler
through the field, droping off   sp
the bales. Edward and I lifted
the bales onto the flat-bed
wagon pulled behind the tractor
that my sister drove.

We always had something to
talk about with each other--the
new calf, the work we would do
that day or the work we had
done, the angus cow who had
butted down a fence post yet
again and run off into the
neighborhood, the king snake my
mother found in the robins mud-   '28
plastered nest in the yard and
the crys all the other birds   pl 31c
made around the snake as he

made his meal on the robin's blue eggs.

We learned what we were good at and what we were bad at. ''Nobody can be good at everything'' my father said. I got to be good at working on engines, but Edward loved to read. ''Just like his namesake, my brother,'' my father said. He was proud of the good grades Edward made in school. But he was also proud because Peggy loved engines, and by the time she was eleven, he had taught her to be a fine mechanic.

My father always wore a suit to his job at the high school. When he put on his suit in the morning he became a different person. He stood up straight and got quiet and seemed to think about everything he was going to say before he said anything. He drove us to school in his old Ford. He never had much to say to us on those mornings. He seemed absorbed in the work he was going to have to do that day--''suit work,'' we called it, the work of being a school principal. And when my

father put on his suit, we took
it as a signal that we should
be quiet.

We came home on the school
bus because he always worked
late. He always had papers to
fill out and letters and reports
to write. Around five o'clock
he came home, changed into blue
jeans or khakis and an old
flannel shirt, and he went out
to the garden or to the barn or
to the fields to work.

Everything about him changed
<u>then</u>. He was relaxed and calm
and happy. He wasn't the school
principal <u>then</u>; he was our
teacher, and the farm was our
book. He taught us about the
different kinds of trees on the
place and the different kinds
of birds and different kinds of
cows and chickens and even the
different kinds of grass.

*You repeat these
thens very close to
each other.
Another word?*

He seemed to know the <u>names
of everything</u>. He knew the
loblolly pine and the Virginia
pine and the white pine. He
knew the red maple and the
silver maple and the mountain
maple. He knew poison ivy and
poison oak and taught us how to

plural

**3b
rev**

know them and avoid them and how to tell the difference between the poison sumac that grew in a marshy place along the creek in the lower field and the harmless, smooth sumac that grew in the woods.

Plants that were weeds to me were wild flowers to him. He could hold a dandelion and admire it as if it were a star fallen to earth. Sometimes we drove over to the mountains a few miles from our house and took hikes on Sunday afternoons, especially in the Spring when *Cap 32* it was first getting warm. He always carried a little notebook in his shirt pocket, and he wrote down the names of all the flowers he saw. It was a contest with himself to see how many flowers he could see in a day. When the honeysuckle was *frag 18* blooming. He'd pull of some of the little blossoms and show us how to suck the nectar out of them. ''It's natural candy,'' he said. ''And it doesn't rot your teeth.''

He saw things we sometimes might have missed. Once we were

walking along the edge of a
field, and he suddenly laid a
hand on my arm and made me stop
and put his other hand up in a
gesture of silence, and he
pointed towards the ground. I
couldn't see anything at first
except the dried grass, but
then I saw a bird the color of
leaves sitting on a nest. ''It's
a woodcock,'' he said real   adj 22d
quiet. And he made me walk
around so we wouldn't disturb
her.

He loved to plant things and
to watch them grow up. He
planted peas on Valentine's
Day, and when the first shoots
came up out of the soil of his
garden, he said, ''I don't care
what the calendar says; its
spring. Its really spring.''   us
And he was happy. He always
said we were his finest crop,
and he couldn't wait see what
fruit we'd bear.

My father was killed in a
wreck during my sophomore year
in high school. A drunk driver
hit him one night when he was
coming home after a school board
meeting. My father had a bag of

corn seed in the back seat of
the car when he was killed. His
last thoughts must have been
about planting something.

A developer bought our farm.
My mother moved us back to
Richmond, to her family, and
she went back to being an
architect. And we have lived
well.

This last summer for the
first time in almost three
years, I went back to visit my
father's brother, my Uncle
Edward, in Knoxville. He drove
me back to the old homeplace.
Nothing was the same. The house
had vanished--bulldozed away,
Uncle Edward said. Streets had
been laid out through our
fields. Houses were built or
being built along the streets.

My grandfather was wrong.
True, my father did not leave
me any money. But he left me
the memory of his pleasure at
hard work and growing things,
his good humor, his love, his
silent wonder at the sight of
the woodcock nesting in the
grass against a background of
leaves. I remember all the times

Much better ending. It matches your introduction.

```
he said, ''Good job. Good job.''
He made me believe I can do a
good job and be happy with what
I have, and that is a legacy
beyond anything my grandfather
can imagine.
```

This is a very nice piece that evokes both sadness and pleasure. You have a clear thesis now, and you stay with it all the way through. I like the way you begin with the word legacy and end with it. I enjoyed the many good stories you tell. But you never do tell us any of your father's faults. Surely he had some. You might talk about them just enough to make more believable all the good memories you have of him. He sounds like a great person, and he will still be great if you admit some shortcomings.

Now and then your language is a little too informal. And I think some parts of the essay don't fit together as well as they should. I've marked some places where you might weave things together a little better. Try to work on the comma splices.

But this is a good paper, and I enjoyed reading it.

■ **Exercise 3.2** Study the final draft of Tim's paper at 3e. Compare your draft with his and discuss the places where your changes are different and where they are similar.

■ **Exercise 3.3** Divide your class into small groups, and compare this final draft of Tim Lee's paper with the rough draft. Where has he revised sentences? Where has he changed paragraphs around? Where has he added new information? Where has he deleted material? Why do you think he has made each of the changes he had made? Do you approve of all the changes, or do you think he has deleted some things that he should have kept? Why?

3c
Proofreading

Both before and after you prepare your final draft, comb your paper for mechanical mistakes and correct them. This step is called **proofreading.** Proofreading requires careful examination of each line on the page.

Proofread your last rough draft before you turn it into your final draft, and proofread again as you prepare your final draft for submission. Hold a ruler or a blank sheet of paper beneath the line you are studying. Examine each sentence carefully for missing words and punctuation. Check each word carefully for missing or incorrect letters. Proofreading a paper by reading backward from the last sentence to the first is another good technique. It helps you to focus on isolated units and to catch errors easily overlooked in the context of surrounding sentences. Some writers touch the point of a pencil to each syllable to help them read more slowly. It is always a good idea to read your paper slowly aloud to yourself.

Tim has an advantage in that a classmate read a rough draft of his essay and made some suggestions about changes. You may be on your own when you prepare your final draft. That is all the more reason for you to pay careful attention to what you do.

3d
Preparing the Final Draft

Remember that your instructor must grade many papers, remaining alert and careful through them all. Messy papers make life hard for the busy teacher. But sometimes you will find a mistake in a paper just as you are ready to hand it in. Always correct the mistake, but do so as neatly as you can.

Follow your instructor's guidelines for correct manuscript preparation in each course. The papers you submit for your instructor's evaluation must be clean and relatively free of handwritten corrections. But it is *always* better to write in a correction than to turn in clean pages with misspellings or other obvious errors.

✓ CHECKLIST: GENERAL MANUSCRIPT RECOMMENDATIONS

Margins

1. Leave margins of 1¼ or 1½ inches at the top, sides, and bottom of each page. Do not fold margins. You can mark off the four marginal areas with light pencil lines to keep your words from straying into them.
2. Indent all paragraphs.

Title

1. Center the title on the first page, 1½ inches below the top margin, or on the first line for handwritten copies.

2. Leave one line of space below the title.
3. Capitalize the first letter of all *major* words in the title, including the first and last words, no matter what part of speech they are.

> Jumping for Fitness and Popularity

4. Capitalize the first letter of prepositions of five or more letters.

> Once upon Life's Highway; Through Time

5. Do not use a period at the end of the title; do not underline the title or enclose it in quotation marks. (The title of a book, an article, or a poem that appears within your title does need correct punctuation. See 29c and 34a.)
6. If you use a cover page, repeat the title at the top of the first page of your manuscript.

Cover page

The cover page usually includes your name, your class number, the submission date, and the professor's name. However, your instructor may have different requirements.

Format

1. Write on one side of each page only.
2. Number all pages consecutively, starting with page 2 of your composition. The first page is not numbered but is considered page 1 nonetheless. (Do not count the cover page or, if you submit one, the outline page.)
3. Use arabic numbers in the upper right-hand corner or centered at the top of each page. Be consistent in whatever form of pagination you use.

Typed and word-processed papers

1. Use 8½ × 11 unlined white bond paper, not onionskin, and not the paper treated to allow corrections with pencil erasers. (Erasable paper smudges easily and often becomes unreadable.)
2. Use *only* black ribbon; if the type looks faded, change the ribbon. Nothing is so hard for a teacher as to be forced to read an almost illegible paper typed with an exhausted ribbon.
3. Double-space between lines; indent paragraphs five spaces.
4. After periods, question marks, exclamation points, and colons, use two spaces; after commas and semicolons, use one space.
5. Do not use a space before or after a hyphen. To type a dash, use two consecutive hyphens (--) without any spacing between the dash and the words on each side.

(continued)

```
Dashes--as in this example--set off thoughts
for emphasis.
```

6. Make corrections with a typewriter eraser, a correcting tape on the typewriter, or correction fluid. Do not strike over incorrect letters. For minor errors discovered after you have removed your pages from the typewriter, use a pen with blue or black ink.

7. If you use a computer, be sure you have not left in words you intended to delete or deleted words you intended to leave in.

8. Type should be clean enough to make clear, sharp letters.

9. Dot matrix printers used with word processors should have true descenders. That is, the tails on the letters, g, j, p, q, and y should come down below the baseline for the rest of the type. (See Appendix B.)

10. Remember to use adequate margins. (A left margin set at 10 and a right margin set at 70 are acceptable.)

11. In general, a manuscript prepared on a word processor is more readable if the right margin is *not* justified. Printers with proportional spacing may justify the right margin.

12. If you use a computer printer with tractor-fed continuous-form paper, be sure you tear off the perforated strip on each side of the paper, and be sure to separate each page.

Handwritten papers

1. Use 8½ × 11 paper with lines spaced about ⅜ inch apart. (For a clear layout, you can skip every other line.)

2. Use blue or black ink; write on one side only.

3. Indent the first line of every paragraph about an inch.

4. Make occasional corrections with an ink eraser or correction fluid, or draw a neat line through words you want to delete. Write in the new words above the deletions, using skipped lines and marginal space for additions.

5. Make your handwriting readable. Use a firm, clear period at the end of each sentence, and leave space before the next sentence. Dot *i*'s and *j*'s directly above the letter. Avoid loops and curlicues, especially when you make capital letters. Make sure readers can distinguish between the *r* and the *n*, the *v* and the *u*, the *o* and the *a*, the *l* and the *t*, and the *e* and the *i*. Be careful to round off the letter *h* so it does not look like the letters *l* and *i*. Be sure to make the letters *m* and *n* so they do not look like the letter *u* combined with another letter or standing alone.

■ **Exercise 3.4** Choose a topic from your own personal experience and prepare a composition based on it. Try to write about an experience that shaped you as a person or that marked a turning point in your life.

Follow guidelines 1a through 3d. As you write, be sure to save the following materials that you can put in a large envelope to present to your teacher.

1. Notes made during your prewriting
2. A limited topic
3. A statement of purpose for your paper, a description of the kind of people you would like to read the paper, and a description of the nature and sources of your supporting details
4. A thesis statement
5. An outline, if required (Outlines are discussed in 36b.)
6. A first draft
7. A second draft and any subsequent drafts that may be necessary
8. A final draft

3e
Making Necessary Changes and Corrections

When your instructor returns your graded paper, read it over carefully. Study the summary remarks that describe the strengths and weaknesses of your work. Examine the marginal notations, and be prepared to make revisions on the basis of the commentary you find there.

You can learn to prevent errors next time around by correcting your mistakes and by responding to suggestions about style, form, and content.

Your instructor may evaluate your paper with a combination of comments, questions, and marking symbols. An alphabetical list of common correction symbols keyed to this handbook appears on the inside front cover of your book. If you see / / in the margin of your paper, for example, the list on the inside cover tells you that / / is a shorthand notation for faulty parallelism and that Chapter 8 explains the problem and how to correct it.

If your instructor writes chapter and section numbers only, check the inside back covers of this handbook for a quick guide to the plan of the text. If your instructor writes ¶ coh in the margin of your paper, for example, the plan on the inside back cover tells you that ¶ coh refers to paragraph coherence. After you read that section, you should understand the problem and some strategies for correcting it.

As you reread your paper, correct all the errors and make required revisions. Pay special attention to places where your instructor may have asked for more information. If, for example, you mention a name, your

3e

rev

✓ **CHECKLIST: MAKING CORRECTIONS ON EVALUATED PAPERS**

1. Follow your instructor's guidelines for revisions. Some instructors read drafts and make comments *before* the paper goes into final form. Others encourage full rewriting based on comments written on final drafts. Be sure to correct errors before you do complete revisions of graded papers.

2. Learn the symbol and comment system your instructor uses.

3. Make all corrections called for by marking symbols and comments. Use a pencil or a different color ink to make corrections so that your instructor can readily see what you have done.

4. As you make corrections, draw a line through the marginal symbol to help yourself keep track of what you have finished.

5. Write short corrections clearly, directly above the error noted by your instructor.

6. Rewrite any weak sentences in the margin (if there is room) or on the reverse side of the page. If you rewrite on the reverse side of the page, put an arrow in the margin to signal your instructor to turn the page over to see your revision.

7. Keep a record of your mistakes from theme to theme. Any writer tends to fall into patterns of error. If you keep a record of your errors, you can discover your own patterns and so be on the lookout for the errors you are most likely to make.

instructor may ask for some identification. You may have written this: "According to John Simon, the English language is in decline." Your instructor may write, "Who is John Simon?" You should revise by saying, "According to John Simon, literary critic and author of *Paradigms Lost,* the English language is in decline." If you don't understand a comment or a symbol, make an appointment to discuss the paper with your instructor.

■ **Exercise 3.5** Following the instructor's comments on the theme on pages 38–47, make corrections and any necessary revisions.

■ **Exercise 3.6** When your instructor returns the composition you prepared for Exercise 3.4, follow the instructor's guidelines and make all necessary corrections and revisions.

CHAPTER

4

WRITING STRONG
PARAGRAPHS

Paragraphs divide a text up into manageable units that organize writing and make reading easier. The first sentence of a paragraph is indented several spaces from the left margin of the page. The indentation serves as a signal; it tells us that the paragraph preceding the indent has ended.

Paragraphs do not stand alone; they are not essays in themselves. Once in a while you may write a single paragraph for some special purpose — as a caption to a picture, for example, or as a brief memo in an office setting. But much more commonly, paragraphs are written not for their own sake, but as part of the flow of a larger text. In a college writing course, paragraphs form steps along the way to the point that the writer wants an essay to make. Paragraphs have meaning as they are joined together to reach the goal of the essay.

How long should a paragraph be? There are no absolute rules. When writing for newspapers and magazines, writers often favor short paragraphs of a few sentences (a total of a hundred words or so). Many professional essayists prefer paragraphs that fill a half page or a full printed page. As you read the sample paragraphs in this chapter, you will find that they vary widely in length.

A new paragraph signals a change in subject — slight or large — so a paragraph should be long enough to let readers absorb and remember its subject. Introductory paragraphs are generally shorter than paragraphs in the body of a paper. Within the body of your papers, it is a good idea to strike a balance between short and long paragraphs. A good general rule is to have one indentation on each typed page — but you can use your own judgment to decide how long your paragraphs will be.

4a
Building Unified Paragraphs

We expect a paragraph to have some single purpose, some point that all the sentences of the paragraph work together to make. A paragraph achieves unity if it supports a controlling idea.

Giving Each Paragraph a Controlling Idea

Every paragraph should have a **controlling idea,** a main thought that all of its sentences support and clarify. Often a lead sentence will express that controlling idea as a generalization:

> Everyone knows that sports teams must have nicknames, but selecting an appropriate one is fraught with peril. Alabama, for instance, may be proud of the Crimson Tide, but it sounds like a bloodbath or a serious algae problem. Notre Dame's famous jocks are ossified as the Fighting Irish, though Hibernian-American athletes are about as rare in South Bend as they are on the Boston Celtics. Nothing exposed the nickname crisis more than the 1982 NCAA basketball championship game played between the Georgetown Hoyas and the North Carolina Tar Heels. Even if you know what a hoya or a tarheel is, the only sensible strategy is to forget it. (For those overwhelmed by a need to know, hoya is short for *Hoya saxa!* a garbled Greek and Latin cheer meaning "What rocks!," and tarheel originated during the Civil War as a disparaging term for folks from the Carolina pine forests.) Few knew what the Fort Wayne Zollner Pistons were when a pro basketball team played under that name. (They were players owned by Fred Zollner, who also happened to own a piston factory in Fort Wayne.) The early vogue of naming a team for a person seems to have come to an end with Paul Brown, the original coach of the Cleveland Browns. Fans who found the cult of personality distasteful at least were grateful that he wasn't named Stumblebrenner.
>
> —JOHN LEO

How do you define a controlling idea? The traditional method has been to put it into a **topic sentence,** a general statement that usually comes at the beginning of the paragraph and is supported by all the following sentences. A topic sentence may limit and define the topic by presenting a strong opinion or an attitude about it. That is what writer John Leo does in the humorous paragraph quoted above. Or the topic sentence may make a simple statement of fact that will be supported by later sentences in the paragraph.

Wars have been waged over water. In recent decades, India and Pakistan fought over rivers they shared; also Israel and Syria, and Iraq and Syria. In 1964, notes resources expert Richard J. Barnet, in *The Lean Years,* a water dispute between two states of the United States led to a legal battle and "language reminiscent of the sort that France and Germany used to employ just before they went to war." ("The aggressive policies of the State of Iowa," read one Supreme Court brief, "have caused great consternation to the State of Nebraska and its citizens, and have threatened to result in armed conflict on the part of landowners and the State of Iowa and its representatives.")

—Jonathan Weiner

You can often add to the clarity of your writing by shaping the first sentence in a paragraph to express, in exact language, the controlling idea you want to convey. Compare the following topic sentences:

1. My father spent the first years of his childhood in Chicago.
2. My father spent the first years of a difficult childhood in Chicago.

Both of these sentences make a general statement about a topic—the father's childhood in Chicago. But no controlling assertion gives direction to the topic in sentence 1. Many things happen in childhood.

In a good paragraph, the writer selects details that develop a central idea. And in some paragraphs that central idea is expressed by a topic sentence that is a sort of general summary of what the rest of the paragraph is about. In the paragraph below, the first sentence makes a broad and general statement; the second sentence develops the general statement more specifically. The paragraph that comes after it will report difficulties in the father's childhood that will show how hard it was. See how the limited topic sentence works in the following paragraph.

My father spent the first years of a difficult childhood in Chicago. His father deserted the family, leaving a wife and five small children. At age eight, my father was the oldest. His mother had to take in washing and had to clean house for rich people on Michigan Avenue just to keep her family together. My father cleaned up yards for ten cents an hour when he was eleven. He got a paper route when he was twelve and had to crawl out of bed at five in the morning, seven days a week, winter and summer, to deliver the papers before breakfast. He gave all the money he made to his mother for family expenses. Because they could not afford doctors, my father was left partly deaf by a childhood disease.

Many paragraphs do not begin with a summary topic sentence. Paragraphs that tell stories, paragraphs that describe, even some paragraphs that explain do not have a general statement that unites everything else in the paragraph. As we said before, paragraphs do not stand by themselves; they take their place within a flow of discourse, and so the meaning of some paragraphs depends on what comes before them in other paragraphs.

Always the most important sentence in setting the stage for the paragraph is the first sentence, even if it does not tell you much about the topic. The first sentence announces the subject, and the rest of the paragraph develops its controlling idea by building on some thought expressed in the first sentence. The controlling idea may not be specifically expressed in a sentence of its own, but when you read a good paragraph you can always express its controlling idea in a sentence if you set yourself to do so.

Sometimes the first sentence introduces the topic for the paragraph without summarizing what will be said about the topic. The second sentence may then be a summary of what is to come.

The steam locomotive evokes nostalgia among many people. *The nostalgia is better than the experience of the steam locomotive ever was.* The steam locomotive was a dirty, dangerous, and generally disagreeable companion to American life for well over a century. It spread filthy black smoke over large areas of every city it served, and it usually left a thick film of oily grime on the face of every passenger in the cars behind it. It started fires along the sides of the tracks in woods and fields. It was so heavy that it pounded rails until they broke, and when it crashed and turned over — as it frequently did — it poured deadly fire and steam on the fireman and the engineer in the cab. It had so many moving parts under high stress that it often broke down, stranding passengers for hours. And it was absurdly inefficient and costly to operate.

Sometimes the first sentence in the first paragraph of a longer work will begin the description of a scene. Several similar sentences will follow. The final sentence in this type of first paragraph may sum up the scene and explain why it is important to the meaning that the paragraph expresses. Or a following paragraph may explain the scene depicted in the first. Such scene-setting first paragraphs are often used to begin articles in popular magazines because they make readers want to know what is going to happen next. Although the first sentence in such a paragraph is not, strictly speaking, a topic sentence, it sets the direction for what comes next and introduces the controlling idea of the paragraph.

The bands are marching, the tailgates swinging open for the ritual of picnics and parties. The beverages are heady, the boosterism infectious, the old school colors vivid and bright. *This is college football, as the television slogan goes, a great way to spend an autumn afternoon.*

—*Newsweek*

Often an introductory paragraph in an essay or an article simply tells a story. The first sentence begins with a striking detail, and the following sentences build on it. A later paragraph introduces the topic that the story illustrates. The role of the first sentence in such a paragraph is to catch the interest of readers and to make them keep on reading.

Georges Randrianasolo, Madagascar's leading naturalist, grabbed the doorframe of our descending helicopter and stared uneasily at the limestone pinnacles below us. From horizon to horizon, erosion had sculptured rock into spires a hundred feet tall, some whetted so thin at their peaks that the setting sun gleamed as if sinking behind an entire skyline of Empire State Buildings. Malagasy — the people of Madagascar — call these rocks *tsingy*, or spikes, and say that in the tsingy there is hardly enough flat land to plant your whole foot.

—ALISON JOLLY

When a paragraph begins by stating the controlling idea in general terms, the second sentence often limits the idea. The rest of the paragraph builds then on that second sentence. In the following paragraph, the first sentence makes a general statement about how the police of Birmingham, Alabama, handled the arrest of civil rights demonstrators in the 1960s. The second sentence makes a limiting statement about the general subject introduced by the first. The rest of the paragraph flows from that more limiting statement to the topic sentence that is the next to the last sentence in the paragraph.

It is true that they have been rather disciplined in their public handling of the demonstrators. In this sense they have been rather publicly "nonviolent." But for what purpose? To preserve the evil system of segregation. Over the last few years I have consistently preached that nonviolence demands that the means we use must be as pure as the ends we seek. So I have tried to make it clear that it is wrong to use immoral means to attain moral ends. But now I must affirm that it is just as wrong, or even more so, to use moral means to preserve immoral ends. *Maybe Mr. Connor and his policemen have been rather publicly nonviolent as Chief Prichett was in Albany, Georgia, but they have used the moral means of nonviolence to maintain the immoral end of flagrant racial injustice.* T. S. Eliot has said that there is no greater treason than to do the right deed for the wrong reason.

—MARTIN LUTHER KING, JR.

Some paragraphs introduce the topic with a direct quotation that focuses attention on the information to come. But again, the general subject of the paragraph is signaled by the first sentence. Here is a paragraph from David Donald's biography of the writer Thomas Wolfe, introducing the chapter on how Wolfe broke into print. Note how he uses a quotation from a letter to Wolfe's sister Mabel to introduce a paragraph that develops the thesis of this chapter.

"My greatest deficiency is a total lack of salesmanship," Wolfe wrote Mabel while he was still working on his novel. He recalled that in trying to place his plays he had sent the scripts to only two or three producers and, when they did not respond promptly, had peremptorily demanded that they be returned. "I have never known where to go, where to turn, or what to do," he explained, but he predicted: "This time, certain friends will probably attend to that part of it for me."

—DAVID HERBERT DONALD

Some paragraphs introduce the topic by posing a question at the beginning. The rest of the paragraph offers some kind of response to the question. The response may be a firm answer, or it may suggest an answer or report an answer that someone has given. In the following paragraph, the biographer of the poet William Carlos Williams reports on Williams's response to the question in the first sentence. (Ed is the poet's brother.)

But wasn't truth, after all, an act of intuitive faith, something that left poor logic far behind? Truth, he told Ed that same month, was not something reasoned out but something intuitively grasped, something believed in. "Don't reason from feelings or rather don't reason at all," he told his brother. For he saw now that truth was not something arrived at by syllogisms and proofs, but something grasped by a quantum leap of faith. Truth was, after all, an intuitive insight into the essence of a thing, something radiantly perceived in a moment.

—PAUL MARIANI

The standard topic sentence is most valuable when you are writing paragraphs about ideas, when you are explaining something, or when you are making an argument. Such paragraphs usually help an essay develop its thesis step by step. The topic sentences define those steps clearly and help both writer and reader know where they are going. In narratives and in descriptions you may often write paragraphs that do not have a topic sentence. But in all paragraphs, the first sentence should have a word or words that are developed in the following sentences. When you write that first sentence, pause a moment and think of what words in it introduce the main ideas you want to express in the paragraph. Then explore those ideas.

■ **Exercise 4.1** Write a couple of pages very swiftly on something that happened to you recently—a parking problem, a talk with a friend about some important event, some victory that you had, something good or something bad that happened to you. Don't pause much over your composition. Get it on paper quickly. Now study your composition and see how the first sentence in each of your paragraphs introduced the subject you explored in the rest of the paragraph. You will usually discover that when you write quickly about something that happened to you recently, your paragraphs develop naturally.

Now write a couple of pages about something you have been thinking about lately—the ideas expressed in a difficult course, something you have been reading about in the newspapers, some thoughts that have been on your mind. See if the paragraphs you construct develop naturally from the first sentence. How many of your paragraphs have a standard topic sentence in them?

■ **Exercise 4.2** Take each of the following statements as the topic sentence for a paragraph, and write a paragraph developing the subject.

1. My neighborhood was a good (or bad) place to live when I was growing up.
2. The parking problem at this school has been handled badly by the administration.
3. I choose my friends because they have some special qualities.
4. I most fear _____ .

■ **Exercise 4.3** State the topic of each of the following paragraphs in your own words. Then tell whether or not the writer states that topic in a topic sentence. Also, explain what words in the first sentence of each paragraph are developed as the subject for the paragraph itself.

Hutton hiked to the margins of glaciers in the heights of the Alps — great seas of ice, in some places thousands of feet thick. Glaciers can last almost as long as the lofty mountain peaks on which they lie; the ice melts a little each summer but is replenished by fresh snows each winter. Hutton noticed boulders embedded in the ice of some glaciers, and more boulders lying on the slopes just below them, rock and rubble that the ice had apparently picked up from the ground as it grew, and then dropped again when it shrank. Hutton put two and two together. Some of these Swiss glaciers, he decided, must once have flowed down from their eminences and filled more than a few Swiss valleys. The glaciers must have plucked up thousands of boulders as they traveled forward and then dropped their loads when they receded, the way a tide strews pebbles on a beach — hence the misfit boulders lying in the valleys, far from any modern glacier.

This insight, like many of Hutton's finest, was unpopular in his lifetime. Misfit boulders, or *erratic blocks,* had long been considered to be irrefutable evidence of Noah's Flood. They were supposed to have been tumbled up hills and down dales by the churning biblical waters. In those days, many people felt as if a dark crack were slowly widening between the world as explained by science and the world as revealed in Holy Writ. Any hypothesis that threatened to widen the crack was frightening. A theory that both geologists and theologians could respect was accepted with gratitude and relief. So the Flood theory prevailed, and Hutton's was ignored.

—Jonathan Weiner

More than Northerners, civilians of the South found that the war affected every facet of their daily lives. Almost from the beginning Confederates began to feel the pinch of the shortages. Theirs was an agricultural society, primarily devoted to raising cotton and tobacco. When the war closed Northern markets and the Union blockade cut off those in Europe, bales and hogsheads piled up. Confederate authorities urged farmers to grow grain instead. Having the utmost confidence in Jefferson Davis, "our worthy President (at once soldier and statesman)," the Jones family willingly responded to this appeal. Cotton planting at 2,000-acre Arcadia, largest of their plantations, was limited in the 1862 season to one acre for every field hand. Wrote Charles C. Jones, Jr., approvingly: "Every bushel of corn and blade of grass will be greatly needed for the support of our armies."

—*We Americans*

Making All Sentences in a Paragraph Support the Main Idea

Every paragraph needs a logical structure based on the main point of the paragraph. The succession of sentences and the flow of ideas help bring that structure about. Any sentence that distracts readers from the main idea violates the architecture of the paragraph. In the following paragraph, several sentences wander away from the main idea.

> After vigorous exercise, the body enters a dangerous period that cooling off can help prevent. When you are swimming or running, a large blood supply from the heart brings your arms and legs the oxygen required for muscle activity. **The human heart works like a pump. When the right upper chamber of the heart (the *auricle*) fills with blood, blood rushes down into the right lower chamber (the *ventricle*). When this chamber fills, the strong muscles in its wall pump tired blood into an artery that speeds the blood to the lungs.** As you exercise, the muscles squeeze, and blood going back to the heart gets an added push as long as you move your limbs. But if you stop suddenly, all this extra blood stays there: your arm and leg muscles are no longer helping your heart pump the blood around. Blood that remains in the arms and legs is blood kept away from vital organs like the brain. But if you *cool off*, that is, slow down your activity gradually, you'll help bring your pulse rate and your body temperature down slowly, you'll help your muscles rid themselves of metabolic waste, and, most important, you'll keep the blood flowing normally through your body.

The controlling idea of this paragraph may be stated like this: Stopping vigorous exercise suddenly can cause a strain on the heart and other body organs, but a gradual cooling off after activity can prevent serious problems. Now look at the sentences in boldface. These details of how the heart operates are interesting. But they distract the reader from the controlling idea of the paragraph. These sentences have no place here, though they may work well in another part of the paper. The paragraph is clearer and reads more smoothly with the distracting sentences removed.

Check the sentences in your paragraphs carefully against your main idea, and remove any sentences that do not support that main idea.

■ **Exercise 4.4**   The following paragraphs contain sentences that distract from the controlling idea that should direct the paragraph. Locate those sentences, and rewrite the paragraph without them. Although the paragraphs deal with similar information, they have different controlling ideas. Discuss the differences, and show how they help you decide which sentences do not belong.

When I was in high school, I tried out for the baseball team during my sophomore year. I had been a pretty good pitcher in pick-up games where the boys in the neighborhood got together to play on Sunday afternoons. But then there was no pressure. We chose up sides, and we played five or six innings, and when it started to get dark, we quit. If one team got too far ahead, we stopped that game, chose up sides again, and started another. It's not much fun to keep playing a game you know you have no chance of winning. When the Denver Broncos got far behind the San Francisco Forty-Niners in the 1990 Superbowl, I felt disappointed because I had planned to spend that Sunday evening watching a close game, and it was an uninteresting rout. We didn't let that happen in our sandlot games. We played and had fun, and we did not take it seriously. But when I stood on the mound of a real baseball diamond with a coach standing near home-plate and a batter in the box and a catcher squatting to receive my pitch, I went into a panic. Before I stepped off, I hit the batter with one ball, threw another over the catcher's head, hit the coach with yet another, and managed to throw yet another over the backstop. The coach put an X by my name, and that was the end of my baseball career.

When I was in high school, I tried out for the baseball team during my sophomore year. I had been a pretty good pitcher in pick-up games when the boys in the neighborhood played on Sunday afternoons. Pitching a baseball is one of the most difficult feats in sports. In one respect, it is a natural action. It is a lot like throwing a rock, and I suppose people have been throwing rocks at animals and each other ever since our remote ancestors began to hunt and make war. You can control a baseball much better than a rock because the baseball is round and you can get a good grip on it, and it weighs just enough to make you think you can throw it easily, and in fact you can. The trick is to throw it accurately, and that is something only a few people can do. The pitcher stands sixty feet six inches from home plate. Home plate is a rubber slab seventeen inches wide. The batter stands beside it, and the pitcher must throw the ball across that plate between the batter's knees and his armpits. It sounds simple, but to go out there and do it again and again and again with the crowd yelling and the batter trying to knock the ball down your throat is to discover just how difficult it is. For most of us it is not just difficult; it is impossible.

■ **Exercise 4.5**   Write out the controlling idea for each of the following paragraphs. Explain how each sentence in each paragraph supports that controlling idea.

Psychophysicists who study food tastes have found four basic tastes: sweet, sour, salty, and bitter. There are wider variations in what people call sweet or bitter than in what they call sour or salty — variations we are only now beginning to understand. We have found, too, that there is not one but a number of receptor mechanisms in the mouth for bitterness, which may explain why people are sensitive to some bitter foods and not others. We have also discovered that certain substances can suppress one or more of the four tastes.

—LINDA BARTOSHUK

Some children dedicate themselves to being ridiculous, their behavior conjuring up memories of old Mack Sennett comedies and floppy-footed clowns. We have encountered a considerable number of these children in our counselling work over the last two decades. They are usually brought in for evaluation and treatment as "behavior problems"; they may be doing badly in school, be in conflict with everyone in the family, or have threatened to run away from home. Whatever the immediate difficulty, we have been impressed in each case with a theatrical clumsiness, a clownish awkwardness.

—SEYMOUR AND RHODA LEE FISHER

To begin with, there was the nature of the country. The front line, ours and the Fascists', lay in positions of immense natural strength, which as a rule could only be approached from one side. Provided a few trenches have been dug, such places cannot be taken by infantry, except in overwhelming numbers. In our own position or most of those round us a dozen men with two machine-guns could have held off a battalion. Perched on the hill-tops as we were, we should have made lovely marks for artillery; but there was no artillery. Sometimes I used to gaze round the landscape and long — oh how passionately! — for a couple of batteries of guns. One could have destroyed the enemy positions one after another as easily as smashing nuts with a hammer. But on our side the guns simply did not exist. The Fascists did occasionally manage to bring a gun or two from Zaragoza and fire a very few shells, so few that they never even found the range and the shells plunged harmlessly into the empty ravines. Against machine-guns and without artillery there are only three things you can do: dig yourself in at a safe distance — four hundred yards, say — advance across the open and be massacred, or make small-scale night-attacks that will not alter the general situation. Practically, the alternatives are stagnation or suicide.

—GEORGE ORWELL

4b
Building Coherent Paragraphs

In coherent paragraphs, thoughts and pieces of information follow one after the other, connected in ways that are easy for readers to see and understand. Writers use various methods to make these connections and to make ideas flow smoothly so that readers do not feel that something has been left out, that questions have been unanswered, or that new information has been suddenly introduced without reason. As you use these methods, you must think carefully about the sequence of ideas you follow in each paragraph.

You can achieve coherence by carefully arranging the information in a paragraph. That arrangement requires you to look carefully at the first sentence in the paragraph to see what ideas in it you want to develop in the following sentence. To make the paragraph coherent, the ideas in the second sentence must be closely related to the ideas in the first.

Pronouns help coherence by referring to nouns that have already been introduced and identified. You can also help coherence by repeating important words or phrases, by using parallel structures, and by using transitional words and expressions. You should combine these techniques as necessary to write paragraphs that hold together around a central theme or topic.

In the following paragraphs, boldface print indicates some of the devices that lend coherence to the paragraph. Study them carefully to see those ideas that are developed, those words that tie previous information to new information being introduced, and how various thoughts are explained.

Experience gained on the Santa Fe Trail was comparatively 1
unimportant, and might be misleading. Conditions there were 2
very different. The distance was only half as far, and the country 3
was nearly all open and level. **Even more important,** as the ex- 4
pression "Santa Fe trade" indicates, that trail was used by 5
traders, and not by **emigrants.** When the Oregon and California 6
emigrants imitated the Santa Fe traders, **they** nearly always 7
came to grief — as **in using big wagons, forming large compa-** 8
nies, and **organizing in military fashion.** 9
On the other hand, the **emigrants** made use of a general 10
backlog of experience with teams and wagons. Every **farmer** 11
knew a good deal about that sort of thing, and **he** had probably 12
made journeys of several hundred miles. What had to be faced, 13
to get to California, were the new conditions — **the tenfold-long** 14
pull, the untamed Indians, the lack of supply points, the diffi- 15
cult country of deserts and mountains. But in the handling of 16

the wagon itself most of the men were already **proficient,** and 17
this **proficiency** was essential to the success of the covered- 18
wagon migration. 19

— George R. Stewart

4b
¶ coh

In both paragraphs, a logical plan controls the arrangement of information. Each of the two paragraphs starts with a generalization. The most dramatic statement in each paragraph appears last. The pronouns *they* and *he* in lines 7 and 12 connect with nouns stated earlier. Repetition in lines 6, 7, and 10 and in lines 17 and 18 advance the flow of ideas by calling attention to important thoughts. In lines 7 to 9 and 14 to 16, the writer repeats grammatical structures that add coherence to the paragraphs. Finally, the use of the expressions *even more important* (line 4) and *on the other hand* (line 10) and the dramatic use of *but* to open a sentence (line 16) act as transitions, carrying thought smoothly from one idea to another.

Here are some devices that will help you achieve coherence in various kinds of paragraphs that you may write.

Arranging Paragraph Ideas According to a Logical Plan

The way you organize information in a paragraph is related to your main point and what you want to say about it. The arrangements among which you select to present the information in a paragraph are the same as those you considered in organizing your ideas for the paper as a whole (2d).

Spatial Arrangement

You can organize information in a **spatial arrangement** by locating the reader somewhere in a scene and then moving through physical space — from back to front, from top to bottom, from left to right, or in some other logical way. In describing landscapes, paintings, buildings, streets, and various other things, you may choose to move your readers carefully across space.

You may learn to write paragraphs such as the one below by standing in front of the scene you want to describe and mentally blocking it off in sections. If you carry a notebook, you can jot down some things you see in each section.

I walked out on the bridge and looked down at the lock. The canal flowed into the lock through a sprung wooden gate just under the bridge. It ran between two narrowly confining walls for about a hundred feet. Then, with a sudden boil and bubble, it broke against another gate, spilled through, and resumed its sluggish course. The walls of the lock were faced with big blocks of rust-red sandstone.

Some of the stones were so huge that they could have been hoisted into place only with a block and tackle. It was beautiful stone, and it had been beautifully finished and fitted. Time had merely softened it. Here and there along the courses I could even make out the remains of a mason's mark. One device was quite distinct — a double-headed arrow. Another appeared to be two overlapping equilateral triangles. I went on across the bridge to the house. The windows were shuttered and boarded up, and the door was locked. No matter. It was enough just to stand and look at it. It was a lovely house, as beautifully made as the lock, and as firmly designed for function. It gave me a pang to think that there had once been a time when even a lock tender could have so handsome a house. A phoebe called from a sweet-gum tree in the dooryard. Far away, somewhere down by the river, a mourning dove gave an answering sigh. I looked at my watch. It was ten minutes after ten. I started up the towpath.

—BERTON ROUECHÉ

Chronological Arrangement

Another way to present information in a paragraph is chronologically. In a **chronological arrangement,** events are organized as they happen, one after another. Earlier incidents come before later ones. We tell stories in the narrative mode.

The sun rose slowly out of the hazy sea as we hiked through the great olive grove at the foot of Mount Iouktos on Crete. By seven o'clock, we had started our slow climb up the mountain, following a trail that twisted back and forth as it snaked its way toward the summit. We left the olive trees behind quickly and entered a rocky world where a few poplars cast an occasional weak shade. By ten o'clock, the sun had burned the haze off the sea, and its heat bore down on us. We quickly became thirsty, but we had brought no water. By eleven, we were drenched with sweat, and the heat made everything shimmer so that the tumbled rocks seemed to dance crazily in the harsh sunlight. By now we could see for miles down the island of Crete, and to the west the huge bulk of Mount Ida rose into the hot blue sky. By noon, nearly crazy with heat, thirst, and fatigue, we got to the top. There we found a little church, and just beside it was a cistern with a bucket attached to a long rope. We dropped the bucket down into the darkness of the cistern and heard a great, reassuring splash. Quickly we pulled the bucket to the top and drank greedily. Then we sat in the shade of the church and looked out over one of the most beautiful landscapes I had ever seen.

—DICK CURRY

Spatial and chronological arrangements often work together. In both of the sample paragraphs above, chronological and spatial order contribute to the coherence of the paragraph.

4b
¶ coh

Order of Importance

You can arrange paragraph elements by **order of importance,** starting with the least significant or least dramatic information and building to a climax with the most significant or most dramatic.

> Shakespeare came to London at a fortunate time. If he had been born twenty years earlier, he would have arrived in London when underpaid hacks were turning out childish dramas about brown-paper dragons. If he had been born twenty years later, he would have arrived when the drama had begun to lose its hold on ordinary people and was succumbing to a kind of self-conscious cleverness. But his arrival in London coincided with a great wave of excitement and achievement in the theatre, and he rode with it to its crest. William Shakespeare brought great gifts to London, but the city was waiting with gifts of its own to offer him. The root of his genius was Shakespeare's own, but it was London that supplied him with the favoring weather.
>
> —MARCHETTE CHUTE

Inductive and Deductive Arrangements

Paragraphs may be arranged inductively or deductively. An **inductive arrangement** builds through successive instances to support a generalization that comes at the end of a paragraph. In other words, the writer presents details one after the other and finally draws a conclusion from them. In a **deductive arrangement,** the generalization comes first and the particular details succeed it in the paragraph. (See Chapter 36).

Inductive

> We huddled together in the cool spring night, whispering in hoarse voices, thrumming with the excitement that vibrated through the crowd gathering in the parking lot outside the Ames train station. All the way home from Des Moines we had hugged each other, laughed, cried, and hugged each other again. When we passed through the small farming towns between Des Moines and Ames, we rolled down the windows of the Harbingers' station wagon and shouted down the quiet streets, "We beat Marshalltown in seven overtimes! We beat Marshalltown in seven overtimes!" It had a rhythmic beat, a chant we

repeated to each other in unbelieving ecstasy. We beat Marshalltown in seven overtimes! For the first time in ten years, Ames High School had won the state basketball championship. Most of us sophomores felt nothing so important could ever happen to us again.

—SUSAN ALLEN TOTH

Deductive

Other scientific investigations also exerted considerable influence on present-day painters and sculptors. Inventions like the microscope and telescope, with their capacity to enlarge, isolate and probe, offer the artist provocative new worlds to explore. These instruments, which break up structures only to examine them more fully, demonstrate how details can be magnified and separated from the whole and operate as new experiences. Repeatedly, artists in recent years have exploited this idea, allowing one isolated symbol to represent an entire complex organism. Miró often needs merely part of a woman's body to describe all women, or Léger, one magnified letter of the alphabet to conjure up the numberless printed words that daily bombard us.

—KATHERINE KUH

Information in the paragraph about childhood in Chicago (4a) is also arranged deductively.

■ **Exercise 4.6** Explain the method of arrangement used in each paragraph below.

Then a strange blight crept over the area, and everything began to change. Some evil spell had settled on the community; mysterious maladies swept the flocks of chickens; the cattle and sheep sickened and died. Everywhere was a shadow of death. The farmers spoke of much illness among their families. In the town the doctors had become more and more puzzled by new kinds of sickness appearing among their patients. There had been several sudden and unexplained deaths not only among adults but even among children, who would be stricken suddenly while at play and die within a few hours.

—RACHEL CARSON

The preacher preached a wonderful rhythmical sermon, all moans and shouts and lonely cries and dire pictures of hell, and then he sang a song about the ninety and nine safe in the fold, but one little lamb was left out in the cold. Then he said: "Won't you come? Won't you come to Jesus? Young lambs, won't you come?" And he held out his arms to all us young sinners there on the mourners' bench. And the little girls cried. And some of them jumped up and went to Jesus right away. But most of us just sat there.

—LANGSTON HUGHES

Once in a long while, four times so far for me, my mother brings out the metal tube that holds her medical diploma. On the tube are gold circles crossed with seven red lines each—"joy" ideographs in abstract. There are also little flowers that look like gears for a gold machine. According to the scraps of labels with Chinese and American addresses, stamps, and postmarks, the family airmailed the can from Hong Kong in 1950. It got crushed in the middle, and whoever tried to peel the labels off stopped because the red and gold paint came off too, leaving silver scratches that rust. Somebody tried to pry the end off before discovering that the tube pulls apart. When I open it, the smell of China flies out, a thousand-year-old bat flying heavy-headed out of the Chinese caverns where bats are as white as dust, a smell that comes from long ago, far back in the brain. Crates from Canton, Hong Kong, Singapore, and Taiwan have that smell too, only stronger because they are more recently come from the Chinese.

—MAXINE HONG KINGSTON

Linking Ideas with Pronouns

By replacing nouns, pronouns help achieve coherence, joining one part of a paragraph to another. Pronouns with antecedents refer the reader to a previously identified noun and help the writer to connect the ideas in a paragraph without having to mention the nouns again and again.

When you use pronouns, pay special attention to the antecedents. Readers must always find it easy to determine which words pronouns are referring to. When they are used well, pronouns fix attention on the ideas that help hold a paragraph together and make it coherent.

When a mother is afraid that **her** child will die when **it** has only a pimple or a slight cold we speak of anxiety, but if **she** is afraid when the child has a serious illness we call **her** reaction fear. If someone is afraid whenever **he** stands on a height or when **he** has to discuss a topic **he** knows well, we call **his** reaction anxiety; if someone is afraid when **he** loses **his** way high up in the mountains during a heavy thunderstorm we would speak of fear.

—KAREN HORNEY

Linking Ideas by Repetition

Repetition helps bind sentences together in a paragraph. By repeating key words you can help readers follow your line of thought. You want to make sure that every repetition includes some new information along with what is repeated. That information should develop some thought important to your essay.

> We do not **choose** to be born. We do not **choose** our parents. We do not **choose** our historical epoch, or the country of our birth, or the immediate circumstances of our upbringing. We do not, most of us, **choose** to die; nor do we **choose** the time or conditions of our death. But within all this realm of choicelessness, we do **choose** how we shall live; courageously or in cowardice, honorably or dishonorably, with purpose or in drift.
>
> —JOSEPH EPSTEIN

Linking Ideas by Parallel Structure

You can tie thought units together in your paragraphs by repeating the forms of clauses, phrases, or sentences. In the paragraph below, parallelism (discussed in Chapter 7) dramatically links Macaulay's statements about Britain's King Charles I (1600–1649), the only English king to be judged a criminal by his people and executed by beheading.

> We charge him with having broken his coronation oath; and we are told that he kept his marriage vow! We accuse him of having given up his people to the merciless inflictions of the most hot-headed and hard-hearted of prelates; and the defense is, that he took his little son on his knee and kissed him! We censure him for having violated the articles of the Petition of Right, after having, for good and valuable consideration, promised to observe them; and we are informed that he was accustomed to hear prayers at six o'clock in the morning! It is to such considerations as these, together with his Van Dyck dress, his handsome face, and his peaked beard, that he owes, we verily believe, most of his popularity with the present generation.
>
> —THOMAS BABINGTON MACAULAY

Transitional Expressions

Transitional expressions are words or phrases that tell a reader something like this: "I am now leading you carefully from the point that I have just made to the point that I am about to make. Don't let me lose you." The

✓ CHECKLIST: TRANSITIONAL EXPRESSIONS

To show relations in space

above, adjacent to, against, alongside, around, at a distance from, at the, below, beside, beyond, encircling, far off, forward, from the, in front of, in the rear, inside, near the back, near the end, nearby, next to, on, over, surrounding, there, through the, to the left, to the right, up front

To show relations in time

afterward, at last, before, earlier, first, former, formerly, further, furthermore, immediately, in the first place, in the interval, in the meantime, in the next place, in the last, later on, latter, meanwhile, next, now, often, once, previously, second, simultaneously, sometime later, subsequently, suddenly, then, therefore, third, today, tomorrow, until now, when, years ago, yesterday

To show something added to what has come before

again, also, and, and then, besides, further, furthermore, in addition, last, likewise, moreover, next, nor, too

To give examples or to intensify points

after all, as an example, certainly, for example, for instance, indeed, in fact, in truth, it is true, of course, specifically, that is

To show similarities

alike, in the same way, like, likewise, resembling, similarly

To show contrasts

after all, although, but, conversely, differ(s) from, difference, different, dissimilar, even though, granted, however, in contrast, in spite of, nevertheless, notwithstanding, on the contrary, on the other hand, otherwise, still, though, unlike, while this may be true, yet

To indicate cause and effect

accordingly, as a result, because, consequently, hence, since, then, therefore, thus

To conclude or summarize

finally, in brief, in conclusion, in other words, in short, in summary, that is, to summarize most obvious transitional expressions are words such as *moreover, furthermore, and, but, or, nevertheless, the, still,* and *likewise.* These expressions, in boldface in the paragraph below, look back to the thought just expressed and announce that readers will now move to a related but slightly different point.

Many couples who want to adopt a child run into frustrating difficulties. They may have a comfortable home and financial security. **And** they may be loving and generous people. **But** they may be too old for the standards set by the adoption agency. **Or** they may discover that no children are available. **Then,** when a child is available, the couple may be charged an exorbitant fee. **Nevertheless,** couples who want to adopt a child usually persevere, **and** their determination usually pays off.

Well-constructed paragraphs may hold together without obvious transitional words and phrases. You can write sentences like the following and know that readers will assume that you are speaking of cause and effect.

I discovered that he lied to me about where he had been that night. I never trusted him again.

You do not have to say this:

I discovered that he lied to me about where he had been that night. Accordingly, I never trusted him again.

A good general rule to follow in writing holds that prose should be efficient. That is, you should generally delete words not necessary to the meaning you want to convey. Unless transitional words are necessary to express your meaning, you should not use them. Readers mentally may add such words as *for example, thus, however,* and *nevertheless* as they read. Also, you have already seen how linking devices other than transitional expressions can work in your paragraphs.

Even the punctuation in a sentence can serve as a connecting device. Notice how the dash in the example below links ideas without stating a transition directly. (The dash is discussed in 27a.)

Some penny-arcade war machines were also busy—the familiar American sound of the thump and whine of miniature electronic holocausts.

— GEORGE PLIMPTON

The rule comes down to this: don't use transitional expressions unless you *must* use them to be clear. A steady repetition of *moreover, furthermore, nevertheless, but,* and so on can easily bore your readers.

■ **Exercise 4.7** Rewrite the following paragraphs, putting in transitional devices where they are needed and taking them out where they are not needed. Compare your revisions with the revisions done by other members of your class. Be prepared to explain why you have removed a transitional device, why you have put one in, or why you have left one in the original paragraph.

Writing is difficult for almost everybody, even professional writers. Specifically, writing requires hours of concentrated work. Furthermore, writers must usually withdraw from others while they are doing their writing. Moreover, writing exposes many writers to a constant sense of failure because they do not think they are doing well. Consequently, many writers stop writing at the peak of their careers. For example, Thomas Hardy thought that he wrote novels badly and stopped after writing some of the greatest novels in the English language. In the same way, Virginia Woolf fell into such despair about her work that she eventually committed suicide. Accordingly, we can see that both teachers and students who think that a writing course can make writing easy are perhaps pursuing a false hope. In other words, a writing course may make one's writing better, but it may not make it easier to do.

The house stood on a shady street in the suburbs. Surrounding it, the neighborhood was filled with similar houses. It was a comfortable place, large and square, with three floors and a basement and a broad covered porch across the front. In the rear, a large backyard allowed the family to picnic in warm weather. The backyard was surrounded by a pleasant wooden fence, too high for anyone to see over. Therefore, it was a private place, and people could sit there and talk or read or merely think without being disturbed. On the other hand, the house itself was old. As a result, the furnace needed replacing. Furthermore, the windows let in drafts of cold air in winter and, likewise, hot air in summer. Often people told us how much they like our house. And in truth, we liked it, too. But it was not an ideal place. Still, I am glad to have lived there growing up, and, not withstanding its disadvantages, I miss it.

Linking Ideas from One Paragraph to the Next

In an essay, coherence *between* paragraphs is as important as coherence *within* paragraphs. You can help your readers follow the direction of your

4b

¶ coh

thought as you move from one paragraph to the next in your writing.

The opening sentence of a paragraph in the body of an essay usually looks back to information in the previous paragraph and forward to information about to be disclosed. Boldface print in the excerpts below shows how that first sentence in a paragraph looks both backward and forward.

> When Africans first got to New York, or New Amsterdam as the Dutch called it, they lived in the farthest downtown portions of the city, near what is now called The Bowery. Later, they shifted, and were shifted, as their numbers grew, to the section known as Greenwich Village. The Civil War Draft Riots in 1863 accounted for the next move by New York's growing Negro population.
>
> **After this violence** (a few million dollars' worth of property was destroyed, and a Negro orphanage was burned to the ground) a great many Negroes moved across the river into Brooklyn. . . .
>
> —LeRoi Jones

> Among those who now take a dim view of marijuana are Dr. Sidney Cohen, a drug expert at the University of California at Los Angeles, who once described marijuana as "a trivial weed," and Dr. Robert L. DuPont, former director of the National Institute on Drug Abuse, who had lobbied for marijuana's legalization.
>
> **According to these and other experts,** it is no longer possible to say that marijuana is an innocuous drug with few if any health effects aside from intoxication.
>
> —Jane E. Brody

In the body of an essay, the first sentence of a new paragraph usually provides the link to ideas in the preceding paragraph. Occasionally, however, the last sentence in a paragraph will point forward.

> Why is marking up a book indispensable to reading it? First, it keeps you awake. (And I don't mean merely conscious; I mean wide awake.) In the second place, reading, if it is active, is thinking, and thinking tends to express itself in words, spoken or written. The marked book is usually the thought-through book. Finally, writing helps you remember the thoughts you had, or the thoughts the author expressed. **Let me develop these three points.**
>
> If reading is to accomplish anything more than passing time, it must be active. . . .
>
> —Mortimer J. Adler

tion to do that. Modern medicine has increased longevity to some degree, but, just as important, it has alleviated some of the persistent, nonfatal maladies of the body. Throughout history, of course, some people have reached their eighties in excellent health, but until this century the majority of Europeans and Americans aged as many people still do in the poorest countries of the world—suffering irreversible physical decay in their forties and fifties. Philippe Ariès reminds us that until recently chronological age had very little meaning in European society; the word "old" was associated with the loss of teeth, eyesight, and so on. The very novelty of health and physical vigor in those past sixty-five is reflected in the current struggle over nomenclature. Since the passage of the Social Security Act, in 1935, demographers have used the age of sixty-five as a benchmark and labeled those at or over it as "the old" or "the elderly." The terms are meant to be objective, but because of their connotations they have proved unacceptable to those designated by them. Sensitive to their audience, gerontologists and government agencies have substituted "older people," "the aging," or "senior citizens." These terms, being relative, could apply to anyone of almost any age, but, by a kind of linguistic somersault, they have come to denote a precise chronological category.

People now over sixty-five live on a frontier also in the sense that the territory is fast filling up behind them. By the end of the century, if current demographic trends hold, one in eight Americans, or slightly more than 12 percent of the population, will be sixty-five or over. The increase will at first be relatively small, because the number of children born in the thirties was a relatively small one; but then, baring catastrophe or large-scale immigration, the numbers will start to climb. In the years between 2020 and 2030, after the baby-boom generation reaches its seniority, some fifty-five million Americans, or nearly 20 percent of the projected population, will be sixty-five or over. How the society will support these people is a problem that Americans are just beginning to think about. Politicians have been considering the implications for Social Security and federal retirement benefits, but they have not yet begun to imagine all the consequences in other realms.

The younger generation assumes that at sixty-five people leave their jobs and spend five, ten, or fifteen years of their lives in a condition called retirement. But there, too, the generation now around sixty-five has broken new ground. Historically speaking, the very notion of retirement—on a mass scale at any rate—is new, and dates only from the industrial revolution, from the time when a majority of workers (and not just a few professionals) became replaceable parts in organizations outside the family. The possibility of re-

The following paragraph is used as a bridge leading from one part of a critical essay to another. Such paragraphs may serve to carry readers over material where they might otherwise be lost.

> I have, I hope, cleared the ground for a dispassionate comparison of certain aspects of Shakespeare's technique in the Henry VI plays with his technique in the "romance" histories. Now, perhaps, some general remarks about the structure of the trilogy will be helpful.
>
> —PAUL DEAN

This short paragraph joins two parts of an essay about the three plays Shakespeare wrote about the English king, Henry VI. The first sentence reminds readers of points made earlier about some of the dramatic techniques Shakespeare used in those plays. Now Dean, the author of the essay, announces a fairly major shift from that discussion to another, this one bearing on the structure of the three plays, called a *trilogy*.

> There is an expression called "the peak experience," a moment which, emotionally, can never again be equalled in your life. I had mine, that first day in the village of Juffure, in the back country in black West Africa.
>
> —ALEX HALEY

This two-sentence paragraph provides a dramatic link for what is clearly a turning point in the essay. The device is especially useful when you think that the two parts of an essay are very different from each other and you want to be sure that the reader sees the connection.

■ **Exercise 4.8** Discuss in class the various devices used to build coherence within and between paragraphs in the following selection from Frances Fitzgerald's article on a retirement community called Sun C near Tampa, Florida.

Ask yourself these questions: What major theme joins all these graphs? What words carry the theme from one paragraph to th How do the last sentences in each paragraph look forward to paragraph? How do the first sentences in each paragraph look last paragraph?

> The younger generation in this country has grow notion that people should reach the age of sixty-five good health. But Americans now over sixty belong to

The following paragraph is used as a bridge leading from one part of a critical essay to another. Such paragraphs may serve to carry readers over material where they might otherwise be lost.

4b
¶ coh

> I have, I hope, cleared the ground for a dispassionate comparison of certain aspects of Shakespeare's technique in the Henry VI plays with his technique in the "romance" histories. Now, perhaps, some general remarks about the structure of the trilogy will be helpful.
>
> —PAUL DEAN

This short paragraph joins two parts of an essay about the three plays Shakespeare wrote about the English king, Henry VI. The first sentence reminds readers of points made earlier about some of the dramatic techniques Shakespeare used in those plays. Now Dean, the author of the essay, announces a fairly major shift from that discussion to another, this one bearing on the structure of the three plays, called a *trilogy*.

> There is an expression called "the peak experience," a moment which, emotionally, can never again be equalled in your life. I had mine, that first day in the village of Juffure, in the back country in black West Africa.
>
> —ALEX HALEY

This two-sentence paragraph provides a dramatic link for what is clearly a turning point in the essay. The device is especially useful when you think that the two parts of an essay are very different from each other and you want to be sure that the reader sees the connection.

■ **Exercise 4.8** Discuss in class the various devices used to build coherence within and between paragraphs in the following selection from Frances Fitzgerald's article on a retirement community called Sun City near Tampa, Florida.

Ask yourself these questions: What major theme joins all these paragraphs? What words carry the theme from one paragraph to the next? How do the last sentences in each paragraph look forward to the next paragraph? How do the first sentences in each paragraph look back to the last paragraph?

> The younger generation in this country has grown up with the notion that people should reach the age of sixty-five and reach it in good health. But Americans now over sixty belong to the first genera-

tion to do that. Modern medicine has increased longevity to some degree, but, just as important, it has alleviated some of the persistent, nonfatal maladies of the body. Throughout history, of course, some people have reached their eighties in excellent health, but until this century the majority of Europeans and Americans aged as many people still do in the poorest countries of the world—suffering irreversible physical decay in their forties and fifties. Philippe Ariès reminds us that until recently chronological age had very little meaning in European society; the word "old" was associated with the loss of teeth, eyesight, and so on. The very novelty of health and physical vigor in those past sixty-five is reflected in the current struggle over nomenclature. Since the passage of the Social Security Act, in 1935, demographers have used the age of sixty-five as a benchmark and labeled those at or over it as "the old" or "the elderly." The terms are meant to be objective, but because of their connotations they have proved unacceptable to those designated by them. Sensitive to their audience, gerontologists and government agencies have substituted "older people," "the aging," or "senior citizens." These terms, being relative, could apply to anyone of almost any age, but, by a kind of linguistic somersault, they have come to denote a precise chronological category.

People now over sixty-five live on a frontier also in the sense that the territory is fast filling up behind them. By the end of the century, if current demographic trends hold, one in eight Americans, or slightly more than 12 percent of the population, will be sixty-five or over. The increase will at first be relatively small, because the number of children born in the thirties was a relatively small one; but then, baring catastrophe or large-scale immigration, the numbers will start to climb. In the years between 2020 and 2030, after the baby-boom generation reaches its seniority, some fifty-five million Americans, or nearly 20 percent of the projected population, will be sixty-five or over. How the society will support these people is a problem that Americans are just beginning to think about. Politicians have been considering the implications for Social Security and federal retirement benefits, but they have not yet begun to imagine all the consequences in other realms.

The younger generation assumes that at sixty-five people leave their jobs and spend five, ten, or fifteen years of their lives in a condition called retirement. But there, too, the generation now around sixty-five has broken new ground. Historically speaking, the very notion of retirement—on a mass scale at any rate—is new, and dates only from the industrial revolution, from the time when a majority of workers (and not just a few professionals) became replaceable parts in organizations outside the family. The possibility of retirement for large numbers of people depended, of course, on the establishment of adequate social-insurance systems, and these were not created until long after the building of industry. In this country, whose industrial evolution lagged behind that of Western Europe, the possibility came only with the New Deal. The Social Security Act of 1935 created an economic floor for those who could not work. More important, it created the presumption that American workers had a right to retire—a right to live without working after the age of sixty-five. This presumption led, in turn, to the establishment of government, corporate, and union pension plans that allowed workers to retire without a disastrous loss of income. But these pension plans did not cover very many people until some time after World War II. Even in 1950, 46 percent of all American men sixty-five and over were still working or looking for work. In 1980, only 20 percent were.

—FRANCES FITZGERALD

4c
Using Supporting Details

Paragraphs are usually weak when they contain nothing but general statements.

> The parking problem here at school is terrible. It sometimes takes hours and hours to find a space. Why can't the administration do something about it? Students are late to class because they can't find a parking space, and then they miss things in the lecture, and they do poorly on their final exams. With all the money the university is spending on football, you would think that they could put a little of it into student parking. It's especially hard on commuter students.

Compare that general paragraph with this one, which is much more specific:

> On Friday of last week, I drove to school, arriving at 9:45 for a ten o'clock class. A parking sticker that cost me $250 for the year announces from the windshield of my car that I have the right to park in any student parking lot. But on Friday, I drove around parking lot A,

parking lot B, and parking lot C without finding a space. Finally, in desperation, I drove up to parking lot M a mile away from my class. There I found plenty of parking, but by the time I raced to the Mahan Building, where my accounting class was in progress, it was 10:20, and Professor Lewis stopped his lecture as I came in and said, "Well, we are certainly happy that Mr. Jenkins has decided to join us this morning. I hope you didn't disturb your sleep just to be with us, Mr. Jenkins." I felt my face turn hot, and I knew I was blushing from anger and embarrassment. I should have come earlier and parked in lot M at the beginning. But my own problem did lead me on a greater quest that is the subject of this paper. What is the nature of the parking problem here, and what can be done about it?

Sensory Details

Sensory details support paragraphs well—mention of colors, actions, sounds, and sensations of taste, touch, and smell. Concrete details are more effective than a series of generalizations. The more specific the details, the better. Sensory language helps readers to join their experience to that of the writer.

An essential quality of fiction, sensory language also adds life, clarity, and vividness to nonfiction prose, as you can see in this paragraph:

> We rode through landscapes of almost surreal beauty. Once we stopped for lunch in a deep stand of cottonwood and surprised a nesting colony of great blue herons; they circled and cried over our heads. Later we flushed a family of javelinas and sent them snorting and grunting into a field of tumbleweed. Other images are imprinted on my mind: blood-red arroyos slicing through curtains of green mesquite; distant blue mountains seen through a screen of cottonwood; an antelope bounding through grass as white as snow. Every evening, while the crowns of the trees filled with golden light, Walter and I would whoop and roll about in the shallow river, letting the cold water wash off the dust and sweat of the day.
>
> —DOUGLAS PRESTON

Statistics and Cases

Statistics and cases are the language of facts and figures. You can often use them effectively to support a topic. **Statistics** are numerical data; **cases** are specific instances involving real people and events. Statistics give authority to your statements and can often help your interpretation of a situation. Notice how the numbers in the first paragraph of the following selection help the writer make his point that although many American Indian children leave the reservation to attend public schools, some tribes feel a strong need to preserve their traditional schools on their reservations.

In 1969 there were 178,476 Indian students, ages five to eighteen, enrolled in public, Federal, private and mission schools. Approximately 12,000 children of this age group were not in school. Of the total in school, 119,000 were in public schools, 36,263 in boarding schools operated by the Bureau of Indian Affairs, 16,100 in Bureau day schools, 108 in Bureau hospital schools, and 4,089 in dormitories maintained by the Bureau for children attending public schools. The Bureau operated 77 boarding schools, 144 day schools, 2 hospital schools, and 18 dormitories. The number of Indian children being educated in public schools has steadily increased, aided by the financial assistance provided local school districts under the Johnson-O'Malley Act of 1934 (which provided financial support, in cooperation with the Department of Health, Education, and Welfare, to aid federally affected areas). The closer relationship between state school systems and the Indian system has been welcomed by many Indian groups. Sixty-one tribes have established compulsory education regulations that conform with those of the states where they live.

On the other hand, some more traditional Indian groups have rebelled at efforts to close down reservation schools. The attempt of the Bureau of Indian Affairs to close down, on July 1, 1968, a small grade-school at Tama, Iowa, created an instant reaction. Forty-five Mesquakie Indian children were attending school there on the reservation purchased by their ancestors, a separate body of the Sac tribe which, with the Fox, had a hundred years earlier been pushed out of Iowa into Kansas. The Mesquakie Indians, who had not been consulted about the closing of the school, promptly sought judicial relief. They got it in September 1968, in the Federal District Court at Cedar Rapids, when United States District Court Judge Edward J. McManus ordered the school reopened in the fall. The Mesquakie were able to call upon a number of influential white friends in their attempt to retain their Indian school. The validity of integration into a white school system that is often both distant from and cold toward Indian values can be questioned, as the Mesquakie questioned it.

—Wilcomb E. Washburn

Always try to think of specific examples to support your generalizations. Readers want to know why you think the way you do, why you make the general statements that you make, and why you look on the world as you do. You can help them by telling them incidents that have formed your opinions.

Of course, not every point that you make in a paragraph can or should be supported by concrete details. Especially in a long essay, a paragraph may present a series of generalizations or abstractions without supporting data. But effective writing uses details. Without them, readers remain vague about what the writer is trying to say, and if they do understand, they may not be convinced.

■ **Exercise 4.9** Read the following selection and identify the details that support the controlling idea of the paragraph.

> When I first saw a water shrew swimming, I was most struck by the thing which I ought to have expected but did not; at the moment of diving, the little black and white beast appears to be made of silver. Like the plumage of ducks and grebes, but quite unlike the fur of most water mammals, such as seals, otters, beaver or coypus, the fur of the water shrew remains absolutely dry under water; that is to say, it retains a thick layer of air while the animal is below the surface. In the other mammals mentioned above, it is only the short, woolly undercoat that remains dry, the superficial hair tips becoming wet, wherefore the animal looks its natural color when underwater and is superficially wet when it emerges. I was already aware of the peculiar qualities of the waterproof fur of the shrew, and, had I given it a thought, I should have known that it would look, under water, exactly like the air-retaining fur on the underside of a water beetle or on the abdomen of a water spider. Nevertheless the wonderful, transparent silver coat of the shrew was, to me, one of those delicious surprises that nature has in store for her admirers.
>
> —KONRAD Z. LORENZ

4d
Using Appropriate Paragraph Forms

The following examples of paragraph forms offer several varieties for study and imitation. The forms we illustrate here include narration, or telling a story of events that happen one after another; process analysis, or how a process works; classification, or sorting data and facts into groups; causal analysis, or showing cause and effect; and definition, or explaining the meaning of terms and words.

As you encounter paragraphs in your own reading, try to see what they do in the essay — do they tell a story, explain a fact, analyze an event? And as you construct your own essays, use the examples here to help you build the kinds of paragraphs you need to develop your topic.

4d
¶ form

Narration

Use narrative paragraphs to tell a story in chronological order. Relate the events one after the other as they happened in time.

> Banyan Street was the route Lucille Miller took home from the twenty-four-hour Mayfair Market on the night of October 7, 1964, a night when the moon was dark and the wind was blowing and she was out of milk, and Banyan Street was where, at about 12:20 A.M., her 1964 Volkswagen came to a sudden stop, caught fire, and began to burn. For an hour and fifteen minutes, Lucille Miller ran up and down Banyan Street calling for help, but no cars passed and no help came. At three o'clock that morning, when the fire had been put out and the California Highway Patrol officers were completing their report, Lucille Miller was still sobbing and incoherent, for her husband had been asleep in the Volkswagen. "What will I tell the children, when there's nothing left, nothing left in the casket," she cried to the friend who called to comfort her. "How can I tell them there's nothing left?"
>
> —JOAN DIDION

Process Analysis

Use process analysis in paragraphs to explain how to do something or how to make something. Here is a paragraph on how to check the inflation on your bike tires if you don't have an air pressure gauge with you:

> There's a great *curb-edge test* you can do to make sure your tires are inflated just right. Rest the wheel on the edge of a curb or stair, so the bike sticks out into the street or path, perpendicular to the curb or stair edge. Get the wheel so you can push down on it at about a 45 degree angle from above the bike. Push hard on the handlebars or seat, depending on which wheel you're testing. The curb should flare the tire a bit but shouldn't push right through the tire and clunk against the rim. You want the tire to have a little give when you ride over chuckholes and rocks, in other words, but you don't want it so soft that you bottom out. If you are a hot-shot who wants tires so hard that they don't have any give, you'll have to stick to riding on clean-

swept Velodrome tracks, or watch very carefully for little sharp objects on the road. Or you'll have to get used to that sudden riding-on-the-rim feeling that follows the blowout of an overblown tire.

—TOM CUTHBERTSON

Comparison and Contrast

Organize paragraphs by using comparisons that may include both similarities and differences.

You may make comparisons between conditions existing at two or more times or between people, places, or things existing at the same time. But be sure that your comparisons are sensible. You can compare any two things with each other—a freight train with a short story, for example. Both have a beginning, a middle, and an end. But such meaningless and trivial comparisons will annoy your readers. Annoyed readers usually stop reading.

The following paragraph compares a Russian tank, the T-34 of 1942, with earlier Russian tanks and also with the German tanks that the Russians encountered in World War II. Because the comparison involves weapons of two armies at war with each other, it is clearly a meaningful comparison.

The new T-34s coming into action in 1942 had better guns and engines. And they retained the broad tracks that made them more mobile and more weatherworthy than German vehicles. In mud or snow they could—quite literally—run rings around the panzers. The turret of the earlier T-34 had been difficult to operate, and its large hatch was vulnerable to grenades and satchel charges; the hatch had been replaced by a smaller opening for the commander and a second one for the gunner. The rear overhang over the turret—a favorite place for the German tank-killer squads to plant their mines—was eliminated, and handrails were welded onto the rear deck so that infantrymen could be carried to counter enemy antitank teams.

—JOHN SHAW

Classification

Use classification to divide a large group into several smaller parts so that readers can see different elements in a group that, at first glance, may seem to be without variation.

Classification helps organize complicated information so that you can manage it in steps.

People who understand high finance are of two kinds: those who have vast fortunes of their own and those who have nothing at all. To an actual millionaire a million pounds is something real and comprehensible. To the applied mathematician and the lecturer in economics (assuming both to be practically starving) a million pounds is at least as real as a thousand, they having never possessed either sum. But the world is full of people who fall between these two categories, knowing nothing of millions but well accustomed to think in thousands, and it is of these that finance committees are mostly composed. The result is a phenomenon that has often been observed but never yet investigated. It might be termed the Law of Triviality. Briefly stated, it means that the time spent on any item of the agenda will be in inverse proportion to the sum involved.

—C. NORTHCOTE PARKINSON

Causal Analysis

Organize paragraphs around an explanation of cause and effect when you want to explain why something happened or when you want to explain the effects of some happening. Here are two paragraphs that give the cause and effect of the plague called the Black Death, which ravaged Europe in the fourteenth century:

In October 1347, a fleet of Genoese merchant ships from the Orient arrived at the harbor of Messina in northeast Sicily. All aboard the ships were dead or dying of a ghastly disease. The harbor masters tried to quarantine the fleet, but the source of the pestilence was borne by rats, not men, and these were quick to scurry ashore. Within six months, half of the population of the region around Messina had fled their homes or succumbed to the disease. Four years later, between one-quarter and one-half of the population of Europe was dead.

The Black Death, or plague, that devastated Europe in the 14th century was caused by bacteria that live in the digestive tract of fleas, and in particular the fleas of rats. But at that time, the disease seemed arbitrary and capricious, and to strike from nowhere. One commentator wrote: "Father abandoned child, wife husband, one brother another, for the plague seemed to strike through breath and sight." The pestilence was widely held to be a scourge sent by God to chasten a sinful people.

—CHET RAYMO

Definition

Use paragraphs to define objects, concepts, ideas, terms, political movements, and anything else that may be important to your essay. A useful definition first identifies something as a member of a class of similar things; then it states how it differs from everything else in its class. Simple, concrete objects may often be identified in a single sentence if they require definition at all.

> A typewriter is a small tabletop machine — operated by a keyboard activated by human fingers — that allows a writer to produce writing on paper more quickly and more legibly than by handwriting.

Here a typewriter is first classified as a small tabletop machine. What distinguishes it from a copier, a stapler, a table saw, or whatever is that it is operated by a keyboard activated by human fingers and that its purpose is to allow a writer to produce writing on paper more quickly and more legibly than by handwriting.

Definitions of more abstract terms may require an entire paragraph or several paragraphs. A paragraph that defines usually comes near the beginning of an essay so that the writer may be sure that readers understand a term to be used throughout.

> We have a roster of diseases which medicine calls "idiopathic," meaning that we do not know what causes them. The list is much shorter than it used to be; a century ago, common infections like typhus fever and tuberculous meningitis were classed as idiopathic illnesses. Originally, when it first came into the language of medicine, the term had a different, highly theoretical meaning. It was assumed that most human diseases were intrinsic, due to inbuilt failures of one sort or another, things gone wrong with various internal humors. The word "idiopathic" was intended to mean, literally, a disease having its own origin, a primary disease without any external cause. The list of such disorders has become progressively shorter as medical science has advanced, especially within this century, and the meaning of the term has lost its doctrinal flavor; we use "idiopathic" now to indicate simply that the cause of a particular disease is unknown. Very likely, before we are finished with medical science, and with luck, we will have found that all varieties of disease are the result of one or another sort of meddling, and there will be no more idiopathic illness.

—LEWIS THOMAS

Writers frequently combine patterns. The paragraphs by Chet Raymo and Lewis Thomas, for example, use narrative to help develop cause and effect and definition. The paragraph by C. Northcote Parkinson (page 83) involves causal analysis as well as classification. When you write an essay, you should not feel obligated to use only one method of development in each paragraph. But your paragraphs will be more coherent if you decide which method of development should be most important in that paragraph for your purposes.

4d
¶ form

■ **Exercise 4.10** Discuss the various techniques used in the following paragraphs — narrative, process analysis, comparison, classification, cause and effect, or definition.

The figure that comes to me oftenest, out of the shadows of that vanished time, is that of Brown of the steamer *Pennsylvania* — the man referred to in a former chapter, whose memory was so good and tiresome. He was a middle-aged, long, slim, bony, smooth-shaven, horse-faced, ignorant, stingy, malicious, snarling, fault-hunting, mote-magnifying tyrant. I early got the habit of coming on watch with dread at my heart. No matter how good a time I might have been having with the off-watch below, and no matter how high my spirits might be when I started aloft, my soul became lead in my body the moment I approached the pilot-house.

I still remember the first time I ever entered the presence of that man. The boat had backed out from St. Louis and was "straightening down." I ascended to the pilot-house in high feather, and very proud to be semi-officially a member of the executive family of so fast and famous a boat. Brown was at the wheel. I paused in the middle of the room, all fixed to make my bow, but Brown did not look around. I thought he took a furtive glance at me out of the corner of his eye, but as not even this notice was repeated, I judged I had been mistaken. By this time he was picking his way among some dangerous "breaks" abreast the woodyards; therefore it would not be proper to interrupt him; so I stepped softly to the high bench and took a seat.

—MARK TWAIN

In December of 1862, Benjamin Butler was replaced in New Orleans by General Nathaniel Banks — who was immediately offered a bribe of $100,000 to approve a shady deal. A disillusioned Banks wrote his wife that "everybody connected with the government has been employed in stealing." He commented sadly: "I never despaired of my country until I came here."

Banks was by no means the only one who despaired of what he witnessed in the free-spending wartime years. The New York *Herald* coined a new epithet—"shoddy"—to describe the whole era. Originally, the word referred to a flimsy material used by profiteering contractors to make Army uniforms that were so poor they tended to disintegrate in the rain. "The world has seen its iron age, its silver age, its golden age and its brazen age," pronounced the *Herald.* "This is the age of shoddy." It was characterized by "shoddy brokers in Wall Street, or shoddy manufacturers of shoddy goods, or shoddy contractors for shoddy articles." On Sundays, concluded the *Herald,* these men became "shoddy Christians."

—DALE JACKSON AND THE EDITORS OF TIME-LIFE BOOKS

People react strongly and variously to being queued. Russians line themselves up without being told. Moscow theater audiences file out, last row first, like school children marching out of assemblies. In America, on the contrary, theatrical performances break up like the Arctic ice in springtime. Commuters and the constitutionally impatient gather themselves for a dash up the aisle, while the rest of the audience is still applauding. Fidgeters and people who can't bear having anyone ahead of them sidle across rows to emergency exits, while placid souls who seem to enjoy the presence of others drift happily up the aisle with the crowd. In Moscow, the theater is emptied faster. In New York, you can get out fast if you're willing to work at it.

—CAROLINE BIRD

■ **Exercise 4.11** Discuss what paragraph form you would use to develop these topics. Choose from narration, process analysis, comparison and contrast, classification, causal analysis, and definition.

1. The meaning of intelligence
2. An embarrassing or humorous moment
3. Types of teachers
4. How to repair a flat tire
5. American democracy and ancient Greek democracy
6. Why teenagers drop out of school

■ **Exercise 4.12** Use the topics below to practice writing paragraphs according to the method listed by each number.

1. *Narration: (a)* a picnic, *(b)* what you did last Monday morning, *(c)* a time you were lost, *(d)* your first dance

2. *Process analysis:* (a) cooking a simple recipe, (b) changing a flat tire, (c) how to study for an exam, (d) throwing a curve ball, (e) learning to type
3. *Comparison:* (a) a novel and a film based on the novel, (b) a pet dog and a pet cat, (c) two college courses, (d) downhill skiing and cross-country skiing, (e) rowing and canoeing, (f) German war aims in 1914 and in 1939
4. *Classification:* (a) supermarket shoppers, (b) clothing styles for different sorts of people, (c) kinds of television watchers, (d) planets in the solar system, (e) fantastic movies and police movies
5. *Causal analysis:* (a) some effects of nuclear war, (b) why some children have trouble learning to write, (c) why more women are smoking cigarettes, (d) how high unemployment rates affect teenagers
6. *Definition:* (a) racism, (b) fascism, (c) religion, (d) women's rights, (e) rock music, (f) jazz, (g) humanity, (h) spectator sports, (i) a fan

---

4e
Constructing Opening and Closing Paragraphs

Your opening paragraph should announce the general topic of your essay and be interesting enough to make people want to read on; the opening paragraph usually implies a promise you make to the reader to do something in your essay. Your concluding paragraph should end with that promise kept.

Writing Opening Paragraphs That Seize Readers' Attention

Your opening paragraphs must win over readers trying to decide whether to read your work. Your opening paragraphs set the tone for everything else in your essay, announcing not only your subject but also the sort of audience you want to read your work.

A few audiences may expect your opening paragraphs to outline everything you intend to do in your essay. Descriptions of scientific experiments almost always start with such an outline, called an **abstract** in scientific circles. But if you are writing about some personal topic or about something you wish to explain or report, your first paragraphs usually give only an inviting glimpse of what lies in store for the reader.

Note how the opening paragraphs that follow introduce a subject and set the tone for the piece.

Nearly 70 percent of Americans are worried about the quality of their drinking water, according to a recent survey. Much of their concern centers on how water looks, tastes, or smells. Unfortunately, water that is hazardous to your health usually looks, tastes, and smells just fine.

— Consumer Reports

Spring is a glorious time to be in the Kansas Flint Hills, especially if the rains have been plentiful. The bluestem grasses have lost their winter gray and brown in favor of a deep rich green, a color that will soon fade with the coming of the hot summer sun. Even if spring is brief, as it is in some years, it is sufficient. The clean sweet smells carried on the gentle warm breeze blowing up from the southwest carry a freshness that the nostrils have not sensed since the Indian summer days of fall. "The hills," as the local cattlemen call the land, have none of the flaming beauty of the forested New England mountains or the majesty of the Rocky Mountains. Rather, the gentle contour of the rolling carpet of grass stretching from horizon to horizon is soft and restfully inviting. It is peaceful because the hand of man is little in evidence. Most of the Flint Hills are still virgin prairie, much as they were a century or more ago when the Indian's cattle— buffalo — grazed on the tall grasses. Today the white man's cattle have replaced the shaggy monsters of the past.

—David Dary

I spent several days and nights in mid-September with my ailing pig, and I feel driven to account for this stretch of time, more particularly since the pig died at last, and I lived, and things might easily have gone the other way round and none left to do the accounting. Even now, so close to the event, I cannot recall the hours sharply and am not ready to say whether death came on the third night or the fourth night. This uncertainty afflicts me with a sense of personal deterioration; if I were in decent health I would know how many nights I had sat up with a pig.

—E. B. White

Introductory paragraphs that summarize the paper to follow are especially popular among science writers. They assume a previous interest by the specialists who will read those papers. People who have an interest in the topic can quickly see the argument of the paper and decide if they want to keep reading.

In this paper I shall consider several educational issues growing out of A. R. Jensen's paper, "How Much Can We Boost IQ and Scholastic Achievement?" (Jensen, 1969). The first deals with the question of how education should adjust to the incontestable fact that approximately half the children in our schools are and always will be below average in IQ. Following this, I take up some of the more moot points of the "Jensen controversy"—what does heritability tell us about teachability? What are the prospects for reducing the spread of individual differences in intelligence? And what are the educational implications of possible hereditary differences in intelligence associated with social class and race?— ending with some implications that these issues have for educational research.

—CARL BEREITER

Writing Concluding Paragraphs That Complete Your Essay Without Summarizing It

Most professional writers make it a rule never to end a story or an essay with a summary. A good concluding paragraph will complete the paper logically and clearly, perhaps drawing a conclusion that expresses some meaning to be found in the information presented in the essay. The following paragraphs express the general meaning of the essays they conclude. You read the first paragraph of each essay above.

Does this terrible tale have a moral? Yes. In the past two decades one of the fondest boasts of medical science has been the conquest of infectious disease, at least in the wealthy countries of the industrialized world. The advent of retroviruses with the capacity to cause extraordinarily complex and devastating disease has exposed that claim for what it was: hubris. Nature is never truly conquered. The human retroviruses and their intricate interrelation with the human cell are but one example of that fact. Indeed, perhaps conquest is the wrong metaphor to describe our relation to nature, which not only surrounds but in the deepest sense also constitutes our being.

—ROBERT C. GALLO

As the sixteenth century was ending, the ranching industry was firmly established in the New World. It had spread northward on two fronts, one up the western and one up the eastern slope of the majestic Sierra Madre. It had swept more than a thousand miles from where it began southwest of Mexico City less than a century before. And the *vaquero* had become an integral part of the spreading cattle-related culture that emphasized the mounted horseman.

—DAVID DARY

The news of the death of my pig traveled fast and far, and I received many expressions of sympathy from friends and neighbors, for no one took the event lightly, and the premature expiration of a pig is, I soon discovered, a departure which the community marks solemnly to its calendar, a sorrow in which it feels fully involved. I have written this account in penitence and in grief, as a man who failed to raise his pig, and to explain my deviation from the classic course of so many raised pigs. The grave in the woods is unmarked, but Fred can direct the mourner to it unerringly and with immense good will, and I know he and I shall often revisit it, singly and together, in seasons of reflection and despair, on flagless memorial days of our own choosing.

—E. B. WHITE

■ **Exercise 4.13** Take any popular magazine that you enjoy reading and look at all the articles in it, carefully comparing the first and last paragraphs of each article. What relation do you see between the two paragraphs even before you read the article? Discuss in class or with friends interested in writing the connections between each first and last paragraph that you survey.

■ **Exercise 4.14** Take one of your own essays and compare the first and last paragraphs. What similarities do you note between them?

4f

Revising Paragraphs for Unity, Coherence, and Development

As you revise the rough draft of your essay, make sure that your paragraphs are unified, coherent, and well developed. You may want to add elements, eliminate elements, or subordinate one element to another. Because the controlling idea of your paragraph should guide any changes you make, start by rereading your paragraph carefully to determine the controlling idea that you want to express. A paragraph such as the one that follows requires revision.

> Wood-burning stoves are helping many Americans beat the cost of fossil fuels and save money. Wood is still plentiful in the United States. Many states set off parts of their state forests where residents can cut designated trees at no charge. Some wood stoves give off emissions that may cause cancer. But the technology of wood stoves has improved so that they can be very safe as well as efficient. The federal government now has standards that wood stove manufacturers must meet. Unfortunately, wood stoves are sometimes bulky and ugly and take up too much space in small rooms. Sometimes they make rooms too hot. Many homeowners who have gone to wood stoves for heat report savings of hundreds of dollars each year over the former price of heating their houses with oil. And many of them enjoy the exercise of cutting wood.

Here the paragraph has been revised.

> Wood-burning stoves are helping many Americans beat the high costs of fossil fuels. In recent years, the prices of oil and gas have come down, but these are limited fuels, and the prices are bound to rise again. So the availability of cheap fuel is still worth considering — and wood is cheap in some parts of the United States. A cord of wood, a stack measuring $4 \times 4 \times 8$ feet, costs just over a hundred dollars in a typical heating season. Many states like Massachusetts and Montana set off parts of their state forests where residents can cut designated trees at no charge. On a warm summer morning, one may see dozens of families sawing trees and loading vans or pickup trucks with logs for use as a winter fuel. Not only can wood be obtained cheaply, but also the technology of wood stoves has improved; the new models are far more efficient than the old ones. Now a family can heat a house with a wood stove with a minimum of waste or expense. A good airtight wood stove heats a room far more efficiently than does a conventional fireplace or a Franklin stove. Many homeowners who have turned to wood stoves for heat report savings of hundreds of dollars each year over the price of heating their houses with oil.

■ **Exercise 4.15** Revise the following paragraph for unity, coherence, and development.

The blizzard began early on the morning of February 6. The snow began falling before dawn. The flakes were small and hard. The snow itself was very thick. By nine o'clock, six inches of white covered the streets. Commuting traffic was reduced to a crawl. None of this affected me, since the schools were closed, and I stayed home, warm and cozy by the fire. I read the morning newspaper and kept refilling the coffee mug that sat beside me on a glass-topped table. By ten-thirty, the streets were impassable, and motorists were abandoning their cars. By noon, the offices in the city that had opened despite the storm were closing and sending workers home. At three o'clock, the mayor declared a state of emergency and asked schools, churches, and synagogues to give shelter to people stranded by the storm. Seeing all those people gathered together in houses of worship gave you a nice feeling about human nature, which some writers have claimed is evil. By six o'clock, the city was locked in the enchantment of a profound silence. Two feet of snow lay in the streets, and more was falling.

PART
TWO

WRITING CLEAR AND EFFECTIVE SENTENCES

93

CHAPTER

5

BASIC SENTENCE GRAMMAR

To write well, you must know how to use the elements of the English sentence — elements traditionally called grammar. **Grammar** is two things:

1. A collection of forms that make sense in sentences
2. The language we use to talk about such forms

5a
Recognizing Basic Sentence Forms

The first definition of grammar is much more important than the second. We use grammar all the time as a set of forms that make sense. Most of us use grammar well enough to make people understand the language we use. We learn the forms of the English sentence when we learn to talk, and we use them every day all our lives.

The word *forms* is essential to understanding grammar. We react to sentences as forms, familiar patterns that we recognize because they are so common. We have heard them since we first heard language, and we have used them since we first began using words in sentences. We cannot change them on whim because everyone else who uses English knows them and uses them by habit.

We probably started by giving something a name that got results. "Milk!" we shouted, and somebody gave us milk. A little later we said, "Give me milk." Still later we said, "Will you please give me some milk?" or "I prefer milk, please."

As we grow older, we learn to work many kinds of thoughts into the basic sentence forms. If you hear somebody say, "I picked up the telephone," you know what the speaker means. But if somebody says, "Picked I the telephone up," you run it through your mind again. What is this person saying? The form is not right. People don't say, "Drove I the car this morning to work" or "Stood bravely he the last until."

The sense of form is so strong in us that we can frequently understand a sentence even when we don't know what every word means. "If somebody says, "Give me the phlumpis on the table," we hear the form or pattern, recognize it as a request or a command, and look on the table to see what the "phlumpis" is. The form tells us to do something with something called a "phlumpis," and we do it. The sentence form is grammar in action.

There are only a few basic sentence forms, although as you will see, you can make some changes in the basic form of any sentence.

5a gram

☐ The most common form tells us that someone or something does something to something or someone else.

The man next door kills ants by spraying them with window cleaner.

This is a simple pattern. The man next door does something to the ants. It may seem odd to kill them with window cleaner. Even so, the sentence tells you he does it, and you can imagine him pumping away with a little spray bottle aimed at the ants.

You can substitute nonsense words and still have an idea of what the sentence means:

The aardcam next door grinks ants by cooming them with dab.

You know that something called an "aardcam" is the actor in the sentence. You know that "grinks" expresses the main act and that "cooming" expresses a helping act to the main act. "Dab" is some kind of tool, some instrument, something used in the action. You know that something is doing something to the ants because you recognize a basic pattern of the English sentence.

☐ Another form tells us that something acts but that nothing receives the action.

The telephone is ringing.

The thermometer exploded.

The flowers bloomed.

☐ Another form describes a state or condition of being. The actor in the sentence exists in a certain way. The sentence expresses no action; it is simply a statement that something *is* (or was or will be), or that it exists with a certain quality.

The telephone is black.

The man was old and feeble but still witty and interesting.

☐ Another form tells that something is acted upon. When you read such a sentence, you expect to discover that from the viewpoint of the writer, the recipient of the action is the most important object or person in the sentence.

My brother was hit by a wheelbarrow this morning.

The striking airline workers were ordered back to work.

5a
gram

These basic forms help sentences make sense. That is what the word **sentence** means — a group of words that make sense. They make sense because they communicate by using patterns that we recognize and expect. We can easily understand the sense of the following statements:

It rained last night.

The dust on the book made me sneeze.

Bicycle racing is becoming popular in the United States.

The Boston Red Sox lost the 1986 World Series.

She wrote three books before she was thirty.

When we don't have a sentence, we don't have a familiar pattern or form that communicates. We are not fooled by words pretending to be sentences. Each word group below looks like a sentence at first glance. It begins with a capital letter and ends with a period. But we cannot make sense of any group.

Shafts of light into the valley.

Favor capital punishment.

The most frequently abused drugs.

None of these groups has a form we recognize as a sentence. In each case, we must add words to make a pattern that communicates a sensible statement.

The rising sun threw shafts of light into the valley.

Polls show that most Americans favor capital punishment.

The most frequently abused drugs are alcohol and tobacco.

To recognize sentence patterns, you do not have to know any grammatical terms — *subject, verb, participle, direct object, indirect object,* and all the rest. But if you know the terms, you can talk more precisely about grammar and you can understand better what your writing teachers say to you. The rest of this chapter will focus on basic grammatical terms.

5b
Reviewing Basic Sentence Structure

The part of the sentence that names what the sentence is about is called the **subject.** The part of the sentence that makes a statement or asks a question about the subject is called the **predicate.** Two qualities are necessary for a sentence:

1. The boundaries of the sentence are clearly marked off by a capital letter at the beginning and a period, a question mark, or an exclamation point at the end.
2. Within these boundaries, every sentence contains at least one subject and one predicate that fit together to make a statement, ask a question, or give a command.

Here are some examples of basic English sentences:

The sun shines today.

Communism is decaying around the world.

Our dog died last summer.

The cold war may be over.

Sarah repairs automobiles.

Is Charles allergic to cigarette smoke?

Does Sarah own her own business?

[You] Bring me the report.

[You] Pass the spaghetti.

The Subject

The subject and the words that describe it are often called the **complete subject.** Within the complete subject, the word (or words) that serve as the focus of the sentence may be called the **simple subject.**

In the following examples, the complete subjects are in italics and the simple subjects are in boldface:

*The quick brown **fox*** jumps over the lazy dog.

Buckner lost the game with his error in the last of the ninth.

*The huge black **clouds** in the west* told of the coming storm.

A **compound subject** consists of two or more subjects connected by a conjunction such as *and* or *but* (discussed in 5c).

*Original **thinking** and bold **design*** have distinguished her architectural career.

**5b
gram**

The Predicate

The predicate asserts something about the subject. The predicate, together with all the words that help it make a statement about the subject, is often called the **complete predicate.** Within the complete predicate, the word (or words) that reports or states conditions, with all describing words removed, is called the **simple predicate** or the **verb.** The word *predicate* can be used for the complete predicate or for the simple predicate, and *verb* can be used instead of *simple predicate.*

In the following sentences, the complete predicates are in italics and the simple predicates (the *verbs*) are in boldface.

The quick brown fox ***jumps*** *over the lazy dog.*

Buckner ***lost*** *the game with his error in the last of the ninth.*

The huge black clouds in the west ***told*** *of the coming storm.*

Original thinking and bold design ***have distinguished*** *her architectural career.*

Like subjects, predicates may also be compound. In a compound predicate, two or more verbs are joined by a conjunction:

The huge black clouds in the west ***told*** *of the coming storm and **ended*** *our picnic.*

Sometimes a verb combines with an **auxiliary verb** (also called a **helping verb**) to form a verb of more than one word, a **verb phrase.** The verb phrases are in boldface in the sentences that follow.

Original thinking and bold design **have distinguished** her architectural career and **have made** her rich.

Gold **was discovered** in California in 1848.

He **might have seen** that film before.

The oldest building on campus **would have been demolished** if not for her generous contribution to save it.

One way to find the subject and the predicate components is to look at what the sentence says and to ask two questions about its meaning:

**5b
gram**

□ Who or what is the sentence about? *(subject)*
□ What statement is the sentence making about the subject? *(predicate)*

Simple Predicates

Perhaps the best way to find basic sentence components is to first look for the verb (the *simple predicate*).
    Remember that verbs express action or state of being.

Churchill **spoke** to England.

The hippopotamus **was** beautiful.

It is even easier to find verbs if you remember that they change their form in accordance with the way they are used in a sentence. Because verbs change their forms to show time, or *tense* (discussed in 5c), you can locate verbs easily by forcing such a change in a sentence. If you use a word like *yesterday*, *today*, or *tomorrow* at the start of a sentence whose verb you are trying to identify, the only word that changes will be the verb.

I eat green vegetables.
Yesterday, I **ate** green vegetables.

Mr. Smith goes to Washington.
Tomorrow, Mr. Smith **will go** to Washington.

Another way to locate verbs is to memorize the verbs that serve as **auxiliaries** — that is, helpers to other verbs. These auxiliaries are always verbs and never anything else. The most common helping verbs are *am, is, are, was, were, shall, will, could, would, have, has, had, do, does, did, be, been, might, can, may,* and *must*. (Verbs are discussed further in Chapters 16 and 17.)

✓ CHECKLIST: IDENTIFYING A VERB

Another good way to test a word you think may be a verb is to use *I, he, she, it, you, we,* or *they* before the word. If you make sense with this combination, the word you are testing is a verb.

Word	Test	Verb?
try	I try she tries	yes
olive	I olive (?) they olive (?)	no
laugh	they laugh	yes
laughing	I laughing they laughing	no

5b gram

✓ CHECKLIST: FINDING AND TESTING VERBS

1. Change a sentence by using *yesterday, today,* and *tomorrow* at the beginning. The word that changes is a verb.

   He played shortstop.
   Tomorrow he will play shortstop.
   Today he plays shortstop.

2. Learn the most familiar helping verbs.

3. Use *I, she, it, you, we,* or *they* before the word you think is a verb.

Simple Subjects

Once you find the verb, you can find the subject easily. Just put the verb in a question asking who or what does the action of a verb. Say the word *who* or *what;* then say the verb. The answer to your question will be the subject of the sentence. Generally, subjects of verbs are **nouns** or **pronouns,** words that name persons, places, things, ideas, or objects (see section 5b). But other words may sometimes be subjects.

We **have been working** all night.
Who has been working all night? **We.**

Trout fishing **is** a popular sport in northern New England.
What is a popular sport in northern New England? **Trout fishing.**

Lee **invaded** the north twice during the Civil War.
Who invaded the north twice during the Civil War? **Lee.**

■ **Exercise 5.1** Write five sentences. Draw a dividing line between the complete subject and the complete predicate. Then draw one line under the simple subject and two lines under the simple predicate, as in the following example.

My writing <u>assignments</u> in school/<u><u>have always caused</u></u> me much difficulty.

Other Predicate Parts

Complete predicates may also include objects, complements, and various words called *modifiers* that help describe other elements.

Direct objects

The **direct object** tells who or what receives the action done by the subject and expressed by the verb. Not every sentence has a direct object, but many verbs require one to complete their meaning. Such verbs are called transitive verbs, from the Latin *trans-*, meaning "across." A **transitive verb** carries action from the subject across to the direct object. In the examples below, direct objects are in boldface.

Catholic missionaries established the **school.**

Snopes burned **barns** all over the county.

The Jets beat the **Colts** in famous Super Bowl III.

I have read that **story.**

We heard the distant **voice.**

In the examples, the verbs are transitive. They report actions done by the subject to the direct object.

A verb that does not carry action to a direct object is an **intransitive verb.** An intransitive verb reports action done by a subject, but it is not action done to anything. These verbs are intransitive:

The ship **sank** within three hours after the collision.

Our dog **died** in the summer.

She **jogs** to keep fit.

In looking for direct objects in sentences, ask *what* or *whom* after the verb. The answer to the question will be the direct object.

The children crossed the **street.**

Indirect objects

Often a verb will report an action on a direct object and will tell for whom or for what the action is done. An **indirect object** is a noun or pronoun placed before a direct object and used to show for whom or to whom the action is conveyed by the verb.

5b
gram

The Miss Liberty celebration gave **us** pride in America.

Ask **the teacher** your question.

Jack told **George** the whole funny story.

If you ask *to whom* (or *to what*) or *for whom* (or *for what*), you can find the indirect object. Indirect objects occur fairly infrequently and are usually used with verbs such as *give, ask, tell, sing,* and *wrote.*

He sang **me** a song.

Direct objects and indirect objects, like subjects, are generally nouns or pronouns (which are discussed in 5c), or they are word groups that act like nouns or pronouns.

Complements

Complements complete descriptions of subjects and objects.

A **subject complement** is located on the other side of the verb from the subject and adds information about the subject. The verb that joins a subject and its complement is called a linking verb. A **linking verb** joins a subject to some further description of itself not included in the subject.

The most common linking verbs are the "to be" verbs — *is, are, was,* and *were.* But many other verbs also link a subject to a descriptive word. Observe the subject complements after the linking verbs in the following sentences.

My father is **a welder.**

America looked **good** to me after my long absence.

✓ CHECKLIST: TYPICAL SENTENCE PATTERNS

You have already seen how important sentence patterns are in our language. We learn to talk not by studying grammar, but by hearing patterns in action and then learning to use these patterns to make "sentence sense." Here are the most typical sentence patterns:

5b gram

Pattern 1 **Subject + Verb**

We	laughed.
The flowers	bloomed.
The house	was destroyed.

Pattern 2 **Subject + Verb + Direct object**

Ann	used	the jackhammer.
Dickens	wrote	*David Copperfield.*
She	told	the story.

Pattern 3 **Subject + Verb + Subject complement**

Our house	was	large and cold.
He	looked	good.
The crowd	became	noisy.
The contract	seemed	fair.

Pattern 4 **Subject + Verb + Direct object + Object complement**

| They | called | Lindbergh | a fool. |
| He | named | his son | John. |

Pattern 5 **Subject + Verb + Indirect object + Direct object**

| Lee | gave | Longstreet | the orders. |
| Smoke | gives | me | a headache. |

The basic patterns can be rearranged in a variety of ways.

Subject complement + Verb + Subject

Fair   lie   the fields of England.

Direct object + Subject + Verb

These bones   he   removed.

An **object complement** comes immediately after a direct object and helps complete the description of the direct object by the verb.

She called me **a bonehead.**

She said I drove her **crazy.**

My aunt dyed her hair **blue.**

I liked my eggs **scrambled.**

Like subject complements, object complements add to the description of the object. Complements may be nouns, pronouns, or adjectives (discussed in 5c).

■ **Exercise 5.2**   Complete the following sentences in any appropriate manner and indicate whether you have supplied a subject complement or an object complement by writing *SC* or *OC* after each sentence.

    1. The university was _____.
    2. The parking permit was _____.
    3. He got the answers _____.
    4. I was often _____.
    5. My professors were _____.
    6. I shut the door _____.
    7. She became _____.
    8. You look _____.
    9. I'll give you _____.
    10. He took his coffee _____.

5c
Reviewing the Eight Parts of Speech

When we say that each word in English can be classified as a **part of speech,** we mean that it can do some things in a sentence but not other things. The eight parts of speech are verbs, nouns, pronouns, adjectives, adverbs, conjunctions, prepositions, and interjections.

Verbs

Verbs report action, condition, or state of being. Verbs are the controlling words in predicates, but verbs themselves are controlled by subjects. The subject determines the person and number of its verb.

Verbs have three persons. In the **first person singular,** I speak of myself. In the **first person plural,** we speak or write of ourselves. In the **second person singular and plural** (the forms are the same), you are addressed. In the **third person singular,** someone speaks or writes about somebody or something who is not being addressed. In the **third person plural,** someone speaks or writes about more than one person or about more than one object.

The form of the verb (discussed in Chapter 17) changes according to the person and number of the subject. If a subject mentions only one thing, we say that it is *singular.* If it mentions more than one thing, we say that it is *plural.* "A dog" is singular. The plural form is "the dogs." Verbs must reflect these differences in subjects by having a singular or a plural form.

Verbs also show whether the action of the sentence is taking place now, took place in the past, or will take place in the future. Study the following examples.

**5c
gram**

	Singular	Plural
First person:	I read.	We read.
Second person:	You read.	You read.
Third person:	She reads.	They read.
First person:	I loosen.	We loosen.
Second person:	You loosen.	You loosen.
Third person:	It loosens.	They loosen.
First person:	I build.	We build.
Second person:	You build.	You build.
Third person:	He builds.	They build.

All these verbs are in the present tense. Notice that the only change that takes place is in the third person singular; a final -*s* is added to the common form of the verb. Most — but not all — verbs will add this -*s* in the third person singular.

Verbs must agree with the person of the subject. In the present tense the rule usually requires you to add an -*s* to the verb in the third person singular. In other tenses the rule usually means making a change in the helping verb.

I run	he runs
I am running	he **is** running

Helping Verbs and Verb Phrases

Helping (or **auxiliary**) **verbs** help a single verb express a meaning that it could not express by itself. A **verb phrase** is the helping verb plus the main verb. The final word in a verb phrase, the **main verb,** carries the primary meaning of the verb phrase. Sometimes more than one helping verb accompanies the main verb. In the following sentences, the verb phrases are in boldface; HV appears over each helping verb, and MV appears over each main verb.

         HV MV   HV MV

The plane **will have left** before we **can get** to the airport.

      HV   MV   HV MV

He **had been walking** for hours before he **was found**.

    HV MV

He **is biking** to Vermont from Boston.

    HV   MV

They **will arrive** in time for the game.

             HV   MV

Contrary to his opinion, he **does** not **have** any imagination.

      HV   HV   MV

Cy Young **has** always **been considered** one of the best pitchers in baseball history.

Notice that sometimes words not part of the verb phrase come between the helping verb and the main verb.

Some typical helping verbs are:

be	do	can
being	did	shall
been	does	will
is	has	might

am	have	could
are	had	would
was	must	should
were	may	

Sometimes particles are added to verbs. **Particles** are short words that never change their form no matter how the main verb changes. They sometimes look like other parts of speech, but they always go with the verb to add a meaning that the verb does not have by itself.

Harry made **up** with Gloria.

He made **off** with my pen.

She made **out** her application.

Verb Tenses

Verbs have three simple times, or **tenses**. (The word *tense* means "time.")

Present: She works every day.

Past: She worked yesterday.

Future: She will work tomorrow.

You can form the simple past tense of most verbs by adding a final -*ed* to the common form of the present or a simple -*d* if the common form of the present ends in -*e*.

Present: I **save** a little money every month.
The dogs in our neighborhood **bark** at night.

Past: I **saved** a thousand dollars last year.
The dog next door **barked** all night long.

But many verbs in English are irregular. That is, the simple past tense is very different from the common form of the present.

Present: We **grow** tomatoes every year on our back porch.
I **run** four miles every day.

Past: We **grew** corn back in Iowa.
Coe **ran** the mile in three minutes and forty-six seconds in August 1981.

The future tense of verbs is always formed by the addition of **shall** or **will** to the common form of the present.

Present: I often **read** in bed.

Future: I **will read** you a story before bedtime.

Chapters 16 and 17 provide a detailed discussion of verbs.

**5c
gram**

■ **Exercise 5.3**   Underline the verb phrases in the following sentences. Include particles as part of the verb phrase. Write HV over the helping verbs and MV over the main verbs.

1. Nomads in Arabia are now wearing sunglasses.

2. Has she rebuilt the Jeep engine?

3. Fees rise every year at universities in America.

4. She ought to be here any minute.

5. We sent out for pizza every Saturday night.

6. Our friend Tom White has spent Thanksgiving with us for years.

7. They used up all the ribbons for the printer.

8. He was running after the car.

9. People are moving to California every day.

10. They made out their route to northern Burma.

Nouns

Nouns are the names we use for people, places, animals, things, ideas, actions, states of existence, colors, and so forth.

In sentences, nouns serve as subjects, objects, and complements.

Common nouns name ordinary things. Common nouns include the following words and thousands more:

profession, color, man, beauty, woman, democracy, philosophy, rope, students, desks, cattle, library, justice, baseball, music, geometry, synagogue, car, glove, showcases, horses, proficiency, ability, tension, glory, defeat, smell, house

Proper nouns are the names given to persons, places, and things to set them off from others in a group. Proper nouns always are capitalized. Proper nouns include the following—and thousands more:

Germany, Department of Transportation, Greek Orthodox, Helen, Ms. Howard, General Dynamics, Belmont, Tennessee, Amtrak, Donald A. Stone, Frenchman, New York, Omaha

5c
gram

Compound nouns consist of two or more words that function as a unit. They include such common nouns as *heartache, mother-in-law, father-in-law, great-grandmother,* and *world view.* Compound nouns also may be proper nouns—*International Business Machines, Federal Bureau of Investigation, Suez Canal.*

How do you recognize nouns? Sometimes nouns reveal themselves by their endings. Words that end in *-ty, -tion, -sion, -or, -ism, -ist, -ment, -ness, -ship, -ture, -ance,* and *-ence* are usually nouns. But be careful! Some words with these endings may also be verbs.

Jackson made **mention** of you in his letter. (noun)

I hope you will **mention** my request to him. (verb)

One of the best ways to test whether a word in a sentence is a noun is to see if you can put the article *a, an,* or *the* in front of the word and still make sense of your sentence.

Nouns can be singular or plural. In sentences they are typically subjects, objects, and complements. (Nouns also may be appositions; see pp. 268–269.) You usually form the plural by adding *-s* or *-es.* (Regular and irregular plural forms are discussed in Chapter 28.)

✓ **CHECKLIST:** TESTING FOR NOUNS

Word	Test	Noun
razor	a razor, the razor	yes
waltzed	a waltzed, the waltzed	no
laughingly	a laughingly, the laughingly	no
horsefly	a horsefly, the horsefly	yes

Singular	Plural
nest	nests
dog	dogs
humanist	humanists
bush	bushes
church	churches

5c
gram

You can form the possessive of nouns by adding *-'s* or a simple apostrophe (') to show ownership or special relation.

Singular	Possessive
girl	girl's
guests	guests'
insect	insect's
neighbors	neighbors'

These qualities of plurality and possession can help you identify nouns in sentences. If you can make a word plural or make it show possession, it is a noun.

✓ **CHECKLIST: THREE TESTS FOR NOUNS**

1. Use *a, an,* or *the* before the word.

Word	Test	Noun?
book	the book	yes
injure	an injure	no

2. Make the word plural.

Word	Test	Noun?
egg	eggs	yes
soon	soons	no

3. Make the word show possession.

Word	Test	Noun?
child	the child's blanket	yes
criticize	the criticize's thing	no

■ **Exercise 5.4** Write a short paragraph about something you did yesterday. Underline all the nouns.

Pronouns

Like nouns, pronouns serve as subjects, objects, and complements in sentences.

There are numerous kinds of pronouns, and we use them for different purposes.

Most pronouns stand for nouns. Always be sure your readers know what nouns your pronouns stand for. A pronoun that lacks a clear antecedent causes great confusion.

Personal pronouns refer to one or more persons: *I, you, he, she, it, we, they.*

Indefinite pronouns make statements about a member of a group when we are unable to name which one we mean: *all, any, anyone, each, everybody, everyone, few, nobody, one, someone.*

Reflexive pronouns refer to the noun or pronoun that is the subject of the sentence; they always end in *-self: myself, himself, herself, yourself, ourselves.*

She allowed **herself** no rest.

He loved **himself** more than he loved anyone else.

Intensive pronouns have the same form as reflexive pronouns; they add special emphasis to nouns and other pronouns.

I **myself** have often made that mistake.

President Harding **himself** played poker and drank whiskey in the White House during Prohibition.

Demonstrative pronouns point out nouns or other pronouns that come after them: *this, that, these, those.*

That is the book I want.

Are **those** the books you bought?

Relative pronouns join word groups containing a subject and verb to nouns or pronouns that the word groups describe: *who, that, which.*

Dravot in Kipling's story was the man **who** would be king.

The tools **that** I lost in the lake cost me a fortune to replace.

The doctor **whom** you recommended has been suspended for malpractice.

Possessive pronouns show possession or special relations: *my, his, her, your, our, their, its.*

She was **my** aunt.

Their cat sets off **my** allergies.

The fault was **ours,** and the worst mistake was **mine.**

Interrogative pronouns introduce questions: *who, which, what.*

What courses are you taking?

Who kept score?

Which of the glasses is mine?

The various kinds of pronouns are grouped in the checklist on the facing page. Review them briefly and think of ways you might use them in sentences. (Pronouns are discussed more fully in Chapter 18.)

■ **Exercise 5.5** Fill in the blanks with any pronouns that make sense. See how many different pronouns you can use in each blank.

1. _____ always wanted to put a small motor on _____ hang glider.
2. _____ house is on the street next to _____ school.
3. _____ who can square-dance is welcome to _____ party.
4. The president _____ said he would be at the party.
5. _____ is in charge of _____ goat?
6. _____ must we do to pay _____ mechanic?
7. _____ of the parts must be replaced?
8. The snake was _____, but I kept quiet when _____ was found on the couch of the adjoining apartment.
9. "The most important principle in dancing," _____ told _____, "is to think of the music and not _____ feet."
10. When _____ drove the car through _____ kitchen window, the impact ruined _____ cake _____ happened to be in the oven at the time.

✓ CHECKLIST: KINDS OF PRONOUNS

Personal pronouns	Indefinite pronouns	Reflexive pronouns	Intensive pronouns
I	all	myself	myself
you	any	yourself	yourself
she	anybody	herself	herself
he	anyone	himself	himself
it	anything	itself	itself
we	each	oneself	oneself
they	everybody	ourselves	ourselves
me	everyone	yourselves	yourselves
her	few	themselves	themselves
him	many		
them	nobody		
	no one		
	one		
	ones		
	somebody		
	someone		
	whichever		
	whoever		
	whomever		

5c gram

Demonstrative pronouns	Relative pronouns	Possessive pronouns	Interrogative pronouns
this	that	my	what
that	which	mine	who
these	who	your	which
those	whom	yours	
		her	
		hers	
		his	
		its	
		our	
		ours	
		their	
		theirs	

Adjectives, Articles, Adverbs

Adjectives and adverbs describe other words more fully or more definitely. Adjectives and adverbs **modify** other words; that is, they change, expand, limit, or otherwise help describe the words to which they relate. You can sometimes recognize adjectives and adverbs because they have **comparative** and **superlative forms;** that is, forms that indicate degree. The comparative degree singles out one object in a set of two. The superlative degree singles out one object among three or more.

5c
gram

Adjective: **large**

Positive degree: She owned a **large** hat.

Comparative degree: Her hat was **larger** than mine.

Superlative degree: She owned the **largest** hat in the theater.

Adverb: **sadly**

Positive degree: My visitors said goodbye **sadly.**

Comparative degree: They spoke **more sadly** than I did.

Superlative degree: I spoke **most sadly** when they told me they had decided not to leave.

Adjectives

Adjectives modify nouns and pronouns. That is, they help describe nouns and pronouns in a sentence by answering questions: Which one? What kind? How many? What size? What color? What condition? Whose? Adjectives appear in boldface in the sentences below:

The **pale** sun shone through the **gloomy** clouds.

Six camels trudged across a **vast white** desert.

Harry's little blue Volkswagen died **one icy winter** morning.

Adjectives may be located immediately before or immediately after the words they modify, although they usually come before.

The **tired, thirsty,** and **impatient** horse threw its rider and went back to the barn.

The horse, **tired, thirsty,** and **impatient,** threw its rider and went back to the barn.

✓ CHECKLIST: A TEST FOR ADJECTIVES

Ask *"Which one?" "What kind?" "How many?" "What size?" "What color?" "What condition?" "Whose?"*

Which one? **That** man was the murderer.

What kind? The **dead** leaves clung to the old tree.

How many? The train had **six** cars.

What size? The **tall** building is Holyoke Center.

What color? The **brown** grass showed that we needed rain.

What condition? **Sick** people often have no energy.

Whose? **My** coat is the one with the rip in the sleeve.

**5c
gram**

An adjective modifying the subject of a sentence sometimes appears on the opposite side of a linking verb from the subject.

The horse looked **tired, thirsty,** and **impatient.**

My friend was **late,** and I was **worried.**

Articles

An **article** is a word used with a noun to limit or specify its application. The articles *a, an,* and *the* function as adjectives. The articles *a* and *an* are indefinite and singular; they call attention to any one of several things.

He sent me **a** card.

Richard III cried, "**A** horse, **a** horse, my kingdom for **a** horse!"

The article *a* appears before words that begin with a consonant sound; *an* appears before words that begin with a vowel sound.

a dish, a rose, a year, an apple, an entreaty, an hour, an ideal, an enemy, a friend, an umbrella, a union, an understanding

The word *Europe* begins with the vowels *eu,* which in this case are sounded as *yu.* So we speak of "*a* Europe at peace" or "*a* European in America." A few English words that begin with the consonant *h* have a vowel sound and are preceded by *an.*

an hour, an honest man, an honor, an honorable schoolboy

The article *the* is used with both singular and plural nouns. It always means "this and not any other." Often the difference between using *a* or *an* and using *the* depends on the writer's idea of how specific the following noun is.

> He came down off **the** mountain and found **the** road.

> No other mountain and no other road will do.

> He came down off **a** mountain and found **a** road.

The writer does not know or care what mountain the man descended or what road he found. Maybe the man himself didn't know.

Adverbs

Adverbs add shades of meaning to words or sentence elements that cannot be modified by adjectives.

Since adjectives can modify only nouns and pronouns, adverbs are left to modify anything else in the sentence that can be modified. They usually modify verbs, adjectives, and other adverbs, but they sometimes modify prepositions, phrases, clauses, and even whole sentences. (Adverbs are discussed more fully in 20b and c.)

Adverbs answer several questions, such as *how, how often, to what degree (how much), where,* and *when.*

> **Wearily** he drifted **away.**

> She did **not** speak **much today.**

Adverbs may modify by affirmation or negation. *Not* is always an adverb.

> He will **surely** call home before he leaves.

> They shall **not** pass.

> We will **never** see anyone like her again.

Many adverbs end in *-ly*, and you can make adverbs of most adjectives simply by adding *-ly* to the adjective form.

large	largely
crude	crudely
beautiful	beautifully

✓ CHECKLIST: A TEST FOR ADVERBS

Ask *"How?"* *"How often?"* *"To what degree?"* *"Where?"* *"When?"* A word that answers one of these questions to describe a verb, an adjective, or another adverb is an **adverb.**

He **cheerfully** gave up the money. (How?)

Sometimes I wonder what she means. (How often?)

I **intensely** dislike having to look for a parking place. (To what degree?)

Odysseus, following the defeat of Troy, turned **homeward.** (Where?)

Yesterday I took my last exam. (When?)

**5c
gram**

But beware! A great many adverbs do not end in *-ly.*

> often, sometimes, then, when, anywhere, anyplace, somewhere, somehow, somewhat, yesterday, Sunday, before, behind, ahead, seldom

And many adjectives end in *-ly:*

> costly, stately, lowly, homely, measly, manly, womanly

Some adverbs can serve to connect ideas between clauses. These are the **conjunctive adverbs,** such words and phrases as *accordingly, consequently, hence, however, indeed, meanwhile, moreover, nevertheless, on the other hand,* and *therefore.* (See 15e.)

Descartes said, "I think; **therefore** I am."

He opposed her before she won the primary election; **however,** he supported her afterward in her campaign.

Swimming is an excellent exercise for the heart and for the muscles; *on the other hand,* swimming does not strengthen the bones as jogging and biking do.

Unlike *coordinating conjunctions* or transitional expressions (discussed in 4b), conjunctive adverbs cannot bind clauses together. If you use one of the conjunctive adverbs between clauses, you must also use a semicolon or a period. This rule makes it easy to tell a conjunctive adverb from a coordinating conjunction. Conjunctive adverbs may shift positions within a clause:

Coordinating Conjunction: Swimming is an excellent exercise for the heart and for the muscles, **but** swimming does not strengthen the bones as jogging and biking do.

Conjunctive Adverb: Swimming is an excellent exercise for the heart and for the muscles; **on the other hand,** swimming does not strengthen the bones as jogging and biking do.

5c
gram

The best test for an adverb is to find what it modifies and then to ask yourself the appropriate adverb questions. If a modifier does not help describe a noun, a pronoun, or some other noun substitute, it has to be an adverb. If it does modify a noun, a pronoun, or some other noun substitute, it cannot be an adverb.

■ **Exercise 5.6**   In the following sentences, underline the adverbs and draw a circle around the adjectives.

1. Later he walked the dog happily down the silent, moonlit street.
2. Clearly solar heat offers many advantages, but both the equipment and its installation have high costs.
3. Japanese planes roared swiftly over the motionless battleships at Pearl Harbor early on Sunday, December 7, 1941.
4. English handbooks are very valuable instruments for sharpening your knowledge of grammar and writing.
5. I learned to appreciate Hebrew by hearing our cantor sing during the Friday-night Sabbath services, but I never understood exactly what the songs meant because I did not know the language well enough.

Conjunctions

Conjunctions join elements within a sentence.

These elements may be words, or they may be groups of words like clauses or phrases (see 5d).

Coordinating conjunctions (or, simply, **coordinators**) join elements of equal weight or function. The common coordinating conjunctions are *and, but, or, for,* and *nor.* Some writers now include *yet* and *so.*

She was tired **and** happy.

The town was small **but** pretty.

They must be tired, **for** they have climbed all day long.

You may take the green **or** the red.

He would not leave the table, **nor** would he stop insulting his host.

Correlative conjunctions are conjunctions used in pairs. They also connect sentence elements of equal value. The familiar correlatives are *both . . . and, either . . . or, neither . . . nor,* and *not only . . . but also.*

Neither the doctor **nor** the police believed his story.

The year 1927 was **not only** the year Lindbergh flew solo nonstop across the Atlantic **but also** the year Babe Ruth hit sixty home runs.

**5c
gram**

Subordinating conjunctions (or **subordinators**) join dependent or subordinate sections of a sentence to independent sections or to other dependent sections. (See 5e.) The common subordinating conjunctions are *after, although, as, because, before, if, rather than, since, that, unless, until, when, whenever, where, wherever,* and *while.*

The stylus will not track records **if** there is not enough weight on it.

Although the desert may look barren and dead, a vigorous life goes on there.

He always wore a hat **when** he went out in the sun.

Stories about divorce are common on television and in the movies **because** so many Americans have been divorced.

Using conjunctions to improve your writing is discussed in Chapter 7.

Prepositions

Prepositions are short words that unite a noun or pronoun into a prepositional phrase. The noun or pronoun is the **object** of the preposition. In the following sentence the prepositions are in boldface and their objects are in italics.

Suburban yards now provide homes **for** *wildlife* that once lived only **in** the *country.*

The preposition, its noun, and any modifiers attached to the noun make up a **prepositional phrase.** Prepositional phrases act as adjectives and adverbs. The main function of prepositions is to allow nouns and pronouns to modify other words in the sentence. Here are common prepositions:

5c gram

about	beyond	on
above	by	over
across	despite	since
after	down	through
against	during	to
along	except	toward
amid	excluding	under
among	following	underneath
as	from	until
at	in	up
before	including	upon
behind	inside	via
below	into	with
beneath	like	within
beside	near	without
between	of	

Some prepositions consist of more than one word:

according to	except for	instead of
along with	in addition to	on account of
apart from	in case of	up to
as to	in front of	with respect to
because of	in place of	with reference to
by means of	in regard to	
by way of	in spite of	

Prepositions usually come before their objects. But sometimes, especially in questions, they do not. Grammarians debate whether or not prepositions should end a sentence. Most writers favoring an informal style will now and then use a preposition to end a sentence.

Which college do you go **to?**

Which lake does she live **by?**

For more formal choices you could restate these questions as "To which college do you go?" and "By which lake does she live?"

Many words used as prepositions can be used as other parts of speech. They also often serve as adverbs or as subordinating conjunctions.

He arrived **after** midnight. (preposition)

Jill came tumbling **after**. (adverb)

After Jack broke his crown, Jill fell down, too. (subordinating conjunction)

Interjections

5c
gram

Interjections are forceful expressions, usually written with an exclamation point, though mild ones may be set off with commas.

They are not used often in formal writing except in quotations of dialogue.

Oh, no!   Wow!
Ouch!   Hooray!

"Wow!" Davis said. "Are you telling me that there's a former presidential adviser who hasn't written a book?"

How Words Act as Different Parts of Speech

A word that acts as a certain part of speech in one sentence may act as other parts of speech in other sentences or in other parts of the same sentence. The way the word is used will determine what part of speech it is.

The **light** drizzle foretold heavy rain. (*adjective*)
The **light** glowed at the end of the pier. (*noun*).
As you **light** the candle, say a prayer. (*verb*)

The cobra glided **outside**. (*adverb*)
The child played on the **outside**. (*noun*)
The mongoose waited **outside** the house. (*preposition*)
The famous **outside** linebacker was terrified by this scene. (*adjective*)

When will he come home? (*adverb*)
He will come **when** he is ready. (*conjunction*)
They decided the where and **when** immediately. (*noun*)

■ **Exercise 5.7** Fill in the blanks in the following sentences with any words that make sense. The word in parentheses at the end of each sentence tells you the part of speech that will go in the blank. But don't worry about that. Look at the names of the parts of speech, but use your own intuition to fill in the blanks. The exercise will prove that you have a feeling for the parts of speech even if you don't readily come up with the names. You will build confidence as you study the other sentences.

**5c
gram**

1. The dinosaurs _____ extinct millions of years ago. (verb)
2. Emma bought _____ a hamburger for lunch. (pronoun or noun)
3. The _____ broke on the car. (noun)
4. The leaves on the maple tree in the yard _____ red. (verb)
5. The English poet Coventry Patmore _____ many poems about young love. (verb)
6. "_____ ," he cried. "That hurt." (interjection)
7. The English troops retreated _____ from Lexington. (adverb)
8. Collecting guidebooks was _____ hobby. (pronoun)
9. I had to buy textbooks _____ supplies on the first day of the semester. (conjunction)
10. Alcohol is one of the _____ dangerous common drugs. (adverb)
11. He wanted me to stay, _____ I had to go. (conjunction)
12. Our arrival was delayed _____ we had a flat tire. (conjunction)
13. The _____ that he found in his driveway turned out to be stolen. (noun)
14. She welded the _____ to the bicycle. (noun)
15. Come _____ my house for the party. (preposition)
16. It rained all _____ the game. (preposition)
17. France _____ California produce some of the finest wines on earth. (conjunction)
18. The buffalo _____ the wide green plains of the West. (verb)
19. The _____ problem was how to buy a car without going into debt. (adjective)
20. The _____ bicycle is much more complicated than its ancestors. (adjective)
21. His father bought him a _____ coat for his birthday. (adjective)
22. We painted the house _____. (adjective)
23. The game turned into a _____. (noun)
24. The New York Mets began playing baseball _____ 1962. (preposition)

■ **Exercise 5.8** Write original sentences in which you use each word below according to the directions. Use a dictionary when you need help. The dictionary will always show the various ways words are used, and it will often give examples that will help you create sentences of your own.

1. Use *jump* as a noun, a verb, and an adjective.
2. Use *beyond* as an adverb, a preposition, and a noun.
3. Use *after* as an adverb, a preposition, and a conjunction.
4. Use *book* as a noun, a verb, and an adjective.
5. Use *lapse* as a noun and a verb.

**5d
gram**

5d
Identifying Phrases and Clauses

A **phrase** is a group of related words without a subject and a predicate.

They **were watching** the game.

The child ran **into the lake.**

Grinning happily, she made a three-point shot.

To succeed in writing, you must be willing to revise again and again.

Diving for treasure is sometimes dangerous.

A **clause** is a group of grammatically related words containing both a subject and a predicate. An **independent clause** can usually stand by itself as a complete sentence. A **dependent,** or **subordinate, clause** often cannot stand by itself because it is introduced by a subordinating conjunction or a relative pronoun and therefore the clause alone does not make sense. In the sentences below, the independent clauses are in boldface, the dependent clauses in italics.

She ran in the marathon *because she wanted to test herself.*

She said *that she felt exhausted after fifteen miles.*

They took *what they could find.*

When we had done everything possible, **we left the wounded to the enemy.**

5e
Reviewing Types of Phrases and Their Uses

English sentences contain three basic types of phrases: prepositional phrases, verbal phrases, and absolute phrases.

Prepositional Phrases

Prepositional phrases always begin with a preposition and always end with a noun or pronoun that serves as the object of the preposition. The noun or pronoun in the phrase can then help to describe something else in the sentence. A prepositional phrase generally serves as an adjective or an adverb in the sentence where it occurs.

> Adjective prepositional phrase: Which tree?
> The tree **in the yard** is an oak.

> Adverb prepositional phrase: When did he arrive?
> He arrived **before breakfast.**

To identify an adjective prepositional phrase or an adverb prepositional phrase, use the same tests you used for simple adjectives and adverbs (5c). In the sentence below, the adjective prepositional phrase (in italics) answers the question "Which book?"; the adverb prepositional phrase (in boldface) answers the question "Why?"

> Ditmars's book *about North American snakes* sold well **because of its outstanding photographs.**

Verbal Phrases

Verbal phrases, or **verbals,** are words formed from verbs, but they do not function as verbs in sentences. Verbals can stand alone as parts of speech, or they can be part of words attached to them to make a verbal phrase. There are three kinds of verbals—infinitives, participials, and gerunds.

Infinitives and infinitive phrases

The infinitive of any verb except the verb *to be* is formed when the infinitive marker *to* is placed before the common form of the verb in the first person present tense.

Verb	Infinitive
go	to go
make	to make

Infinitives and infinitive phrases function as nouns, adjectives, and adverbs. Here too, the tests for adjectives and adverbs come in handy.

To finish his novel was his greatest ambition.

The infinitive phrase functions as a noun, the subject of the sentence.

He made many efforts **to finish his novel.**

The infinitive phrase functions as an adjective modifying the noun *efforts.* Which efforts? The efforts to finish his novel.

He rushed **to finish his novel.**

The infinitive phrase functions as an adverb modifying the verb *rushed.* Why did he rush? To finish his novel.

Participles and participial phrases

Participles are made from verbs. **Present participles** suggest some continuing action. **Past participles** suggest completed action. The present participle of verbs is formed when -*ing* is added to the common present form of the verb. The past participle is usually made by the addition of -*ed* to the common present form of the verb, but past participles are frequently irregular. That is, some past participles are formed not by an added -*ed*, but by a change in the root of the verb.

I have **biked** five hundred miles in two weeks.

I have **driven** five hundred miles in a morning.

Because they do represent action, participles can be used in a wide variety of ways. In the sentences above, the participle is part of a verb phrase. But participles also can act as adjectives. In the sentences below, the participial phrases modify the subjects (*messenger* and *team*).

Creeping through heavy traffic, the messenger on the bike yelled angrily at pedestrians.

Insulted by the joke, the team walked out of the banquet.

Gerunds and gerund phrases

The **gerund** is simply the present participle used as a noun. The **gerund phrase** includes any words and phrases attached to the gerund so that the whole serves as a noun.

Walking is one of life's great pleasures.

Walking swiftly an hour a day will keep you fit.

She praised his **typing.**

He worked hard at **typing the paper.**

Absolute Phrases

An **absolute phrase** modifies the whole sentence in which it appears. An absolute phrase is formed when a noun or pronoun is attached to a participle without a helping verb. Remember: a helping verb would make the participle part of a verb phrase.

Her body falling nearly a hundred miles an hour, she pulled the rip cord, and the parachute opened with a heavy jerk.

Falling nearly a hundred miles an hour, she pulled the rip cord, and the parachute opened with a heavy jerk.

The storm came suddenly, **the clouds boiling across the sky.**

■ **Exercise 5.9** Write sentences using the following phrases.

1. was leaving (verb phrase)
2. on the head (prepositional phrase)
3. the train having arrived (absolute phrase)
4. to use a computer (infinitive phrase)
5. lying in the dark (participial phrase)

■ **Exercise 5.10** Identify the clauses in each of the following sentences. Draw one line under the dependent clause and two lines under the independent clause.

Example

When he was a pilot on the Mississippi River in his youth, <u>Samuel Clemens learned the lore of the people along its banks.</u>

1. Before she set out on the Appalachian Trail, she had to buy a good backpack.
2. Movies are often made from successful novels.
3. Although Americans feel nostalgic about trains, they don't ride them very often.
4. When knighthood was in flower, life was bloody and short.
5. Women now do many things that society prevented them from doing only a few years ago.
6. In college football, the running game is more important than it is in professional football.
7. Soccer is a coming sport in the United States because it is much cheaper and safer to play than high school football.
8. The state of Texas has decided that high school athletes must pass all their academic work if they are to play sports.
9. George Armstrong Custer and the Seventh Cavalry perished because they attacked a village where thousands of Indian braves were ready to fight.
10. Medical evidence has been building up for years to prove that cigarette smoking causes lung cancer and heart disease.

5e gram

■ **Exercise 5.11** Identify the phrases in boldface in the following sentences. Tell what kind of phrase each one is and how it is used in the sentence.

1. The sheriff entered the bar, **his hands hovering over his pistols.**
2. "Where is that cat?" he shouted, **his eyes darting around the room.**
3. **Whispered softly and urgently,** the question rippled down the bar.
4. **Opening the door softly,** the cat walked into the room.
5. **Over the barroom** a great hush fell as the sheriff and the cat stared at each other.
6. The sheriff wiped his eyes **to see better.**
7. "Time's up for you, cat," the sheriff shouted **in the great, expectant silence.**
8. **Licking his fur indifferently and sitting down,** the cat seemed to nod behind the sheriff.
9. **Frightened and dismayed,** the sheriff looked behind him.
10. A thousand cats were softly padding **through the open door.**

5f
Reviewing the Basic Kinds of Clauses

Clauses have subjects and predicates and may be independent or dependent. Sometimes we call independent clauses *main clauses* and dependent clauses *subordinate clauses.*

An **independent clause** usually can stand on its own as a complete sentence. A dependent clause cannot. In the sentences below, the independent clause is in boldface, the dependent clause in italics.

**5f
gram**

> **He swam across the lake** *after the sun set.*

> **He claimed** *that he swam across the lake after the sun set.*

An easy test for dependent clauses is to see if they are introduced by a subordinating word or group of words. (See "Conjunctions," 5c, and "Subordination Within Sentences," 7b.) A **dependent clause** is subordinate to another clause. That is, it serves another clause as an adjective, an adverb, or a noun. The subordinator tells you that the clause to follow is to serve another clause. In the following sentence, the subordinate clause (in boldface) serves as an adverb answering the question *Why?*

> I am going to bed **because I am tired.**

Here are some subordinating conjunctions: after, although, as, because, before, if, once, since, that, though, till, unless, until, when, whenever, where, wherever, while, as if, as soon as, as though, even after, even if, even though, even when, for as much as, in order that, in that, so that, sooner than.

Some subordinators are relative pronouns: what, which, who, whom, whose, that.

The subordinators *that* and *which* are sometimes left out of sentences before dependent clauses. In the following sentences, the dependent clauses are in boldface, and the subordinator has been omitted.

> Many poor people in Latin America believe **they can gain dignity only by revolution.**

> She said **she would enroll in evening school and work during the day.**

> We thought **the Mets might win the pennant this year.**

Noun Clauses

A **noun clause** may act as a subject:

That English is a flexible language is both glory and pain.

or as an object:

He told me **that English is a flexible language.**

or as a complement:

His response was **that no response was necessary.**

Adjective Clauses

An **adjective clause** modifies a noun or pronoun; a relative pronoun is used to connect it to the word it modifies.

The contestant **whom he most wanted to beat** was his father.

Here the adjective clause modifies the noun *contestant.* (Which contestant?) The relative pronoun *whom*, which stands for its antecedent *contestant*, serves as the direct object of the infinitive *to beat.* Compare: "He most wanted to beat the contestant."

The computer **that I wanted** cost too much money.

The adjective clause modifies the noun *computer.* (Which computer?) The relative pronoun *that* serves as the direct object of *wanted.* Compare: "I wanted the computer."

The journey of Odysseus, **which can be traced today on a map of Greece and the Aegean Sea,** made an age of giants and miracles seem close to the ancient Greeks.

The adjective clause modified *journey.* (Which journey?) The relative pronoun *which* serves as the subject of *can be traced.*

Adverbial Clauses

An **adverbial clause** serves as an adverb, frequently (but not always) modifying the verb in another clause. Adverbial clauses are often introduced by the subordinators *after, when, before, because, although, if, though, whenever, where,* and *wherever,* as well as by many others.

After we had talked for an hour, he began to look at his watch.

The adverbial clause modifies the verb *began*. (Began when?)

He reacted as swiftly **as he could.**

The adverbial clause modifies the adverb *swiftly*. (How swiftly?)

The desert was more yellow **than he remembered.**

5g
gram

The adverbial clause modifies the adjective *yellow*. (How yellow?)

■ **Exercise 5.12** Write sentences using the following dependent clauses. Tell whether you make each an adjective, an adverb, or a noun.

1. because we were afraid
2. when he saw the elephant
3. as soon as she could
4. after she had won the state lottery
5. although he wrecked the car
6. where the dinosaur bones were found
7. wherever she drew the plans
8. before the fire started
9. though the night had long since fallen
10. if she would turn down her radio

5g
Identifying Types of Sentences

The basic sentence types are: simple, compound, complex, and compound-complex.

The Simple Sentence

A **simple sentence** contains only one clause, and that clause is independent, able to stand alone grammatically. A simple sentence may have several phrases. It may have a compound subject or a compound verb. It can even have both a compound subject and a compound verb. But it can have only one *clause*— one subject and one verb that combine to make a clear statement. The following are simple sentences. Some are quite complicated, but they are *all* simple sentences, each with one independent clause.

Large land reptiles have been unable to evolve in the presence of large land mammals.

The bloodhound is the oldest known breed of dog.

He staked out a plot of high ground in the mountains, cut down the trees, and built his own house with a fine view of the valley below.

Historians, novelists, short-story writers, and playwrights write about characters, design plots, and usually seek the dramatic resolution of a problem.

The LaSalle, the DeSoto, and the Pierce Arrow once flourished as American automobiles but then, like dinosaurs meeting a new climate, declined and finally became extinct.

Singing, brawling, shouting, laughing, crying, and clapping every moment, the fans turned out every night hungry for a pennant.

5g gram

The Compound Sentence

A **compound sentence** contains two or more independent clauses, usually joined by a comma and a coordinating conjunction — *and, but, nor, or, for, yet,* or *so.* A compound sentence does not contain a dependent clause. Sometimes the independent clauses are joined by a semicolon, a dash, or a colon:

> The sun blasted the earth, and the plants withered and died.

> He asked directions at the end of every street — but he never listened to them.

> The trees on the ridge behind our house change in September: the oaks start to redden; the maples pass from green to orange; the pines become more dark.

A compound sentence also may consist of a series of independent clauses joined by commas, with a conjunction before the last clause.

> They searched the want ads, she visited real estate agents, he drove through neighborhoods looking for for-sale signs, and they finally located a house big enough for them and their dogs.

The Complex Sentence

A **complex sentence** contains one independent clause and one or more dependent clauses. In the following sentences, the dependent clause is in boldface type.

He consulted the dictionary **because he did not know how to pronounce the word.**

She asked people **if they approved of what the speaker said.**

Although football players are reputed to be the most powerful athletes in team sports, the winners of the World Series beat the winners of the Super Bowl in a tug-of-war on network TV one year.

The Compound-Complex Sentence

A **compound-complex sentence** contains two or more independent clauses and at least one dependent clause. In the following sentences, boldface type indicates dependent clauses.

She discovered a new world in historical fiction, but she read so much **that she had no time to write anything of her own.**

Although Carrie Nation may seem ridiculous in retrospect, her belief **that God had called her to break up saloons with her hatchet** was widely applauded in her time.

After Abraham Lincoln was killed, the government could not determine **how many conspirators there were,** and **since John Wilkes Booth, the assassin, was himself soon killed,** he could not clarify the mystery, **which remains to this day.**

■ **Exercise 5.13** Classify the following sentences as simple (S), complex (CX), compound (CD), or compound-complex (CC).

1. The winter of 1542 was marked by tempestuous weather throughout the British Isles: in the north, on the borders of Scotland and England, there were heavy snowfalls in December and frost so savage that by January the ships were frozen into the harbor at Newcastle.

   —Antonia Fraser

2. Prints, with woodblocks as the oldest form, began life humbly, not as works of art but as substitutes for drawings or paintings when multiples of a single image were needed, probably as long ago as the fifth century A.D. in China.

   —John Canaday

3. The female belted kingfisher, distinguished by a rusty band across her breast, lays six to eight pure white eggs on a bed of sand or regurgitated fish bones.

—ALEXANDER WETMORE

4. Although America has some fine native cherries, some of the very best wild cherries to be found came originally from seedlings of cultivated varieties, and the birds have been the chief agents of scattering the seeds.

—EUELL GIBBONS

5. The notion of the painter as a sort of boon companion to the hangman is carried on by Leonardo, who was fond of attending executions, perhaps to study the muscular contortions of the hanged.

—MARY MCCARTHY

6. Once a month I would ride ten miles down the wretched mountain road to Winchester, go to confession, hear mass, and take communion.

—WILLIAM ALEXANDER PERCY

7. Huey had found another issue that would help to move him along the path to the governorship.

—T. HARRY WILLIAMS

8. When he had eaten seven bananas, Mr. Biswas was sick, whereupon Soanie, silently crying, carried him to the back verandah.

—V. S. NAIPAUL

9. The people who developed the English language were more interested in making distinctions between boats than they were in the differences between colors and feelings, not to speak of tastes and smells.

—WALTER KAUFMANN

10. Inside the tough-talking, hard-jogging man of 40 who is identified largely by his work, there is a boy trying not to cry, "Time is running out."

—GAIL SHEEHY

■ **Exercise 5.14**   Combine the following groups of sentences into complex, compound, or compound-complex sentences. You will often have to add conjunctions or relative pronouns. Sometimes you will want to delete some words. See how many combinations you can work out from each group.

1. A pitcher can throw a baseball faster than ninety miles an hour. Batters may be severely injured if they are hit. Every batter must wear a helmet at the plate.

2. Ultralight planes now swoop down valleys and soar over mountains. They are hardly more than hang gliders with engines. The engines are small. The ultralights may fly at thirty to forty miles an hour.

3. Orson Welles terrified America with his radio presentation of *War of the Worlds* in 1938. Hitler was pushing Europe into war. News bulletins regularly interrupted broadcasts. Welles made the program sound like a news broadcast. He made people think that Earth was being invaded from Mars.

4. The Mississippi Delta has some of the richest farmland in the world. It grows more cotton than any comparable area on earth. It was not thickly settled until after the Civil War. Mosquitoes gave people in the Delta yellow fever.

5. Almost a million accountants now work in the United States. The profession is still growing. Positions will increase by 30 percent over the next ten years. These figures have been reported by the Bureau of Labor Statistics.

CHAPTER

6

SENTENCE LOGIC

Every sentence should make a statement that readers can understand.

Sentences should clearly answer all or some of the five questions we ask when we read anything: Who? Where? What? When? Why?

Short, simple sentences like these offer little difficulty:

The world came to life at dawn.

The Mets won the 1986 World Series.

The snow fell softly all night long.

Even when your sentences are long and complicated, you can simplify your thinking by asking which of the five questions they answer. In writing, you need to strive for clarity and logic. To write clear and logical sentences and paragraphs you can use five strategies that most writers know: (1) Prune irrelevant details that can derail your readers. (2) Give proper emphasis to the most important parts of your sentence. (3) Clearly establish cause-and-effect relations. (4) Limit your generalizations. (5) Use concrete terms when you define a word. In this chapter we will apply these strategies in a variety of examples.

6a
Pruning Irrelevant Details

Unnecessary information may confuse your readers by blurring the central thought of your sentence. Everything in a sentence must support the central statement.

In a first draft, you may throw in irrelevant details as you try to put down everything you know about a topic. When you revise, cut out these details so that everything in each of your sentences will contribute to the major statement you wish it to make.

> **Draft:**   *The Adventures of Huckleberry Finn,* by Mark Twain, who lectured widely in the United States and Great Britain, received only one review when it was published in 1884.

> **Revised:**   *The Adventures of Huckleberry Finn,* by Mark Twain, received only one review when it was published in 1884.

Often you can revise a sentence so that all the details in your first draft can be made to support the major purpose of the sentence:

> Although Mark Twain lectured widely in the United States and Great Britain and was well known to the public, *The Adventures of Huckleberry Finn* received only one review when it was published in 1884.

But you should never cram too many ideas in a sentence. As a general rule, you should aim at stating one central idea in every sentence. When you have several important ideas to communicate, put them in separate sentences.

> **Draft:**   World War I began on July 28, 1914, when the Austrians, whose army was huge but badly commanded and badly supplied and was also made up of many rival nationalities, attacked the city of Belgrade, in what was then called Serbia, though today it is a part of the nation of Yugoslavia.

This sentence contains too much information. What is its purpose? Is it to tell us when the war began? Or is it to tell us why the Austrian army was much weaker than it appeared? Or is it to tell us where Belgrade is?

> **Revised:**   World War I began on July 28, 1914, when the Austrians attacked the city of Belgrade in what was then called Serbia. The Austrian army was huge, badly commanded, and badly supplied, but the Serbians were no match for it by themselves, and so they had to call on the Russians for help. The Austrians thereupon called upon the Germans for help against the Russians. The Germans decided to defeat the French first before turning their attention to fighting Russia. In that way, the Germans hoped to avoid war on two fronts. Suddenly all Europe was in conflict.

■ **Exercise 6.1** Rewrite the following sentences to clarify the main statement in each of them. You may choose to revise to make two sentences with related thoughts if you want to express two distinct main statements. You may want to leave out some of the information given in the sentences so that the statements you preserve will be clear.

6b
logic

1. My mother, who always hated to wash windows or clean house but preferred to work in her flower garden, worked on newspapers for twenty years in places as diverse as Beaumont, Texas, and Montgomery, Alabama.
2. Notoriously hard to spell and difficult grammatically, the English language has spread all over the world largely because of the power and influence of the United States and the British Empire and Commonwealth.
3. Scurvy, a disease once common among sailors who spent many weeks at sea, can be prevented by eating citrus fruits, which grow in warm climates and can be preserved at sea because of their thick skins.
4. If Lincoln had not sent ships to supply the federal garrison at Fort Sumter in Charleston Harbor, the British might have recognized the Confederacy as an independent nation so that they might ensure a steady supply of southern cotton to British textile mills, which by 1861 were using steam engines.
5. Terrorism is one of the frightening symbols of modern society because it is violent, bloody, and merciless and often completely anonymous, since the terrorists sometimes do not know and do not care who their victims are, but they know that a bomb exploding in an airport or a bullet tearing through the body of a police officer will get publicity, which they think will make them look important in the eyes of the world, and they think that if they are important, they may be able to get their way.

6b
Deciding on Proper Emphasis

The most emphatic places in a sentence are the beginning and the end. Most sentences begin with the subject. The person, place, or thing that the sentence is going to be about comes first so that readers will have it in their minds for the rest of the sentence. Think about your sentences enough to have a clear idea about the elements you most want to emphasize. Here is an example:

Weak: When you are looking for a good book, try *The Adventures of Huckleberry Finn,* which you will find to be a great one.

Revised: *The Adventures of Huckleberry Finn* is one of the greatest books in American literature.

6c
logic

6c
Expressing Cause and Effect

Be logical when you attribute an effect to a cause, and avoid statements that imply causal relations that you do not intend. Confusion may arise when you put two ideas together so that readers think some cause-and-effect relation exists between them when in fact you intend no such thing.

Confusing: In 1950 the most popular song in American was "Tennessee Waltz," and the United States went to war in Korea.

Was the popularity of "Tennessee Waltz" the cause of the Korean War? The thought needs filling out to clarify the writer's point: that two contradictory things were happening at the same time.

Revised: In 1950, when the most popular song in America was the slow, dreamy "Tennessee Waltz," the United States went to war in Korea, and a peaceful dream ended for thousands of young men.

Confusion may also result from joining a dependent clause to an independent clause in such a way that a cause-and-effect relation seems to be implied.

Confusing: When he saw the movie *Casablanca* my friend Bert had a heart attack.

Did the movie *Casablanca* cause Bert to have a heart attack? Probably not. But a rapid reader might think that it did. Again, a solution is to fill out the thought so that readers will not think you are implying cause and effect.

Revised: While he was watching the movie *Casablanca* last week, my friend Bert had a heart attack. He seemed to be in perfect health, and he was enjoying himself, but suddenly he was doubled over with a near-fatal seizure.

Some words establish negative relations — such words as *but, although,* and *however.* Often we wish to make a statement that sets up certain expectations in the minds of readers. But we wish to tell them that these expectations will not be fulfilled. Such words as *but, however,* and *although* tell us that we may expect some cause-and-effect relation, but that in fact the relation does not exist. Use these words only when you are trying to set up an expectation that you wish to contradict. Confusion results if you use one of these words to join two statements that are unrelated to each other.

6d logic

Confusing: Although I like to read, television is exciting.

Revised: Although I like to read, it is easier for me to watch an exciting television show in the evening when I am too tired to concentrate on the printed page.

■ **Exercise 6.2** Rewrite the following sentences to eliminate faulty patterns of cause and effect. Add information when it is necessary to establish sentence logic.

1. Personal computers were unknown twenty years ago, and Elvis Presley was in his prime.
2. Steroids have been shown to produce a host of illnesses including cancer while they are helping build huge, muscular bodies for weight lifters and football players, and athletes often use them.
3. Aspirin is a potent pain reliever because some doctors believe that too much aspirin may damage the kidneys.
4. If you see a Woody Allen movie, he captures the humor and suffering of middle-class urban men and women today.
5. When you go to college, many teachers love to write and talk to students about research and writing.

6d
Limiting Generalizations

Avoid sweeping statements that assert too much on too little evidence. Sweeping generalizations give the impression that the writer has not studied the material enough to be aware of the exceptions serious observers know about. If you make sweeping generalizations, you will risk losing authority with your readers. Be especially careful when you use *all, always,* and *never.*

> **Misleading:**   Students nowadays lack dedication and seriousness, and they seldom read anything but the sports pages and the comics.

> **Revised:**   Some students I have known lack dedication and seriousness, and they seldom read anything but the sports pages and the comics.

> **Misleading:**   There never has been another play as good as *Macbeth.*

> **Revised:**   *Macbeth* is an excellent play because Macbeth's flaws are the flaws of all of us.

6d logic

■ **Exercise 6.3**   Rewrite the following sentences to qualify sweeping generalizations. Don't be afraid to change words if the changes help you improve the sentences.

> **Example:**   Everyone is agreed that Faulkner's story "A Rose for Emily" is not one of his better works because it is too melodramatic.

> **Revised:**   Some critics believe that Faulkner's story "A Rose for Emily" is not one of his better works because, they say, it is too melodramatic.

1. On the expressway the other day, the driver of one car shot another driver who dented his fender. This kind of thing happens because people in big cities carry pistols in the glove compartments of their cars.
2. My cousin Charles was furious because he could not get anybody to speak English when he asked directions in Paris no matter how much he shouted at them. His experience proves that the French all hate the Americans except when France needs American help in time of war.
3. Members of the crime syndicate are always photographed smoking cigars, and the cigar has long been regarded as a symbol of success by everyone who thinks about such things.
4. The photographs of the ship *Titanic* lying on the bottom of the Atlantic Ocean since it sank in 1912 prove that travel by ship was much more dangerous than travel by airplane is today.
5. Colstrop's necktie was found at the scene of the murder along with his wristwatch, his notebook, and a pair of his trousers. So he was the killer, and the police have arrested him.

6e
Defining Terms

Don't define a word by repeating it or by using one of its cognates. **Cognates** are words that come from the same root. *Grammar* and *grammatical* are cognates. So are *describe* and *description, narrate* and *narration, compute* and *computer,* and *nostalgic* and *nostalgia.* Here are some examples:

**6e
logic**

Poor: A grammar book teaches you grammar.

Revised: A grammar book explains the system of rules about word endings and word order that allows a language to communicate.

Poor: A community is a group with communal interests.

Revised: A community is a group that shares similar ceremonies, goals, habits, and patterns of work.

Avoid using the words *is when.*

Awkward: Fascism is when a military dictator rules with the help of secret police and won't allow freedom of the press or assembly.

Revised: Fascism is a political system ruled by a military dictator with the help of secret police and characterized by terror and strict censorship of the press to limit popular assemblies and suppress freedom of speech.

■ **Exercise 6.4**   Rewrite the following sentences to give proper definitions. Use the dictionary when necessary (see 14b).

1. An accident is when you have something happen accidentally that is unexpected and usually harmful, although accidents can be lucky, too.
2. A traffic jam is when traffic is jammed up on the streets.
3. Inflation is when you have inflated prices.
4. A quarterback is a back on a football team.
5. A poet is a man or a woman who writes poetry.

CHAPTER

7

COORDINATION, SUBORDINATION, PARALLELISM

To develop sentences effectively, take care to distinguish between main ideas and subordinate ideas and to bind related thoughts together with parallel construction. Your readers should be able to follow your train of ideas from the beginning of a sentence through to the end. Improper coordination or subordination can interrupt the flow and can make your readers struggle to understand the main points you are trying to make. A lack of parallelism disrupts the relation between the parts of a sentence and weakens its force.

7a
Expressing Equal Ideas: Coordination

Establish equal emphasis between parts of a sentence by using coordinating conjunctions or suitable punctuation or both.

Coordinating Words, Phrases, or Clauses

The conjunction *and* always calls for equal emphasis on the elements that it joins.

The bear **and** her cubs ate the food in camp.

The bear **and** her cubs ate the food in camp **and** destroyed our tent.

At the end of our climb we were hot **and** tired.

He drank only coffee, tea, **and** milk for a week.

A comma can sometimes replace the **and** in a series:

He zigzagged, fell, rolled, ran into my waiting hand.

—E. B. WHITE

Wistfully, admiringly, the old voice added, "It's snug in here, upon my word!"

—KATHERINE MANSFIELD

7a

coord

The conjunction *or* also joins equal sentence elements:

He could go by bus **or** by train.

They knew that they must work out their differences over money **or** else get a divorce.

Coordinating Thoughts by Joining Short Consecutive Sentences

Coordination can establish clear relations among equal elements in a sentence.

They hesitate, and they regret, and sometimes they petition; but they do nothing in earnest and with effect.

—HENRY DAVID THOREAU

When you use *and, but, or, for, nor, yet,* or *so* to connect independent clauses and thus coordinate related statements of equal importance, use a comma.

To act is to be committed, and to be committed is to be in danger.

—JAMES BALDWIN

I buried my head under the quilts, but my aunt heard me.

—LANGSTON HUGHES

You can also use a semicolon to connect related statements that are equally important.

We walked, and he talked; the musical irresistible voice seemed to set the pace of our march.

—EMLYN WILLIAMS

Sometimes both a semicolon and a coordinating conjunction introduce an independent clause (as discussed in 24a).

7b
subord

The hands of the man who sawed the wood left red marks on the billets; and the forehead of the woman who nursed the baby was stained with the stain of the old rag she wound around her head again.

—CHARLES DICKENS

■ **Exercise 7.1** Rewrite the following sentences to provide proper coordination. You may want to write more than a sentence for some of the examples.

1. He loved to shave in the morning because he liked the softness of shaving cream, the clean feel of the razor on his cheek, the smell of his after-shave, and he enjoyed taking a shower, too.
2. We drove to Baltimore last month, and to Wilmington the month before that, and next month we hope to drive to Providence.
3. Police officers in old movies often seem hard, cynical, and yet they are honest.
4. Truck drivers in this country complained bitterly about the 55-mile-an-hour speed limit, the high price of diesel fuel, and many of them refused to slow down.
5. Our friends would eat out on Saturday night, go to a movie, visit with each other, or they would do something else to have a relaxing good time.

7b
Expressing Unequal Ideas: Subordination

In many sentences, some ideas depend on others. For example, one condition or event may cause another; one event may come before another; one observation may explain another. Subordination establishes the dependence of one idea on another by shifting emphasis away from supporting elements so that major statements become clear.

Clauses, phrases, and single words can all be subordinate units in a sentence. The subordinate element usually enlarges on some element in the main part of the sentence. As you rethink your first drafts, keep clearly in mind the main thoughts you want to communicate. Then subordinate other elements to those main thoughts.

Subordination within Sentences

In the following paragraph, readers would have trouble finding the statements that carry the writer's major line of thought. Each sentence in this paragraph is clear, but the sentences create confusion because they do not show proper subordination.

**7b
subord**

Columbus discovered the New World in 1492. He made his voyage in three tiny ships. No educated person at that time believed that the world was flat. Columbus was well educated. The Greeks had taught that the world was round. They had taught that two thousand years before Columbus. On a round world, a sailor might head west to lands others had found by sailing east. Columbus wanted to find a new route to China and to other lands in Asia. Others had reached those lands. They had sailed around the southern tip of Africa to get there. Columbus thought the world was much smaller than it is. He thought he could get to Asia in about a month. Suppose America had not been in the way. He would have had a voyage of three or four months. He did not find the East Indies or China or Japan. America was in the way. It is a good thing America was in the way. Columbus might have sailed his three ships into an enormous ocean. His sailors might have starved to death. The ocean would have been far larger than anything Columbus could have imagined.

Revised: With tiny ships, Christopher Columbus discovered the New World in 1492, although he never understood just what he had done. Neither he nor any other educated person in his time believed that the world was flat. From the time of the ancient Greeks, two thousand years earlier, educated people had believed that the world was round, and that a ship might reach Asia by sailing west, around the tip of Africa. Because Columbus thought the world was much smaller than it is, he expected to find the East Indies, China, or Japan. Instead he found America. Had this continent not been in the way, he might have sailed his crews to starvation in an enormous ocean far larger than any sea he had imagined.

Key words, often called *subordinators* (p. 119), help to build subordinate clauses. Commas may also set off subordinate sections from a part they modify, especially when a subordinated element opens the sentence (as discussed in 23b).

> **Where** the road forks, you will find the graveyard.

> **Unless you object,** I will plug my ears at the rock concert.

> **Because great horned owls are so big,** they can sometimes kill and eat cats.

> **Until you remove the engine head,** you cannot see the pistons.

> He taught me **how to throw a curve.**

> **Although she looked tiny,** she was a superb police officer.

**7b
subord**

The position of a subordinator in relation to the clause it introduces will affect the meaning of a sentence.

> She did not eat **because she was angry.**

> She was angry **because she did not eat.**

> **When the police arrived,** the burglars ran away.

> **When the burglars ran away,** the police arrived.

> **After he completed a fifty-yard pass,** we cheered him.

> **After we cheered him,** he completed a fifty-yard pass.

Relative pronouns — *who, whom, that, which, what, whoever, whomever, whose* — also signal subordinate elements in a sentence. Notice how the use of subordinators speeds up the pace of the following sentences.

Without subordinators: My cousin does my taxes every year. He is an accountant. He helps me with many suggestions. These suggestions allow me to take several deductions. These deductions reduce my tax bill considerably.

With subordinators: Because my cousin is an accountant, he does my taxes every year, suggesting several deductions that reduce my tax bill considerably.

Embedding

Short sentences are easy to understand, but several of them in a row may be monotonous, even if they are all clear and correct. Good writers can compress a great deal of information into a few words by using embedding techniques. Look at these examples:

> She was sad. She did not look back. She mounted the seawall. She was bowed by her burden of failure, sorrow, and self-contempt.

> Sadly, without looking back, she mounted the seawall, bowed by her burden of failure, sorrow, and self-contempt.

> — CONSTANCE HOLME

**7b
subord**

Several of the sentences in the first version have been reduced to modifiers in the second version. We say that the ideas expressed in the several sentences in the first version have been *embedded* in the second.

> We can turn poetry toward biology. We can suggest a closer relationship between them. This creation of a relationship would follow a long line of similar suggestions. Other disciplines have made these suggestions.

> To turn poetry toward biology and to suggest a closer relationship between them is only to follow in a long line of similar suggestions made by other disciplines.

> — ELIZABETH SEWELL

> The White Star liner *Titanic* was the largest ship the world had ever known. The *Titanic* sailed from Southampton on her maiden voyage to New York on April 10, 1912.

> The White Star liner *Titanic*, largest ship the world had ever known, sailed from Southampton on her maiden voyage to New York on April 10, 1912.

> — HANSON W. BALDWIN

> She was falling asleep. Her head was bowed over the child. She was still aware of a strange, wakeful happiness.

> Even as she was falling asleep, head bowed over the child, she was still aware of a strange, wakeful happiness.

> — KATHERINE ANNE PORTER

You can embed several enriching thoughts within one base sentence and transform a whole group of ideas into a statement in which unstressed elements modify main ideas precisely. By using coordination along with subordination, you can expand your options for embedding and transforming sentences. Look at these examples:

> The fissions generate heat, and in a power reactor this heat produces steam, which drives electric turbines.
>
> —JEREMY BERNSTEIN

> Equality with whites will not solve the problems of either whites or Negroes if it means equality in a world society stricken by poverty and in a universe doomed to extinction by war.
>
> —MARTIN LUTHER KING, JR.

■ **Exercise 7.2** Using the subordination techniques illustrated in 7b, revise the following sets of sentences. Make any necessary changes to create logical, correct sentences. You may want to see how many different combinations you can make of each example.

1. Bilingual education is expanding in many schools. It is designed for children. The native language of these children is not English. It may be Spanish. It may be Chinese. It may be Vietnamese. It may be Korean. It may be some other language.

2. This auditorium was huge. The acoustics were terrible. The tenor nearly screamed at us. But no one could hear him beyond the ninth row. The soprano looked as if she was trying. But her voice sounded like a whisper in the balcony. The singers walked off the stage. They had played only two-thirds of the first act. The baritone was in tears.

3. Henry James began his novel *The Portrait of a Lady* in the spring of 1879. He wrote parts of the preface more than twenty-five years later. The novel has been one of his most enduring works. It is still in print.

4. A uniform can symbolize a worker's status. Status means power. People see authority in some uniforms. A doorman in an apartment building shows by his uniform that he can let people in. He can also keep people out. A policeman by his uniform shows that he has authority to make people stop. Sometimes uniforms are not prescribed. But people try to wear clothing that makes them look as if they belong. Male college professors used to wear tweed jackets. Their tweed jackets were a kind of uniform.

5. I read the same want ads over and over. I was looking for a job as a word processor in Dallas. I wanted to work at night. I had moved to Dallas the day before. I did not have a job. Finally I found the right ad. It asked for someone to do word processing. The hours were

from midnight until 8:00 A.M. I love to work at night when it is quiet and to sleep during the day.

Avoiding Too Many Subordinate Structures

Too much subordination may distract readers and confuse your main statement. Be sure not to overload your sentences.

7b subord

Overloaded: He was a stamp collector of considerable zeal who bought stamps at the post office on the day they were issued and fixed them with loving care in large books which had leather bindings, treasuring them not merely for themselves but for the enormous profit that he hoped to gain from them in the passage of years when they had increased in value.

Revised: A stamp collector of considerable zeal, he bought stamps at the post office on the day they were issued and fixed them carefully in large, leatherbound books. He prized them not only for themselves but for the enormous profit he hoped to gain from them, when, after many years, they had increased in value.

Overloaded: Jackson Bingle, leader of the rock group called the Howlers, who had been known for his ability to scream over the sound of drums, a primal shriek that had amazed critics and delighted audiences while dismaying parents, learned during his annual physical, administered by Dr. T. J. Summers, head of Whooping Crane Hospital, that he had lost seven-eighths of his hearing, so he told reporters this morning.

Revised: Jackson Bingle told reporters this morning that he had lost seven-eights of his hearing. Bingle, leader of the rock group called the Howlers, had been known for his ability to scream over the sound of the drums. His was a primal shriek that had amazed critics and delighted audiences. It also dismayed parents. Bingle said he learned of his hearing loss during his annual physical administered by Dr. T. J. Summers, head physician of Whooping Crane Hospital.

■ **Exercise 7.3** Revise the following sentences to eliminate excessive subordination. You will have to write at least two sentences for each one that appears below.

1. The Paul Newman movies, which nearly always end with an upbeat final scene, have beguiled Americans for years, during which time

many movies have been either somber or else nonsensical, causing many adults to quit going to see movies at all.

2. The new sun creams, which contain various sun-blocking chemicals, help protect against skin cancer, long a hazard to people who spend much time in the sun, and against aging, which seems to be at least partly a consequence of the ultraviolet rays of the sun, and they have also been shown to retard the graying of hair.

3. Literacy should mean not only the ability to read and write, which is an essential skill in our culture, but also the ability, which is very much appreciated by academics, businesspeople, and professionals, to talk about many topics with intelligence—which may be another way of saying that true literacy embraces curiosity and the love of learning.

**7c
parallel**

7c
Writing Balanced Constructions: Parallelism

In parallel constructions, the same form is repeated for balance. The elements in a parallel construction are equal or nearly equal in grammatical structures and importance. Parallel constructions may help you make lists, join similar ideas, or build emphasis. The coordinating conjunctions *and, but, or, nor,* and *yet* always join parallel structures.

The simple parallel structure is the series with two or more elements in it:

She loved to read **magazines** and **newspapers.**

She loved to read **books, magazines,** and **newspapers.**

At Gettysburg in 1863, Abraham Lincoln said that the Civil War was being fought to make sure that government **of the people, by the people,** and **for the people** might not perish from the earth.

He did the dishes, ran the vacuum, put out the garbage, and **swept the walk.**

He runs marathons and she runs sprints, but **they train** together.

Many performers live **to hear** the roar of the crowd, **to feel** the love of their fans, and **to enjoy** the attentions of reporters.

Comparison and Contrast

Parallelism helps make comparisons and contrasts more emphatic.

> **Weak:** She preferred **to buy** a house rather than **renting** one.

> **Parallel:** She preferred **to buy** a house rather than **to rent** one.

> **Better:** She preferred **buying** a house to **renting** one.

> **Weak:** The new library was larger than the old one, more beautiful than any other building on campus, and **it cost too much money.**

> **Parallel:** The new library was **larger** than the old one, **more beautiful** than any other building on campus, and **more expensive** to build than anyone had imagined.

**7c
parallel**

Coordinating Elements

Use parallel forms to coordinate such elements as *both . . . and, either . . . or, neither . . . nor, not only . . . but also,* and *whether . . . or.* Such pairs, often called **correlatives,** always indicate a choice or a balance between equal elements. If you use these pairs to join unequal elements, you disrupt the relation between those elements and lose the grammatical sense of the sentence.

> **Faulty:** Most soldiers in the Civil War were **neither heroic nor were they cowardly.**

> **Parallel:** Most soldiers in the Civil War were **neither heroic nor cowardly.**

> **Faulty:** The parking lot for commuters was **both small and it was crowded.**

> **Parallel:** The parking lot for commuters was **both small and crowded.**

When you use a single coordinating element, such as *and* or *or,* be sure that you join equal elements.

> His favorite pastimes were reading, walking, **and he liked to skate on frozen ponds in winter.**

In this sentence, the words *reading* and *walking* prepare us to find a similar word after *and* — a gerund, such as *skating* or *thinking.* Instead we find not another gerund but an independent clause, and we feel that something has been left out. We can amend the sentence in this way:

His favorite pastimes were reading, walking, **and skating.**

Confusion and a breakdown in parallelism can arise when *or* joins unequal elements.

They could see a movie, a play, **or** talk all night.

We feel that something is missing in such a sentence. We hesitate, go back over it to see if we have read it correctly, and then see that the breakdown in parallelism makes it seem that they could "see talk" all night. The writer must mean this instead:

They could see a movie or a play, **or** they could talk all night.

Lists and Outlines

In lists and outlines the meaning is clear only when the items are parallel.

Faulty:

Americans now rely on the automobile because:

1. cities are sprawling; public transport poor.
2. habit.
3. the cheapness of gasoline for so long.
4. parking lots provided for employees and students by businesses and schools.

Parallel:

Americans now rely on the automobile because

1. cities are sprawling and public transport is poor.
2. they have formed the habit of driving cars everywhere.
3. gasoline was cheap for a long time.
4. businesses and schools provide parking lots for employees and students, encouraging them to drive.

Repeating Words

Note that the sentences *without* the repeated elements in the following examples are correct and parallel. But repetition of an element may help you add a certain kind of emphasis to your sentences. You do not always have to make that choice, but from time to time, repetition will strengthen your style.

They thought it was better **to** agree than quarrel.

Parallel: They thought it was better **to** agree than **to** quarrel.

They searched for the lost keys **in** the house, yard, and street.

Parallel: They searched for the lost keys **in** the house, **in** the yard, and **in** the street.

For the handicapped, getting an education is often **a** tribulation, necessity, and victory.

Parallel: For the handicapped, getting an education is often **a** tribulation, **a** necessity, and **a** victory.

I decided to leave when I realized **that** I had offended him, he was angry, and my apology would do no good.

Parallel: I decided to leave when I realized **that** I had offended him, **that** he was angry, and **that** my apology would do no good.

■ **Exercise 7.4** Rewrite the following sentences to create parallel forms.

1. Harrison Ford was a hot-rod driver in *American Graffiti,* a rocket-ship pilot in *Star Wars,* and he played Indiana Jones, the archaeologist in *Raiders of the Lost Ark.*
2. Orson Welles starred on radio, he directed and appeared in movies, and toward the end of his life advertised wine on television.
3. We biked around the reservoir, over the hills, enjoyed the country roads, and we ended at the ice cream store.
4. He was not a good writer, and he couldn't speak very well either.
5. Many people in America are unhappy because of jobs not leading anywhere, with their families, and they don't like where they live either.

■ **Exercise 7.5** Revise the following sentences to repeat introductory words before parallel forms to make the parallelism more striking.

1. The new ultralight aircraft can land on a sandbar, back lot, or open field.
2. She promised to help out in the day or night.
3. They piled their books on the sofa, tables, and beds.
4. She made three promises — that she would try the machine out, write up a report about it, and tell her friends if she liked it.

7c
parallel

5. The railroad tracks passed through a tunnel and then over a river and highway.

Parallel Clauses

If you begin a clause with *and which, and that, and who,* or *and whom,* be sure that it follows a clause that begins with *which, that, who,* or *whom.*

The peach tree, with its sugary fruit and which was not known in the Middle Ages, seems to have developed from the almond.

Parallel: The peach tree, which has a sugary fruit and which was not known in the Middle Ages, seems to have developed from the almond.

Walt Whitman, influenced by Emerson and whom multitudes loved, was the first great American poet to praise cities in his verse.

Parallel: Walt Whitman, whom Emerson influenced and whom multitudes loved, was the first great American poet to praise cities in his verse.

Walt Whitman, whom Emerson influenced and multitudes loved, was the first great American poet to praise cities in his verse.

■ **Exercise 7.6** Revise the following sentences to make good parallel constructions.

1. The movie *Gone with the Wind,* filmed in Technicolor and which cost millions of dollars to make, was the first talking movie about the Civil War to be a success at the box office.
2. Television, the great rival to the movies and which movie people hated at first, was not allowed to show the Academy Awards until 1952.
3. General Douglas MacArthur, American leader against Japan in World War II, maker of the Japanese Constitution afterward, and who was fired by President Harry Truman during the Korean war, wanted to become president.
4. She hoped to win her first marathon, the one she entered at Boston and which led over a hilly course.
5. He brought home a new car, large, fire-engine red, expensive, and which he could not afford.

CHAPTER

8

EMPHASIS AND VARIETY

Two ways to gain and keep readers' attention are to provide proper emphasis and to supply variety. When you arrange information carefully in a sentence, you can emphasize important ideas and put less emphasis on less important ideas. When sentences vary in pattern and length, readers will not be distracted by the monotonous repetition of the same forms.

8a
Using Periodic Sentences

A **periodic sentence** has a strong word or phrase at the end, just before the period. The complete meaning is apparent only when you come to the end and have read the last few words.

> If asked to name the central quality in Faulkner's work, one is likely to give the quick answer "Imagination."
>
> —MALCOLM COWLEY

Sometimes a periodic sentence ends with a striking thought rather than with a striking word.

> The original Hopalong Cassidy was created by Clarence E. Mulford, a Brooklyn marriage-license clerk who at the time had never even seen the West.
>
> —JAMES HORWITZ

When you have several facts to convey in a sentence, it is nearly always a good idea to put the more important ones toward the end to give a sense of building toward a climax. The most important fact in the following sentence is the part played by John Muir in establishing Yosemite National Park, not the fact of his wearing a beard:

> **Wrong emphasis:** John Muir, the naturalist who was more responsible than any other single person for establishing Yosemite National Park, took long, solitary walks and let his beard grow long and tangled.

> **Revised:** John Muir, a naturalist who took long, solitary walks and let his beard grow long and tangled, was more responsible than any other person for establishing Yosemite National Park.

8b
Avoiding Weak Endings

A weak ending lets readers down because it leaves them with a sense of unfinished business or a sense that they've been taken in — that the writer had no real goal in mind.

> **Weak:** Young people in 1946 and 1947 turned from the horrors of World War II to a love affair with the jukebox, however.

> **Better:** Young people in 1946 and 1947, however, turned from the horrors of World War II to a love affair with the jukebox.

> **Weak:** The huge demonstrations in Washington against the Vietnamese war in the 1960s may not have been supported by a majority of the American people, nevertheless.

> **Better:** Nevertheless, the huge demonstrations in Washington against the Vietnamese war in the 1960s may not have been supported by a majority of the American people.

■ **Exercise 8.1** Rewrite the sentences below to make periodic sentences. If necessary, delete some words and phrases or invent others than capture the central idea.

1. Adlai Stevenson, laboring against the awesome power of Dwight Eisenhower's smile, lost the presidential elections of 1952 and 1956, as everyone knows.
2. Fiction writers do not often talk very well to interviewers about how they write, so Malcolm Cowley says.

3. The inspector found the body in the kitchen. When she had arrived on the scene, the house was locked and silent. She had the officers break down the door.

8c
Using Free Modifiers and Absolutes

In a **cumulative sentence,** several free modifiers or absolutes are appended to the predicate, thus giving new layers of meaning to the basic assertion of the clause.

A **free modifier** is a participle or participial phrase that occurs at the end of a clause and modifies the subject. The free modifiers in the following sentences are in boldface type.

> The motorcycle spun out of control, **leaving the highway, plunging down the ravine, crashing through a fence, coming to rest at last on its side.**

> The ocean beat against the shore in long swells, **roaring above the sound of the wind, threatening the tiny houses, slamming against the great rocks on the beach.**

An **absolute** (discussed in 5c) consists of a noun and a participle. At the end of the clause it modifies, an absolute adds meaning to the whole. The absolutes in the following sentences are in boldface.

> He crossed the finish line in record time, **his lungs nearly bursting with his effort.**

> The barn burned, **the flames rising two hundred feet into the night sky.**

A cumulative sentence may use absolutes or free modifiers or both. A noncumulative sentence completes its thought with a subject complement, a direct object, or an adverb with an adverbial phrase. The sentence below concludes its thought with an adverbial phrase.

> The house stood silently **on the hill.**

But the sentence can be revised so that it completes its thought with absolutes and free modifiers.

> The house stood silently on the hill, baking in the hot sunshine, its broken windows gaping open to the ragged fields, its roof collapsing, its rotting doors hanging open, its glory departed.

Study the following cumulative sentences, and see how elements added to the end of the predicate help them accumulate force.

> He emptied them thoroughly, **unhurried, his face completely cold, masklike almost.**

> —WILLIAM FAULKNER

> Another characteristic was that once a Veragua had caught and gored a man or a horse he would not leave him but would attack again and again, **seeming to want to destroy his victim entirely.**

> —ERNEST HEMINGWAY

■ **Exercise 8.2** Combine the following sentences to make cumulative sentences.

Example:
He sat at the typewriter. His teacup was at his left. The wind was blowing outside. The clock was ticking over the fireplace.

He sat at the typewriter, his teacup at his left, the clock ticking over the fireplace, the wind blowing outside.

1. She studied the map of the block. She was thinking of the fine old buildings that would have to be torn down. She was thinking of her own creation that would take their place. Her ideas were rushing in her head like a flood.
2. He got down from the train and looked around. He saw the courthouse. He saw the city square. It was vacant at this hour of the morning.
3. She saw him. He was sitting in a rocking chair. He was holding a large black book. It was his family Bible.

■ **Exercise 8.3** Look around the room where you are sitting and write three cumulative sentences that describe some of the things you see.

8d
Using the Active Voice

In general, use the active rather than the passive voice. The subject of a sentence in the active voice performs the action of the verb; the subject of a sentence in the passive voice is acted upon. (The active and passive voices of verbs are discussed in 18c.) Look at the difference:

Weak: His decision not to run for reelection to the presidency in 1968 was announced on television on March 31 of that year by Lyndon Johnson.

Revised: On March 31, 1968, President Lyndon Johnson announced on television that he would not run for reelection in the fall.

As a rule, use the passive voice only when the actor or agent in the sentence is much less important to your statement than the recipient of the action.

Estes Kefauver **was elected** to the Senate in 1948.

She **was taken** to the hospital last night.

8e
Emphasizing with Repetition

Add emphasis by repeating key words or phrases in consecutive clauses or sentences.

Let every nation know, whether it wishes us well or ill, that we shall pay *any* price, bear *any* burden, meet *any* hardship, support *any* friend, oppose *any* foe to assure the survival and the success of liberty.

—JOHN F. KENNEDY

8f
Varying Sentence Length

Give special emphasis to ideas by writing a very short sentence to follow several long ones.

The real objection to capital punishment doesn't lie against the actual extermination of the condemned, but against our brutal American habit of putting it off so long. After all, every one of us must die soon or late, and a murderer, it must be assumed, is one who makes that sad fact the cornerstone of his metaphysic. But it is one thing to die, and quite another thing to lie for long months and even years under the shadow of death. *No sane man would choose such a finish.*

—H. L. MENCKEN

8g
variety

■ **Exercise 8.4** Rewrite the following sentences to emphasize the elements you think are most important or most dramatic. You may change or delete words and phrases as long as you keep the central idea. Try to find several ways of dealing with each sentence.

1. The college library was locked up by the head librarian, G. W. Cranshaw, who said he got tired of seeing all those careless and sweaty students handling the books.
2. How strongly we believe in something, especially when it is something we think we ought to believe and maybe don't but won't admit it, and somebody comes and asks us if we believe it, is not measured well by statistics.
3. Now swimmers can buy little floats with bright colors on the top and clamps on the bottom under the water, and they can swim out to sea and take off their bathing suits and clamp them with the clamps and go skinny dipping if they want to.

8g
Varying Sentence Type

Sentence variety is the spice of lively writing, and you should strive to write sentences varied enough to hold your readers' attention throughout your paper.

Vary the patterns and the lengths of sentences to keep readers alert and involved. If you repeat any sentence pattern too often, you will bore your readers. It is a good idea to learn and practice variations in the basic writing pattern. The basic pattern in modern English writing is *subject* + *predicate* (discussed in 5b). In this example, the subject is in bold and the predicate is in regular type.

My father and my stepmother left on the noon plane to Atlanta.

The most common variation on this pattern is to begin with some kind of adverbial opener.

By the late afternoon, they will be at home.

Because they live so far away, we see them only once or twice a year.

Tomorrow they will telephone.

Another variation is to begin with a participle or a participial phrase that serves as an adjective.

8g variety

Smiling, he walked confidently into the room.

Stunned by the stock market crash, many brokers committed suicide.

Sentences also can open with an infinitive phrase or a coordinating conjunction.

To protect my mother, I'd made up stories of a secret marriage that for some strange reason never got known.

—SHERWOOD ANDERSON

But, say you, it is a question of interest, and if you make it your interest, you have the right to enslave another. Very well. *And* if he can make it his interest, he has the right to enslave you.

—ABRAHAM LINCOLN

In the first passage below, the sentences all begin with the subject; they are all about the same length; and they are all short. They are clear and understandable, but notice the improvement in the second passage, where the combined and embedded elements create a pleasing variety in both length and sentence structure.

He dived quickly into the sea. He peered through his mask. The watery world turned darker. A school of fish went by. The distant light glittered on their bodies. He stopped swimming. He waited. He thought the fish might be chased by a shark. He satisfied himself that there was no shark. He continued down. He heard only one sound. That was his breathing apparatus. It made a bubbling noise in operation.

He dived quickly into the sea, peering through his mask at a watery world that turned darker as he went down. A school of fish went by, the distant light glittering on their bodies, and he stopped swimming and waited a moment to see if the fish might be chased by a shark. Satisfying himself that there was no shark, he continued down. The only sound he heard was the bubbling noise of his breathing apparatus.

8h
variety

The improved version combines thoughts and reduces the number of sentences. The repetition of the pronoun *he* is also reduced, and the sentence patterns are more varied and interesting.

8h
Using Rhetorical Questions

A **rhetorical question** heightens attention by suddenly requiring the reader to participate more actively. A rhetorical question allows you to give an answer, as the writer does in the following example:

> The movie is called *Rock 'n Roll High School,* and for anyone not into punk, it has only one conceivable point of interest: Can Van Patten act as well as he hits a tennis ball? The answer is no, which is not to say that he isn't a promising young actor. It's just that as a tennis player he is a good deal more than fine.
>
> — *Sports Illustrated*

Sometimes writers ask a question or even a series of questions without giving an answer because to them the answer is obvious:

> Is not marriage an open question, when it is alleged, from the beginning of the world, that such as are in the institution wish to get out; and such as are out wish to get in?
>
> —Ralph Waldo Emerson

Avoid beginning an essay with broad rhetorical questions that might better be phrased as sharp thesis statements. "Why should we study *Huckleberry Finn?*" "How did TVA begin?" "Was Alger Hiss guilty as charged?" Readers may suspect that the writer did not take the trouble to think of a better opening. Save your rhetorical questions for an occasional paragraph that comes in the body of a paper after the subject has been introduced in some other way.

8i
Using Exclamations

Use an exclamation on rare occasions for special effects. Occasionally an exclamation helps you vary a series of declarative sentences:

> Clearly, even if there were a limit on the length of sentences to twenty words, it would not be possible to characterize any individual's knowledge of English by claiming that he carried around a list of all its sentences in his head! But there is in fact no limit to the length of a sentence. A sentence twenty-one words in length can be made longer by adding another modifier or a subordinate of some kind—and so on.

> —HELEN S. CAIRNS AND CHARLES E. CAIRNS

8j
Inverting Subject and Verb

For variety, you can put the verb before the subject. This is another device that should be used only rarely:

> Beyond is another country.

> —ROBERT M. PIRSIG

> From high above in the swirl of raging wind and snow came a frightening, wonderful, mysterious sound.

> —MARK HELPRIN

■ **Exercise 8.5** Revise the following set of simple sentences to form two coherent paragraphs made up of sentences that are varied in style and in length. You may change or add words but not facts. Look for places where you can subordinate one idea to another, both to reduce the number of words and to create a pleasing style.

Experiment. Rearrange some sentences to make the verb come before the subject. Convert a sentence into a question, and either begin an answer or point your reader toward an answer. Compare your version with the work of others in your class.

1. Bluegrass music was popular in the rural south before World War II.
2. Radio and recordings have made it popular everywhere.
3. It features hand-held instruments.
4. These include the banjo, the guitar, the fiddle, the mandolin, and sometimes the dulcimer and the bass fiddle.
5. Bluegrass does not use drums.
6. Bluegrass songs are in the tradition of the mountain ballad and the Protestant hymn.
7. It began as the music of poor southern American mountaineers.
8. They had to make their own entertainment.
9. Bluegrass songs are about love affairs gone wrong.
10. Sometimes they speak about the fear of hell.
11. Sometimes they describe conversion experiences.
12. Sometimes they express the yearning of the soul for heaven.
13. Bluegrass bands never use electrified instruments.

8i/j
variety

PART
THREE

USING
WORDS
EFFECTIVELY

CHAPTER

9

APPROPRIATE DICTION

In writing, use language that is appropriate to your subject by choosing words that state your meaning exactly and that convey a clear sense of it to your readers. Avoid a writing style that is too informal or chatty, but beware of being stiff and pompous.

The best way to gain a sense of appropriate language is to read as much as you can. Whether you are preparing to write about literature or natural science or history, take some time to read what writers who know the subject have written. Try to use their tone as a model for your own style.

Always choose the tone and the diction that fit your subject. Do not use a breezy, informal tone for a paper on cancer or an essay on famine in Africa. Do not use a sober, humorless tone in writing about the World Series or the Super Bowl.

9a
Using Slang

Use slang sparingly and only when it is appropriate to the subject and the tone you choose for your essay. Consider the following pairs of sentences.

> In *Heart of Darkness*, we hear a lot about a dude named Kurtz, but we don't see the guy much.

> In *Heart of Darkness*, Marlow, the narrator, talks almost continually about Kurtz, but we see Kurtz himself only at the end.

> When Thomas More saw how Henry VIII was going, he might have run off to France to save his hide, but he stayed on and got his head chopped off for his trouble.

When he saw the direction of Henry's mind, Thomas More might have fled to France to save himself, but he stayed on until he was imprisoned and put to death.

Some slang terms are always entering the mainstream of the language, and many American journalists adopt a breezy, informal tone. But even these journalists do not fill their prose with slang. Instead, they use slang to fit a special mood that they are trying to convey.

But Boston is also a city that historically has pricked the social conscience of many well-heeled undergraduates.

— HOWARD HUSOCK, *New York Times Magazine*

Minutes before the camera's ruby light flashed on, cable TV's garrulous impresario was already well into his inaugural address before a gathering of Atlanta VIPs.

—*Time*

You must use slang if it is part of a direct quotation. There the prose is not yours but that of your source, and you must quote that source exactly if you are using quotation marks.

"He whopped me good," Turner said of the tackle that made him fumble.

9b
Using Dialect

Some inexperienced writers try to use dialect to show the ethnic or regional origins of people, but dialect is very difficult to do correctly. Inexperienced writers frequently get it wrong and may appear to be making fun of the people they are writing about.

Dialect: "Ah'm a-goin' raght over thar," she said, "an if'n you'd go along, hit'ud be a big hep, and Ah'd be much obleeged."

Revised: "I'm going right over there," she said with a strong Appalachian accent, "and if you'd go along, it'd be a big help, and I'd be much obliged."

9c
Avoiding Jargon

Jargon is a language that uses ordinary English words in ways that are unfamiliar to most people. Sometimes jargon enables people with specialized interests to talk with each other. For example, people who use computers speak of "booting a disk" and of making "hard copies" and of "accessing the program."

All too often, though, writers use jargon to make simple thoughts seem complicated and to imply that they have special knowledge. Experienced readers rarely take jargon seriously. Consider this paragraph written by an academic author:

> Romantic love is characterized by a preoccupation with a deliberately restricted set of perceived characteristics in the love object which are viewed as a means to some ideal ends. In the process of selecting the set of perceived characteristics and the process of determining the ideal ends, there is also a systematic failure to assess the accuracy of the perceived characteristics and the feasibility of achieving the ideal ends given the selected set of means and other pre-existing ends.

**9c/d
diction**

The paragraph means something like the following:

> People in love see only what they want to see in the beloved. They want to believe in an ideal, so they do not question the accuracy of what they see or ask themselves if the ideal they imagine can be attained.

When you think you may be using unnecessary jargon, break your sentences down into simple core assertions, keeping subjects close to verbs, limiting modifiers, removing repetitions. Write the simplest sentences that will still keep the meaning you want to convey. See if you can make them so direct that any literate person can understand them.

9d
Avoiding Obsolete, Foreign, and Technical Words

Avoid obsolete or archaic words and expressions that confuse your reader or misstate your meaning.

> It was clear ere she left that the problems had not been resolved.

Use foreign words only when they are necessary. It is pretentious to use foreign expressions when English will do.

Pretentious: Her collection of exotic clamshells was her only *raison d'être.*

Better: Her collection of exotic clamshells was her only reason for living.

Pretentious: Sarah's *Weltanschauung* extended no further than her daily whims.

Better: Sarah's view of the world extended no further than her daily whims.

Avoid using technical terms unless you are writing for an audience that understands what those terms mean. The advice that applies to jargon (9c) applies here. Sometimes technical terms work well when they are used for a specialized audience that understands them. But technical terms thrown into a paper for a general audience often seem pompous and only confuse the average reader.

9d diction

> The potential audience for the existentialists consists of those who feel that, when they ask for bread, the most competent English-speaking philosophers offer them a stone.
>
> —WALTER KAUFMANN

Pretentious: Baxter felt a pang of existential anxiety when he contemplated his English exam.

Better: Baxter worried about his English exam when he thought about it.

■ **Exercise 9.1** Rewrite the following sentences to change language that might be inappropriate in a formal paper. Try to keep the meaning of each sentence. To do so, you will need to consider what we mean when we use some common slang words—words that are often emotional but inexact.

1. When the ump called nine consecutive strikes on three batters, Manager Sparky Anderson got his back up.
2. When the Germans were presented with the Treaty of Versailles in 1919, they really got sore.
3. Maybe the concert of the Boston Symphony Orchestra will be so wicked that the audience will fork over megabucks to go with the flow.

4. John Foster Dulles, Eisenhower's first secretary of state, was a shrewd old geezer who saw red whenever the Commies did some dirt.

5. Some people think that if Marie Antoinette had not been so stuck up, the French mobs might not have cut her head off in the revolution, but maybe the Frenchies were so riled up over everything in general that they would have beheaded her if she had been as pure as Julie Andrews.

■ **Exercise 9.2** Rewrite the following sentences to eliminate foreign words or stilted expressions. You may need to look up words in your desk dictionary. Don't try to translate the foreign words literally; try to put their meaning into fresh, idiomatic English.

1. The freshmen thought that the *summum bonum* of college life was to own a convertible.

2. Max said that if his roommate kept on smoking cigars in bed at night, it would be a *casus belli*.

3. A common multidimensional learning problem for students of the typewriter and the violin is the dexterity factor, for in both cases erroneous application of the fingers has the end result of a negative production response.

4. A sophomore is a kind of *tertium quid* between freshmen and upper-class students.

**9e
diction**

9e
Using Idioms Correctly

Idioms are habitual ways of saying things, and they usually cannot be translated from one language to another. Sometimes they cannot be transferred from one region to another within a country. If you say in French to a Frenchman, "I'm going to eat a hot dog with mustard," he will probably be appalled at your taste. If you ask a mountain southerner in the United States for a poke, he will hand you a paper bag; if you ask a New Yorker, he may hit you in the mouth.

Teachers often write *id* (for incorrect idiom) in the margin of a paper when the student has mangled some standard English word or phrase. If you write, "The South was angry against Lincoln," your teacher may write id because we commonly say that we are *angry with* someone or *angry at* someone, not angry *against* the person. The same objection can be made to the phrase *different than*. We say, "Fred is *different from* his older brother," not "Fred is *different than* his older brother."

From these examples you can see that idioms often involve prepositions, and that getting an idiom right is often a matter of using a preposition correctly. There is a big difference between these two sentences: "He made off with the money." "He made up with his friend." There is also a big difference between these two sentences: "He bet on the horses every week." "He bet at a window at the racetrack." Sometimes we use the wrong idiom by using the wrong preposition. We should not say, "He stayed *to* Boston last Sunday afternoon." We should say rather, "He stayed *in* Boston last Sunday afternoon." Sometimes we use a preposition when none is necessary. We should not say, "We will meet *up with* him in Denver." We should say, "We will meet him in Denver."

Inexperienced writers most often have trouble with idioms when they use unfamiliar words or expressions and do not know how to put them together the way experienced writers use them. We learn idioms one at a time, and we remember them as we grow in experience with language and as we use them in our writing and speaking.

9e diction

■ **Exercise 9.3** Rewrite the following sentences to correct mistakes in idiom. Don't be afraid to make a mistake. Idiom is difficult because it often has no logic. It is a reflection of customary speech patterns, and custom often refuses to obey logical rules. You may wish to consult a dictionary that includes examples of how words are used.

Wrong:
Jack was angry against Leo.
Right:
Jack was angry with Leo.

1. We celebrate Labor Day at the first Monday after the first Sunday in September.
2. Lyndon Johnson became president on November 1963.
3. My mother introduced me with her friend.
4. Previous to the meeting, we agreed to talk only an hour before adjourning.
5. Newton's general principle states that all bodies have a force of gravity proportionate with their mass.
6. Jazz music has been traditionally centered around the experience of black musicians playing in small groups.
7. He deaned the faculty for ten years and then returned to teaching because he wanted to make something of himself.
8. The sun arose that morning at six o'clock.

9. They promised to meet up with our group on the trail.
10. Computers promise to us much more efficiency than typewriters could ever give.

9f
Understanding Connotations and Denotations

Words have both primary meanings, called **denotations,** and secondary meanings, called **connotations.** Connotations allow some words to work in some contexts and not in others. You can say that your friend Murdock *evaded* the requirement that everyone learn how to swim before graduation, or you can say that he *flouted* it, or you can say that he *escaped* it. Each way we know that Murdock did not learn how to swim and that he did not obey the rule. But if he *evaded* the rule, he slipped away from it slyly. If he *flouted* the requirement, he may have announced publicly and arrogantly that he did not intend to observe the requirement. If he *escaped* the requirement, something may have happened to make the college forget to enforce the rule for him.

Here are some words with similar denotations but different connotations:

requested	demanded
ignored	neglected
unsympathetic	intolerant
confused	dazed

Beginning writers often have trouble with connotations. The best remedies are to note how experienced writers use different words and to study the dictionary for the use of **synonyms** — words having similar meanings but different connotations.

■ **Exercise 9.4**   Write sentences that use the following words correctly. You may use several of the words in one sentence if you can do so gracefully.

1. ambitious, greedy
2. successful, enterprising
3. proud, arrogant, haughty
4. hit, smash, collide
5. drink, guzzle, sip
6. eat, gobble, pick at

IMAGERY AND FIGURATIVE LANGUAGE

You can enliven your writing by creating word pictures for the reader. With concrete nouns and verbs that appeal to the senses, you can change an abstract idea into something vivid and specific. If you write, "The trees were affected by the bad weather," you do not give your readers much to picture in their minds. But if you write, "The small pines shook in the wind," the concrete nouns and the verb create an image.

Figurative language helps you build images. A **figure** states or implies a comparison between your subject and something else. If you write, "The small pines shook in the wind," you are being literal. If you write, "The small pines trembled with fear like children scolded by the wind," you are being figurative. The figure compares the trees to frightened children and the wind to a person scolding them. Our language is rich in figures because they help us express ideas clearly and succinctly.

10a
Using Concrete Nouns and Verbs

Use nouns and verbs that convey clear, concrete images or that report action. Some nouns and verbs merely report the existence of something but not that something happens. Examine this paragraph:

> Often the positions people take on energy are an index to how they stand on other issues. Conservatives, liberals, and radicals tend to group their causes, and if you tell me where you think we ought to get our energy, I can probably tell you what you think about what we ought to eat and how we ought to spend our time. But nearly everybody on every side of every current issue agrees that we should use solar energy.

This paragraph contains no errors in grammar, and it is fairly clear. But its prose style does not engage our attention, and when we finish reading it, we have a hard time remembering it.

Now study this version (italics added):

Every source of energy seems to have become a political issue. Tell me whether you think the path to a happy future lies with *solar heating* or with *nuclear furnaces,* tell me how you feel about *oil shale* and *coal* and *corn-fed gasohol,* and I'll tell you where you stand on *welfare reform, environmental policy, vegetarianism, busing, back-packing,* and *abortion.* But there is one kind of energy that attracts a diverse following: *photovoltaics,* the art of converting *sunlight* into *electricity.*

—TRACY KIDDER

10b

image

■ **Exercise 10.1**   Read the following paragraph and pick out the concrete details.

In the smallest of these huts lived old Berl, a man in his eighties, and his wife, who was called Berlcha (wife of Berl). Old Berl was one of the Jews who had been driven from their villages in Russia and had settled in Poland. In Lentshin, they mocked the mistakes he made while praying aloud. He spoke with a sharp "r." He was short, broad-shouldered, and he had a small white beard, and summer and winter he wore a sheepskin hat, a padded cotton jacket, and stout boots. He walked slowly, shuffling his feet. He had a half acre of field, a cow, a goat, and chickens.

—ISAAC BASHEVIS SINGER

10b
Using Metaphors and Similes

Use metaphors and similes to make your prose more vivid, but be sure that these devices are appropriate to your subject, your tone, and your audience. Similes and metaphors make comparisons. **Simile** uses the word *like* or *as.*

My love is **like** a red, red rose.

—ROBERT BURNS

Tom Birch is as brisk **as** a bee in conversation.

—SAMUEL JOHNSON

Mortality weighs heavily upon me **like** an unwilling sleep.

—JOHN KEATS

A **metaphor,** or implied comparison, speaks of things or of actions as if they were something other than what they are. Because of its compression, a metaphor may have stronger force than a simile.

The dice are the gods of the backgammon wars.

—E. J. KAHN, JR.

**10b
image**

Marcel Duchamp once referred to dealers as "lice on the backs of artists"—useful and necessary lice, he added, but lice all the same.

—*The New Yorker*

At least half of all writers, major or minor, have suffered from writing blocks—from inner resistance to dragging oneself, hour after hour, to the bar of self-judgment, and forcing oneself, before it, to confront that most intimidating of objects to any writer: the blank page waiting to be filled.

—WALTER JACKSON BATE

■ **Exercise 10.2** Complete the simile that will describe each of the following actions or objects. Try to avoid any similes that you have heard before. Add as many words as you need.

1. My mother was as angry as _____.
2. The biscuits were as light and fluffy as _____.
3. The coin gleamed in his hand like _____.
4. My flower garden was as wild as _____.
5. Our football team was as inept as a group of _____.

■ **Exercise 10.3**   Write a descriptive paragraph on two of the following subjects, using a simile and a metaphor in each.

1. A sunny dawn in the spring
2. A child learning that her parents will be divorced
3. The announcement that your father has won a beauty contest
4. Deciding to buy a new car
5. Realizing suddenly that you have a friend who is an alcoholic

10c
Avoiding Clichés

10c
image

A **cliché** is an overworked expression. The moment we read the first word or two of a cliché, we know how it will end. If someone says, "She was as mad as a _____," we expect the sentence to be completed by the words *wet hen* or *hornet*. If someone says, "My biscuits were as light as _____," we expect the sentence to be completed by *a feather*. If someone says, "His prose is as heavy as _____," we expect the sentence to end with *lead*.

We have heard these expressions so often that our minds are dead to them even when we understand what they mean, and they no longer create vivid pictures in our imaginations. The checklist shows some common clichés. You can probably think of others.

Usually it's best to rephrase a cliché as simply as you can in plain language.

Cliché: When John turned his papers in three weeks late, he had to *face the music.*

Better: When John turned his papers in three weeks late, he had to take the consequences.

Cliché: Harvey *kept his nose to the grindstone.*

Better: Harvey gave close and unceasing attention to his work.

✓ CHECKLIST: COMMON CLICHÉS

abreast of the times
acid test
add insult to injury
agony of suspense
beat a hasty retreat
better half
beyond the shadow of a doubt
blind as a bat
blue as the sky
bolt from the blue
brave as a lion
brown as a nut
brutal murder
bustling cities
calm, cool, and collected
cold, hard facts
come to grips with
cool as a cucumber
crazy as a loon
dead as a doornail
deaf as a post
deep, dark secret
depths of despair
diabolical skill
distaff side
doomed to disappointment
drunk as a lord
every dog has his day

face the music
fair sex
few and far between
fire-engine red
flat as a pancake
gild the lily
green with envy
heave a sigh of relief
heavy as lead
hit the nail on the head
in this day and age
ladder of success
last but not least
little lady
live from hand to mouth
livid with rage
nose to the grindstone
one hundred and ten percent
the other side of the coin
paint the town red
pale as a ghost
pass the buck
poor but honest
poor but proud
pretty as a picture
primrose path
proud possessor of

quick as a flash
quiet as a churchmouse
reigns supreme
right as rain
rise and shine
rise to the occasion
sadder but wiser
sharp as a tack
shoulder to the wheel
sink or swim
smart as a whip
sneaking suspicion
sober as a judge
straight and narrow
tempest in a teapot
tired but happy
tried and true
ugly as sin
undercurrent of excitement
walk the line
wax eloquent
white as a ghost
white as a sheet
worth its weight in gold

10c
image

■ **Exercise 10.4** Rewrite the following sentences and eliminate the clichés. Be adventurous. Try to think up some similes or metaphors that convey the meaning of a cliché without repeating its tired words.

1. Although he had worked like a dog all week long, the conductor seemed as cool as a cucumber and as fresh as a daisy when he mounted the podium and raised his baton to his orchestra.

2. The letter announcing the prize came to her like a bolt from the blue, making her friends green with envy, while she herself felt worth her weight in gold.

3. Bollinger believed that he had a right to be president of the university, since he had paid his dues as a lower functionary for years, sometimes feeling in the depths of despair over the way people treated him like a dog, believing often that he was doomed to disappointment in life, but determined to put his shoulder to the wheel.

10c
image

CHAPTER

11

INCLUDING NEEDED WORDS AND AVOIDING WORDINESS

One of the keys to good writing is making sure you have all the words you need to make your meaning clear—and only all the words you need. Extra words are something to avoid.

11a
Including Necessary Words

Include all the words that are necessary to make sentences clear and complete.

Parts of Verbs

Many forms of the verb require more than one word to make clear English sense. Be sure to include necessary helpers.

In some dialects of English, past participles serve as **finite verbs**— that is, verbs that report the actions of subjects and that control predicates. Correct written English requires helping verbs with these forms.

He **is writing** about the beehives.

I **have seen** what he **has done.**

She **has taken** a minute to rest.

If you have trouble with the principal parts of verbs, consult 17a, and study your dictionary when you are in doubt about correct forms.

Do not leave out part of a compound verb when the tense of one part of the verb varies from the tense of the other part.

> Caldwell has long and always will be sympathetic to those who think jogging is boring.

> Caldwell has long **been** and always will be sympathetic to those who think jogging is boring.

The Subordinating Conjunction *That*

When necessary, include the subordinating conjunction *that* for clarity. Omit it only if the subordinate clause is so simple that its meaning is instantly clear.

> He sent the message **that** canoes were unable to navigate the Platte River.

> Loretta Lynn sang songs women love.

■ **Exercise 11.1** Check the following sentences for missing words. Add words where they are needed. Place a check mark by the numbers of sentences that are clear and grammatical as they stand.

1. He told the staff men and women deserve equal pensions.
2. He taken the car to a junkyard and found many people in suits now go to junkyards to get parts for old cars they want to keep running a few more years.
3. I been here now for thirty years and never seen so little rain.
4. Air travel getting so expensive only the rich and people on business able to afford it now.
5. She told her daughter driving across the country and staying in motels were much more expensive than flying.

Articles, Prepositions, and Pronouns

Include the articles, prepositions, and pronouns that are necessary for idiomatic expressions.

> All **the** people in the room had quit smoking.

> A dog that bites should be kept on **a** leash.

> He gave me **the** books he liked best.

This type **of** dog is noted for its affection.

He did not like taking **from** or giving **to** the fund.

You do not have to repeat a preposition before every word in a series, but if you do repeat it before any of those words, you must repeat it before all the words in the series.

He loved her for her intelligence, her beauty, and her money.

Revised: He loved her **for** her intelligence, **for** her beauty, and **for** her money.

Making Comparisons Clear

Include a possessive form when you are comparing possessions or attributes.

Plato's philosophy is easier to read than **that of** Aristotle.

Revised: Plato's philosophy is easier to read than Aristotle's.

**11a
clarity**

Use *other* and *else* to show that people or things belong to a group with which they are being compared.

Gone with the Wind won more awards than any **other** film in Hollywood history.

Professor Koonig wrote more books than anyone **else** in the department.

Use the word *as* twice when you use it to compare people or things.

His temper was **as** mild **as** milk.

Avoid the vague comparison implied in the word *that* used as a weak synonym for *very*.

Professor Koonig was not **that** dull.

Revised: Professor Koonig was not **very** dull.

When you are tempted to use *that* as a vague comparative, think of something concrete and lively, and use the comparative form *as . . . as* instead of *that*. Or use *so . . . that* and a clause:

Professor Koonig was not **as** dull **as** some cows I have known.

Professor Koonig was **so** dull **that** he could make flowers droop.

Be sure your comparisons are always complete. If you have just said, "Professor Koonig is dull," you can say immediately afterward, "Professor Donovan is more interesting." But you cannot say in isolation, "Professor Donovan is more interesting." You need to name who or what forms the rest of the comparison. You may say, "Professor Donovan is more interesting than Professor Koonig."

■ **Exercise 11.2**   Add words as they are needed in the following sentences. If a sentence is correct as it stands, put a check by the number.

1. She was happy as I have ever seen anyone when she graduated from West Point.
2. He took the car in to have the transmission replaced, the body painted, and seats covered.
3. This type grass seed does not do that well in shade.
4. The car I drove to the beach was worse than any car I have ever driven.
5. Pete Rose was not that fast, but he always played hard as a boy even when he was forty years old.

11b
Avoiding Wordiness

If you can eliminate words that do not add anything to your prose, you can make every word count. Avoiding wordiness does not mean that you must write in short, choppy sentences or that you must reduce your prose to its bare bones. It does mean that every word should add something significant to your thought, because words that add nothing will obscure your meaning and bore your readers.

Eliminating Unnecessary Words

The following paragraph, a response to an assignment requiring an explanation of **expository writing,** is a good first draft, but it is entirely too wordy. The writer correctly tried to put down thoughts as fast as they came to mind, without pausing to edit. Then she revised the draft to eliminate wordiness and to make her points more effectively.

> Briefly, expository writing is the kind of writing that develops an idea. It is not quite the same as narration, which tells a story, though you and I both know that narratives may contain many ideas. But that is not their main purpose. If I tell you that last night I was eating in a restaurant and found a pearl in my oyster, that is narration. And expository writing is not the kind of writing that describes something, though descriptions may include several of the most important ideas that a writer considers significant. If I describe how the campus looks under a deep, thick white snow and describe the way people wade through the snow and leave tracks on its pure and immaculate surface, then that is description. But if I go to the theater and see a play and come home and write down an interpretation of it, then I am doing expository writing even if part of the exposition is to describe the action of the play itself. And if I go on and talk about the aforesaid snow that I have talked about falling on the campus and if I tell the story about how the history department got out in it and started aggressively and energetically throwing snowballs at the dean, and if I then go on and try to explain why historians on this campus are at this point in time and always have been bellicose, then I am combining description, narration, and expository writing. But the main thing I want you to be conscious of is how you should classify the kinds of writing that are likely to go on in a single piece of writing and you've simply got to remember that it is not an example of expository writing unless it is writing about expounding an idea.

11b clarity

Revised

> Expository writing develops ideas; narration tells stories; descriptions tell how things look. If I tell you that last night in a restaurant I found a pearl in my oyster, I am narrating. If I write of a deep snow on campus and how people wade through it and leave tracks, I am describing. But if I interpret a play, I am writing exposition, even if part of my essay describes the action of the play itself. And if I describe snow, and tell how the history department threw snowballs at the dean, and try to explain why historians at this university are bellicose, I am combining description, narration, and exposition. Remember that all three kinds of writing may appear in a single piece, but only expository writing interprets an idea.

The writer has recast the entire paragraph as well as several of its sentences. She has found ways to shorten sentences. She has presented her definitions at the beginning, as quickly as possible, and she has combined sentences to save words. (Helpful discussions are found in Chapters 6 and 7.)

Redundant Constructions

As you revise for wordiness, look out for redundant words and phrases, the unnecessary repetitions that slip so easily into first drafts. Conscious, deliberate repetition can help you emphasize ideas (see 8c); meaningless repetition only makes for flabby sentences. Avoid redundant constructions such as the following:

> The candidate repeated the answer again.

> He expressed a number of clever expressions much to the audience's delight.

> Her dress was blue in color.

**11b
clarity**

■ **Exercise 11.3** Edit the following paragraphs and make them more concise:

> I am going to tell you how much fun and profit there is in it for you to build your own house. If you have the time and a little energy and common sense, then you can build your very own house, save a ton of money, and have lots and lots of fun as you build your house. When it's all done and your house is standing there, built by you and maybe some members of your family, you will be proud of it, really proud. And think of all the fun you've had!
>
> Most of us, including probably you and me, usually think there is some kind of strange, secret mystery to the occult art of carpentry, but building things with wood is not a mystery at all. It takes lots and lots of care and lots and lots of hard work, but just about anybody can do it. You can do it too. The enjoyment you'll experience as well as all the money you'll save will make you enjoy this experience.

■ **Exercise 11.4** Underline the redundancies in the following examples.

1. at three A.M. in the morning
2. in modern times in the twentieth century today
3. return to the old neighborhood again
4. in my opinion, I think

    5. the autobiography of her life
    6. resultant effect of the report
    7. quite tiny in size
    8. the surrounding environment
    9. unemployed workers now out of work
  10. rectangular in shape

Eliminating Fillers and "Waiting Words"

When we speak, we often use phrases that serve as "waiting words"—they let us keep talking while we think of something more to say. These waiting words often creep into writing, where they take up valuable room without doing any work. Common waiting words include *like, you know, sort of, kind of, what I mean is, so to speak, in other words,* and *in the final analysis.*

    Other common phrases are cumbersome, roundabout, habitual ways of saying something when we need only a word or two. And some of them are junk—words we can get rid of altogether without losing any real meaning.

    Study the checklist and the recommended substitutions.

**11b
clarity**

✓ CHECKLIST: PHRASES TO AVOID

Don't use	Substitute
at the present time in the present circumstances at this point in time at this moment in this day and age	now, today, nowadays
at that point in time in those days in that period	then
in many cases in some cases in exceptional cases in most cases	often sometimes rarely usually

consider as, consider as being
  I consider study as being neces-
    sary to success.
	I consider study necessary to suc-
	cess.

prior to subsequent to	before after
despite the fact that regardless of the fact that	although

(continued)

due to the fact that for the purpose of by virtue of the fact that the reason is because	because
in a position to, in order to	can
in the area of	near, in
in the event that in the event of in case of	if *(with a verb)*: If fire breaks out . . .

in terms of
    The new curriculum was designed in terms of student needs and faculty ability.
	Usually recast sentence to eliminate:
	    The new curriculum considers both student needs and faculty ability.
	    The new curriculum was designed to match faculty ability with student needs.

11b
clarity

in the final analysis	finally, *or drop entirely*
in no uncertain terms	firmly, clearly, *or eliminate*
in the nature of	like
things of that nature	thing of that sort
refer back	refer
He is of a complex character. She is of a generous nature. The car was of a green color.	He is complex. She is generous. The car was green.
The weather conditions are bad. Traffic conditions are congested.	The weather is bad. Traffic is congested.

■ **Exercise 11.5** Edit the following paragraphs to eliminate unnecessary words and phrases. You may find some words and phrases that are not in the checklist. Think hard about each sentence to see if you can eliminate padding and wordiness.

    Due to the fact that at this point in time we have an energy crisis of a severe nature, we need to devote ourselves to a good rethinking of the academic calendar. At the present time, schools in the area of the United States begin in September and end in May or June. The reason is because schools once upon a time used to begin right after the harvest in societies of an agricultural character. But by virtue of the fact that buildings must be heated in the wintertime, schools in the cold regions of the earth are now paying out millions of dollars for fuel bills — money that might do much more good if it were put into faculty salaries, student scholarships, the library fund, the athletic program, or things of these kinds and of that nature. A solution to the problem may be of a simple nature: make the academic calendar according to the weather conditions prevailing in the different areas where the schools happen to be located.

Word Inflation

Do not inflate simple thoughts with overblown language (see 9e).

Inflated: Owning a gun for protection could be a consequence of several other factors. It could be the logical extension of a general home defense orientation. One mode of behavior for individuals who are vulnerable to crime is to increase their personal security, which leads them to a general home defense orientation and the acquisition of a gun.

Better: Some people buy guns to defend their homes, especially when they feel threatened by crime.

11b
clarity

Inflated: Lucinda Childs' early development as a choreographer in the 1960s paralleled the rise of minimalist art. And while her work is extremely complex in its patterning and ordering, this complexity is grounded in the permutations of simplicity expressed in a few steps and their repetition.

Better: Lucinda Childs' early choreography in the 1960s developed alongside the work of the minimalist painters. Although she created complex patterns and sequences, she uses only a few simple steps repeated with slight changes.

■ **Exercise 11.6** Edit the following sentences to make them more concise and clear. You may want to make two sentences where the writers have written one. Use the dictionary when you must.

1. A total site signage program is being studied, and if the study analysis dictates to relocate the stop sign, it will be done as a part of the total signage program and not as a result of your suggestion.
2. Dissatisfaction over the lack of responsiveness and accountability of decision makers is itself a primary source of the recent precipitous decline in confidence and trust that citizens hold for the national government.
3. We were not micromanaging Grenada intelligencewise until about that time frame.

CHAPTER

12

AVOIDING BIAS

Sensitive writers avoid all kinds of inappropriate bias in their writing. **Biased writing** is writing that fosters stereotypes or that demeans, ignores, or patronizes people on the basis of gender, race, religion, country of origin, physical abilities, sexual preference, or any other human attribute.

12a
Avoiding Sexist Labels and Clichés

Many clichés imply that women are not fully functional and mature in the same sense that men are. Consider the implications of such terms and phrases as *lady, the weaker sex, the fair sex, the little woman, girl, gal, broad, dame, working mother, housewife.*

All such terms imply that women have only one proper role in society. *Ladylike,* for example, is often intended as a compliment, but may in fact disparage women: a "ladylike" woman is polite and cooperative, but she does not assert herself as men are expected to do and is not taken quite so seriously. Behavior that in a man is admired as *assertive* is often criticized in women as *abrasive* or *aggressive.*

Careful writers avoid clichés and labels that stereotype either women or men.

Women as Appendages

Do not refer to women as if they were appendages to men.

Lily Roundtree, wife of the insurance agent John T. Roundtree, has joined Filmore, Inc., as an account executive.

Revised: Lily Roundtree, formerly promotion manager of Whitby Mills, has joined Filmore, Inc., as an account executive.

Do not make the false assumption that all women and children are non-productive dependents, or that homemakers do not do real work.

Farmers had to labor long hours to support their wives and children.

Revised: Farm families had to labor long hours to sustain their way of life.

She was a housewife for ten years, but now she works.

Revised: She was a homemaker for ten years, and now she works outside the home as well.

Women as Mothers

Avoid identifying a woman by reference to her children if they have nothing to do with the subject you are discussing.

Molly Burdine, mother of six, will represent Sourmash State University at the national meeting of the American Association of University Professors in Washington.

Revised: Molly Burdine, professor of government, will represent Sourmash University at the national meeting of the American Association of University Professors in Washington.

Women as Invisible

When you use the word *man,* be sure you are referring to an adult male and no one else. Avoid the use of *man* and *mankind* to stand for all members of the human species.

The professor lectured on man and his environment.

Revised: The professor lectured on humans and their environment.

**12b
bias**

12b
Avoiding Masculine Pronouns and Nouns

Whenever possible avoid using the pronouns *he, him, his,* and *himself* as indefinite personal pronouns. One satisfactory way to avoid masculine pronouns is to use the plural forms.

Every student who signed up for the class had to pay his fee in advance and pledge himself to attend every session.

Revised: Students who signed up for the class had to pay their fees in advance and pledge themselves to attend every session.

Often you can avoid the masculine pronouns by revising the sentence to eliminate the pronouns altogether:

Every student who signed up for the class had to pay the fee in advance and pledge to attend every session.

Avoiding Cumbersome Constructions

In general, avoid such constructions as *his or her, his/her,* and *s/he.* Sometimes, to be sure, it may be perfectly natural to use *he or she* or *his or her.* Consider the following sentence:

The student who spray-painted the insulting graffiti on the chalkboard last night may have thought that he or she was being original and bold, but it was a cowardly act.

In this case the writer means to make it clear that the vandal could have been either male or female.

Such usage generally is cumbersome, though, and it becomes unbearable when it is repeated several times in succession:

Each student in the psychology class was to pick up a different book according to his or her interests, to read the book overnight and do without his or her normal sleep, to write a short summary of what he or she had read the next morning, and then to see if he or she dreamed about the book on the following night.

You can eliminate the cumbersome *he or she* easily when you revise the paragraph to eliminate the other unnecessary wordiness:

Each student in the psychology class was to choose a book to read overnight. After a night without sleep, the students were to write a short summary of what they had read and then see if they dreamed about it the following night.

You can alternate *he* and *she, him* and *her,* using one gender in one paragraph and the other gender in the next. This alternative is sometimes effective, especially when combined with plural forms and with sentences constructed in such a way that no indefinite personal pronoun is required. But switching back and forth also can become distracting, so use this alternative carefully.

Many speakers and some writers use a plural pronoun to refer to an impersonal singular antecedent: "The person who left *their* suitcase on the bus can call for it at the office." However, many writers and editors consider such usage nonstandard. You can revise the sentence to avoid the pronoun: "The person who left a suitcase on the bus can call for it at the office."

Using the neuter impersonal pronoun *one* can often help you avoid the masculine pronoun.

> The American creed has always held that if anyone is willing to work, he can succeed in life.

> **Revised:** The American creed has always held that if one is willing to work, one can succeed in life.

Perhaps the most graceful way to avoid the masculine pronoun is to recast the sentence:

> The American creed has always held that anyone who is willing to work can succeed in life.

It may seem difficult at first to avoid the masculine pronoun, but it becomes increasingly easy to do with practice, and it is well worth doing to avoid offending any of your readers.

Avoiding Artificial Coinages

Many English words end in *-man* because at one time all those who occupied the positions the words describe were men: *freshman, chairman, councilman, sportsman, workman, policeman, fireman, repairman, statesman,* and *salesman,* for example. All of these terms, of course, now apply to women as well, so in most situations the old words are no longer appropriate.

Many writers and editors substitute *-person* for *-man* in such words. Unfortunately, the result is often clumsy. The best course seems to be to choose synonyms that use neither *-person* nor *-man.* A *newsman* becomes a *reporter* or a *journalist* or a *writer.* The *chairman* becomes the *chair,* the *weatherman* the *weather forecaster* or the *weather reporter* or the *meteorologist,* the *freshman* the *first-year student,* the *policeman* the *police officer,* and so forth.

12b bias

12c
Avoiding Other Kinds of Bias

You should avoid stereotyping people because of their racial, religious, or ethnic attributes or because of their abilities, sexual orientations, or occupations.

Ethnic or Religious Bias

Do not ascribe qualities to people based on their racial, religious, or ethnic backgrounds. In all the examples of bias below, the writer makes unwarranted assumptions about people.

> Like many other wealthy Italian families, the Bonfiglios probably got their money through Mafia connections.

> Black people never come on time for a party, but they sure like to have fun!

> The Jews have a knack for making money and control most of the world's financial systems.

**12c
bias**

Stereotyping

Do not make generalizations about people because of their abilities, disabilities, occupations, or sexual orientations.

> A clerk confined to a wheelchair will not be as productive on the job as someone who is not physically handicapped.

> Football players are not known for their great intelligence, so don't be surprised if he can't answer your question.

> I knew that she would not deliver on her promise once she was elected: Gay men and women are simply unreliable.

■ **Exercise 12.1** Rewrite the following sentences to eliminate sexist language.

1. An ambassador must learn the customs of the country where he is stationed. He should also learn the language.
2. When machinery breaks down in the home, we must grit our teeth and call the repairman, knowing that he will charge too much money and that we may have to call him again soon.

3. Any country musician worth his guitar knows that true bluegrass music does not use drums. He would also not use an electric guitar.
4. Every organization man knows the value of pleasing the boss. The boss may be a fool or a beast, but he is still the boss.
5. Anybody who goes to college knows that he has to work hard to earn good grades and that his grades do not always show how much he has learned.

■ **Exercise 12.2** For each of the following words, supply a gender-free synonym. (Avoid using -*person*.)

1. policeman
2. fireman
3. newspaperboy
4. mailman
5. mankind
6. sportsman
7. repairman
8. congressman

**12c
bias**

■ **Exercise 12.3** Look at the examples of biased writing on page 192. Explain the nature of the bias in each case.

CHAPTER

13

USING A DICTIONARY AND THESAURUS

A good dictionary is an essential tool for every writer. You should consult your dictionary every time you have the slightest doubt about the spelling, meaning, proper use, pronunciation, or syllabication of a word.

13a
Choosing Useful Dictionaries

The most useful dictionaries for college writers are desk dictionaries — books of a convenient size to keep on the desk, handy to consult as the need arises. Words and usages that do not appear in the standard desk dictionaries may be found in an unabridged dictionary or in an appropriate specialized dictionary. Any good library has a variety of such dictionaries.

Desk Dictionaries

A standard desk dictionary contains 140,000 to 170,000 entries. It may include drawings as well. Illustrations are useful because they can show something that otherwise cannot be defined easily in words.

The following desk dictionaries are all useful for the college student.

☐ *The American Heritage Dictionary of the English Language.* 2d College ed. Boston: Houghton Mifflin, 1982.

The American Heritage Dictionary has more than 200,000 entries, including biographical and geographical listings set alphabetically in the body of the work, among the other words and expressions. It lists definitions in order of common usage, beginning with the primary meaning suggested by the etymology or source of the word and proceeding through other senses that are progressively less common.

☐ Webster's *Ninth New Collegiate Dictionary*. Springfield, MA: Merriam-Webster, 1983.

The Merriam-Webster desk dictionary is based on *Webster's Third New International Dictionary,* generally regarded as the standard one-volume unabridged dictionary in English. Biographical and geographical entries appear in appendixes. The dictionary has about 160,000 entries, many from the sciences. It lists the meanings of words in the order in which they came into use. Exemplary sentences from works of well-known writers illustrate usage, and an occasional usage note offers guidance in the different connotations of synonyms.

☐ *The Random House College Dictionary,* revised edition. New York: Random House, 1988.

The Random House dictionary has 170,000 entries, a great number of them geographical and biographical. It is rich in scientific vocabulary and in entries that contain more than one word. The typeface is small, and there are few drawings. It does not contain nearly as many examples of usage as the Merriam-Webster and American Heritage dictionaries, and the examples it does include are not from well-known writers.

**13a
dict**

Unabridged Dictionaries

In theory, an unabridged dictionary should include every word in the language. In practice, such inclusiveness is impossible. Yet a couple of unabridged dictionaries come close to the ideal, and college writers should learn about them and continue to use them long after college.

☐ *Webster's Third New International Dictionary of the English Language.* Springfield, Mass.: G. & C. Merriam, 1967.

Webster's enormous unabridged dictionary occupies a prominent place in the reference room of any respectable library. When it first appeared in 1961, purists greeted it with howls of outrage, and a few people burned it in protest. The dictionary includes *ain't* and other words not regarded as standard English, and some people thought that it symbolized the decay of the language. The dictionary takes a relaxed attitude toward usages of standard words. The *Third New International Dictionary,* in the opinion of many authorities, can lead inexperienced writers astray because it does not warn them that certain usages are unacceptably casual, confusing, or avoided by careful writers. To *Webster's* nothing is substandard.

☐ *The Oxford English Dictionary.* 13 vols. Oxford, England: Oxford University Press, completed 1933.

The *OED*, as it is known to its devotees, has four supplements. Volume 1, A – G, appeared in 1972; Volume 2, H – N, appeared in 1976; Volume 3, O – S, appeared in 1982; the last volume appeared in 1986. The original thirteen volumes have been available since 1971 in a photographically reduced two-volume edition printed on opaque paper, easily read with the strong magnifying glass furnished with the set.

Indisputably the greatest dictionary of the English language, the *OED* traces each word from its first known appearance in writing to the present. Each variety of meaning is illustrated by sentences drawn from works that originated in the period when the word was so used. Variations appear in the citations from century to century. The thirteen original volumes include no words that might have offended proper Victorians, but the modern supplements include all such words.

Despite its great reputation, the *Oxford English Dictionary* is more valuable for the literary historian than for the general college writer. Spellings are those standard in England, not in the United States.

**13a
dict**

Specialized Dictionaries

Many highly specialized dictionaries may be found in the reference room of any good library — biographical and geographical dictionaries; foreign-language dictionaries; medical dictionaries; dictionaries of legal terms; dictionaries of philosophy, sociology, engineering, and other disciplines; dictionaries of slang, of word origins, of famous quotations. These dictionaries may often help you write an essay, and you should always browse through them when you are deciding on a topic. Your reference librarian can help you locate the dictionaries that will be most helpful.

These dictionaries may prove especially interesting or helpful in your general writing:

Dictionaries of slang

☐ Partridge, Eric. *Dictionary of Slang and Unconventional English.* 7th ed. New York: Macmillan, 1970.

☐ Wentworth, Harold, and Stuart Berg Flexner. *Dictionary of American Slang.* 2d ed. New York: Thomas Y. Crowell, 1975.

Dictionaries of usage

Dictionaries of usage answer questions that all writers ask now and then about the appropriate use of words. If you don't know whether to use *like* or *as* or whether to use *infer* or *imply* or whether you should split an infinitive or whether to use *slow* as an adverb, a dictionary of usage will give you helpful advice and offer alternatives. The three leading dictionaries of usage are the following:

☐ Follett, Wilson. *Modern American Usage.* Ed. Jacques Barzun. New York: Hill & Wang, 1966.

☐ Fowler, H. W. *A Dictionary of Modern English Usage,* 2d ed., revised and edited by Sir Ernest Gowers. Oxford and New York: Oxford University Press, 1965.

☐ Morris, William, and Mary Morris. *Harper Dictionary of Contemporary Usage.* New York: Harper & Row, 1975.

13b
Reading Entries in a Standard Desk Dictionary

All dictionaries contain guides to their use. In these guides, usually located in the front, you will find the meanings of the abbreviations used in the entries, and you will also find a list of the special cautions dictionaries use for words that the editors consider *slang, vulgar, informal, nonstandard,* or something else worthy of notation. When you use a dictionary for the first time, study these instructions carefully. They usually contain sample entries that will help you get the most from the time you spend consulting the dictionary.

Here is an entry in the *American Heritage Dictionary,* 2d College edition. Study it, the accompanying labels, and the following suggestions to see what you can learn from a good desk dictionary.

13b
dict

[pronunciation] — **com·pare** (kəm-pâr′) *v.* **-pared, -paring, -pares.** —*tr.* **1.** To represent — [part of speech]

[main entry, word division] — as similar, equal, or analogous; liken. Used with *to.* See Usage note below. **2.** *Abbr.* **cf., cp.** To examine in order to note the similarities or — [abbreviation] differences of. Used with *with.* See Usage note below. **3.** *Grammar.* To — [special use] form the positive, comparative, or superlative degrees of (an adjective or adverb). —*intr.* **1.** To be worthy of comparison; be considered as

[definitions] — similar. Used with *with.* See Usage note below. **2.** To vie; compete. —**compare notes.** To exchange impressions. —*n.* Comparison. Usually used in the phrase *beyond* or *without compare.* [Middle English *comparen,* from Old French *comparer,* from Latin *comparāre,* to pair, match, — [etymology] from *compar,* like, equal : *com-,* mutually + *pār,* equal (see **pere-** in Appendix*).] —**com·par′er** *n.* — [cross-reference]

[usage note] — **Usage:** In formal usage, *compare to* is the only acceptable form when *compare* means representing as similar or likening, according to 71 per cent of the Usage Panel: *compare a voice to thunder.* In such comparisons the similarities are often metaphorical rather than real; the things compared are of fundamentally unlike orders, and a general likeness is intended rather than a detailed accounting. *Compare with* is the only acceptable form in the sense of examining in order to note similarities or differences, according to 70 per cent of the Panel: *compare Shelley's poetry with Wordsworth's.* Here the things compared are of like kinds, and specific resemblances and differences are examined in detail. Informally, *to* and *with* are often used interchangeably in the foregoing examples. In formal usage, only *compare with* is acceptable when *compare* intransitively means being worthy of comparison, according to 94 per cent of the Panel: *Promises do not compare with deeds.* In such constructions, *compare to* is infrequent, even in informal usage.

Spelling, Syllabication, and Pronunciation

Entries in a dictionary are listed in alphabetical order according to standard spelling. In the *American Heritage Dictionary,* the verb *compare* is entered as **com·pare.** The dot divides the word into two syllables. Phonetic symbols in parentheses show the correct pronunciation; explanations of these symbols appear across the bottom of the pages in this dictionary. The second syllable of *compare* receives the greater stress when you pronounce the word correctly. You say "comPARE." In this dictionary, the syllable that receives the primary stress is given an accent mark at the end, like this: ´. Down the column in this section of the dictionary, you find the word *compartmentalize.* It is pronounced with the heaviest stress on the syllable *men,* and it has a secondary stress on the syllables *com* and *ize.* The syllable with the heaviest stress has the darkest accent mark; the syllables with the secondary stress receive lighter accent marks. Other dictionaries use a simple apostrophe to show accents. Learn the accent marks in the dictionary you use.

13b
dict

Parts of Speech and Various Forms

The symbol *v.* immediately after the pronunciation tells you that *compare* is most frequently used as a verb. The *-pared* shows the simple past and the past participle forms. If the past participle differed from the simple past, both forms would be included. (Look at the verb *drink* in your dictionary; you will see the forms *drank* and *drunk.*) The *-paring* gives you the present participle form and shows that you drop the final *e* in *compare* before you add the *-ing.* The *-pares* tells you the third-person singular form of the verb: she or he compares.

The symbol — *tr.* shows that the verb is used transitively. That is, the verb *compare* can be used to take a direct object. A little farther down in the entry the symbol — *intr.* shows that *compare* is also used as an intransitive verb, one that does not take a direct object. The symbol — *n.* still farther along in the entry shows that *compare* is occasionally used as a noun, and to illustrate this usage the dictionary notes "the phrase *beyond* or *without compare.*" The form *comparer* in boldface at the end of the main entry shows that by adding the simple suffix *-er,* we can get the noun meaning "one who compares."

Definitions

The several meanings of the word are arranged according to the parts of speech that the word plays in various contexts. When it is appropriate to do so, the editors also note in italics whether a word or a particular meaning of a word is *nonstandard, informal, slang, vulgar, rare, poetic, regional,* or *foreign.*

Word Origins

At the end of nearly every entry in this column is an **etymology**—a brief history of the word, usually beginning with its entry into English and tracing its forms from there to the present. We see that *compare* came from *comparen* in Middle English, the English in use in Chaucer's time, in the fourteenth century. *Comparen* came from the French word *comparer*, used by the Normans, who introduced a wealth of French words into Anglo-Saxon speech. *Comparer* came from the Latin verb *comparare*; Latin was the language of the Roman West, and French evolved from it.

Usage

A usage note follows some main entries in the *American Heritage Dictionary*. Here we see the dictionary's panel of experts divided over *compare with* and *compare to;* the majority of the usage panel holds that *compare with* is the more acceptable idiom when "the things compared are of like kinds," but prefers *compare to* when they are not fundamentally alike.

**13b
dict**

■ **Exercise 13.1**   Which of the following words can be used as verbs? What cautions does your desk dictionary offer about using them? Indicate with a *T* or an *I* whether a verb is transitive or intransitive. Put *TI* before verbs that can be used both transitively and intransitively.

1. total	**6.** victory
2. outside	**7.** hipster
3. fritter	**8.** radio
4. freeze	**9.** slop
5. consider	**10.** postulate

■ **Exercise 13.2**   Write out your own short definition for each of the following words, noting the part or parts of speech that you think each word may serve. Then check your definitions with those in a standard desk dictionary. If you don't know a word, try to guess what it means before you look it up.

1. effete	**6.** nomenclature
2. jejune	**7.** manufacture
3. jangle	**8.** relationship
4. parameter	**9.** mucus
5. pestilent	**10.** buckboard

■ **Exercise 13.3**   Look up the etymologies of the following words in your desk dictionary. Do the origins of a word help you understand its modern meaning?

1. gynecologist
2. gymnasium
3. geology
4. manufacture
5. center

6. dimension
7. populist
8. democracy
9. helicopter
10. muck

Synonyms and Antonyms

Here is the synonym entry in the *American Heritage Dictionary,* 2d College edition, for the word *include.* Study the **synonyms,** words that mean the same or nearly the same as the entry word. Note that the editors explain the slightly different sense that each of these synonyms conveys.

Synonyms: *include, comprise, comprehend, embrace, involve.* These verbs mean to take in or contain one or more things as part of something larger. *Include* and *comprise* both take as their objects things or persons that are constituent parts. *Comprise* usually implies that all of the components are stated: *The track meet comprises 15 events* (that is, consists of or is composed of). *Include* can be so used, but, like the remaining terms, more often implies an incomplete listing: *The meet includes among its high points a return match between leading sprinters. Comprehend* and *embrace* usually refer to the taking in of intangibles as part of a broader subject: *Law and order comprehend much more than exercise of police power. A person's tastes in reading need not embrace every subject fashionable at the moment. Involve* usually suggests the relationship of a thing that is a logical consequence or required condition of something more inclusive: *A heavy scholastic schedule involves extra effort.*

An **antonym** has an opposite or nearly opposite meaning from the dictionary definition of any given word. The antonym of *large* is *small.* The antonym of *young* is *old.* Antonyms are generally less useful to writers than synonyms, and many dictionaries do not include them.

■ **Exercise 13.4**   Look up both words in each pair of synonyms below and write a sentence using each to show that you understand the connotation of the word.

Example

mournful/lugubrious

The funeral procession made its **mournful** way to the graveyard under the dripping trees and threatening skies.

He tired of her **lugubrious** outpourings of insincere grief.

1. walk/ramble
2. ask/demand
3. urbane/suave
4. mercenary/pecuniary
5. rebut/refute
6. decline/reject
7. bright/gaudy
8. cheap/tawdry
9. reporter/informer
10. ideal/visionary

Geographical and Biographical Entries

The size of a standard desk dictionary limits the information that each entry can include. But you can find the correct spellings of important place names, the official names of countries with their areas and populations, and the names of capitals. Biographical entries give the birth and death years and enough information about the person to justify a listing in the dictionary.

✓ CHECKLIST: USING A DICTIONARY

13b dict

1. *Use the guide words.* Appearing on top of each dictionary page, *guide words* (usually in boldface) tell you what words to expect on that page. All entries are arranged alphabetically. Guide words save you time.

2. *Use the pronunciation key.* The letters and symbols used to indicate pronunciation are explained at the bottom of the page and, more fully, in a separate section at the front or the back of a dictionary. Always pronounce new words aloud to integrate them into your spoken vocabulary.

3. *In checking definitions, pay attention to the part of speech.* The same word serving as different parts of speech can have different meanings. You have to choose the meaning appropriate to the way the word is being used. Thus you can see a *light* (noun) or a butterfly that *lights* (verb) on a leaf. The first means "an illumination"; the second means "comes to rest." You will find both meanings (among many others) in a dictionary and you have to match the correct meaning with the appropriate word use. Part of speech markers—like *n* for noun, *v.t.* or *v.i.* for transitive and intransitive verbs, and *adj* for adjective—will help you match words to meanings.

4. *Always test the meaning you find.* To check whether you have selected the correct meaning, substitute the meaning for the word in the sentence in which you find it.

5. *Try alternate spellings if you cannot find the spelling for the word you are looking up.* Don't give up if you can't find a word on first try. Use alternate phonetic spellings. For example, if you tried to look up a word you thought was spelled *truff* you wouldn't find it. You also should try *trouf, troff,* and *trough.* (*Trough* is correct.)

13c
Using a Thesaurus

A **thesaurus** (the word means "treasury" or "collection" in Latin) is a dictionary of synonyms, usually without definitions. Three standard thesauruses are available:

☐ *Roget's International Thesaurus.* 4th ed. New York: Thomas Y. Crowell, 1977.

☐ *The Synonym Finder.* Ed. J. I. Rodale. Emmaus, PA: Rodale Press, 1978.

☐ *Webster's Collegiate Thesaurus.* Springfield, MA: Merriam-Webster, 1976.

All three give many synonyms for each listed word, and the words are indexed in the back of each book. Pocket thesauruses arranged in dictionary form are available but are limited in number of entries and hence in usefulness.

13c
thes

Here is an entry from *Roget's International Thesaurus.* Labels identify various features of the entry.

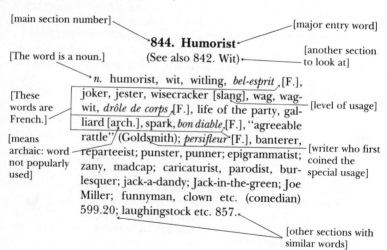

[main section number]   [major entry word]

844. Humorist

[The word is a noun.]   (See also 842. Wit)   [another section to look at]

n. humorist, wit, witling, *bel-esprit* [F.],
[These words are French.] joker, jester, wisecracker [slang], wag, wag-
wit, *drôle de corps* [F.], life of the party, gal-   [level of usage]
liard [arch.], spark, *bon diable* [F.], "agreeable
[means archaic: word not popularly used] rattle" (Goldsmith); *persifleur* [F.], banterer,
reparteeist; punster, punner; epigrammatist;   [writer who first coined the special usage]
zany, madcap; caricaturist, parodist, bur-
lesquer; jack-a-dandy; Jack-in-the-green; Joe
Miller; funnyman, clown etc. (comedian)
599.20; laughingstock etc. 857.

[other sections with similar words]

As you can see, a thesaurus does not define words. It is most useful for someone who already knows the definitions of the words and merely wants to be reminded of synonyms that may add color, variety, or precision to a piece of prose. Thesauruses have misled many inexperienced writers by encouraging them to use a word without understanding its connotations (see 9f). If you read that "the delegates to the convention

✓ **CHECKLIST: USING A THESAURUS**

1. *Know how the words are arranged.* When you check a word in the thesaurus index, it will refer you to a numbered section (like 844 in the sample) or subsection in the book. Words in that section are considered synonyms for the word you are looking up, but other subsections under the same section number may also include a word you could use. Roget's uses a complex system of word categories; *humorist,* for example, is in Subsection 1 ("Passive Affections") of Section II ("Personal Affections") of Class Six "Affections."

2. *Use no unfamiliar synonym without checking it first in a dictionary.* The writer mentioned above found *surpassed* as a synonym for *exceeded* and *call* as a synonym for *mandate.* But in putting them together in a new phrase, "surpassed their call," the writer created an undecipherable expression.

3. *Test the replacement word carefully in your sentence.* Watch particularly for appropriate connotations as well as denotations.

4. *Reject high-sounding or multisyllabic words simply for the impression you think they might create.* Use a thesaurus to find a more precise word, not a fancier one. Inexperienced writers can be seduced by "fine" or unusual language, which is inconsistent with their writing style and often misleading or ridiculous.

13c
thes

surpassed their call," would you have any idea what the delegates did? The writer in this instance was trying to paraphrase a sentence in a history book and found some unfortunate synonyms in a thesaurus. The delegates, it seems, had done more than they had been instructed to do: they had "exceeded their mandate."

Use the thesaurus with extreme caution. If you do not fully understand a synonym that you are thinking of using in your own writing, look it up in a good dictionary.

■ **Exercise 13.5** Find five synonyms for the word *excitement* in a thesaurus. Write a sentence for each of the synonyms, using the words correctly. Use a desk dictionary if you need to check on the connotations of a word.

PART FOUR
UNDERSTANDING GRAMMAR AND WRITING CORRECT SENTENCES

PART FIVE
UNDERSTANDING PUNCTUATION

PART SIX
UNDERSTANDING MECHANICS

BOOK TWO

USAGE RULES AND OPTIONS

PART
FOUR

UNDERSTANDING GRAMMAR AND WRITING CORRECT SENTENCES

CHAPTER

14

CORRECTING RUN-ONS AND COMMA SPLICES

Appropriate punctuation and conjunctions can correct two common sentence errors: run-ons and comma splices. A **run-on error** occurs when two independent clauses run together. A **comma splice** occurs when two independent clauses are linked by a comma. You can see both errors in the example below. *A* is a comma splice; *B* is a run-on.

> Fuel emissions at Yosemite National Park can disrupt the delicate ecological balance, *[A]* authorities have acted firmly against pollution *[B]* they have banned the automobile in Yosemite Valley.

Independent clauses may be joined or separated correctly in several ways: by using end marks, by using a comma and a coordinating conjunction, by using a semicolon, and by using subordination.

14a
Using End Marks to Set Off Independent Clauses

A period at the end of an independent clause, followed by a capital letter at the beginning of the next word, will give you two correct sentences.

> Fuel emissions at Yosemite National Park can disrupt the delicate ecological balance. Authorities have acted firmly against pollution. They have banned the automobile in Yosemite Valley.

Sometimes you can use a question mark or an exclamation point to separate the clauses.

Run-on: Are liberal arts graduates desirable employees in business many corporations report their strong interest in women and men with humanities backgrounds.

Corrected: Are liberal arts graduates desirable employees in business? Many corporations report their strong interest in women and men with humanities backgrounds.

Comma Splice: I made it, I passed the bar exam, I can be a lawyer!

Corrected: I made it! I passed the bar exam! I can be a lawyer!

■ **Exercise 14.1**   The items below contain one or more run-on errors or comma splices. Correct them by creating complete sentences separated by appropriate end punctuation and, where necessary, appropriate capitalization.

1. Many states outlaw the sale of fireworks, every year they cause many children to lose their hands and eyes.
2. Despite the rise in fares, short ocean voyages continue to draw vacationers for all over America now "cruises to nowhere" have grown in popularity.
3. The art of welding is necessary to modern industry welding is an art that requires much care and patience.
4. How can noise ordinances protect city dwellers against loud portable radios cradled like babies in the arms of strolling adolescents the police seem reluctant to arrest young offenders, since a loud radio is not a violent crime.
5. When my mother first got a job, I had to make some sudden adjustments, I had to deal with an unexpected feeling of abandonment the first time I came home from grade school to an empty house and realized that Mom was not there to greet me and that everything seemed still and dead.

**14a/b
run-on**

14b
Using a Comma and a Coordinating Conjunction

A comma alone is not strong enough to mark off one independent clause from another (see 5d). Notice how conjunctions serve correctly in the following examples.

Fuel emissions at Yosemite National Park can disrupt the delicate ecological balance, **so** authorities have acted firmly against pollution.

The comma and the conjunction *so* coordinate the independent clauses, giving us a compound sentence.

Comma Splice: Cortez first introduced chocolate to Europe, the Spaniards later added sugar for sweetening.

Corrected: Cortez first introduced chocolate to Europe, and the Spaniards later added sugar for sweetening.

14c
Using a Semicolon between Independent Clauses

When the ideas in two independent clauses are closely related, a semicolon stresses the relation. The first word after a semicolon begins with a lowercase letter unless the word is a proper noun. When a conjunctive adverb such as *also, however,* or *therefore* or a transitional expression such as *for example* or *on the contrary* (see 14e) appears between two independent clauses, you can separate them with a semicolon. Remember, however, that the period is a more usual mark of separation than a semicolon. When you use a period, you of course have two sentences; if you use the semicolon, you have one sentence.

14c
run-on

Federal authorities in Yosemite National Park have acted firmly against pollution; they have banned the automobile in Yosemite Valley.

By connecting the independent clauses, the semicolon stresses the point that the second clause is a consequence of the first.

Comma Splice: A good researcher may not know all the facts however, she should know where to find them.

Corrected: A good researcher may not know all the facts; however, she should know where to find them.

Occasionally a writer will use both a semicolon and a conjunction to mark off independent clauses (see 24a).

Nothing could be more racy, straightforward, and alive than the prose of Shakespeare; but it must be remembered that this was dialogue written to be spoken.

—W. SOMERSET MAUGHAM

When independent clauses are short and closely related in structure and meaning, some writers occasionally join them with a comma to achieve a special effect.

You fly in with the goods, you fly out with the lucky.

—JOHN LE CARRÉ

■ **Exercise 14.2** Correct run-on errors and comma splices in the following sentences. Use either a coordinating conjunction and a comma or a semicolon, but be sure that your corrections yield logical sentences. Mark any correct sentences *C*.

1. The snow started falling at five o'clock then the wind began to blow hard from the north.
2. The best way to keep warm in icy weather is to wear layers of clothing moreover wool is much warmer than cotton.
3. She saw the cat spring through the air onto the bluebird she yelled.
4. Fewer jobs are open for teachers every year, yet many college students major in education to obtain teaching certificates.
5. The heavy black clouds meant rain, they came on swiftly with thunder and lightning.

**14d
run-on**

14d
Using Subordination

Comma Splice: Fuel emissions at Yosemite National Park can disrupt the delicate ecological balance of the region, authorities there have acted firmly against automobiles.

Corrected by Subordination: Because fuel emissions at Yosemite National Park can disrupt the delicate ecological balance of the region, authorities there have acted firmly against automobiles.

Run-on Sentence: Authorities have acted firmly against pollution —they have banned the automobile in Yosemite Valley.

Corrected by Subordination: Authorities who have banned the automobile in Yosemite Valley have acted firmly against pollution.

Acting firmly against pollution, authorities have banned the automobile in Yosemite Valley.

■ **Exercise 14.3** Use subordination to correct run-on errors and comma splices in the sentences below. Mark any correct sentences *C*.

1. Learning to read lips is not easy young children can adapt to this preferred method of teaching language to the deaf more easily than older people can.
2. At Bourda Market in Georgetown, Guyana, daybreak stirs a rush of activity, vendors set up their wares for the 6:30 A.M. opening.
3. Play, which allows a child's free expression, helps early childhood education. However, children must keep some real control over the situation if play is to encourage real learning.
4. Different careers and different ambitions often separate childhood friends, they share only memories after a while and do not share any common experiences in the present.
5. The Super Bowl in January has now become an unofficial national holiday, people who hardly follow professional football during the regular season gather at parties before huge color television sets, eating and drinking and enjoying each other and sometimes watching the game.

**14e
run-on**

■ **Exercise 14.4** Correct the run-on errors and comma splices in Exercise 14.1, this time by joining complete thoughts either through subordination or through coordination (14b and 14d).

**14e
Recognizing Sources of Run-on Errors or Comma Splices**

Certain conjunctive adverbs (5c), transitional expressions (4b), and subject pronouns (5c) at the beginning of a sentence can mislead you into producing a run-on error or a comma splice.

Adverbs

Conjunctive adverbs in this category include such words as *accordingly, also, anyway, as a result, besides, consequently, finally, furthermore, hence, however, incidentally, indeed, instead, likewise, meanwhile, moreover, nevertheless, nonetheless, now, otherwise, still, suddenly, then, therefore,* and *thus.*

Comma Splice: The price of gold varies greatly every year, nevertheless, speculators purchase precious metals in large quantities and hope always for a price rise.

Corrected: The price of gold varies greatly every year; nevertheless, speculators purchase precious metals in large quantities and hope always for a price rise.

Run-on Sentence: Salt air corrodes metal easily — therefore, automobiles in coastal regions require frequent washing even in cold weather.

Corrected: Salt air corrodes metal easily. Therefore, automobiles in coastal regions require frequent washing even in cold weather.

Transitional Expressions

Some transitional expressions that may lead to comma splice or run-on errors are the following: *after all, after a while, as a result, at any rate, at the same time, for example, for instance, in addition, in fact, in other words, in particular, in the first place, on the contrary,* and *on the other hand.*

**14e
run-on**

Comma Splice: Richard Rodgers's music continues to delight audiences everywhere, in fact, revivals of *Oklahoma!, Carousel,* and *The King and I* pack theaters every year.

Corrected: Richard Rodgers's music continues to delight audiences everywhere. In fact, revivals of *Oklahoma!, Carousel,* and *The King and I* pack theaters every year.

Run-on Sentence: Americans continue their love affair with the automobile — at the same time they are more successful than ever before in restricting its use.

Corrected: Americans continue their love affair with the automobile, but at the same time they are more successful than ever before in restricting its use.

✓ CHECKLIST: HOW TO CORRECT RUN-ON ERRORS AND COMMA SPLICES

1. Use a period, a question mark, or an exclamation point.

2. Use *and, but, or, nor, for, yet,* or *so,* preceded by a comma.

3. Use a semicolon to coordinate closely related ideas in consecutive independent clauses.

4. Use subordination to relate some ideas that might otherwise be expressed in independent clauses.

Subject Pronouns

The subject pronouns that may lead to comma splices and run-on sentences are *I, you, he, she, it, we, they,* and *who.*

> **Comma Splice:** Disneyland is fun for everyone, I think I enjoyed it as much as my ten-year-old niece did.

> **Corrected:** Disneyland is fun for everyone; I think I enjoyed it as much as my ten-year-old niece did.

> **Run-on Sentence:** The weather disappointed Vermont vacationers — they wanted snow in January, not warm, sunny skies.

> **Corrected:** The weather disappointed Vermont vacationers because they wanted snow in January, not warm, sunny skies.

**14e
run-on**

Divided Quotations

In divided quotations or in consecutive sentences within a quotation, be sure to punctuate complete sentences correctly.

In a dialogue, commas are not sufficient to set off independent clauses.

> **Comma Splice:** "Speak up, amigo," Juanita said, "I can't hear you."

> **Corrected:** "Speak up, amigo," Juanita said. "I can't hear you."

■ **Exercise 14.5** Use the words in brackets correctly in the sentences that follow. Correct the punctuation and capitalization where necessary.

1. [they] The use of copying machines has replaced note-taking for many students _____ simply photograph text pages instead of taking notes on their readings.

2. [however] His car skidded and struck the telephone pole _____, he was not hurt.

3. [however] He said _____ that the car would never run again.

4. [it] The dulcimer has a soft, sweet tone _____ was long ago replaced by the guitar in bluegrass music.

5. [I] "Not I," she replied with a scowl "_____ never liked him."

14f
Revising Your Papers

Examine drafts of your papers carefully for run-on errors and comma splices. If you have trouble with these errors, spend extra time trying to locate and correct them. If you read over your drafts with an eye to avoiding these errors, you can locate them before you produce a final draft.

☐ Read your papers aloud slowly. When you read aloud slowly, your ear probably will pick out the independent clauses. They will sound like complete sentences, and you are likely to pause for breath at the end of each one. When your voice clearly stops and drops, look for a period or a semicolon at that point.

☐ Before you write your final draft, count your sentences. Number your sentences all the way through the draft of your paper. Then see if you have separated them with the right punctuation and capitalization. If the number of sentences seems small in relation to the length of the draft, you may have committed some run-on errors.

☐ Read your papers backward from the last sentence to the first. When you use this technique, you can consider each sentence as a separate unit of meaning apart from the surrounding sentences. Each sentence appears as a complete statement on its own, and implied connections, such as those made through transitional phrases, adverbs, and pronouns, cannot trap you into making errors. You must read very carefully, being sure that each group of words you read aloud forms a complete sentence or a complete independent clause.

☐ Watch for the words and phrases that often cause run-on errors or comma splices at sentence junctures. (See 14e.) Subject pronouns, transitional expressions, and conjunctive adverbs frequently appear at sentence junctures. Words and phrases in these groups can trap

14f
run-on

you into writing run-on errors and comma splices. If you look for those words and phrases when you read over your drafts, you can often locate and correct your mistakes.

■ **Exercise 14.6** In each item below, underline the sentence element that gave rise to the run-on error or the comma splice. Correct the errors by using any of the methods explained in this chapter.

1. The deputy mayor enjoys speaking to civic groups, for example, she addressed the Kiwanis Club, the Young Republican Club, and the Daughters of the American Revolution all on one Sunday last month.
2. A hush fell over the crowd then a small man with an empty sleeve on this coat and a hideously scarred face got out of his seat and hobbled to the platform.
3. Public transportation is quick and safe on the other hand it does not offer the flexibility and privacy of travel by car.
4. Sidesaddles allowed women to ride horseback modestly in an age of long, thick skirts, however, such saddles were extremely dangerous because they did not allow women to grip the horse with their legs.
5. A two-cycle gasoline engine is excellent for lawn mowers and for boats equipped with an outboard motor it is not good for larger machines because its lubrication is uneven at the higher temperatures larger machines generate.

CHAPTER

15

CORRECTING SENTENCE FRAGMENTS

End marks — periods, question marks, and exclamation points — separate grammatical units that are complete sentences. To be complete grammatically, a sentence needs both a subject and a predicate. A grammatically incomplete unit starting with a capital letter and closing with an end mark is called a **sentence fragment.**

In the following sentence fragments, the writer makes an incomplete word group look like a sentence by using a capital letter for the first word and by placing a period after the last.

> And tried the hot tamales.

> Watching the ducks on the lake.

You can easily spot sentence fragments when they appear in isolation. But when a fragment is buried in surrounding sentences, you may have trouble seeing it and correcting it.

> We enjoyed our stroll through the park. **Watching the ducks on the lake.** The leaves were changing color.

> We visited a new Mexican restaurant downtown. **And tried the hot tamales.** They burned my mouth for a week.

Each of these fragments can be added to the preceding sentence to form one complete sentence.

> We enjoyed our stroll through the park, watching ducks on the lake.

We visited a new Mexican restaurant downtown and tried the hot tamales.

■ **Exercise 15.1** Identify the fragments and the complete sentences below.

1. Without any funds from the federal government or from foundations.
2. Who found the lost keys.
3. Supported by heavy steel cables.
4. Driving through the California desert with the temperature at 114 degrees.
5. Johnny Cash sings many songs about prisons and prisoners, their loneliness and their hardships.
6. Since she spoke to the child's mother.
7. That woman holds two jobs.
8. Country music wailing with pain and loss.
9. A woman who holds two jobs.
10. Country music wails with pain and loss.

■ **Exercise 15.2** Identify the complete sentences and the fragment or fragments in each selection below.

1. Alcohol can damage heart muscle tissue in a condition called *alcoholic cardiomyopathy*. Which can be fatal. Especially to people who cannot leave alcohol alone.
2. The United States Constitution gives three basic duties to Congress. Enacting laws, representing the people, and limiting the power of the executive branch.
3. Videodiscs and tapes have increased in popularity. As a result of this exciting new technology. Many more people can buy or rent their favorite movies. Seeing them without commercial interruptions on their own TV sets at home.
4. Human beings develop intellectually in leaps from one stage to another, say some important theorists in psychology. Such as Erik Erikson and Jean Piaget.
5. Working for the government sometimes requires great personal sacrifice, but the rewards of public service are great. By hard work and careful attention to detail, a government worker can do much good for the society at large.

15a
Making Fragments into Complete Sentences

No handbook can give a complete set of rules for converting fragments into sentences, but the following examples show some typical problems and ways to remedy them.

☐ Join the fragment to the sentence that comes before it.

Fragment: Television brings current events to life. **Through lively interviews and dramatic images.**

Corrected: Television brings current events to life through lively interviews and dramatic images.

Fragment: Jean Rhys's *Good Morning, Midnight* is a novel about Sasha Jansen. **A lonely woman in Paris.** She searches desperately for escape from a dismal past.

Corrected: Jean Rhys's *Good Morning, Midnight* is a novel about Sasha Jansen, a lonely woman in Paris.

☐ Add the fragment to the beginning of the sentence that follows or precedes it. Your intended meaning determines whether you connect a fragment to the sentence before or to the sentence after it. Sometimes neither option will produce a sentence that makes sense and pleases stylistically.

Fragment: **Watching ducks glide across the lake.** Men and women sit everywhere beneath the flowering dogwoods and talk softly under the afternoon sun.

Corrected: Watching ducks glide across the lake, men and women sit everywhere beneath the flowering dogwoods and talk softly under the afternoon sun.

☐ Add or remove words to convert a fragment into a complete sentence, or change the wording of the fragment itself.

Fragment: On Sundays in May at the seacoast everyone can relax. **Watching the lobster boats come in.**

Corrected: On Sundays in May at the seacoast everyone can relax. Children enjoy watching lobster boats come in.

or

On Sundays in May at the seashore everyone can relax. Children watch lobster boats come in.

■ **Exercise 15.3** Return to Exercise 15.1. Correct each fragment by using the techniques explained in 15a. Be sure that your new sentences make sense. Read them aloud.

**15a
frag**

✓ CHECKLIST: CORRECTING A SENTENCE FRAGMENT

According to sentence logic and to your own stylistic tastes, take one of these steps:

1. Connect the fragment to the sentence *before* or *after* it.
2. Add a new subject, a new verb, or both, and add any other necessary words.
3. Remove any words that keep the fragment from being a complete sentence.
4. Make a present or past participle into a verb by adding a helping verb such as *am, is, are, was,* or *were* before the participle or by changing the participle into a correct verb form.
5. When necessary, add a subject to the fragment to convert it into a complete sentence.
6. Change an infinitive to a verb by removing *to* and using the correct form of the verb. Or you can sometimes use *like, likes, want, wants, plan, plans, try, tries, am, is,* or *are* before the infinitive. Sometimes you will have to add a subject to fragments that contain an infinitive.
7. Make any necessary changes in the wording of the fragment to convert it into a complete sentence.

■ **Exercise 15.4** Find the fragments in the following selection. Correct each one by adding it to an adjacent sentence, by adding words to it, or by removing words from it. Be sure that each sentence has a subject and a predicate.

We knew him as heavyweight boxing champion of the world. A joking, mocking, happy showman. He wrote poems about his foes. Bad poems. But they made people laugh. Paying attention. He bragged about himself in a sport. Where the athletes supposed to be humble. Not telling the world how good they are. But he was good. Maybe the best fighter in boxing history. Now he no longer heavyweight champion. He writes no more poems. On television speaks slowly. Hesitates. Looks puzzled and hurt.

15b
Recognizing Words and Phrases That May Cause Fragments

When you use present and past participles, infinitives, and certain adverbs, connectives, and subordinators as sentence openers, you may trap yourself into producing an incomplete sentence. If you check carefully when you proofread for words in these groups at the beginnings of your sentences, you may spot unwanted fragments.

Present participles are verb forms ending in *-ing*, such as *singing, running, speaking, trying, shouting, working,* and *flying* (see 5d, 17a).

Fragment: Running wildly in the hills. The stallion looked untamed and beautiful and somehow ghostly.

Corrected: Running wildly in the hills, the stallion looked untamed and beautiful and somehow ghostly.

Past participles are verb forms ending in *-ed, t,* or *-n,* such as *dressed, faded, hurt,* and *driven* (see 17a).

Fragment: The toast popped up. **Burned black as coal.** It looked like a piece of volcanic rock.

Corrected: The toast popped up, burned black as coal.

Infinitives are verb forms introduced by the word *to,* which is called the **infinitive marker** (see 5d). Infinitives include such forms as *to play, to scream, to study,* and *to eat.* Like participles and participial phrases, they express action vividly and sometimes seem so strong that writers may think them capable of standing alone as sentences.

Fragment: The mayor spoke forcefully. **To convince her audience of the need for tax reform.**

15b frag

Corrected: The mayor spoke forcefully to convince her audience of the need for tax reform.

Adverbs, subordinators, and connecting words and phrases that often begin fragments include *also, as well as, especially, for example, for instance, just like, mainly,* and *such as.* In speaking we often use fragments along with adverbs and connecting words, but when we write, we must be sure that adverbs and connecting words or phrases lead into complete sentences.

Fragment: An individual spectrum exists for each element. **For example, hydrogen.** It has a red, a blue-green, and a green line.

Corrected: An individual spectrum exists for each element. For example, hydrogen has a red, a blue-green and a green line.

Subordinators that may lead writers into making sentence fragments include conjunctions, such as *as long as, after, although, as, as if, as soon as,*

✓ CHECKLIST: CHECKING FOR INCOMPLETE SENTENCES

1. Read your sentences aloud, or get a friend to read them aloud to you. Distinguish between the pause that a speaker may make for emphasis and the grammatical pause marked off by a period, a question mark, an exclamation point, or a semicolon.

2. Read your paper from the last sentence to the first, or have a friend read the paper aloud in that way to you.
   Stop after you read each sentence and ask: Is it complete? Does it make a complete statement or ask a complete question?

3. Check for subjects and predicates.
   Every complete sentence must have at least one subject and one predicate (see 5b).

4. Look at sentences that begin with present and past participles, connective words and phrases, and subordinators.

because, before, wherever, once, while, how, provided, if, since, so that, though, unless, until, when, where, and *whether,* and relative pronouns, such as *what, which, who, whoever, whose, whom, whomever, whatever,* and *that* (see 5c).

**15c
frag**

> **Fragment:**   The University Government Association gives students a voice in making policy. **Because they too should influence the university administration in matters of academic, social, and cultural welfare.**

> **Corrected:**   The University Government Association gives students a voice in making policy because they too should influence the university administration in matters of academic, social, and cultural welfare.

15c
Using Fragments for Special Effects

Although most formal writing requires complete sentences, sentence fragments occasionally can achieve some special effects. Writers of fiction use fragments to record dialogue, since when we speak, we often use incomplete sentences. However, the context always makes the meaning of the fragment clear.

Although they can be effective and acceptable in the hands of skilled writers, fragments are still rare in the expository writing you will do in college. Use them carefully. In writing for your courses, when you write a fragment, you may even want to mark it as such with an asterisk and a note at the bottom of the page. Your teacher will then know that you have made a deliberate choice, not a mistake.

> Jean leaned back, her hands clasped round a knee, looking at the water below them. "I came to a decision last night, Dan." It was unexpected, and he glanced at her. **"Yes?"** She shrugged. **"Nothing momentous.** But I think I'll definitely try for a teacher training course when I get home. **If I can find a place."**
>
> —JOHN FOWLES

> I had a sudden mad impulse to pack my bags and get away from both of them. Maybe it wasn't a question of choosing between them but just of escaping both entirely. **Released in my own custody. Stop this nonsense of running from one man to the next. Stand on my own two feet for once.**
>
> —ERICA JONG

Fragments may also appear in nonfiction, especially when the writer is striving for an informal, conversational effect.

> But such was Autry's impact that even the action-all-the-way Cowboys had to have somebody in their films who could sing a few cowboy songs while the hero stood around listening and tapping his foot. Charles Starrett was good enough not to need any yodelers slowing up his action. But you couldn't buck the fashion. Anyway, Dick Weston did not exactly stop the show. **And never would if he went on calling himself Dick Weston.** The name was definitely not a bell ringer. **No matter how many times you said it.**
>
> —JAMES HORWITZ

**15c
frag**

Questions and exclamations often have impact when written as fragments. To call attention to an idea, writers can use fragments effectively.

> **American culture?** Wealth is visible, and so, now, is poverty. Both have become intimidating clichés. **But the rest?**
>
> —PETER SCHRAG

> Whatever economic sanctions can achieve will be duly tested. A semblance of Western resolve has been temporarily achieved. **At a considerable price.**
>
> —*The New York Times*

■ **Exercise 15.5** In each selection, correct each fragment by adding it to the sentence that comes before or after or by changing it into an independent sentence. Write *C* by the number of any selection that is correct as it stands.

1. In 1980, the Supreme Court ruled that scientists could patent bacteria made in laboratories. An important decision that has made profitable genetic engineering possible.

2. In and around Boston, the sixty-eight institutions of higher learning draw both full-time and part-time students, numbering more than 150,000. Of these over 60 percent come from states other than Massachusetts.

3. When I approached him after school for extra help with my algebra. He replied that he had already given me enough time. That I should try to find a tutor. Who could explain things slowly and carefully.

4. Although styles change quickly, the jeans phenomenon looks as if it is here to stay. Worn all over the world, jeans are especially popular with teenagers. But adults wear them, too, sometimes with jackets and neckties.

5. Abigail Adams championed women's rights. Writing about new legislation to her husband John early in the history of the United States. She said, "I desire you would remember the ladies and be more generous and favorable to them than your ancestors." A strong remark, considering the times.

15c
frag

■ **Exercise 15.6** Return to Exercise 15.2. Correct each fragment. Do not change correct sentences.

■ **Exercise 15.7** Using the following fragments, construct complete sentences. You may add anything you want to make the sentences complete.

1. Breaking away from the pack.
2. The coiled snake under my bed.
3. A woman of enormous strength and speed.
4. When I had discovered myself walking in my sleep.
5. If he should die before Saturday.

■ **Exercise 15.8**   Identify the fragments in the following passages. Then explain why you think each writer used a fragment instead of a complete sentence. If you wanted to avoid the fragment, what would you do?

1. Mr. Fitzgerald and his wife, Kathy Fitzgerald, realized that if their hopes for filming the script were to be realized, they would need more help. Which they got in the form of Tom Shaw, a well known production manager and old friend of John Huston, who left a big-budget Barbra Streisand picture to take charge of *Wise Blood*.

   —LINDA CHARLTON

2. But how many women can name marriage itself as a source of our turbulence? More often than not, we were the ones who most wanted to bet married. Besides, if not marriage, what *do* we want? Divorce? That is too fearsome.

   —NANCY FRIDAY

3. Milan is quite an attractive little city. A nice cathedral, *The Last Supper*, a very glamorous train station built by Mussolini, La Scala, and many other enjoyable sights.

   —FRAN LEBOWITZ

**15c
frag**

CHAPTER

16

AGREEMENT OF SUBJECT AND VERB

When a verb is singular, its subject must be singular; when a verb is plural, its subject must be plural. When a subject is in the first, second, or third person, the verb must match it (as we saw in 5c). This matching in number and person of subjects and verbs is called **agreement.**

In the present tense, the presence of the *-s* suffix at the end of a subject or verb usually indicates a plural subject or a singular verb.

Our *dog* **sleeps** in the basement.

Our *dogs* **sleep** in the basement.

The suffix *-s* (or *-es*) on a noun subject generally means that the subject is *plural*. The suffix *-s* (or *-es*) on a present-tense verb usually tells you that the verb is *singular*. Singular noun subjects, which usually do not end in *-s*, accompany singular verbs, which usually do end in *-s*.

Agreement: singular noun subject; singular verb, third person, present tense

An *orchid* **costs** too much.

The *house* **needs** paint.

The *day* **goes** by quickly.

Plural noun subjects, which usually do end in *-s* (or *-es*), accompany plural verbs, which usually do not end in *-s*.

Agreement: plural noun subject; plural verb, third person, present tense

Orchids **cost** too much.

The *houses* **need** paint.

The *days* **go** by quickly.

16a
Using Singular Verbs with Singular Noun Subjects Ending in -s

The letter -*s* at the end of a word is not always a suffix denoting the plural form. Some singular nouns end in -*s*, and they, too, must match singular verb forms.

Glass **breaks**

Moss **grows.**

Fungus **spreads.**

16b
Using Plural Verbs with Plural Noun Subjects Not Ending in -s

16a/b/c agree

Some nouns do not use the suffix -*s* for the plural form (see 28c). But no matter what the form is, a plural subject requires a plural verb.

Children **giggle.**

Men **guffaw.**

Alumni **contribute.**

16c
Using Singular Verbs with Singular Pronoun Subjects

The third person singular pronouns *he, she,* and *it,* like the nouns they replace, require singular verbs.

She **raises** tomatoes.

He **keeps** the cat away.

It **eats** all the seedlings.

16d
Using the Present Tense with the Pronouns *I* and *You*

Even though the pronoun *I* is singular, it always takes the present tense without a singular *-s* ending.

I **applaud.**	I **write.**
I **dream.**	I **cry.**

The pronoun *you* functions as both a singular and a plural. Only the verb form without the singular *-s* works correctly with *you,* whether *you* is singular or plural. The right column below shows the form of the verb to be.

You **live.**	I **am.**
You **laugh.**	You **are.**
You **love.**	She **is.**

**16d/e
agree**

16e
Using Plural Verbs with Plural Pronoun Subjects

They **applaud.**

We **love** trains.

■ **Exercise 16.1**   In the sentences below, subjects are in italics and verbs are in boldface. If subjects and verbs are singular, make them plural; if they are plural, make them singular. You may need to change other words as well. Follow the example.
Example:
A *field mouse* **takes** cover in the house when the *temperature* **drops.**

Field mice **take** cover in the house when *temperatures* **drop.**

1. The *horses* **gallop** swiftly over the plains.
2. A *city* **provides** many interesting things for people to do.
3. Cigarette *smokers* **run** a high risk of getting certain diseases.
4. I **drive** her to class on Mondays, but on Thursdays *she* **insists** on taking the bus.
5. *Terror* **stalks** some neighborhoods; *people* **face** the possibility of violence every day.

16f
Using Plural Verbs with Subjects Joined by *and*

Pepper and garlic **flavor** the soup.

Greed and arrogance **disgust** most people.

Queenie and Clarence **work** on cars.

When subjects joined by *and* suggest a single idea, they may take a singular verb, but such uses are rare.

The *tenor and star* of the show **is** out with the flu.

16f
agree

The words *each* and *every* preceding singular subjects that are joined by *and* require a singular verb for the whole subject, even though the subject may sound plural.

In the Nittany Mountains, *each dawn and dusk* **fills** the sky with soft, pink light.

When *every window and every door* **shuts** out drafts, your furnace will burn less oil.

In the rare instances when *each* follows subjects joined by *and*, you may choose either a singular or a plural verb, whichever sounds better to you.

In the Nittany Mountains, dawn and dusk each **fill** (or **fills**) the sky with soft, pink light.

✓ CHECKLIST: AGREEMENT OF SUBJECT AND VERB

Singular subject	Singular verb
I	love
He	loves
The compact disk	was spinning
Our class	laughs
He	sings
The dog	barks
You	are
She	is
Anybody	can
Every one of them	is
Each of us	was
Either Burriss or Ted	is
Neither Dorothy nor John	is
Everyone	is
The friend who	was coming
The committee	is meeting
Mathematics	is

Plural subject	Plural verb
Dogs, walruses, and seals	bark
They	are barking
He and I	sing
All of them	are
All of us	were
Both Burriss and Ted	are sitting
The three friends who	were coming
The committee members	are meeting

16g
agree

16g
Learning a Special Case: The Verb *To Be*

With the verb *to be,* observe the rules of agreement in both the present and past tense (see 17a). In the present tense, the various forms of *to be* are irregular and require selective use with subjects.

am: When *I* **am** tired, I cannot think.

is: The *door* **is rattling.**
             Martha **is** late again.
             He **is serving** tables.
             It **is** drawn, and still *she* **is studying.**

are: The *waves* **are racing** to the shore.
             They **are gardening;** *we* **are resting.**
             When *you* **are finished,** you can go.

In the simple past tense both singular and plural verbs use the same form for all subjects — except for the verb *to be,* which has two past tense forms, *was* (singular) and *were* (plural).

was: The *ball* **was** high.
             He **was** merely pink, but *I* **was** lobster-red

were: As *you* **were reading,** the *children* **were planning** their little surprise.
             The *refugees* **were standing** patiently in line.

The rules of agreement also apply to the present perfect tense (see 17a). In the present perfect tense, the helping verb *has* is singular and the helping verb *have* may be either singular or plural.

I **have biked** across the country twice.

He **has** often **complained** about his back.

They **have been** out all night.

**16h
agree**

16h
Watching Out for Intervening Words

Make your verbs and subjects agree when misleading words or phrases come between them.

Large *sums* of money **go** to national defense.

One *error* in a column of figures **throws** computations off by thousands.

Words such as *in addition to, as well as, along with, plus, including,* and *together with* do not affect the number of the subject. They usually serve as prepositions introducing the object of a preposition, which can never be the subject of a verb (as we saw in 5d).

The price, including the tip and taxes, **was** $45.

Although such a sentence may be grammatically correct, it may still be awkward. Revise awkward sentences whether they are grammatically correct or not.

One of my happiest childhood memories is of a baseball game between the Philadelphia Athletics and the St. Louis Browns. I can still see the bright colors of the grass and the uniforms, and I can still feel the excitement of the crowd.

The *Marx brothers,* including Groucho, still **make** audiences laugh in *A Night at the Opera,* filmed half a century ago.

The plural subject *Marx brothers* requires a plural verb, **make:** the phrase *including Groucho* does not influence the number of the verb.

16i
agree

16i
Making Subject and Verb Agree: *Or, Either-Or, Neither-Nor*

When words such as *or, either . . . or,* and *neither . . . nor* connect singular subjects, use singular verbs.

A simple fungus *infection or a rash* between the toes **is** often extremely painful.

Either running or swimming **improves** the heart's performance significantly.

When a subject with *or* or *nor* contains both a singular and a plural part, the verb agrees with the nearest part of the subject.

Either fine art or old coins **make** a good hedge against inflation.

Either old coins or fine art **makes** a good hedge against inflation.

Neither Jack Miller nor his friends the Stanleys **like** *beer.*

Neither the Stanleys nor their friend Jack Miller **likes** *beer.*

Combined singular and plural subjects often sound awkward. Consider revising them to make compound subjects that may be expressed easily by a plural verb.

Old coins and fine art make a good hedge against inflation.

Both the Stanleys and their friend Jack Miller dislike beer.

16j
Making Indefinite Pronouns Agree

With singular indefinite pronouns such as *anybody, anyone, anything, each, either, everybody, everyone, neither, nobody, none, no one,* and *one,* use singular verbs. Use singular verbs with singular indefinite pronouns even when a prepositional phrase with a plural noun comes between the pronoun subject and the verb.

Everyone **is** on strike.

Nobody **likes** a losing team.

Everyone in all the departments **is** on strike.

Nobody among ardent fans **likes** a losing team.

With the more ambiguous indefinite pronouns *all, any, more, most,* and *some,* use singular or plural verbs, depending on whether their meaning is singular or plural in a particular sentence.

She listens carefully to the children because *some* of them **have** mature ideas.

He made a cake last night; *some* of it **is** still on the table.

The pronoun *none* has been a subject of much debate. Strict grammarians point out that *none* means "no one" and therefore should always take a singular verb. But many writers make the same distinction with *none* that they make with *any*. When *none* refers to a plural noun, some writers use a plural verb. When *none* refers to a singular noun, these writers use a singular verb.

> *None* of my students **are** here yet.

> I read his *novel* and discovered that *none* of it **was** any good.

16k
Watching Agreement in Inverted Sentences

Make verbs agree with their subjects when you invert the normal sentence order.

> Below the waves **lurks** a great white *shark*.

> Beside the brook **grow** *tulips* in a profusion of color.

16l
Beginning a Sentence with *There* or *Here*

16k/l/m agree

When a verb follows *there* or *here* at the beginning of a sentence, make sure that the subject that follows the verb agrees with it.

> Here **lie** the *ruins* of a once-thriving civilization.

> There **are** five broken *pencils* on the desk.

> There **is** a heavy glass *door* at the end of the corridor.

16m
Using Relative Pronouns as Subjects

When the relative pronouns *who, that,* and *which* appear as subjects, use a verb that agrees with the antecedent.

> Readers learn about new products from advertisements *that* sometimes **mislead** by making fantastic claims.

one of those physicians *who* **work** compulsively.

placed before *one* can make a verb singular, even
~~relative~~ pronoun that later refers to it seems to have a plural
antecedent.

The Glass Menagerie is the only one of Tennessee Williams's plays *that*
experiments with slide photography.

16n
Having Linking Verbs Agree

Use linking verbs that agree with their subjects, not with complements of
the subjects.

Scholarship and study **are** her passion.

Her *passion* **is** scholarship and study.

If such sentences sound awkward, you can revise them to make them
smoother.

Her passions are scholarship and study.

She loves scholarship and study.

16n/o
agree

16o
Having Collective Nouns Agree

Use singular verbs with most collective nouns that stand for or suggest a
unit. Such nouns have singular forms, although they have plural meanings. *Army, audience, class, committee, majority, minority, team,* and so on
take singular verbs when the words stand for a single body acting as a unit.

This *class* **meets** too early.

An *army* **needs** good leadership and a good cause.

The parking *committee* **issues** permits to students.

The football *team* **travels** to East Lansing tomorrow.

When such words apply to a group acting not in concert but as individuals or factions, a singular verb can produce a ludicrous effect.

The graduating *class* **was** already going its separate ways.

The *couple* **was** arguing with each other.

Many writers would revise such sentences to make them sound less awkward.

The *members* of the graduating class **were** already going their separate ways.

The *two* **were** arguing with each other.

Some plural nouns that specify quantities require singular verbs because the nouns suggest a single unit.

Ten minutes **is** not enough time to see the Acropolis.

A hundred *dollars* **is** not much to pay for a bike these days.

**16p
agree**

16p
Using Singular Nouns That Look Plural

Use singular verbs for those noun subjects that appear plural in form but are singular in meaning. A book or other work that has a plural title is singular, not plural. *Mathematics, politics, athletics, ethics, kudos, pediatrics,* and many other words are plural in form but nearly always take a singular verb.

Gulliver's Travels **is** both a fantastic narrative and a serious satire on the human condition.

Politics **is** both a science and an art.

Mathematics **is** difficult for many people.

■ **Exercise 16.2** Change the infinitives shown in brackets into the correct forms of the *present tense* verb.

[to do]   **1.** The two books about health care for the senior citizen _____ not provide enough data.

[to like]   **2.** Neither she nor I _____ horror movies.

[to have]   **3.** Each of the children _____ to do some of the housework.

[to win]   **4.** The battery-powered car regularly _____ praise from environmentalists.

[to require] **5.** Economics _____ careful study both for governments and for people planning to buy a new house or car.

[to give]   **6.** She is the only one of the trustees who _____ any consideration to what faculty members and students want.

[to be]   **7.** A pen and pencil _____ all you need.

[to recommend] **8.** Our group unanimously _____ an end to parking fees.

[to need]   **9.** Each man and woman on the boat _____ a life jacket.

[to stand]   **10.** Beyond the elms _____ a small cabin.

**16p
agree**

CHAPTER

17

VERB FORMS

Verbs can take a variety of forms, depending on the ways you use them. This chapter focuses on learning how to make the various verb forms work for you.

17a
Reviewing the Principal Parts of Verbs and Verb Tenses

Tense means "time." Verb tenses show the time of the action described by the verb. To form tenses correctly, you must know the **principal parts** of the verb. The principal parts are the *present* form, the *past* form, and the *past participle.*

The *present* form (the *infinitive* form without the infinitive marker *to*) is listed alphabetically in the dictionary; it is often called the **dictionary form.**

Dictionary Forms: Sing, dance, delight, slice

Infinitive Forms: to sing, to dance, to delight, to slice

To make the *past* form of most verbs, add the suffix *-d* or *-ed* to the dictionary form.

I ask**ed**, you play**ed**, he danc**ed**, she slic**ed**, we calculat**ed**, they open**ed**

Participles and Helping Verbs

The *past participle* also is usually formed by the addition of *-d* or *-ed* to the dictionary form of the verb. But unlike the past form, the past participle always requires a helping verb to complete the phrase. (The past participle form is sometimes used as a verbal; see 5d.)

Helping verbs help form tenses. The common helping verbs are *have, has, had, am, is, are, was, were, be, being, been, do, does, did, shall, will, should, would, can, may, might, must,* and *could.* Helpers may also be groups of words such as *have to, ought to, used to, is going to,* and *is about to.*

I **should have predicted** that result.

We **were finished** by noon.

He **had planted** his garden before he left for work.

The present participle is an essential verb form, but since it is always formed by the suffix *-ing* added to the dictionary form, it is not usually listed among the principal parts. (Spelling changes that occur when *-ing* is added to some verbs are discussed in 28b.) Remember that the *gerund* has the same form as the present participle, but gerunds are always treated as nouns (see Glossary and 5d). Here are some present participles:

singing, dancing, delighting, slicing

A further note: The important helping verb *do* in its various forms helps other verbs to make emphatic statements, to ask questions, or to make negations.

I do work!

Do I work?

I do not work.

17a
verbs

Verb Forms for the Three Simple Tenses

Simple present

The *simple tenses* of any verb are the *present, past,* and *future.* The *simple present* of most verbs is the *dictionary form,* which is also called the **present stem.** To form the third person singular from the simple present, you usually add *-s* or *-es* to the present stem.

I run	I go	I join
you run	you go	you join
he run**s**	she goe**s**	it join**s**
we run	we go	we join
you run	you go	you join
they run	they go	they join

Simple past

To form the simple past of regular verbs, -*d* or -*ed* is added to the present stem. The simple past does not change form.

I escaped	we escaped
you escaped	you escaped
he escaped	they escaped

Sometimes the simple past is irregular. Irregular verbs may not form the simple past tense with -*d* or -*ed*.

I ran	we ran
you ran	you ran
she ran	they ran

Simple future

The simple future is made with the helping verbs *shall* and *will*.

I shall go	we shall go
you will go	you will go
she will go	they will go

Traditional grammar holds that *shall* should be used for the first person, *will* for the second and third persons. In practice, this distinction is often ignored; most people write "I will be twenty-five years old on my next birthday."

**17a
verbs**

Verb Forms for the Three Perfect Tenses

In addition to the simple present, past, and future, verbs have three perfect tenses — the *present perfect,* the *past perfect,* and the *future perfect.* In grammar, the word *perfect* means that an act reported by one verb will be completed before an act reported by another verb. For that reason, a verb in the *perfect tense* should always be thought of as paired with another verb, either expressed or understood.

In the *present perfect* tense, the action of the verb started in the past. The present perfect is formed by the helping verb *has* or *have* plus the past participle.

I **have worked** hard for this diploma.

The work you began in the past has just ended. This compound sentence is implied: "I have worked hard for this diploma, but now my work is ended."

She **has loved** architecture for many years, and now she *takes* architecture courses in night school.

The interest in architecture began in the past and continues into the present.

Past perfect

The *past perfect* tense reports an action completed before another action took place. The past perfect is also formed with the past participle, but it uses the helping verb *had.*

I **had worked** twenty years before I saved any money.

The act of working twenty years has been completed before the act of saving took place.

They thought they **had considered** all the dangers when they decided on the attack.

The act of considering all the dangers had been completed before the act of deciding took place.

The past perfect, like the present perfect, implies another act that is not stated in the sentence.

He **had told** me that he would quit if I yelled at him. I yelled at him, and he quit.

**17a
verbs**

Future perfect

The *future perfect* tense reports an act that will be completed by some specific time in the future. It is formed by the helping verb *shall* or *will* added to *have* or *has* and the past participle.

I **shall have worked** fifty years when I retire.

He **shall have lived** with me ten years next March.

The Progressive Form

The progressive form of the verb is made with the present participle and a helping verb that is a form of *to be.* The progressive form is used with all tenses to show that an action continues during the time that the sentence describes, whether that time is past, present, or future.

Present: I am working.

Past: I was working.

Future: They will be working.

Present Perfect: She has been working.

Past Perfect: We had been working.

Future Perfect: They will have been working.

Here are some examples of progressive forms:

I **am working** on a new book.

I **was working** in the kitchen when the house caught fire.

They **will be working** in the garage tomorrow afternoon.

Principal Parts of the Most Common Irregular Verbs

Although the principal parts of most verbs are formed quite regularly, many of the most frequently used verbs are irregular. That is, their past tense and their past participle are not formed simply by an added -*ed*. The only way to master these irregular verbs is to memorize them.

If you are unsure of the principal parts of a verb, always look in a dictionary. If the verb is regular, a dictionary will list only the present form, and you will know that you should form both the past and the past participle by adding -*d* or -*ed*. If the verb is irregular, a dictionary will give the forms of the principal parts.

17a verbs

The most important irregular verb is *to be,* often used as a helping verb. It is the only English verb that does not use the infinitive as the basic form for the present tense. Study the following forms:

TO BE

	Singular	Plural
Present:	I am	we are
	you are	you are
	she is	they are
Past:	I was	we were
	you were	you were
	it was	they were
Past perfect:	I had been	we had been
	you had been	you had been
	he had been	they had been

The following is a list of the principal parts of the most common irregular verbs. (Some verbs in this list are not irregular but are included because they confuse many people.) Notice that the past or the past participles of some irregular verbs have more than one form.

COMMON IRREGULAR VERBS

Present stem	Past stem	Past participle
awake	awoke	awoke/awakened
become	became	become
begin	began	begun
blow	blew	blown
break	broke	broken
bring	brought	brought
burst	burst	burst
choose	chose	chosen
cling	clung	clung
come	came	come
dive	dove/dived	dived
do	did	done
draw	drew	drawn
drink	drank	drunk
drive	drove	driven
eat	ate	eaten
fall	fell	fallen
fly	flew	flown
forget	forgot	forgotten/forgot
forgive	forgave	forgiven
freeze	froze	frozen
get	got	gotten/got
give	gave	given
go	went	gone
grow	grew	grown
hang (things)	hung	hung
hang (people)	hanged	hanged
know	knew	known
lay (to put)	laid	laid
lie (to recline)	lay	lain
lose	lost	lost
pay	paid	paid
ride	rode	ridden
ring	rang	rung
rise	rose	risen
say	said	said
see	saw	seen
set	set	set
shake	shook	shaken
shine	shone/shined	shone/shined

**17a
verbs**

COMMON IRREGULAR VERBS

Present stem	Past stem	Past participle
show	showed	shown
sing	sang	sung
sink	sank	sunk
sit	sat	sat
speak	spoke	spoken
spin	spun	spun
spit	spat/spit	spat/spit
steal	stole	stolen
strive	strove/strived	striven/strived
swear	swore	sworn
swim	swam	swum
swing	swung	swung
take	took	taken
tear	tore	torn
tread	trod	trod/trodden
wake	woke	waked/woke/wakened
wear	wore	worn
weave	wove	woven
wring	wrung	wrung
write	wrote	written

17a verbs

■ **Exercise 17.1** In the following sentences, supply the correct form of the verb that appears in parentheses at the end of the sentence.

Example:
The book had <u>been published</u> before he knew anything about it. (publish)

1. The plane _____ before we can get to the airport. (go)
2. He will _____ the house by the time we get back from our vacation. (paint)
3. He _____ while we were singing in the living room. (cook)
4. They had often _____ together in the same place where the shark attacked. (swim)
5. On the western frontier, horse thieves were sometimes _____ without a trial. (hang)
6. Every day she comes down to the ocean and _____ out to sea. (look)
7. Macbeth was _____ from a great victory when he met the three witches. (return)
8. She _____ for you at this very moment. (search)

9. Johnson, whom you see over there at his desk, has _____ in this office for twenty years. (work)

10. He _____ to escape from his job whenever he can. (like)

17b
Reviewing Special Uses of the Simple Present

The *simple present* has several uses:
It makes an unemphatic statement about something happening or a condition existing right now.

> The earth **revolves** around the sun.

> The car **passes** in the street.

It expresses habitual or continuous or characteristic action.

> Porters **carry** things.

> Dentists **fill** teeth and sometimes **pull** them.

> Rocky McKnuckle **fights** with everybody.

> The organization of his government always **seems** more important to an incoming president than the organization of his White House.

> —THEODORE H. WHITE

**17b
verbs**

It expresses a command indirectly, as a statement of fact.

> Periodicals **are** not to be taken out of the room.

It reports the content of literature, documents, movies, musical compositions, objects of art, or anything else that supposedly comes alive in the present each time it is experienced by an audience.

> Macbeth **is driven** by ambition, and he **is haunted** by ghosts.

> The Parthenon in Athens **embodies** grace, beauty, and calm.

Some writers use the present tense to describe historical action on the theory that history happens to us again each time we read about it. This *historical present* is awkward to sustain in English; in general, you should avoid it. A wise rule is to write about the past in the past tense.

> When Tom Paine **calls** for America's independence, he **is speaking** as an English radical.

17c
Observing Correct Sequence of Tenses

If you use more than one verb in a sentence, be sure that the time of the verbs flows logically from one to the next. This means that past, present, and future actions must appear in sequences in a logical order.

> While I **am writing,** I **like** to listen to the radio.

Two actions take place at the same time—the present. Both are reported in verbs using the present tense.

> He **says** that Hamlet **felt** only self-pity.

The action of saying appears in the present; it is a comment of something that happened in the past.

> Dickens **was** already famous when he **made** his first trip to America.

The two verbs both report past action; both are in the simple past.

> The child **was crossing** the street when I **saw** the car bearing down on her.

The past progressive is used with the simple past, the action *crossing* continuing to the definite point when I *saw.*

> He **had been** in Vietnam for a year when he **began** to write his book.

The past perfect *had been* indicates an action in the past that continued before the action expressed in the simple past tense *began.*

When I **get up,** he **will have been gone** for hours.

A future time is indicated by the adverb *when* and the present *get up*. The future perfect *will have been gone* indicates an action that will be completed before the action of getting up takes place.

Ordinarily, a past tense in the first clause of a sentence cannot be followed by the simple present, the present perfect, or a future tense.

Sir Walter Scott **wrote** many novels because he **is** always in debt and **needs** to make money.

Sir Walter Scott **wrote** many novels because he **has been** in debt and **has needed** to make money.

Revised: Sir Walter Scott **wrote** many novels because he **was** always in debt and **needed** to make money.

However, you may use the present tense or the future tense in the second clause if it expresses a general truth always in force and follows a first clause containing a verb such as *say, tell, report, agree,* or *promise.*

They **agreed** that relations between the sexes **are** difficult now.

He **says** that he **will pay** the bill next month.

He **says** that he **has paid** the bill already.

He **says** that he **paid** the bill last month.

**17c
verbs**

■ **Exercise 17.2** Fill in each blank with any verb that makes sense. Use the tense given in parentheses.

Example:
After John *had been dancing* for three hours, he realized that the band had stopped playing. (past perfect progressive)

1. He _____ to New York five times and plans to go again. (present perfect)
2. Tomorrow _____ the first day of the rest of my life. (future)
3. Ralph _____ in the bank when the robbery took place. (past perfect)
4. Hitchcock always _____ in his own movies. (present)
5. Canada geese _____ continually while they fly. (present)

■ **Exercise 17.3**   Fill in each blank with a logical tense of the verb given in parentheses.

1. They were going out the door when she _____. (call)
2. You will _____ home by the time you get this letter. (arrive)
3. They had been _____ for about an hour when the fire broke out in the boat. (sail)
4. Winter will have come and _____ by the time you come home from the army. (go)
5. They _____ supper right now. (eat)

17d
Using Mood Accurately

The **mood** of a verb expresses the attitude of the writer. Verbs have several moods—the *indicative,* the *subjunctive,* the *imperative,* and the *conditional.*

Indicative Mood

The indicative is used for simple statements of fact or for asking questions about the fact. It is by far the most common mood of verbs in English.

The tide **came** in at six o'clock and **swept** almost to the foundation of our house.

Can he **be** serious?

Subjunctive Mood

The subjunctive conveys a wish, a desire, or a demand in the third person, or it makes a statement the writer thinks is contrary to fact.

He requested that his son **use** the money to go to college.

He requested that his sons and daughters **use** the money to go to college.

He asked that they never **forget** him.

Use the subjunctive in a clause beginning with *if* when the clause makes a statement contrary to fact:

If only I **were** in Paris tonight!

The subjunctive form for most verbs differs from the indicative only in the third person singular. The present subjunctive of the verb *to be,* however, does not vary at all. It is *were* for the first, second, and third persons singular and plural.

Were she my daughter, I would not permit her to date a member of a motorcycle gang.

I wish you **were** here.

Use the subjunctive in clauses beginning with *that* after verbs that give orders or advice or that express wishes or requests.

He wishes that she **were** happier.

She asked that he **draw** up a marriage contract before the wedding.

In all these examples, a request is embodied in a *that* clause. Since no one can tell whether a request will be honored or not, the verb in each clause is in the subjunctive.

Should and *had* may also express the subjunctive:

Should he step on a rattlesnake, his boots will protect him.

Had he taken my advice, he would not have bought stock in a dance hall.

Take care not to confuse the conditional with the past subjunctive. Do not say "I wish we *would have* won the tournament." Say "I wish we *had* won the tournament."

Use the subjunctive in some commands or wishes expressed in the third person singular.

May the Good Lord **bless** and **keep** you.

Let there **be** light.

Grammar **be** hanged!

Imperative Mood

The *imperative mood* is a particular kind of subjunctive. The imperative is used only to express commands or entreaties in the second person singu-

**17d
verbs**

lar or plural, and the form of the verb is the same as the indicative. In the imperative sentence, the *subject* of the verb is always *you,* but the *you* is usually understood, not written out:

> **Pass** the bread.

> **Drive** me to the airport, please.

> **Leave** the room!

> **Watch** your step!

Sometimes *you* is included for extra emphasis:

> You **give** me my letter this instant!

■ **Exercise 17.4**   Identify the moods of the verbs in italics in the following sentences. Over each italicized verb, write *I* for indicative, *S* for subjunctive, or *IM* for imperative.

1. If she *was* awake, she must have heard the noise.
2. Prisoners in solitary confinement sometimes *dream* of enormous meals.
3. He said that Japan *has* one of the lowest crime rates in the world.
4. If Carlton Fisk *were* still *playing* for Boston, the Red Sox might not be so blue.
5. *Had* you *been* here, we might not have quarreled.

Conditional Mood

The conditional mood expresses what might be true or false under certain circumstances. A conditional sentence contains a clause that states the condition and another that states the consequence of the condition. Most conditional statements are introduced with *if.*

> **If** Communist governments had been able to produce enough food for their people, they would not have collapsed in 1989.

> **If** you will be home tonight, I'll come over.

> **If** the strike were settled right now, bad feelings between them would still exist.

The subjunctive is used only for conditions clearly contrary to fact.

> If he **were** here right now, we would be happy.

He is not here, we know that he is not here, and we are not happy.

If he **is** there, we will be happy.

We do not know whether he is there or not. We make a simple statement of fact. If we discover he is there, we will be happy.

If the circumstances are in the past, use the subjunctive for conditions that were clearly not factual and the indicative for conditions that may have been true. The verb *would* is used as a helping verb for statements that give the supposed consequences of conditions that were not factual.

If he **were** there that night, he **would have had** no excuse.

He was not there; the conditional clause uses the subjunctive, and the clause stating the consequences uses *would*.

If he **was** there, he **had** no excuse.

He may have been there; we do not know. If he was indeed there, he had no excuse. The indicative mood is used in both clauses as a simple statement of fact.

The past perfect can be used as a subjunctive form in past conditional statements when the condition states something that was not true.

If Hitler **had stopped** in 1938, World War II **would not have come** as it did.

17e verbs

Avoid using the conditional in both clauses.

Incorrect: If she **would have gone** to Paris, she **would have had** a good time.

Correct: If she **had gone** to Paris, she **would have had** a good time.

17e
Using Active and Passive Voice

Learn the difference between the active voice and the passive voice. Use verbs in the active voice in most sentences; use verbs in the passive voice sparingly and only for good reason.

✓ CHECKLIST: COMMON ERRORS IN THE USE OF VERBS

	Faulty	Correct
Irregular verbs		
Confusing simple past with past participle	I **seen** her last night. He **done** it himself.	I **saw** her last night. He **did** it himself. He **had done** it himself.
Trying to make irregular verbs regular	She **drawed** my picture. We **payed** for everything.	She **drew** my picture. We **paid** for everything.
Transitive and intransitive verbs		
Confusing *lay* (trans.) with *lie* (intrans.)	I **lay** awake every night. I **lay** my books on the desk when I come in. I **laid** down for an hour.	I **lie** awake every night. I **laid** my books on the desk when I came in. I **lay** down for an hour.
Confusing *set* (trans.) with *sit* (intrans.)	He pointed to a chair, so I **set** down. She **sat** the vase on the table.	He pointed to a chair, so I **sat** down. She **set** the vase on the table.
Illogical shifts in tense		
	The car **bounced** over the curb and **comes** crashing through the window. I **asked** him not to do it, but he **does** it anyhow.	The car **bounced** over the curb and **came** crashing through the window. I **asked** him not to do it, but he **did** it anyhow.
Mood		
Confusing conditional with past subjunctive	I wish he **would have come** sooner. I would have been here if you **would have told** me you were coming.	I wish he **had come** sooner. I would have been here if you **had told** me you were coming.

17e verbs

The voice of a transitive verb tells us whether the subject is the actor in the sentence or is acted upon. (A transitive verb carries action from an agent to an object. A transitive verb can take a direct object; an intransitive verb does not take a direct object. See 5b.)

When transitive verbs are in the **active voice,** the subject does the acting. When transitive verbs are in the **passive voice,** the subject is acted upon by an agent that is implied, or an agent that is expressed in a prepositional phrase. (Intransitive verbs cannot be passive. You can say "My brother *brooded* too much," but you cannot say "My brother *was brooded*.") In the passive voice, the transitive verb phrase includes some form of the verb *to be*.

Active: She **mailed** the letter.
John **washed** the dishes.

Passive: The letter **was mailed** by her.
The dishes **were washed** by John.

Readers usually want to know the agent of an action; that is, they want to know *who* or *what* does the acting. Since the passive often fails to identify the agent of an action, it may be a means of evading responsibility.

Active: The senator **misplaced** the memo.
The Mustangs lost because Al Tennyson **missed** a tackle on the punt return.

Passive: The memo **was misplaced.**
The Mustangs lost because a tackle **was missed** on the punt return.

**17e
verbs**

Use the passive only when the recipient of the action in the sentence is much more important to your statement than the doer of the action.

My car **was stolen** last night.

Who stole your car is not important; you don't know who took it. The important thing is that your car was stolen.

After her heart attack, she **was taken** to the hospital in an ambulance.

Who took her to the hospital is unimportant; the important fact is that she was taken.

Scientific researchers generally use the passive voice throughout reports on experiments to keep the focus on the experiment rather than on the experimenters.

When the bacteria **were isolated,** they were treated carefully with nicotine and **were observed** to stop reproducing.

■ **Exercise 17.5** Rewrite the following sentences to put the passive verbs in the active voice.

1. The paintings on the wall of my kitchen were done by my daughter.
2. The song "9 to 5" was written by Dolly Parton.
3. The movie *Citizen Kane* was made by Orson Welles, was the recipient of many awards, but was not viewed by Welles himself for years afterward.
4. In the 1950s, color was used by filmmakers to compete with television, where all the programs were still being shown in black and white.
5. The house was painted by Mr. Johnson last summer.

■ **Exercise 17.6** The following sentences were all written by professional writers. Analyze each verb to see whether it is in the active or the passive voice. Tell why the passive is used when you do find it.

1. Some birds can be identified by color alone.

   —ROGER TORY PETERSON

2. The radio was silenced, and all that could be heard was the echo of the Mayor's voice.

   —MARK HELPRIN

3. If you are bitten and the dog gets away, make every effort to find the dog and its owner.

   —RICHARD BALLANTINE

4. At this point, a doctor was summoned; a formal pronouncement of death was made; and Big Jim's carcass was dragged, feet first, and for the last time, through the front door of his saloon.

   —JOE MCGINNISS

5. Many statesmen feel that weapons are in themselves evil, and that they should be eliminated, as you would crush a snake.

   —E. B. WHITE

17f
Using the Infinitive

Use the infinitive form of the verb to complete the sense of other verbs, to serve as a noun, and to form the basis of some phrases.

The word *to*, sometimes called the infinitive marker, is placed before the verb to identify the infinitive form.

The **present infinitive** describes action that takes place at the same time as the action in the verb the infinitive completes:

> He **wants** to go.

> He **wanted** to go.

> He **will want** to go.

The present infinitive uses the infinitive marker *to* along with the simple present tense of the verb:

> to write, to dance, to play, to sing

The **present perfect infinitive** uses the infinitive marker *to*, the verb *have,* and a past participle:

> to have written, to have danced, to have sung, to have swum, to have run

The present perfect infinitive describes action prior to the action of the verb whose sense is completed by the infinitive. The present perfect infinitive often follows verb phrases that include *should* or *would.*

> I would like **to have seen** her face when she found the duck in her bathtub.

An **infinitive phrase** includes the infinitive and the words that complete its meaning:

> Her attempt **to bicycle through a New York subway tunnel** was frustrated by an express train.

> **To take such an immense journey** required courage and money.

> **To dance** was his whole reason for living.

> Her only aim was **to dodge his flying feet.**

**17f
verbs**

He studied **to improve his voice.**

Sometimes the infinitive marker is omitted before the verb, especially after such verbs as *hear, help, let, see,* and *watch.*

She heard him **come** in.

They watched the ship **sail** out to sea.

She made him **treat** her with respect.

In general, *avoid split infinitives.* A **split infinitive** has one or more words awkwardly placed between the infinitive marker *to* and the verb form. The rule against split infinitives is not absolute: some writers split infinitives and others do not. But the words used to split infinitives can usually go outside the infinitive, or they can be omitted altogether.

Split Infinitive: He told me **to** really **try** to do better.

Better: He told me **to try** to do better.

Some writers believe that split infinitives are acceptable:

The government was little altered as Mr. Bush touched down at Andrews Air Force Base at 6:30 P.M. **to** gracefully **assume** the duties but not the powers of the Presidency.

—Time

**17f
verbs**

■ **Exercise 17.7** Fill in the blank in each of the following sentences with the proper form of the infinitive of the verb in parentheses at the end of the sentence.

1. He asked her _____ his plane at 7:07 P.M. (meet)
2. I promise _____ your plane tomorrow. (meet)
3. He would have preferred _____ his education before he bought a car. (complete)
4. We often heard him _____ late at night in his shower. (sing)
5. She was not one _____ for opportunity to knock. (wait)

■ **Exercise 17.8** Rewrite the following sentences to eliminate split infinitives.

1. She claimed to truly mean her promise to work hard.
2. They intended to speedily complete the job.
3. The pilot wanted to safely and happily complete the trip.
4. The United States Football League vowed to strictly refuse to sign college football players before they had played in their senior year.
5. The Red Sox seemed to really enjoy losing.

■ **Exercise 17.9** Correct the errors in the following sentences. If a sentence is correct as it stands, place a check mark beside the number.

1. He come home last night and find the dog sick.
2. They taken the kickoff and get to work and have a touchdown in five minutes of the first quarter.
3. She worked hard and done a good job.
4. After a long day it's always good to lay down.
5. He lay his pants over the back of the chair last night and go right to sleep and don't wake up until this morning at ten o'clock.

**17f
verbs**

CHAPTER

18

PRONOUNS

Pronouns take the places of nouns in sentences. If we had to repeat the noun *house* every time we wrote about the idea *house* in the sentence below, we would have awkward and unwieldy prose.

> The house stood on a shady street, and the house looked large and comfortable, as if the house were perfectly suited for a large family and for two sets of grandparents who might visit the house for long periods.

We use pronouns to avoid awkwardness, to simplify style, and to express certain ideas clearly. (See 5c on identifying pronouns.)

We could not express some ideas without pronouns. Many sentences require first-person pronouns (*I, we, our,* and *ours*) or second-person pronouns (*you, your,* and *yours*), and no other words can serve in their place.

By themselves, pronouns are indefinite words; therefore, most pronouns require an antecedent to give them content and meaning. The **antecedent** is the word that the pronoun substitutes for. The antecedent usually appears earlier in the same sentence or in the same passage.

> The *snow* fell all day long, and by nightfall **it** was three feet deep.

Some pronouns take their meaning not from an antecedent but from the sentences in which they are located.

> **Anybody** who wants to see the concert should get a ticket two months in advance.

Some pronouns are **reflexive.** They end in *-self,* and they add emphasis to the noun or pronoun they follow.

> John **himself** admitted his error.

The legal battle about who owned the field went on for years while the field **itself** grew like a jungle.

No matter how you may judge my actions, you **yourself** would have done the same thing in my situation.

I hurt **myself.**

18a
Making Pronouns Refer Clearly to Antecedents

Pronouns that do not refer clearly to their antecedents or that are widely separated from them may confuse your readers. Often the only way to remedy such confusion is to rewrite the sentence.

Weak: Albert was with Beauregard when he got the news that his rare books had arrived.

Who got the news? Did the rare books belong to Beauregard, or did they belong to Albert?

Improved: When Albert got the news that his rare books had arrived, he was with Beauregard.

Now the sentence is clear. The rare books belong to Albert, and he got the news of their arrival while he was with Beauregard.

**18a/b
pron**

18b
Avoiding *They* and *It* Without a Referent

In constructions such as *they say* or *it says*, *they* and *it* as indefinite pronouns may be both awkward and unclear.

Vague: They say that the heat wave will break tomorrow.

They say he dyes his hair.

It says in the paper that we can expect a higher rate of inflation next year.

Better: The weather forecast is that the heat wave will break tomorrow.

His former wife says he dyes his hair.

The front-page article in today's paper says we can expect a higher rate of inflation next year.

18c
Making Pronouns Agree in Number with Their Antecedents

Singular antecedents require singular pronouns. Plural antecedents require plural pronouns.

The *house* was dark and gloomy, and **it** sat in a grove of tall cedars that made **it** seem darker still.

The *cars* swept by on the highway, all of **them** doing more than 55 miles per hour.

Roosevelt and Churchill found radio a perfect medium for **their** speaking talents.

Use a singular pronoun when all the parts of a compound antecedent are singular and the parts are joined by *or* or *nor*.

**18c
pron**

Either *Ted* or *John* will take **his** car.

Neither *Judy* nor *Linda* will lend you **her** horn.

But if Ted and John own one car in partnership, you should write, "Either Ted or John will take *their* car." And if Judy and Linda own only one horn between them, you should write, "Neither Judy nor Linda will lend you *their* horn."

Sometimes you must revise a sentence because a single pronoun will not do.

Weak: Neither *Patricia* nor *John* would let me borrow **his** lawn mower.

Revised: Neither Patricia nor John would let me borrow a lawn mower. John would not lend me his lawn mower, and Patricia would not lend me hers.

When referring to collective nouns — *team, family, audience, majority, minority, committee, group, government, flock, herd,* and many others — Americans usually use a singular pronoun.

The *team* won **its** victory gratefully.

In elections, the *majority* has **its** way.

The *committee* disbanded when **it** finished **its** business.

However, if the members of the group indicated by a collective noun are being considered as individuals, a plural pronoun is appropriate.

The hard-rock *band* broke up and began fighting among **themselves** when **their** leader was converted to Mozart.

In British English, collective nouns usually take plural pronouns and plural verbs.

The cricket *team* quit playing when **they** discovered that **their** spectators had fallen into a profound sleep.

The *government* have refused to elaborate on **their** earlier brief announcement.

Books on writing used to direct us to use masculine singular pronouns to refer to nouns and pronouns of unknown gender.

**18c
pron**

Any *teacher* must sometimes despair at the indifference of **his** students.

Everybody can have what **he** wants to eat.

Such language, though grammatically correct, is now often viewed as sexist. Writers who are sensitive to the implications of the words they use avoid sexist language. The problem apparent in these sentences is not difficult to fix:

Any teacher must sometimes despair at the indifference of students.

You can all have what you want to eat.

Everybody, order anything you want!

We can all have what we want to eat.

All participants can have what they want to eat.

Chapter 12 explores biased language and describes the various remedies for it.

■ **Exercise 18.1** Rewrite the following sentences to correct errors in pronoun reference. If you find no error in a sentence, put a check by it. You may rewrite a sentence to keep some pronouns, or you may eliminate the pronouns altogether.

1. The ship sailed under the Golden Gate Bridge as it put out to sea.
2. The painter complained to her model that she was too pale.
3. Blodgett met Whitney as he was returning from the swim meet.
4. It says on the menu that the special is fried eggplant.
5. The traveler bought a melon from the peasant as he stood in the shade on the road below Lamia, the city on the hill.
6. Anyone who loses their token will have to buy a new one if they want to ride the subway.
7. Neither Lewis nor Alfred brought their toothbrush.
8. If one wears polyester shirts, he will be much hotter in summer and much colder in winter than with cotton shirts, but he can enjoy them for years.
9. The gold team used the indoor tennis courts when they practiced in winter.
10. Neither Ellen nor Mike rode her bicycle to school that day, although they usually rode in together every morning.

**18d
pron**

18d
Avoiding Pronouns Without References

Some writers use such pronouns as *this, that, they, it, which,* and *such* to refer not to a specific antecedent, but to the general idea expressed by the whole clause or sentence. But broad reference with pronouns is imprecise and is often misleading.

Andy Warhol once made a movie of a man sleeping for a whole night, **which** was a tiresome experience.

Was the movie tiresome to watch? Or was making the movie the tiresome experience?

Andy Warhol once made a tiresome movie of a man sleeping for a whole night.

Andy Warhol once went through the tiresome experience of making a movie of a man sleeping for a whole night.

18e
Differentiating Between the Expletive *It* and the Pronoun *It*

The pronoun *it* always has an antecedent; the expletive *it* serves as a grammatical subject when the real subject is placed after the verb or is understood.

Pronoun *It*: When a barn burned in rural America, **it** often took with **it** a year's hard work for a farm family.

Expletive *It*: When a barn burned, **it** was difficult for a farm family to recover from the loss.

The expletive *it* does not have an antecedent but serves as the grammatical subject of the independent clause that it begins. The sentence could read, "When a barn burned, to recover from the loss was difficult for a farm family." But such a sentence, although correct grammatically, sounds awkward in comparison with the sentence that uses the expletive *it*.

Try to avoid using the expletive *it* and the pronoun *it* one after the other.

Weak: What will happen to the kite? If **it** is windy, **it** will fly.

Improved: What will happen to the kite? It will fly if the wind blows.

**18e/f
pron**

18f
Addressing Your Readers

In the first example below the writer announces that he will talk with the reader throughout as though in a discussion. The tone is informal and the pronoun *you* appropriate. In the second example, the writer chooses a more formal tone. The pronoun *one* does the service that *you* might perform in a less formal piece.

The book's no good to you now. Neither is scientific reason. You don't need any scientific experiments to find out what's wrong.

—Robert M. Pirsig

One might have supposed that Abraham Lincoln's Gettysburg Address was disappointing because it was so short.

18g
Using the First Person Singular

Let the tone and intention of your essay determine whether you will use the pronouns *I*, *my*, *me*, and *mine*. Many teachers tell students to avoid using pronouns in the first person singular. The intention of these teachers is to prevent student writers from calling attention to themselves and getting in the way of the subject they should be writing about.

Intrusive

I think Carew is a handsome man, but I don't mean that in the conventional sense. I think that the most arresting features on his face are a tiny turned-up nose and a mouth that in my opinion is a mile wide, and I believe it can exaggerate the mildest emotion. When he smiles, I believe the light can be seen as far away as Newport Beach. When he's downcast, I'd say there's an eclipse of the sun.

Nonintrusive

Carew is a handsome man, but not in the conventional sense. The most arresting features on his face are a tiny turned-up nose and a mile-wide mouth that can exaggerate the mildest emotion. When he smiles, the light can be seen as far away as Newport Beach. When he's downcast, there's an eclipse of the sun.

—Ron Fimrite

The first person singular pronouns are appropriate when you are writing about some experience of yours that is the center of your prose.

From all available evidence no black man had ever set foot in this tiny Swiss village before I came. I was told before arriving that I would probably be a "sight" for the village; I took this to mean that people of

**18g
pron**

my complexion were rarely seen in Switzerland, and also that city people are always something of a "sight" outside of the city. It did not occur to me — possibly because I am an American — that there could be people anywhere who had never seen a Negro.

—JAMES BALDWIN

First person singular pronouns are also acceptable when you are weighing two contradictory opinions and want to let readers know which side you are on.

Many scientists believe that all matter in the universe will fall back to a central mass, which will eventually explode again in a "big bang" like the one that created the universe. Others believe that the universe will end in the solitary deaths of all those stars scattered at an infinite distance from one another in space. I am inclined to accept the second view.

Avoiding the first person can help you avoid wordiness, but when you believe you must use it, you may do so with a good conscience. No rule of English or good taste holds that you should always avoid saying *I, me, my,* and *mine.*

18h
Avoiding the Unnecessary Pronoun after a Noun

In the following sentences the pronouns in boldface are redundant and should be omitted.

George Bush **he** liked to fish.

My mother **she** graduated from college when I graduated from high school.

The newspapers **they** admitted that advertising sometimes influences their editorial policy.

■ **Exercise 18.2** Rewrite the following sentences to eliminate pronoun errors. If a sentence is correct, put a check beside it.

1. He liked to read in the bathtub in the summer and to regulate the water temperature with his toes and to keep the door shut and

locked, which was inconvenient for others in the family, since the house had only one bathroom.

2. The movie *Apocalypse Now* was based partly on a novel by Joseph Conrad. It is likely that it suffered because Marlon Brando was so fat in it that it was hard to take him seriously. It looked as if he himself had not taken the movie seriously, and despite the money spent on promoting it, it is clear that it failed to meet expectations about it.

3. The movies *The Godfather* and *The Godfather, Part II* made millions of dollars, which proves that crime does pay if it is possible to make it exciting on film.

4. The house it was small and cramped for a family of four, and my mother and father, they loved each other, and they made the house seem as big as all creation.

5. The readers of this page will forgive this writer perhaps if he indulges himself in a personal recollection of hearing Hank Williams sing at the Grand Ole Opry in Nashville.

18i
Using the Proper Cases of Pronouns

18i

pron

The **case** of a pronoun is a form that shows the pronoun's grammatical relation to other words in the sentence. English has only three cases — the *subjective* (sometimes called the *nominative*), the *possessive* (sometimes called the *genitive*), and the *objective* (sometimes called the *accusative*).

Indefinite pronouns (*anybody, everybody:* see 5c), the pronoun *it,* and the pronoun *you* change form only for the *possessive* case. We speak of *anybody's* guess, *its* color, and *your* writing. The pronouns *I, we, he, she, they,* and *who* change form in each of the three cases.

Subjective Case

Pronouns in the *subjective case* act as subjects or as subject complements.

He and **I** read books all summer long.

She was the candidate **who** I thought deserved the victory.

It could have been **anyone.**

Mark's best friends were **she** and **I.**

Possessive Case

Pronouns in the *possessive case* show ownership or a special relation.

Their cat climbed up on **his** roof and ate **our** bird.

Her critics were louder than **her** admirers.

My uncle was **my** only relative **whose** tastes were like **mine.**

The decision was **theirs** to make after we had made **ours.**

Objective Case

Pronouns in the *objective case* are indirect objects, direct objects, objects of prepositions, or the subjects or objects of infinitives.

The company gave **her** a contract to design the building.

The team chose **me.**

Just between **you** and **me,** I thought the play was terrible.

They believed **him** to be better qualified.

She asked **him** to call **her** that evening.

18j
Using Pronouns Correctly

The checklist below provides useful hints for correct pronoun use in places that sometimes give writers trouble.

✓ CHECKLIST: SOME USEFUL PRONOUN RULES

☐ The subject of a dependent clause is always in the subjective case, even when the dependent clause serves as the object for another clause.

Dr. Hiromichi promised the prize to **whoever** made the best grades.
She was the writer **who** I thought deserved to win the Pulitzer Prize.
Leave the message for **whoever** comes into the house first.
The child **who** we believed had fallen from the bridge in fact had jumped to retrieve her ball.

☐ Objects of prepositions, direct objects, and indirect objects always take the objective case.

(continued)

✓ **CHECKLIST: SOME USEFUL PRONOUN RULES**

She called **him** and **me** fools.
It was a secret between **you** and **me**.
A package arrived for Beverly and **him**.
The old man pushed Rocco and **her** aside and then hobbled down the stairs.
She glared at Pei Ching and **me**.
She gave the driver and **me** quite a lecture on road safety and courtesy.
Who's kicking **whom?**

☐ When a noun follows a pronoun in an appositive construction, use the case for the pronoun that you would use if the noun were not present. Note that in these examples the presence of the noun does not change the case of the pronoun.

He gave the test to **us** students.
Freedom of speech is very important to **us** lawyers.
We students said that the test was too hard.
We lawyers must protect freedom of speech.

☐ *Than* and *as* often serve as conjunctions introducing implied clauses. In these constructions, we understand the idea that follows a pronoun at the end of a sentence. The case of the pronoun depends on how the pronoun is used in the clause we would write if we expressed the thought. (Implied clauses are sometimes called elliptical clauses.)

Throughout elementary school, Elizabeth was taller than **he**.
I always thought I was smarter than **she**.
The Sanchezes are much richer and more miserable than **they**.

☐ Differences in case can cause differences in meaning. In the first sentence below, *Odetta* likes *Jorge* more than *I* like Jorge. In the second sentence, *Odetta* likes *Jorge* more than *she* likes *me*. Notice how the difference in case changes the meanings of these two sentences.

Odetta likes *Jorge* more than **I**.
Odetta likes *Jorge* more than **me**.

☐ Pronouns that are the subjects or the objects of infinitives take the objective case.

They thought **her** to be an excellent choice for department head.
I believe **them** to be boring and ordinary.
Lincoln decided to consult Johnson and **him**.
The conference leaders wanted to choose Martinez and **her**.

☐ Use the possessive case before gerunds. Use the subjective or objective case with present participles used as adjectives.

Gerund (an *-ing* verb form used as a noun; see 5d)
His returning the punt 96 yards for a touchdown spoiled the bets made by the gamblers.
Her hanging a light above the painting softened the reds and darkened the blues.

(continued)

18j
pron

Present participle
They remembered **him** laughing as he said goodbye.
Through the wall they heard **him** sighing with pain.

☐ Pronouns agree in case with the nouns or pronouns with which they are paired.

Compound
He and Juan Sebastian del Cano sailed around the world.
She and Carla ran a design studio.

Appositive
The captain chose two crew members, **her** and **me,** to attempt the rescue.
The state honored two women, Carla and **her,** for their contribution to the project.
The last two crew members on board, **he** and **I,** drew the first watch.
Two teachers in the audience, my mother and **I,** whistled through our fingers.

■ **Exercise 18.3** Circle the correct pronoun within the parentheses in the following sentences.

1. He wrote the book for Nini, for (she, her) of the quick quip.
2. Of all the English kings, Henry VIII was the one (who, whom) I think was most cruel.
3. Between her and (I, me) little difference appeared.
4. I had no objection to (she, her) walking across the country.
5. The candidates seemed to most Americans, including (I, me), to represent a choice between foolishness and stupidity.
6. Just between you and (I, me), I have to say that Hawley was to blame.
7. Jackson is the sculptor (who, whom) I believe to be worthy of the Sting Memorial Award.
8. Clark Gable played the same role again and again for (whoever, whomever) directed him.
9. Unfortunately, he built (we, us) a solar house in the shade of Mount Tom.
10. Eisenhower was the president for (who, whom) the college was named.

**18j
pron**

CHAPTER

19

ADJECTIVE AND ADVERB MODIFIERS

Adjectives and adverbs are describing words. Because they qualify the meanings of other words, we say that they *modify* other parts of speech.

Adjectives tell us what kind or how many. Adverbs tell us where, when, why, and how. Adjectives modify nouns and pronouns; they do not modify anything else. Adverbs modify verbs (including verb phrases), adjectives, other adverbs, and sometimes whole sentences.

19a
Modifying Nouns and Pronouns with Adjectives

You can identify adjectives by locating words that answer one or more of these questions about nouns or pronouns: *Which one? How many? What color? What size? What kind?*

The adjectives in the following sentences are in boldface.

The road was **long, hard,** and **twisting.**

She was a **brilliant** architect and a **good** person.

The **red** Buick belonged to my aunt.

The **six large** men were brothers.

Writing is always **difficult.**

The **American hockey** team beat the Russians in the Olympics of 1980.

You may use adjectives before or after the noun or pronoun they modify.

The building, **ugly** and **tall,** burned down last night.

The **tall, ugly** building burned down last night.

The **old** car, **battered** and **rusty,** finally died.

Present and past participles of verbs often serve as adjectives:

Running hard, the bank robber fired back over his shoulder at the police.

The trip was both **exhausting** and **rewarding.**

The **gathering** night was **filled** with stars.

Buried alive for days, he survived to tell about the earthquake.

Tired and **discouraged,** she dropped out of the marathon.

A noun can be used as an adjective:

Cigarette smoking harms your lungs.

The **energy** crisis is not helped by people who drive six miles for a six-pack.

The **Marshall** Plan helped rebuild Europe after World War II.

Adjectives can serve as nouns. All of the words in boldface in the sentence below are normally adjectives, but here they clearly modify a noun that is implicit though not stated: *people* or *persons.* The words therefore assume the function of the implicit noun and become nouns themselves.

19a adj/adv

The **unemployed** are not always the **lazy** and the **inept.**

Using Adjectives after Linking Verbs

A linking verb always links a subject with an adjective or a noun that adds to the description of the subject.

Charles was **fast** and **reliable.**

The road became **difficult.**

Avoiding Jargon

Bureaucratic jargon teems with nouns used as adjectives when perfectly good adjectives are available or when the sentence is better recast in standard English.

An **opposition education** theory holds that children learn Latin best under strict **discipline** conditions.

In the hands of a seasoned bureaucrat, a multitude of nouns used as adjectives can serve much the same function as the passive voice (see 17e): it can obscure facts that the writer prefers not to make clear.

Pursuant to the environmental protection regulations enforcement policy of the Bureau of Natural Resources, special management area land use permit issuance procedures have been instituted.

We may surmise that the bureau is issuing permits for use of lands designated as "special management areas." But what are "special management areas"? They are ecologically fragile lands that the government had decided to protect against development. In other words, the bureau is inviting firms that want to develop those lands to go ahead and do so now. They need only secure a permit, which the bureau is prepared to issue to them. The bureau's "policy" is to ignore regulations established to protect the environment. The bureaucrat who wrote the statement knows that the developers' lawyers will understand it, and that the public will not.

■ Exercise 19.1

1. Write a sentence in which the adjective *gigantic* appears before a noun subject and the adjectives *frightening* and *dreamy* appear as subject complements.
2. Write a sentence in which the adjective *happy* is used in a phrase immediately after the noun or pronoun that it modifies.
3. Write a sentence in which the adjective *young* is used as a noun.
4. Write a sentence in which the adjective *unwilling* is used to modify the subject.
5. Write a sentence in which the noun *baseball* is used as an adjective.

**19b
adj/adv**

19b
Using Adverbs
to Modify Verbs, Adjectives, and Other Adverbs

The child ran **quickly** into the house.

The game was **hotly** contested.

He spoke **more** slowly at the end than at the beginning.

Adverbs answer the questions *When? Where? How? How often? How much? To what degree?* and *Why?*

Yesterday she was in Chicago.

The lamp is right **there.**

He came **painfully** to the door.

She **seldom** comes to visit anymore.

We were **greatly** relieved to receive your letter.

She was **completely** surprised at the results.

Dickens mixed humor and pathos **better** than any other English writer after Shakespeare; **consequently** he is still read by millions.

Most adverbs are formed by the addition of *-ly* to the adjective form, but adverbs may also end in *-wise, -where,* or *-ward.* And many adverbs have no special ending. Among them are *anew, soon, never, ever, almost, already, well, very, often, rather, yesterday,* and *tomorrow.*
The surest way to recognize adverbs is by understanding how they work in a sentence.

■ **Exercise 19.2** Fill in the blanks in the following sentences with adverbs that make sense.

19c adj/adv

1. She waited _____ at the airport for the team to make its way _____ home.
2. Lincoln was _____ witty, but he was also _____ sad.
3. _____ the sun was shining when I got up, and a great blue heron flew _____ over the waters of the lake.
4. Doctors have _____ accused boxing of being responsible for serious brain injuries among fighters.
5. She was _____ careful after the accident.

19c
Avoiding Adjectives When Adverbs Are Called For

In common speech we sometimes use adjectival forms in an adverbial way; in writing, this colloquial usage should be avoided.

Nonstandard: He hit that one **real good,** Howard.
Both *real* and *good* are adjectives, but they are used here as adverbs, *real* modifying *good* and *good* modifying the verb *hit.*

Revised: He hit that one to the warning track, Howard.

Nonstandard: She **sure** made me work hard for my grade.
The adjective *sure* here tries to do the work of an adverb modifying the verb *made.*

Revised: She made me write a five-page paper every week.

19d
Using Adverbs and Adjectives with Verbs of Sense

Verbs of sense (*smell, taste, feel,* and so on) can be linking or nonlinking. You must decide whether the modifier after a verb of sense serves the verb or the subject. Study the following examples:

Adverb: The dog smelled **badly.**
The dog had lost its sense of smell and could not track anything.

Adjective: The dog smelled **bad.**
The dog needed a bath.

Adverb: I felt **badly.**
My sense of touch was bad, perhaps because my fingers were numb.

Adjective: I felt **bad** because she heard me say that her baby looked like a baboon.
The person is saying, "I felt that I was bad because she heard me make such a terrible remark." A similar expression would be this: "I felt *guilty* because she heard me make that remark." You would not say "I felt *guiltily* because I hurt her feelings."

19e
Distinguishing Adjectives and Adverbs Spelled Alike

Some words have the same spelling in the adjectival and adverbial forms. Not every adverb is an adjective with -*ly* tacked to the end of it. In standard

English, many adverbs do not require the *-ly*, and some words have the same form whether they are used as adjectives or as adverbs. When you are in doubt, consult your dictionary (see 13b).

Adjective	Adverb
fast	fast
hard	hard
only	only
right	right or rightly
straight	straight

■ **Exercise 19.3**   In each of the following sentences, locate the words misused as adjectives and put the proper adverbs in their place or vice versa. You may simplify the sentence by eliminating the misused adjective or adverb.

1. I felt badly because he took my advice about the horse race and lost all his money.
2. He did terrific on the exam, and I sure was unhappy about his success.
3. John felt real good because he ran so fast in the race.
4. McDonald looked greedy at the fried chicken on his neighbor's plate and decided he would go to Kentucky real fast.
5. She sat still while the poisonous snake twined silent in the arbor just over her head, but she was real scared.

**19e
adj/adv**

■ **Exercise 19.4**   Fill in the blanks in the sentences below with any adverb that makes sense. Avoid the easy choices of *very, well,* and *badly.*

1. As the rains grew heavier, the houses were _____ damaged by the flood.
2. The procession wound _____ through the narrow streets and across the square, where the police had _____ blocked off traffic.
3. One by one the graduates walked _____ across the stage, shook hands _____ with the college president, received their diplomas, and stood _____ for a moment while relatives snapped their pictures.

4. She ate _____, saying that diets might help some but that eating _____ did her much more good.

5. Jokes are _____ funny because we do not expect the punch line.

19f

Forming the Comparative and Superlative Degrees of Adjectives and Adverbs

Adjectives and adverbs are often used to compare. Usually an -*er* or an -*est* ending on the word or the use of *more* or *most* along with the word indicates the degree of amount or quality.

The simplest form of the adjective or the adverb is the *positive* degree, the form of an adjective or adverb used when no comparison is involved. This is the form you find in the dictionary.

> The dog ran **quickly** out of the house. (*adverb*)

> The dog was **quick.** (*adjective*)

The *comparative degree* is used when two things are being compared. You form the comparative degree of many adjectives by adding the suffix -*er*, but you can also form the comparative degree by using the secondary adverb *more* or *less*. The adverb *more* or *less* is also used to form the comparative of most adverbs.

> The dog was **quicker** than the rabbit.

> The dog was **more quick** than the rabbit.

> The dog ran **more quickly** than the rabbit.

> The rabbit ran **less quickly** than the dog.

Use the *superlative degree* of both adjectives and adverbs when you compare more than two things. You may form the superlative degree of an adjective by adding the suffix -*est* to the positive form, or by using the adverb *most* or *least* with the positive form. The adverb *most* or *least* is used to form the superlative degree of an adverb.

> She was the **happiest** of the three women.

George was the **most gloomy** person I ever knew.

They sang **most happily** when they had eaten well.

✓ CHECKLIST: FORMS OF IRREGULAR ADJECTIVES AND ADVERBS

Positive	Comparative	Superlative
bad	worse	worst
good	better	best
little	less	least
many/much	more	most
far	farther	farthest

Some Rules for Using Degrees

☐ Do not use the superlative for only two things or units.
Not: Of the two brothers, John was **quickest.**
But: Of the two brothers, John was **quicker.**
☐ Do not use the comparative and superlative degrees with absolute adjectives. **Absolutes** are words that in themselves mean something complete or ideal, such words as *unique, infinite, impossible, perfect, round, square, destroyed,* and *demolished.* If something is *unique,* it is the only one of its kind. We cannot say, "Her dresses were *more unique* than his neckties." Either something is unique or it is not. "The answer to your question is *more impossible* than you think," is also wrong. Something is either possible or impossible; it cannot be *more* or *less* impossible.
☐ Avoid using the superlative when you are not making a comparison.
Dracula is the **scariest** movie!
The scariest movie ever filmed? The scariest movie you have ever seen? The scariest movie ever shown in town? In common speech, we frequently use expressions such as *scariest movie* or *silliest thing* when we are not in fact comparing the movie or the thing with anything else. In writing, such expressions lack the vocal emphasis we can give them when we speak. They become merely wordy and imprecise, taking up space without conveying any meaning.
☐ Avoid adding an unnecessary adverb to the superlative degree of adjectives.
Not: She was the **very** brightest person in the room.
But: She was the brightest person in the room.

Not: The interstate was the **most** shortest way to Nashville.
But: The interstate was the shortest way to Nashville.

**19f
adj/adv**

☐ Avoid making illogical comparisons with adjectives and adverbs. Illogical comparisons occur when writers leave out some necessary words.

Illogical: The story of the *Titanic* is more interesting than the story of any disaster at sea.

This comparison makes it seem that the story of the *Titanic* is one thing and that the story of any disaster at sea is something different. In fact, the story of the *Titanic* is about a disaster at sea. Is the story of the *Titanic* more interesting than itself?

Illogical: Building houses with brick is harder than lumber.

What is being compared here? Is the *act* of building harder than the *thing* we call lumber? The comparison is illogical because acts are different from things and so cannot be compared with them.

Illogical: Mr. Lincoln's speech was shorter than Mr. Everett.

In this sentence, one might suppose that Mr. Everett was six feet tall but that Mr. Lincoln's speech was only five feet.

Avoid the Overuse of Adjectives

Too many adjectives in a sentence weaken the force of a statement. Strong writers put an adjective before a noun or pronoun only when the adjective is truly needed. They rarely put more than one adjective before a noun unless they need to create some special effect or unless one of the adjectives is a number or part of a compound noun, such as *high school* or *living room*.

**19f
adj/adv**

Weak

The **sleek-looking high-speed jet** airplane has radically altered the **slow** and **unsteady** rate at which our **current Western** technology and today's **apparent** culture have spread.

The **clean** and brightly **lit** dining car left a **cold** and **snowy** Moscow well stocked with **large** and **sweet fresh red** apples, **many** oranges, **long green** cucumbers, **delicious chocolate** candy, and **countless other** well-**loved** delicacies.

Improved

The jet has radically altered the rate at which **Western** technology and culture have spread.

—JAMES BURKE

The dining car left Moscow well stocked with **fresh** apples, oranges, cucumbers, **chocolate** candy and **other little** delicacies.

—HEDRICK SMITH

■ **Exercise 19.5** In the following sentences, use any adjectives you choose to fill in the blanks. But whatever adjective you write in must be in the proper degree—positive, comparative, or superlative. Be adventurous. Avoid common adjectives such as *good* and *bad*.

1. President Franklin D. Roosevelt was a _____ man than many presidents who served before him.
2. Rhode Island is the _____ of all the states.
3. Lassie is a _____ actor than John Travolta.
4. Steam radiators are _____ .
5. Percy owned the _____ leather vest in his motorcycle gang.
6. Rock records are generally the _____ of all records sold.
7. Rain is generally _____ than snow or ice.
8. The president of the university is _____ than the faculty.
9. The sea is _____ than the desert.
10. Dick Tracy was _____ than Batman.

■ **Exercise 19.6** Revise the sentences below to correct inappropriate use of adjectives and/or adverbs.

1. She felt badly that his cat was voted more cuter than hers.
2. Hopefully, I can find a real good job when I graduate.
3. Her long, thin, red-nailed fingers quickly raced silently over the polished white ivory keyboard.
4. Run to town right quick and find Dr. Clemson.
5. The most happiest days of my life were spent when I was a tiny tough troublemaking child on the large, wide-open ranch owned by my uncle Huey.

**19f
adj/adv**

■ **Exercise 19.7** Eliminate as many adjectives as you can in the following paragraph:

The old, bent, gray man stood still and thoughtful on the crowded edge of the crowded, busy, narrow street and looked down to the tall, lighted, brick building which loomed up in the thick, damp, gray mist of the early, chill, autumn, overcast, threatening night. He felt in the deep, warm, dark pocket of his new wool black tweed overcoat for the hard, blue, loaded automatic pistol and checked the tiny metal safety catch on the lethal, heavy, criminal weapon. The important, threatening, dangerous gun was there, ready, waiting, eager to be fired.

CHAPTER

20

DANGLING MODIFIERS AND MISPLACED PARTS

In English, clarity depends on the word order within sentences. We expect most adjectives and adjectival clauses and phrases to stand as close as possible to the words they modify. But adverbs and adverbial phrases are often separated by other words from the words or phrases they modify. We say, "They began their job yesterday," not "They began yesterday their job." And we also write sentences such as "When she was young, she played softball every Saturday," in which the adverbial clause and the simple adverb are separated from the verb by other words.

We have to know when we can separate modifiers from the words or phrases they modify and when we cannot. And in general we can separate adverbs and adverbials from the words they modify more easily than we can separate adjectives from the words they modify.

Yet even adverbs and adverbial phrases can be misplaced. In general, an adverbial phrase modifies the nearest verb. It may be separated from that verb by other words, but English idiom joins adverbs and adverbials to the nearest possible verb. When another verb gets in the way, our sentences get into trouble, as in the following sentences from a humorous squib in *The New Yorker:*

> Wednesday morning, Lee's oldest son Mike signed a national letter of intent with Indiana University to play football for the Hoosiers in the family kitchen at 3838 Ashland Drive in West Lafayette.

The writer intended to make the adverbial prepositional phrase *in the family kitchen* modify the verb *signed*. But since it is nearer to the infinitive phrase *to play football*, it seems to modify that phrase, giving the impression that Mike is going to be running for touchdowns over the kitchen sink.

During the lecture, Johanson will describe the discovery of a band of the new species of hominids who appeared to have been killed simultaneously by some disaster with color slides.

The writer has intended to make the prepositional phrase *with color slides* modify the verb phrase *will describe*. But it is nearer to and appears to describe the noun *disaster* and seems to be an adjectival phrase.

These errors should remind you to keep the related parts of a sentence as close to each other as you can. Otherwise you may confuse your readers.

20a
Avoiding Dangling Participles

Introductory participles and participial phrases must modify the grammatical subject of the sentence. Participles that do not modify the grammatical subject are called **dangling** or **misplaced participles.** A dangling participle lacks a noun to modify.

Having studied small-engine repair in night school, fixing the lawn mower was easy.

Driving along Route 10, the sun shone in Carmela's face.

Using elaborate charts and graphs, the audience understood the plan.

Running down the street, the fallen lamppost stopped her suddenly.

Having thought for a long time, the idea of a community patrol group emerged.

The work was hard, sweating over hot machinery, bending in cramped spaces, sometimes mashing his fingers, skinning his knees, twisting heavy wrenches, and getting home late and exhausted every night.

**20a
dangler**

Revised

Having studied small-engine repair at night school, Jane found that fixing the lawn mower was easy.

or

After Jane studied small-engine repair in night school, fixing the lawn mower was easy.

Driving along Route 10, Carmela found the sun shining in her face.
or
As Carmela drove along Route 10, the sun shone in her face.

Using elaborate charts and graphs, the mayor explained the plan to the audience.
or
Because the mayor used elaborate charts and graphs, the audience understood the plan.

Running down the street, she saw the fallen lamp post, which stopped her suddenly.
or
As she ran down the street, the lamp post stopped her suddenly.

Having thought for a long time, the committee finally developed the idea of a community patrol group.
or
After the committee thought for a long time, the idea of a community patrol group emerged.

He worked hard, sweating over hot machinery, bending in cramped spaces, sometimes mashing his fingers, skinning his knees, twisting heavy wrenches, and getting home late and exhausted every night.

**20a
dangler**

Usage Note

Informal usage frequently accepts the following forms that combine an introductory participle with the expletive *it* (see 18e), especially when the participle expresses a habitual or general action.

Walking in the country at dawn, it is easy to see many species of birds.

The statement is general, expressing something that might be done by anyone. Many writers and editors would prefer this revision: "Walking in the country at dawn is an easy way to see many species of birds."

When beginning a new exercise program, it is good to have a complete physical examination by a doctor.

The statement is general, and to many writers it seems preferable to an informal statement like this one: "When you begin a new exercise program, you should have a complete physical examination by a doctor." But many other writers — perhaps a majority — would revise the sentence to read like this: "Anyone who begins a new exercise program should have a complete physical examination by a doctor."

■ **Exercise 20.1**   Rewrite any of the following sentences that have dangling participles. If a sentence is correct, put a check beside it.

1. Daydreaming about his new job, the doorbell startled him.
2. Working hard through the night, the job was finished by daybreak.
3. Looking up, the long V-shaped flock of geese could be seen by everyone in the valley.
4. Riding hard through the night, Paul Revere spread the alarm through Middlesex County to the sleeping town of Lexington.
5. Backed into a corner and hurt, the bell barely saved him.
6. Walking along the street, the city seemed calm.
7. Using a word processor, he was able to revise his paper in a couple of hours and turn in the finished product the next day.
8. Having played hard, the loss was bitter.
9. Taking the ship from New York, the trip was now under way.
10. Having been aged in an oak barrel for twelve years, he discovered that the wine was exactly to his taste.

20b
Avoiding Misplaced Prepositional Phrases

Prepositional phrases used as adjectives seldom give trouble. We use them commonly in speech, and these speech habits transfer readily to writing:

The book **on the table** belongs to me.

We lived in a house **near the school.**

Prepositional phrases used as adverbs are harder to place in sentences, and sometimes writers are led astray by their adverbial phrases.

He saw the first dive bombers approaching **from the bridge of the battleship.**

The German chancellor was introduced to Americans **on television.**

He ran the ten-kilometer race from the shopping mall through the center of town to the finish line by the monument **in his bare feet.**

Revised

From the bridge of the battleship, he saw the first dive bombers approaching.

The German chancellor was introduced on television to Americans.

In his bare feet he ran the ten-kilometer race from the shopping mall through the center of town to the finish line by the monument.
or
From the shopping mall through the center of town to the finish line by the monument he ran the ten-kilometer race in his bare feet.

20c
Avoiding Misplaced Clauses

**20c
modifier**

A misplaced clause is one that modifies the wrong element of the sentence.

Professor Peebles taught the course on the English novel that most students dropped after three weeks.

For five years Dixon worked all day as an accountant to support her family and after supper went to night school to study law, which was hard, but finally she got her degree.

Revised

Professor Peebles taught the course on the English novel, a course that most students dropped after three weeks.

For five years Dixon worked all day as an accountant to support her family and after supper went to night school to study law. It was a hard schedule, but she finally got her degree.

■ **Exercise 20.2**   Rewrite the following sentences to correct errors in modification.

1. Marco Polo traveled overland to China with his father and his uncle to visit the Mongol Empire, which was very dangerous.
2. He stood in the middle of the room and shouted at everyone in his pajamas.
3. He bought a digital watch at the jewelry shop which ran on tiny batteries.
4. She wrote the outline of her book on the wall in the kitchen with a black crayon.
5. When she was a little girl, she used to lie awake at night wishing that she had a horse in her bedroom.

20d
Placing Adverbs Correctly

Avoid the confusing adverb or adverbial phrase that seems to modify both the element that comes immediately before it and the element that comes immediately after it.

To read a good book **completely** satisfies her.

Changing gears **continually** gives mental exercise to people who ride bicycles.

To speak in public **often** makes her uncomfortable.

**20d
modifier**

Revised

She is completely satisfied when she reads a good book.
or
She is satisfied when she reads a good book completely.

Continually changing gears gives mental exercise to people who ride bicycles.
or
Changing gears gives continual mental exercise to people who ride bicycles.

When she speaks in public often, she feels uncomfortable.
or
Often she feels uncomfortable when she speaks in public.

Be cautious when you use adverbs to modify whole sentences.

Unfortunately, *The Quiz Kids* lost its popularity as an afternoon game show.

Presumably, the climber was killed in an avalanche three years ago, although his body was never found.

Some authorities maintain that these adverbs modify the entire sentence; others insist that these adverbs modify only the verbs in the clauses where they appear. In either case, the meanings of these sentences are clear. But other adverbs are much more ambiguous when they modify full sentences.

Hopefully he will change his job before this one gives him an ulcer.

Who is doing the hoping? Is it the person who speaks the sentence or the person who is the subject of the sentence?

Revised: We hope he will change his job before this one gives him an ulcer.

20d
modifier

Similar confusions occur when other adverbs modify whole sentences:

Briefly, Tom was the source of the trouble.

Does the writer wish to say briefly that Tom was the source of the trouble? Or was Tom briefly the source of the trouble but he then mended his ways?

Revised: To put it briefly, I think Tom was the source of the trouble.

The following sentence does not mean what it says:

Happily, the mad dog fell dead before it could bite anybody.

The grammar of this sentence indicates that the mad dog fell dead very happily before it could bite anybody. The writer doubtless means that people on the street were happy that the mad dog fell dead before it could bite one of them. Why not write that?

■ **Exercise 20.3**   Rewrite the following sentences to eliminate the confusion of adverbs that may modify two elements. If a sentence is correct, place a *C* beside it.

1. The car starting easily made this the best day of my trip.
2. People who disliked long hair very much liked having ten-dollar bills with long-haired Alexander Hamilton's picture on the front.
3. Hopefully, she will be able to buy another red coat like the one she lost on the train.
4. A scholar who studies often goes to sleep over her books.
5. People who love to criticize books sometimes do not write books themselves.
6. Sadly the old man waved goodbye to the child he knew he'd never see again.

20e
Putting Limiting Modifiers in Logical Places

Such words as *merely, completely, fully, perfectly, hardly, nearly, almost, even, just simply, scarcely,* and *only* must be placed before the words or phrases they modify.

The **almost** exhausted man finished the marathon.

The exhausted man **almost** finished the marathon.

The **completely** restored antique cars paraded proudly through the admiring town.

The restored antique cars paraded proudly through the **completely** admiring town.

In speaking we sometimes put limiting modifiers in illogical places, but the sense of what we say is clear from tone of voice, gestures, or general context. In writing, the lack of logic that results from misplacement of modifiers can cause confusion.

He **only** had one bad habit, but it **just** was enough to keep him in trouble.

They were all **nearly** about to graduate, but they wouldn't **even** send one invitation because all of them decided **almost** that the commencement speaker would insult the intelligence of the audience.

Revised

He had **only** one bad habit, but it was **just** enough to keep him in trouble.

They were **nearly** all about to graduate, but they wouldn't send **even** one invitation because all of them decided that the commencement speaker would insult the intelligence of the audience.

■ **Exercise 20.4**   Explain the meaning conveyed by the placement of the adverb in each of the following sentences. Make any revisions necessary to clear up the confusion.

1. He *just* ate half a sandwich before nodding off to sleep.
2. The lawyer *only* spoke to her client after he quieted down.
3. The lawyer spoke *only* to her client after he quieted down.
4. *Only* the lawyer spoke to her client after he quieted down.
5. The lawyer spoke to her client *only* after he quieted down.

**20e
modifier**

CHAPTER

21

CONFUSING SHIFTS

To keep your sentences clear and harmonious, you must be consistent in your use of verbs and nouns. You should avoid jarring shifts in point of view and sudden outbursts of emotion — what is sometimes called purple prose.

21a
Being Consistent in Verb Tenses

When you write about the content of any piece of literature, you usually use the present tense. Be careful not to shift out of the present tense when you have decided to use it for such a purpose. Make sure your tenses are consistent not only within sentences, but from one sentence to another. Be especially careful when you quote a passage that is in the past tense. Do not shift your description of the passage into the past tense if you have been using the present. Here is an example:

> David Copperfield **observes** other people with a fine and sympathetic eye. He **describes** villains such as Mr. Murdstone and improbable heroes such as Mr. Micawber with unforgettable sharpness of detail. But David Copperfield **was** not himself an especially interesting person.

Being Consistent in Narrative

Avoid the temptation to lapse into inconsistent tenses when you are telling a story. Sometimes the events you are relating become so vivid to you as you speak or write that you slip into the present tense. The inconsistency may be acceptable in conversation, but it confuses readers.

Inconsistent: The wind **was howling** and **blowing** a hundred miles an hour when suddenly there **is** a big crash, and a tree **falls** into Rocky's living room.

Consistent: The wind **was howling** and **blowing** a hundred miles an hour when suddenly there **was** a big crash, and a tree **fell** into Rocky's living room.

Inconsistent: Every day the parking lot **fills** up by eight in the morning, and commuting students arriving after that **could** not find parking places.

Consistent: The parking lot **fills** up by eight in the morning, and commuting students arriving after that **cannot find** parking places.

Being Consistent in Successive Clauses

Inconsistency may creep into your writing when you combine present perfect and past perfect tenses with present and past tenses of verbs.

Inconsistent: She **has admired** many strange buildings at the university, but she **thought** that the Science Center **looked** completely out of place.

Consistent: She **has admired** many strange buildings at the university, but she **thinks** that the Science Center **looks** completely out of place.

21a
shifts

In writing successive clauses, you must be sure that you take into account the continuing action of the first clause. The thought expressed in the consistent sentence is like this: *She has admired and still admires many strange buildings at the university, but she thinks now that the Science Center looks completely out of place.* Verbs in successive clauses do not have to be in the same tense, but they should follow each other in tenses that make good grammatical sense and say what the writer wants them to say.

Some Rules for Successive Tenses

☐ The present tense may be followed by another present tense:
Dogs **bark** to show that they **are** interested in something, or to show that they **are** afraid, or to announce that someone—perhaps another dog—**is invading** their territory.

☐ The present tense may be followed by a past tense:
Michaelson **says** that transistors **made** stereo systems cheaper but **reduced** the fidelity of sound created by vacuum tubes.

□ The present can be used with the present perfect:
Quality control in the American automobile industry **is** a long-standing problem that **has made** millions of Americans think that Japanese cars **are** better.

□ The present can be used with the future tense:
We **predict** that word processors **will replace** electric typewriters in most offices by the end of this decade.

✓ CHECKLIST: TIPS FOR TENSE CONSISTENCY

Do not use the present tense with the past perfect tense unless a suitable tense follows the past perfect.

Inconsistent: She swears that she **had registered** her car properly.
Consistent: She swears that she **had registered** her car properly before she **received** a ticket for having an improper license plate.

If you are not going to follow the past perfect with a clause that contains a verb in the past tense, change the past perfect tense to a more suitable form.

She **swears** that she **registered** her car properly.

The simple past can be followed by another simple past:

College football **was** so violent early in this century that President Theodore Roosevelt **threatened** to abolish it.

The simple past can be used with the imperfect:

Everyone **was** eager to know if she **was going** to enter the fifty-mile road race.

The simple past can be used with the future:

They **told** me that the tire shipment **will arrive** next week.

The simple past should not be used with the present perfect, although in informal speech we sometimes do use the two tenses together.

She **reports** that she **runs** nine miles every morning.
She **reported** that she **had been running** nine miles every morning.

21b
Being Consistent in Moods of Verbs

The mood of a verb is a distinguishing form that indicates whether or not an assertion is intended as a statement of fact (see 17e). The indicative mood makes simple statements or asks simple questions. The conditional mood makes statements that would be true if something else were true. The subjunctive mood is now used rarely in English, but when it is used, it often makes conditional statements known to be contrary to fact. (If I *were* in Rome on Easter morning, I would hear thousands of church bells. I am not in Rome on Easter morning, and I may not be there when Easter comes; so I use the subjunctive mood in the clause *if I were*.)

Inconsistent shifts from the indicative to the conditional or from the conditional to the indicative often cause trouble.

Inconsistent

He **will go** to night school and **would take** a course in hotel management.

If he **goes** to night school, he **would take** a course in hotel management.

If he **were** absent, he **will fail** the course.

Consistent

If he **could go** to night school, he **would take** a course in hotel management.

He **would go** to night school, and he **would take** a course in hotel management, if he **could get** out of jail.

He **will go** to night school and **will take** a course in hotel management if he **gets out** of jail.

If he **is** absent, he **will fail** the course.

If he **were** absent, he **would fail** the course.

21b
shifts

■ **Exercise 21.1** Correct the confusing shifts in the following sentences. If a sentence is correct as it stands, put a check by the number.

1. Hamlet has been in school in Wittenberg, and he came home to find his father dead and his mother married to his father's brother.

2. Mercutio has to die in *Romeo and Juliet,* or else he would have carried the play off from the two young lovers, who are not nearly as interesting as he was.

3. The band hit a sour note, and the drum major gets sore at the tuba section.

4. Parents who often get drunk embarrassed their children.

5. King James I, who died in 1625, had never taken a bath in his adult

life, and those who prepared him for burial have to scour his underwear off his body.

21c
Being Consistent in Voice

The voice of a transitive verb is either active or passive. In clauses with active verbs, the subject does the acting; in clauses with passive verbs, the subject is acted upon (see 17e). Inconsistency in voice sometimes arises from a writer's desire to use variety in sentence forms. But when the actor remains the same, you should not change voice.

Inconsistent

The Impressionist painters **hated** black. Violet, green, blue, pink, and red **were favored** by them.

The bulldozer **clanked** into the woods and **bit** into the ground. The trees and the earth **were ripped** up.

Consistent

The Impressionist painters **hated** black. They **favored** violet, green, blue, pink, and red.

The bulldozer **clanked** into the woods, **bit** into the ground, and **ripped** up the trees and the earth.

Note that you can go easily from a linking verb of simple description in the active voice to a verb in the passive voice in the next clause, thereby keeping attention on the subject of greatest interest:

Today the majority of American Indians **are** poor, uneducated, and unhealthy. They **have been isolated** from the rest of the country, **deprived** of the benefits of the land that **was taken** away from them by force, and **forgotten** by the people who robbed them.

McNabb **rode** his motorcycle through the plate-glass window and **was taken** to the hospital as soon as the ambulance could get there.

**21c
shifts**

The best advice about the passive voice is try to use it infrequently and only with good reason.

21d
Being Consistent
in Person and Number of Nouns and Pronouns

In speaking and writing in an informal tone, we often use the pronoun *you* instead of the more formal pronoun *one* (see 18f).

> If **you** smoke cigarettes, **you** run a high risk of getting lung cancer.
> *not*
> If **one** smokes cigarettes, **you** run a high risk of getting lung cancer.

Here are some consistent alternatives:

> If **one** smokes cigarettes, **one** runs a high risk of getting lung cancer.
> *or*
> **Anyone** who smokes cigarettes runs a high risk of getting lung cancer.
> *or*
> **People** who smoke cigarettes run a high risk of getting lung cancer.

21d
shifts

If you address your reader directly as *you,* you may write in the third person from time to time. But you cannot shift from the third person to the second person or from the second person to the third person in the same sentence.

> **Consistent:** **You** will always find good writing to be hard work. **Good writers** never think that their craft is easy.

> **Inconsistent:** **People** flying across the country nowadays discover that **you** can get many different fares to the same destination.

Make your pronouns agree with their antecedents, but avoid sexist language (see Chapters 12 and 18).

> **Anyone** who rides a bicycle every day will discover that **they** develop some muscles not developed by jogging.

You can substitute consistent plural forms:

People who ride bicycles every day will discover that **they** develop some muscles not developed by jogging.

Or you can avoid the need for a pronoun:

Anyone who rides a bicycle every day will discover that some muscles that are little used in jogging are being developed.

Anyone who rides a bicycle every day will discover that the exercise develops some muscles that are not developed by jogging.

You can make a much more sweeping revision:

Bike riders do not exercise some of the muscles used in jogging and usually discover that they get sore quickly when they try to run around the neighborhood at night.

Or a simpler one:

Daily bicycle riding develops some muscles not used in jogging.

21e
Avoiding Shifts in Point of View

He sat idly in his seat and looked down at the land pouring beneath the low-flying plane like some immense sea whose waters reached to the sky. The green of the forest enchanted him. Everything was primitive and nearly unspoiled. Here and there a house stood in a solitary clearing that, from above, looked like a raft afloat on the great ocean of green. He saw it for a moment, and then it was whisked away behind him. In the houses, people were sitting down to supper, unfolding napkins, looking expectantly at the head of the table where the father gravely bowed his head to say grace.

The point of view is of someone in an airplane looking down on the land passing underneath. But in the last sentence we shift to a scene that such a traveler cannot see. The last sentence can be fixed to match the point of view of the rest of the passage.

He could imagine that in the houses people were sitting down to supper, unfolding napkins, looking expectantly at the head of the table where the father gravely bowed his head to say grace.

■ **Exercise 21.2** Rewrite the following sentences to eliminate confusing shifts. If a sentence is correct as it stands, put a check beside it.

1. American landscape painters of the nineteenth century viewed the American wilderness as the handiwork of God; signs of God's work were seen by them in lakes, mountains, and prairies.
2. Government paperwork costs forty billion dollars a year, and government accountants are working to trim those costs — and making more paperwork as they do so; you can see the problem.
3. If anyone carries a pack on your back while they ride a bicycle up a mountain in the summer, be prepared to be hot and tired.
4. People who take a lot of pictures sometimes find that you get tired carrying a camera, and they often stop taking pictures all at once, the way some people stop smoking.
5. Anyone who writes a long letter of complaint is frustrated when they get a form letter in return.

■ **Exercise 21.3** Rewrite the following paragraph to correct the confusing shifts.

**21f
shifts**

In Thomas More's book *Utopia*, which is the name he gave to an island supposedly located off the coast of the New World, the people of his commonwealth wear unbleached wool, eat together in great halls, punish adultery with death when one is convicted twice of the offense, and allow husbands and wives to inspect each other naked before they are married so one will not be deceived by the other. The Utopians had no individuality. They tried as hard as they could to eliminate passion. More made no mention of any artists among them.

21f
Avoiding Excessive Emotionalism

You may have strong feelings about a subject, and having discussed some of the issues in an essay, you may be tempted to conclude with a highly emotional ending so readers will know where you stand. Emotionalism in writing is almost always a mistake. Readers tend to dismiss the opinions of ranters and to laugh at their "purple prose." You may embarrass even those people who agree with you if you present your opinions in an irrational way. Readers want to like the person who has written the prose they read; otherwise they will not enjoy spending time in the writer's company. Few readers like to spend time with an angry or overwrought or sarcastic person.

Consider the excessive emotionalism in this paragraph:

Lord Crenshaw strode mightily into the room, his bushy eyebrows looking like forests waving in the mightiest of all God's storms, his cold blue eyes flashing like bolts of lightning as he looked around at the assembled guests. Philippa felt her heart go bang in her chest with a wild emotion, wilder than anything she had ever felt before, wild as the incandescent lava that bursts from a volcano and pours down the mountainside, burning up all the reserve and all the hesitation that she might have felt. This was the famous Lord Crenshaw, dauntless leader of Wellington's right at Waterloo, the bold, brave man who flung his great arms skyward and shouted at his troops to hold fast while all around his gallant head the bullets whizzed and whirled, the thunderhead of a hero whose voice sounded like ten thousand organs booming through ten thousand cathedrals. People nodded gravely to him, knowing his reputation for sudden anger, for the outburst that could lead to the duel at sunrise that had more than once snuffed out the tender flower of a young life before it could grow and flourish and become a mighty tree. As he entered the room, a silence like that of Judgment Day itself fell over everyone, and it seemed that the world held its breath while he walked to the buffet and thundered a command to the trembling waiter here. "Give me a ham sandwich." he said. "And hold the pickles."

■ **Exercise 21.4** Rewrite the passage about Lord Crenshaw.

**21f
shifts**

PART
FIVE

UNDERSTANDING PUNCTUATION

299

CHAPTER

22

END MARKS

In English as in most other languages, the system of end marks gives writers a means to separate sentences and to indicate other special operations.

22a
Using the Period

Use a period after a sentence that makes a statement, that gives a mild command or makes a mild request, or that asks a question indirectly. Commands showing strong emotion require exclamation points, discussed in 22c. Direct questions require question marks, discussed in 22b. The use of ellipses is discussed in 27f.

Statements

Soap melts in the bathtub.

Every year Americans buy more bicycles than cars.

The building burned down last night.

Mild Commands

Please go with me to the lecture.

Consider your opponent's views carefully when you are making an argument.

Lend me the car, and I'll do the shopping.

Indirect Questions

People wonder why they have to pay such high taxes.

She asked me where I had gone to college.

They demanded to know who was responsible for the killings.

He wanted to know how I had come to that conclusion.

The words *why, where, who,* and *how* in these sentences ask questions indirectly.

22b
Using the Question Mark

Use a question mark after a direct question but not after an indirect question.

Who wrote *One of Ours?*

She wanted to know who wrote *One of Ours.*

If a question ends with a quoted question, one question mark serves for both the question in the main clause and the question that is quoted.

What did Juliet mean when she cried, "O Romeo, Romeo! Wherefore art thou Romeo?"

If a question is quoted before the end of a sentence that makes a statement, place a question mark before the last quotation mark and put a period at the end of the sentence.

"What was Henry Ford's greatest contribution to the industrial revolution in America?" he asked.

"What did the president know and when did he know it?" became the great question of the Watergate hearings.

Occasionally a question mark changes a statement into a question.

You expect me to believe a story like that?

22a/b

. / ?

He drove my car into your living room?

To emphasize parts of a series of questions, you can use question marks to separate them into fragments.

> And what will we leave behind us when we are long dead? Temples? Amphora? Sunken treasure?
>
> —MARYA MANNES

To express uncertainty about a word or a date, you may use a question mark. In such usage the question mark means that no one can be sure if the date or word is correct. You should never use such question marks merely to show that you have not bothered to look up the information.

> Napoleon Bonaparte's brother-in-law, Joachim Murat (1767?–1815), was king of Naples for seven years.

22c
Using the Exclamation Point

Use exclamation points sparingly to convey surprise, shock, or some other strong emotion.

> The land of the free! This is the land of the free! Why, if I say anything that displeases them, the free mob will lynch me, and that's my freedom.
>
> —D. H. LAWRENCE

> Moon, rise! Wind, hit the trees, blow up the leaves! Up, now, run! Tricks! Treats! Gangway!
>
> —RAY BRADBURY

22c
!

Avoid using too many exclamation marks because readers will not respond with the excitement that an exclamation mark is supposed to call up. For a mild statement, use a comma or a period.

> "Ah, what a beautiful morning," she said, throwing the windows open onto the new day.

> Socrates said, "Know thyself."

■ **Exercise 22.1** Use periods, question marks, and exclamation points where they are required in the sentences below.

1. He wanted to know if Mr. Kuhns worked for UNESCO or for the FBI
2. "Was it you," she asked, "who painted that wall purple"
3. What did he mean when he asked me, "Is your car an antique"
4. Stolen The money was stolen Right before our eyes, somebody snatched my purse and ran off with it
5. "Help me" he said "I want to learn how to dance"
6. "Isn't the true folk instrument the dulcimer" she asked
7. You expect me to believe that computers can think
8. Pick up the papers Don't you think it's fair for each of us to try to keep this room clean
9. She asked if the theft of credit cards has become a major crime in this country
10. "Where will it end" he asked

■ **Exercise 22.2** Compare the effects of different punctuation marks on the sentences in each pair below. Imagine situations in which you might have used each version of each sentence.

1. **a.** You don't have to tell me.
   b. You don't have to tell me!
   c. You don't have to tell me?
2. **a.** You mowed the lawn!
   b. You mowed the lawn?
   c. You mowed the lawn.
3. **a.** What will you contribute, your time, your talent, or your money?
   b. What will you contribute? Your time? Your talent? Your money?

**22c
!**

CHAPTER

23

COMMAS

When you speak, you pause to emphasize elements of a sentence and to catch your breath. Commas show these pauses within written sentences. Commas also set off sentence elements, clarify the relations of some sentence elements to others, and serve in standard ways in dates, addresses, and other conventional forms.

23a
Setting Off Independent Clauses

Use commas to set off independent clauses joined by the common coordinating junctions: *and, but, or, nor, so, yet, for.*

Her computer broke down, and she had to write with a pencil.

He won the Heisman Trophy, but no pro team drafted him.

The art majors could paint portraits, or they could paint houses.

Many Americans did not at first understand jazz, nor did they enjoy listening to it.

He strained to hear her, for she spoke barely above a whisper.

Many people don't understand punctuation, yet they use it correctly anyway.

Printing has made language much less flexible than it once was, so the rules of English grammar will probably not change much from now on.

Some writers do not separate short independent clauses with a comma.

He stayed at home and she went to work.

23b
Setting Off Long Introductory Phrases and Clauses

Use commas after long introductory phrases and clauses. A long introductory phrase or clause is easier to read and understand when a comma separates it from the rest of the sentence.

After he had sat in the hot tub for three hours, the fire department had to revive him.

If you plan to lose fifty or more pounds, you should take the advice of a doctor.

After standing as a symbol of oppression and fear for twenty-six years, the Berlin Wall at last was broken down.

Packed into Candlestick Park awaiting the third game of the World Series, 64,000 fans suddenly felt the San Francisco earthquake of 1989 give the city a terrifying jolt.

Short opening phrases do not have to be set off by commas.

After the game I drifted along with the happy crowd.

Before the wedding they discussed household duties.

In their coffeehouses eighteenth-century Englishmen conducted many of their business affairs.

Always put a comma after an introductory subordinate clause (as explained in 7b).

When we came out, we were not on the busiest Chinatown street but on a side street across from the park.

—MAXINE HONG KINGSTON

23a/b

؛

Although the struggle and competition for national or international power may not be explained wholly and simply as analogous to the power drive in personal relations, the personal may provide significant insight into the political.

—KENNETH B. CLARK

Commas set off interjections and transitional adverbs.

Yes, a fight broke out after the game.

Nevertheless, we should look on the bright side.

To be sure, no one was killed.

Consequently, we will play again next year.

23c
Setting Off Absolutes

Use commas to set off absolutes. Any absolute—a phrase that combines a noun with a present or past participle and that serves to modify the entire sentence (as discussed in 5d)—must be set off from the rest of the sentence by a comma.

The bridge now built, the British set out to destroy it.

The snake slithered through the tall grass, **the sunlight shining now and then on its green skin.**

23d
Setting Off Participial Modifiers

Use commas to set off participial modifiers at the end of a sentence.

They toiled all night on the engine, grinding and adjusting the valves, polishing the cylinders, cleaning the pistons, replacing the rings, installing a new fuel pump, and putting in new spark plugs and points.

She rushed down the corridor, holding the report in her hand.

We climbed the mountain, feeling the spring sunshine and intoxicated by the view.

23e
Separating Elements of a Sentence

Use commas to separate elements of a sentence to avoid confusion.

Unclear

Every time John raced small boys could leave him behind.

No matter how fast he ran the course was too hard for him.

To John Smith seemed odd.

Clear

Every time John raced, small boys could leave him behind.

No matter how fast he ran, the course was too hard for him.

To John, Smith looked odd.

■ **Exercise 23.1** Put commas where they are needed in the following sentences.

1. Many young people want to write fiction but they lack the patience to revise.
2. Having missed the plane we had to take the bus to New York.
3. Although you need to know grammar exercises in grammar cannot help you write well unless you read a lot.
4. Steve was to be sure a steady performer.
5. Nevertheless Greek wine has become popular in America and is often sold in restaurants that he said do not specialize in Greek food.
6. He fired to second his throw beating Henderson to the bag by a step.
7. Pay something if you can but if you cannot go in and enjoy the exhibit anyway.

23e

⌃
,

8. After he had watched television all night long his eyes turned to egg white and his brain became glue.
9. With student populations increasing people with the Ph.D. degree can get jobs again.
10. Turning their backs on the medieval world scholars in the Renaissance tried to recapture the classical age of Greece and Rome.

23f
Setting Off Nonrestrictive Clauses and Phrases

Use commas to set off nonrestrictive clauses and phrases. Nonrestrictive clauses and phrases can be lifted out of the sentences where they appear without any resultant change in the primary meaning of the sentences. The paired commas that set off a nonrestrictive clause or phrase announce that these words provide additional information.

My dog Lady, who treed a cat last week, treed the mailman this morning.

In the middle of the forest, hidden from the rest of the world, stood a small cabin.

Setting off a phrase or a clause with commas can often change the meaning of a sentence. In the first sentence below, the commas make the clauses nonrestrictive. There was only one commencement speaker, and that speaker happened to be a sleep therapist. In the second sentence, the absence of commas makes us suppose there must have been several speakers. The writer must single out the one who spoke for three hours. By calling the speaker a sleep therapist, the writer says that although there were several speakers, there was only one who was a sleep therapist, and that person was the one who spoke for three hours.

The commencement speaker, who was a sleep therapist, spoke for three hours.

The commencement speaker who was a sleep therapist spoke for three hours.

■ **Exercise 23.2** Use commas to set off nonrestrictive clauses and phrases in the following sentences. In some you have a choice. You can make the clause or phrase restrictive by not setting it off with commas. In such cases, discuss the changes in meaning so that you may be clear as to what they are and why they occur. At times simple common sense will tell you whether to make the clause restrictive or nonrestrictive.

1. The chain saw which had a two-cycle engine gave him a sense of immense power as he took it in his hand and walked into the woods filled with oaks and maples.
2. Fly fishing a difficult and sometimes dangerous sport requires much more skill than fishing with worms from a boat on a still lake.
3. The McCormick reaper which was invented by Cyrus Hall McCormick vastly increased wheat production in the nineteenth century.
4. Farmers who are by profession often isolated and independent have never been drawn in large groups to communism, but they have been attracted by fraternal organizations which have helped them meet together to satisfy social and economic needs.
5. Bats flying mammals found all over the world probably seem odious to many people because they look like rats that fly.

23g
Separating Items in a Series

Use commas to separate items in a series. A **series** is a set of nouns, pronouns, adjectives, adverbs, phrases, or clauses joined by commas and —usually—a final coordinating conjunction. Note that American writers put a comma before the coordinating conjunction at the end of a series.

Nouns

In 1940, when he became prime minister, Winston Churchill told the English people that he had nothing to offer them but blood, toil, sweat, and tears.

Carrots, sweet potatoes, and other yellow vegetables help prevent cancer.

Pronouns

You, we, and they all have some things in common

We saw you, him, and her walking on the beach.

23g
,

Adjectives

My teacher's notes were old, yellow, and worn.

She was a helpful, surprising, and amusing person.

Adverbs

The three outlaws walked slowly, silently, and cautiously into the Sunday school.

She played steadily, intently, and cautiously.

Phrases

The college raised fees, reduced maintenance, fired assistant professors, turned down the heat, but went bankrupt anyway.

Lincoln's great address commended government of the people, by the people, and for the people.

Clauses

The traffic was heavy, the parking lot was full, rain drenched the city, and I was late.

She combed the dog's hair, he started the car, Jack brought down the ribbon, and we were all ready for the show.

23h
Separating Two or More Adjectives

23h

̂,

Use commas to separate two or more adjectives before a noun or a pronoun if you can readily imagine the conjunction *and* in place of the commas.

Lyndon Johnson flew a short, dangerous combat mission in the Pacific during World War II.
(Imagine: Lyndon Johnson flew a short and dangerous combat mission in the Pacific during World War II.)

Computers are expensive, necessary, and complicated.
(Imagine: Computers are expensive and necessary and complicated.)

If you cannot make an *and* fit easily between the adjectives, omit the comma.

Six thin green pines stood against the evening sky.

Four old red coats lay piled in a corner.

Adjectives do not require a dividing comma when they mention color, size, age, location, or number. But if you mention several colors or sizes or numbers before nouns, separate the adjectives with commas:

The auto industry first painted its cars a universal black, but now assembly lines turn out thousands of green, silver, gold, blue, crimson, tan, gray, brown, and other colors.

23i
Setting Off Direct Quotations

Use a comma with quotation marks to set off a direct quotation from the clause that names the source of the quotation.

When the source comes first, the comma goes before the quotation marks. When the quotation comes first, the comma goes before the last quotation mark.

She said, "I'm sorry, but all sections are full."

"But I have to have the course to graduate," he said.

"A rule is a rule," she said sweetly, "and you will just have to postpone your graduation."

No comma is used if some other punctuation mark is used within the quotation marks.

"Do you believe in grades?" he asked.

"Believe in them!" she cried. "I've had them."

23i/j

^
,

23j
Setting Off Names in Direct Address

Use a comma to set off a name used in direct address.

I'll say this, Ethel. You understood him first.

Henry, come here right away.

Jack, why are you doing this?

■ **Exercise 23.3** Place commas where they belong in the following sentences.

1. The old gray mare is not the superb creature she used to be says the old song.
2. Three happy little children came to the door shouting "Trick or treat!"
3. The hospital smelled of floor wax linen and iodine.
4. She righted the boat ran up the sail grabbed the rudder and flew before the wind.
5. The storm broke suddenly and furiously the lightning crashed from a black sky and the cattle ran off into the dark.
6. "North Dakota is sky prairie wheat and hospitality" she said. "You must go there Charles. You will never see colors so pure land so vast or cities so clean."
7. The poor the speaker said commit far more violent crimes than do members of the middle class and the saddest thing he thought is that poor people are most likely to kill or maim members of their own families.
8. To be sure violent crime is not limited to the poor.
9. Nevertheless he said the frustrations of poverty often come to the boiling point in assault robbery and murder.
10. He spoke energetically sadly and eloquently.

23k
Substituting for Words

Use a comma to take the place of a word omitted from a sentence. A comma frequently takes the place of the conjunction *and,* and in some constructions it can take the place of other words as well.

Power staggers forward, then falls facedown in the dust.

—PHILIP CAPUTO

The comma can also take the place of *and* in a series.

The joke was stale, flat, vulgar.

In sentences that express a contrast, the comma can stand for several words.

Lincoln was impressive, not handsome.

She said her car was big, bright, and fast, not economical.

23l
Providing Emphasis

Use commas to give special emphasis to words and phrases, even when commas are not grammatically necessary.

> It seems impossible to get a saint, or a philosopher, or a scientist, to stick to this simple truth.
>
> —D. H. LAWRENCE

> He found hamlets of three decaying houses with the corrugated iron of their roofs grinding and clanking in a hot wind, and not a tree for miles.
>
> —WILLIAM GOLDING

23m
Setting Off Parenthetical Elements

Use paired commas to set off parenthetical elements. Parenthetical elements are words, phrases, or clauses set within sentences which add further description to the main statement the sentence makes. Always be sure to set such elements off by paired commas—a comma at the beginning of the element and another at the end.

> Senator Cadwallader, responding to his campaign contributions from the coal industry, introduced a bill to begin strip mining operations in Yellowstone Park.

23l/m

⌃
,

Our Latin teacher, Mr. Harrison, was devoted to making us love the language.

Jeannine is, we agree, a great editor.

The Germans were, however, unprepared for the allied landing at Anzio, near Rome.

23n
Separating Parts of Place Names and Addresses

Use a pair of commas to separate parts of place names and addresses.

At Cleveland, Ohio, the river sometimes catches fire.

The comma separates the city, Cleveland, from its state, Ohio. Another comma comes after Ohio to set off the state from the rest of the sentence.
Commas set off parts of an address in sentences and in addresses on letters and envelopes.

He lived at 1400 Crabgrass Lane, Suburbia, New York.

My address is:
63 Oceanside Drive, Apartment 3
Knoxville, TN 37916

23o
Separating Parts of Dates

Use paired commas in dates when the month, day, and year are included.

On June 6, 1944, British and American armies invaded France.

On October 17, 1989, the largest earthquake in America since 1906 shook San Francisco.

No comma is necessary when the day of the month is omitted.

Germany invaded Poland in September 1939.

✓ CHECKLIST: AVOIDING COMMON ERRORS WITH COMMAS

☐ Do not separate subject, verb, object. A comma should not separate a subject from its verb or a verb from its object or complement unless a nonrestrictive clause or phrase intervenes.
Faulty: The tulips that I planted last year, suddenly died.
Correct: The tulips that I planted last year, which seemed to be doing well, suddenly died.

☐ Do not separate prepositional phrases from what they modify. A prepositional phrase that serves as an adjective is not set off by commas from the noun or pronoun that it modifies.
Faulty: The best part, of the meal, is coffee.
A prepositional phrase that serves as an adverb is not set off from the rest of the sentence by commas.
Faulty: He swam, with the current, rather than against it.

☐ Do not divide a compound verb with a comma.
Faulty: He ran, and walked twenty miles.
But if the parts of a compound verb form a series, set off the parts of the verb with commas.
He ran, walked, and crawled twenty miles.

☐ Do not use a comma after the last item in a series unless the series concludes a clause or phrase set off by commas.
He loved books, flowers, and people and spent much of his time with all of them.
Three "scourges of modern life," as Roberts calls the automobile, the telephone, and the polyester shirt, were unknown little more than a century ago.

☐ Avoid commas that create false parentheses.
Faulty: A song called, "Faded Love," made Bob Wills famous.

☐ Do not use a comma to set off a dependent adverbial clause at the end of a sentence. In practice this rule means that you should not use a comma before words such as *because, when, since, while, as, neither,* and *either.*
Faulty: He looked forward every year to June, because he always made a long bike trip as soon as school was out.
But if the clause beginning with *because* begins the sentence, follow the rule in 23b.
Because he always made a long bike trip as soon as school was out, he looked forward every year to June.

23n/o

$\hat{,}$

British and European writers use a form of the complete date that requires no comma at all.

She graduated from college on 5 June 1980.

■ **Exercise 23.4** Use commas correctly in the sentences below.

1. The speaker was rude pompous tiresome.
2. She purchased eggs rolls and butter from a small corner store in Cincinnati Ohio on June 7 1989 just before her son's birthday.
3. I shall be thirty on April 7 1990 when I shall be in London England.
4. Dugan takes the Ford Martha the Toyota.
5. Water flows over the rocks for a mile then plunges fifty feet into a lake.

■ **Exercise 23.5** Eliminate the unnecessary commas in the following sentences. Be careful! Some of the commas belong where they are. If a sentence is correct as it is written, put a check by it.

1. According to Hedrick Smith of the *New York Times,* life for the average Russian, has been one long round, of corruption, lines, and alcoholism.
2. Events, in Eastern Europe, in the summer, and fall, of 1989, made many people hope that the cold war, might be over.
3. A controversial issue, in 1989, was the "docudrama," on television, which presented fictionalized accounts of historical events as true, stories.
4. A story in the Sunday, *New York Times,* of November 26, 1989, held that crack dealers on the street, did not make much money, and were terrorized, by their overlords, in the illegal, drug trade.
5. The Oakland, Athletics, swept the San Francisco, Giants, in the 1989, World Series, despite the disruption, of the earthquake.
6. Tom Wolfe's, *Bonfire of the Vanities,* was one of the big, paperback, best-sellers of 1989.
7. It is sometimes not easy to tell, when you have drunk, too much beer to drive safely.
8. Since divorce has become common, in America, many children are growing up in homes with only one, parent.
9. With the lessening of restrictions, on travel between East, and West in 1989, many people hoped that the East, German athletes would compete, in more athletic contests, in the West.
10. Laptop computers in 1989 and 1990 became, much, much smaller than ever, some of them weighing less than three, or four, pounds.

CHAPTER

24

SEMICOLONS

The semicolon is a stronger mark of punctuation than the comma, and it can be used to join sentence elements that cannot be joined by a comma alone. Semicolons can join certain independent clauses and set off elements within a series when commas must be used within the elements.

24a
Joining Independent Clauses

Use a semicolon to join independent clauses, either with or without the help of a coordinating conjunction.

> Silence is deep as eternity; speech is shallow as time.
>
> —THOMAS CARLYLE

> Before 8000 B.C. wheat was not the luxuriant plant it is today; it was merely one of many wild grasses that spread throughout the Middle East.
>
> —JACOB BRONOWSKI

In each example, two clauses are closely related to each other — one of the reasons for using the semicolon. Each writer could have separated them with a period, but he chose the semicolon to stress the relation of ideas in the clauses.

> In the first draft I had Bigger going smack to the electric chair; but I felt that two murders were enough for one novel.
>
> —RICHARD WRIGHT

The semicolon adds emphasis to the second independent clause.

24b
Joining Main Clauses

Use a semicolon to join main clauses separated by a conjunctive adverb. Conjunctive adverbs such as *however, nevertheless, moreover, then,* and *consequently* are not coordinating conjunctions and cannot join independent clauses (see 14e). Even a comma placed before them cannot give them the grammatical strength to link clauses. A semicolon is necessary before the conjunctive adverb *nevertheless* to join the two clauses properly.

He had biked 112 miles in ten hours; nevertheless, he now had to do a marathon.

■ **Exercise 24.1**   Review the following sentences for the proper use of semicolons. If a sentence is correct as it stands, place a check beside it. Supply semicolons where they are needed. Eliminate semicolons that are incorrectly used.

1. She was unable to keep the appointment; since she was delayed in traffic; because of the wreck.
2. The sun is our most potent source of energy, nevertheless, research in harnessing solar power has gone slowly.
3. The United Stated and Canada have relatively few varieties of poisonous snakes; but the climate is warm enough to allow many such snakes to flourish should they be accidentally introduced.
4. Western movies once showed hostile Indians attacking covered wagons drawn up in circles on the plains; although no such attack ever occurred in fact.
5. Videocassette recorders allow many people to rent movies on tape and to play them at home through their television sets moreover, the rental fee for the tape is much less than it would cost a family to see a movie in a theater.
6. Nuclear war is a horror that no one wants to imagine; yet imagining it may help us prevent it.
7. November is a month that is much abused and often unfairly so; true, the leaves fall, and cold weather begins; but November gives us three holidays — Election Day, Veterans Day, and Thanksgiving.
8. I like Brian De Palma's films, however, they sometimes scare me.

24a/b

^
;

24c
Separating Elements in a Series

Use a semicolon to separate elements in a series when some of those elements contain commas.

> They are aware of sunrise, noon and sunset; of the full moon and the new; of equinox and solstice; of spring and summer, autumn and winter.
>
> —ALDOUS HUXLEY

Use semicolons to separate elements that contain other marks of punctuation.

> The assignment will be to read Leviticus 21:1-20; Joshua 5:3-6; and Isaiah 55:1-10.

> The committee included Dr. Curtis Youngblood, the county medical examiner; Roberta Collingwood, the director of the bureau's criminal division; and Darcy Coolidge, the chief of police.

24d
Separating Elements in Elliptical Constructions

Use a semicolon to separate elements in elliptical constructions where words left out are clearly understood.

> In America, traffic problems are caused by cars; in China, by bicycles.

> In the Middle Ages, many children were abandoned by their parents; by the nineteenth century, comparatively few.

24c/d
^
;

■ **Exercise 24.2** For each set below, write a single sentence using semicolons correctly. Make reference to all the people and identify them by their jobs.

1. Dr. Mary A. Carter is a professor of history. Mr. Glenn G. Swenson is a football coach. Dean Sylvia Paoli was the moderator of the discussion. Dr. Carter and Mr. Swenson debated the place of intercollegiate athletics in education.

2. Ronald Martin is a designer of computers. Elizabeth Ingersol is an architect. Joseph Greenberg is a science teacher in Bradford High School. The three of them led a discussion on the future of home computers in business and education.

■ **Exercise 24.3** Punctuate the following sentences correctly.

1. Some were satisfied others disgruntled.
2. He needed seven hours of sleep a night she only five.
3. Cancer is more feared heart disease more fatal.
4. In her room there were three pictures in mine one in his none.

■ **Exercise 24.4** Explain the use of the semicolon in each sentence below.

1. The Red Sox last won a World Series in 1918; the Cubs, in 1908.
2. The company had branches in Cleveland, Ohio; Paris, Tennessee; Del Rio, Texas; and Reno, Nevada.
3. Our guests included John Fox, the administrative dean of the Graduate School; Bill Dean, a good friend; and Tom Fox, John's son.
4. She had appeared in summer stock in *Mary, Mary; The Prisoner of Second Avenue;* and *Come Back, Little Sheba.*
5. He visited us at Thanksgiving 1989 with his sister; afterward we never saw him again.
6. We cooked a large meal together; then we sat down together and ate.
7. Elizabeth claimed to despise Darcy; nevertheless, in the end she married him.
8. Alcohol is the most dangerous drug; nicotine kills almost as many.
9. A little exercise each day can lengthen your life; it can be as little as a walk around the block.
10. He asked me what I wanted; I could not tell him.

24c/d
^
•
,

CHAPTER

25

APOSTROPHES

We use apostrophes to show possession and to indicate omitted letters in words written as contractions. Apostrophes are used in such a wide variety of ways that they can be confusing. Contractions offer little difficulty, but be sure to learn the difference between the possessive case and the plural form of nouns. The apostrophe is used to form the possessive case of all nouns and of many pronouns. It is not used to form a plural.

25a
Showing Possession

To indicate ownership — or, in special cases, to show that an entity has a particular attribute, quality, value, or feature — writers can often choose among forms of the possessive case (see p. 110).

Children's toys could mean:	**Everybody's** dreams could mean:
toys *of children*	dreams *of everybody*
toys *for children*	dreams *for everybody*
toys *belonging to children*	dreams *everybody has*
toys *owned by children*	dreams *belonging to everybody*
toys *that children own*	

Most writers would use the first form above without spelling out one of the full phrases. Without such words as *of, for, belonging to,* and *owned by*, only the apostrophe plus *s* ('s) conveys the intended sense of possession. Writers often use possessive forms even when the concept of possession seems uncertain. In the examples above, *everybody* does not possess *dreams* in the same way that *children* possess *toys*. Also, accepted usage requires apostrophes with concepts of duration and of monetary value:

an **hour's** wait	two **minutes'** work
a **dime's** worth	five **dollars'** worth

✓ CHECKLIST: THE POSSESSOR AND THE POSSESSED

	Possessor	Thing, attribute, quality, value, or feature possessed
the woman's shovel	woman's	shovel
a child's bright smile	child's	bright smile
Juanita's son	Juanita's	son
the robbers' clever plan	robbers'	clever plan
five dollars' worth	dollars'	worth
everyone's plans	everyone's	plans
babies' books	babies'	books

Two elements are usually required to show possession correctly with an apostrophe. Someone or something is the possessor, and someone or something is being possessed. The person or entity that possesses something takes an apostrophe, either along with an -s or alone if the word already ends in -s. The person or entity being possessed usually appears just after the word with the apostrophe.

Sometimes the thing possessed precedes the possessor. Sometimes the sentence may not name the thing possessed, but its identity is clearly understood by the reader. Sometimes we indicate possession by using both the *of* form and an apostrophe plus *s* or a personal possessive pronoun.

> The motorcycle is the student's.
> Is the tractor Jan Stewart's?
> I saw your cousin at Nicki's.
> He was a friend of Rocco's.
> This dress of Mother's is out of style.
> That child of **his** rakes our leaves every fall.

25a/b
؛

25b
Distinguishing Between Plurals and Possessives

Most nouns require -s endings to show the plural form: boy/boys; girl/girls; teacher/teachers; song/songs. Possessive forms require the apostro-

phe plus *s* ('s) ending: boy/boy's; girl/girl's; teacher/teacher's. The possessive form and the plural form are not interchangeable.

Incorrect: The teacher's asked the girl's and boy's for attention.

Correct: The teachers asked the girls and boys for attention.

An apostrophe plus *s* at the end of a word makes that word the
possessor of something.

■ **Exercise 25.1** Identify each word in the following list as plural or
possessive; then use each word correctly in a sentence.

1. **a.** women   **b.** women's   **c.** woman's
2. **a.** man's   **b.** men's   **c.** men
3. **a.** child's   **b.** children   **c.** children's
4. **a.** cats   **b.** cat's   **c.** cats'
5. **a.** professor's **b.** professors **c.** professors'

■ **Exercise 25.2** In each of the following sentences, underline the
word that shows possession and put an **X** above the word that names the
entity possessed. (The entity possessed may be understood but not
named.)

1. Plucking feathers on turkeys is not everyone's idea of a good job.
2. If the responsibility is the mayor's, then our citizens' group should
   push her to act.
3. At Mario's, the waiters serve with elegance; the diner's pleasure is
   the staff's only concern.
3. She brought me six dollars' worth of flour.
5. They went on a week's vacation together.
6. Gloria's smile welcomes students to the Writing Center.

25c
ʾ

25c
Forming Possessives

To form a possessive, add an apostrophe plus *s* to a noun or pronoun,
whether it is singular or plural.

Noun/pronoun		As a possessive
baby	singular	a baby's smile
men	plural	the men's club
Wanda	singular	Wanda's sundae
hour	singular	an hour's time
anyone	singular	anyone's idea
children	plural	the children's papers
Dickens	singular	Dickens's books

Add only an apostrophe (') to plurals ending in -s

Word (-s) ending		Word used as a possessive
babies	plural	the babies' smiles
companies	plural	the companies' employees

Most writers add both an apostrophe and a final *s* to one-syllable singular nouns already ending in -*s* and to nouns of any number of syllables if the final -*s* is hard (as in *hiss*).

Keats**'s** art, James**'s** adventure, Ross**'s** flag, Elvis**'s** songs

Note that proper names of geographical locations, associations, organizations, and so forth sometimes do not take apostrophes:

Kings Point, Veterans Highway, St. Marks Place, Harpers Ferry

25c

For hyphenated words and compound words and word groups, add an apostrophe plus *s* to the last word only.

my father-in-law**'s** job

the editor-in-chief**'s** responsibilities

the union leader**'s** supporters

To express joint ownership by two or more people, use the possessive form for the last name only; to express individual ownership, use the possessive form for each name.

Felicia and Elias's house

McGraw-Hill's catalog

Felicia's and Elias's houses

the city's and the state's finances

■ **Exercise 25.3** Change each word in parentheses into the correct possessive form by adding an apostrophe alone or an apostrophe plus *s*. A word may require a plural form before you change it to a possessive.
Example:
The two (woman) <u>women's</u> cars blocked the driveway.

1. (Mr. Cass) _____ contribution to the primaries brought praise from the (governor) _____ reelection committee.
2. The (assistant editor) _____ idea was to run three (student) _____ biographies in each issue.
3. The (Lady) _____ Auxiliary League drew hundreds to its Fourth of July picnic; (everyone) _____ praise meant that the tradition would continue next year.
4. In (Dickens) _____ novel *Great Expectations*, (Pip) _____ adventures hold every (reader) _____ attention.

■ **Exercise 25.4** Change the structures that show ownership to possessive forms that use apostrophes.
Example:
The announcement of the Secretary of State
The Secretary of State's announcement

1. the car of Kim and Thai
2. a business belonging to my brother-in-law
3. the houses of Mr. Garcia and Mr. Youngblood
4. the smile of Doris
5. the value of three dollars

25d
v

25d
Showing Omission

Use an apostrophe to indicate letters or numbers left out of contractions, or letters omitted from words to show regional pronunciation. In a contraction—a shortened word or group of words formed when some letters or sounds are omitted—use an apostrophe in place of the omissions.

it's	(for *it is* or *it has*)
weren't	(for *were not*)
here's	(for *here is*)
comin'	(for *coming*)

Sometimes we abbreviate the numbers of years, using the apostrophe. For example, we say, "The '50s were a decade of relative calm; the '60s were much more turbulent." But it is usually better to spell out the decades. "Many people claim that the fifties were much more turbulent than we remember and that the sixties only continued trends begun a decade earlier."

✓ CHECKLIST: SOME RULES FOR PROPER USE

☐ Don't use an apostrophe plus *s* ('s) to show the plural of a letter, number, or word used as a word rather than as a symbol of the meaning it conveys. Underline such elements (to indicate that they would be set in italics if your story or essay were set in type) and add -s, without an underline.
Committee has two *m*s, two *t*s, and two *e*s.
There are twelve *no*s in the first paragraph.
He makes his 2s look like 5s.

☐ To show possession with personal and relative pronouns and the pronoun *it*, use the special possessive forms, which never require apostrophes (my/mine, your/yours, his, her/hers, our/ours, their/theirs, whose, and its).
His cooking won a prize
Its fur was shedding.
They knew **our** secret.
Is he a friend of **yours?**
The rake is **hers.**

☐ When an apostrophe appears with an *s* in a pronoun, the apostrophe probably marks omissions in a contraction.
It's too hot (It + is)
Who's there? (Who + is)
If **you're** awake, please call. (you + are)

25d
;

■ **Exercise 25.5**   Correct any words in italics either by removing incorrectly used apostrophes or by adding apostrophes where they belong. Some words are correct and require no change.

1. *Iris* cat lost *its* way, but one *neighbors* boy helped her find it.
2. There *wasnt* enough attention placed on writing *skills'* in college English curricula in the *60s.*
3. In the word *occurrence,* the two *c*s and two *r*s confuse many grade school *students'.*
4. If the *ideas'* are *hers', it's* wise to give her credit for them.
5. Many *childrens parents'* bought these *dolls* before the *companies* recalled them at the *governments* request.

CHAPTER

26

QUOTATION MARKS

Quotation marks (". . .") always work in pairs. They are used to enclose words, phrases, and sentences that are quoted directly. Titles of short works such as poems, articles, songs, and short stories, when cited with other words, also require quotation marks, as do some words and phrases that you wish to use in a special sense.

26a
Enclosing Direct Quotations

A **direct quotation** repeats the exact words of a speaker or of a text. Direct quotations from written material may include whole sentences or only a few words or phrases.

James Baldwin wrote of his experience of whites during his childhood, "The only white people who came to our house were welfare workers and bill collectors."

James Baldwin wrote that the only white visitors he saw in his home as a child were "welfare workers and bill collectors."

The examples in the table at the right will help you see how direct quotations are used and punctuated in sentences.

In writing dialogue, use quotation marks to enclose everything a speaker says. When one person continues speaking, use quotation marks again if the quoted sentence is interrupted.

Sentence: Quoted Words First

Quotation mark — Capital letter

"The first thing that strikes one about Plath's journals is what

End quotation mark   End mark

they leave out," writes Katha Pollitt in *The Atlantic.*

Comma inside quote   Small letter

Sentence: Quoted Words Last

Comma

Small letter   Capital letter

In *The Atlantic* Katha Pollitt writes, "The first thing that

Quotation mark

strikes one about Plath's journals is what they leave out."

End mark inside quote

Sentence: Quoted Words Interrupted

Quotation mark

Quotation mark   Comma inside quote

Capital letter   Small letter

"The first thing that strikes one about Plath's journals," writes

Quotation mark   End mark inside quote

Katha Pollitt in *The Atlantic,* "is what they leave out."

Comma   Small letter   Quotation mark

26a
" "

"I don't know what you're talking about," he said. "I did listen to everything you told me."

"You listened," she said, "but you did not try to understand."

An **indirect quotation** is a **paraphrase.** That is, you express in your own words the meaning of someone else's words. Quotation marks are not used with an indirect quotation.

Casey confessed that he enjoyed blowing the whistle more than anything else he did as a locomotive engineer.

Odette asked if she could borrow my chain saw.

When you quote more than five lines, type them double-spaced and set every line off by a five-space indentation from the left margin. Triple space above and below the quotation. *Be sure that you indent every line in a block quotation.*

Block quotations are *not* set off by quotation marks. If the block includes a direct quotation, however, use quotation marks as they are found in the text. The example that follows shows you how to do this.

Some of the most interesting pages in Schorske's book describe how Sigmund Freud arrived at psychoanalysis and the interpretation of dreams and so made a revolution in our understanding of how the mind works. But as Schorske points out, the young Freud's first passion was not the working of the mind but classical archeology:

> He consumed with avidity Jakob Burckhardt's newly published *History of Greek Culture,* so rich in materials on primitive myth and religion. He read with envy the biography of Heinrich Schliemann, who fulfilled a childhood wish by his discovery of Troy. Freud began the famous collection of ancient artifacts which were soon to grace his office in the Berggasse. And he cultivated a new friendship in the Viennese professional elite — especially rare in those days of withdrawal — with Emanuel Loewy, a professor of archeology. "He keeps me up till three o'clock in the morning," Freud wrote appreciatively to Fliess. "He tells me about Rome."
>
> — CARL SCHORSKE

26a

" "

Use block quotations sparingly because they cut down on the readability of your papers. Try instead to paraphrase the material and include it in the text, giving proper credit to your sources (see 34b, c, and d).

A short quotation of poetry may be run into your text, much like any other short quotation. Line breaks are usually shown with a slash.

> In the nineteenth century Wordsworth wrote of the weary acquisitiveness of our modern age: "The world is too much with us; late and soon,/Getting and spending, we lay waste our powers:/Little we see in Nature that is ours."

Longer verse quotations are indented block-style, like long prose quotations. If you cannot get an entire line of poetry on a single line of your typescript, you may put the end of the line under your typed line near the right margin of your paper.

> Ah, what can ever be more stately and admirable to me
> $\qquad$ than mast-hemm'd Manhattan?
> River and sunset and scallop-edg'd waves of flood-tide?
> The sea-gulls oscillating their bodies, the hay-boat in the twilight,
> $\qquad$ and the belated lighter?
> What gods can exceed these that clasp me by the hand, and with
> $\qquad$ voices
> I love call me promptly and loudly by my nighest name
> $\qquad$ as I approach?
>
> —WALT WHITMAN

A pair of single quotation marks (made with the apostrophe on the typewriter) is used to set off quotations within quotations.

> What happened when the faculty demanded an investigation of dishonest recruiting practices in the athletic department? The president of the university said, "I know you're saying to me, 'We want an honest football team.' But I'm telling you this: 'I want a winning football team.'"

26b
Using Other Punctuation with Quotation Marks

A comma or period at the end of a quotation is always set before the last quotation mark. A question mark is set before the last quotation mark if the quotation itself asks a question. Punctuation marks that come before the quoted material are not included within quotation marks.

> "The worst movie I've ever seen is *Jaws*," he said.

"How can you say that?" she asked. "I loved *Jaws*."

"How can I say that?" he said. "I'll tell you how I can say that; I can say that because I saw it eight times!"

She said, "I think *Jaws II* is even worse."

"Yes," he replied, "I agree. I saw it only four times."

Standard practice is to place the period before the final quotation mark even when the quotation is only one or two words long. A question mark or exclamation point is placed after the last quotation mark if the quoted material is not itself a question or an exclamation.

He had what he called his "special reasons."

Why did he name his car "Buck"?

"Because," she said, "people pass it all the time."

Standard practice is to put colons and semicolons after the final quotation mark.

"I think the jokes in this book are terrible"; she made the remark at the top of her voice, and since I wrote the book, I was hurt.

Dean Wilcox cited the items he called his "daily delights"; a free parking place for his scooter at the faculty club, a special table in the club itself, and friends to laugh with after a day's work.

■ **Exercise 26.1** Punctuate correctly the following sentences. Some sentences require no additional punctuation.

1. I want you to write a book Ted told me one night
2. He said Give me a manuscript, and I'll get it published
3. She told me that she would rather play tennis than eat
4. He said to his friend I bought the car on credit
5. The wind is rising she shouted Make the boats secure The hurricane is coming

26c
" "

26c
Enclosing Titles

Use quotation marks for titles of essays or chapters or other sections within books or periodicals, and for titles of all unpublished works.

"How to Die: The Example of Samuel Johnson" is the title of a recent article in *The Sewanee Review*.

The chapter was called "Another Question of Location."

Note that the titles of songs and short poems are usually put in quotation marks. Titles of long poems are put in italics. In manuscripts, titles of long poems are underlined (see 31a).

Robert Herrick wrote the poem "Upon Julia's Clothes."

George Noel Gordon, Lord Byron, wrote *Childe Harold's Pilgrimage*.

26d
Indicating Special Use

Use quotation marks to show that someone else has used a word or phrase in a special way that you or the general public may not use or agree with completely.

The "workers' paradise" of Stalinist Russia turned out to be a combination of slums, shortages, secret police, and slave-labor camps.

George had the "privilege" of working his way through school by cleaning bathrooms.

For them, getting "saved" is clearly only the first step.

—FRANCES FITZGERALD

The "core curriculum" has now been in effect for several years.

26e
Avoiding Apologetic Quotation Marks

26d/e
" "

Experienced writers rarely enclose slang or clichés in quotation marks. Inexperienced writers sometimes do so to indicate their awareness that such expressions are not usually found in serious writing. They think the quotation marks show readers that they know better. In fact, quotation marks in these cases only mark the writer as inexperienced.

People in California are "laid back."

You can accomplish great things only if you "keep your nose to the grindstone."

I thought he was "cute."

When you are tempted to use apologetic quotation marks, take time to think of a better way of expressing yourself.

People in California pride themselves on living for pleasure without taking anything too seriously.

You can accomplish great things only if you pay attention to what you are doing.

I thought he was attractive.

But if you have a good reason for using a cliché or a slang expression and are sure you can justify its use, use it — without quotation marks.

■ **Exercise 26.2** In some of the following sentences, quotation marks are incorrectly used. Correct any incorrect usages, and put a check by those sentences where the quotation marks are used in the right way.

1. "Traditional Principles of Rhetoric" is the title of a chapter in Kenneth Burke's book *A Rhetoric of Motives.*
2. "Gee whiz," he said, "I could rap with you all night long."
3. When I waited to do my term paper until the night before it was due, I was really "up the creek without a paddle."
4. "Sweet Baby James" is the title of a song James Taylor sings.
5. I wanted to know if I could bring the "kids" to the party.
6. She was "put off" by my reaction to her paper.
7. "To His Coy Mistress" is a celebrated poem by Andrew Marvell.
8. Most "utopian" communities emphasize rigid conformity, hard work, and puritanical ethics.
9. "Lochinvar" is a rousing poem by Sir Walter Scott.
10. The word "trees" can be both a noun and a verb.

26d/e
" "

CHAPTER

27

OTHER MARKS OF PUNCTUATION

27a
Using the Dash

The dash sets off words, phrases, and sometimes whole sentences so that they receive special emphasis. Think of the dash as a very strong pause intended to give special emphasis to what follows—and sometimes to what comes immediately before.

> A Wisconsin man traveling on horseback had the lower parts of his boots—brand-new ones, be it noted—eaten by wolves, but managed to save his toes.
>
> —RICHARD ERDOES

> I think this is the most extraordinary collection of human talent, of human knowledge, that has ever been gathered at the White House —with the possible exception of when Thomas Jefferson dined alone.
>
> —JOHN F. KENNEDY

On the typewriter the dash is made with *two* unspaced hyphens, and there is no space between the dash and the word on either side of it. Handwritten and typeset dashes are single, unbroken lines about as wide as a capital *M*.

```
Beer, cheese, and brevity--these
are the marks of a good study
session in the dorm.
```

Often the dash sets off nouns placed for special emphasis at the beginning of a sentence and then summarized by a pronoun after the dash, as you see in the sentence above. The dash sometimes can set off an independent clause within a sentence. In such sentences, the content of the set-off independent clause is not essential to the main assertion of the sentence. It is added information.

> Love, with Chaucer, is something tender and vulnerable — it must be protected from the sniggers of a callous world, from the cynicism bred by casual conquest, from the damage done by blurted-out ugly words.
>
> —HANS P. GUTH

When used in pairs, dashes serve to separate parenthetical statements more closely related to the sentence than parentheses would allow.

> There's a newspaper in Colorado that I admire, for instance, called *High Country News* —"A Paper for People Who Care About the West" —which is devoted solely to environmental matters.
>
> —WILLIAM ZINSSER

> Age groups and the part they have played in American culture — or indeed in any culture—are a subject that has seldom been thoroughly discussed.
>
> —MALCOLM COWLEY

Overuse of the dash can distract readers. You should use the dash only for special emphasis.

27b
Using the Colon

Use the colon (:) to link independent clauses, to introduce direct quotations and lists, and to set off words and phrases at the end of a sentence. Use the colon also to separate the numbers of chapters and verses of the Bible and in other such specialized forms.

The colon links independent clauses when you want to emphasize the clause that follows the colon; the second clause restates or elaborates on the first.

> Until recently, women in Switzerland had an overwhelming political disadvantage: they could not vote.

Of this I am sure: Martin will arrive late, talk loudly, and eat too much.

You can use a colon to introduce a direct quotation. A colon is more formal than a comma. The use of the colon before a direct quotation can separate the independent clauses.

"Don't speak of it," she said in a reciting voice and choosing her words sadly and carefully: "It was a stroke."

—V. S. PRITCHETT

Later she recalled the hours Faulkner spent helping her to recover hope: "He kept me alive," she said.

—DAVID MINTER

Use a colon to introduce a block quotation:

Dickens had contempt for lazy people. Some of his worst characters are those who lie about, waiting for others to wait on them. Here is the way he introduces Mrs. Witterly in *Nicholas Nickleby:*

The lady had an air of sweet insipidity, and a face of engaging paleness; there was a faded look about her, and about the furniture, and about the house altogether. She was reclining on the sofa in such a very unstudied attitude that she might have been taken for an actress all ready for the first scene in a ballet, and only waiting for the drop curtain to go up.

Colons also introduce itemized lists:

During its first four years the Virginia venture had failed to meet three basic needs: political stability, economic prosperity, and peaceful Indian relations.

—ALDEN T. VAUGHAN

27a/b
— / :

The colon *cannot* be used to introduce a simple series:

Incorrect: During its first four years the Virginia venture had failed to meet: political stability, economic prosperity, and peaceful Indian relations.

Some writers capitalize the first letter of the first word after a colon if a complete sentence follows the colon.

He is kind: Innumerable unknowns in dire need have received financial help from Sinatra.

—ISOBEL SILDEN

But most writers capitalize the first letter of the word following a colon only when they are writing titles. (A proper noun is, of course, capitalized wherever it appears. See 29b.)

Doing Without: Meeting the Energy Crisis in the 1980s

Colons intervene between Bible chapters and verses:

Young writers should take Proverbs 12:1 as a motto.

To indicate the time of day, use a colon between the hour and the minutes:

He woke up at 6:30 in the morning.

Colons follow salutations in business letters:

Dear Mr. Bush:

27c
Using Parentheses

Use parentheses to set off information that breaks the flow of thought within a sentence or a paragraph. Parentheses enclose material that is not as important as material set off by commas or dashes.

The first money you get for a book will probably be your advance; as a rule, half of that is paid when you sign your contract (or as soon thereafter as the legal department and the accounting department fill out the appropriate forms), and the other half comes due when you deliver a satisfactory manuscript.

—JUDITH APPLEBAUM and NANCY EVANS

At another barrier a seaman held back Kathy Gilnagh, Kate Mullins, and Kate Murphy. (On the *Titanic* everyone seemed to be named Katherine.)

—WALTER LORD

27c
( )

When parentheses enclose a whole sentence, a period comes after the sentence but before the final parenthesis, as in the example above. A sentence that appears inside parentheses *within a sentence* is neither capitalized nor closed with a period.

> John Henry (he was the man with the forty-pound hammer) was a hero to miners fearing the loss of their jobs to machines.

But a question mark or an exclamation point may follow a parenthetical sentence within a sentence.

> John Henry (did he really swing a forty-pound hammer?) was a hero to miners fearing the loss of their jobs to machines.

> John Henry (he swung a forty-pound hammer!) was a hero to miners fearing the loss of their jobs to machines.

Parentheses are used to enclose many kinds of numbers within a text. In some forms of annotation (see 34e), parentheses enclose page numbers of a book referred to throughout a paper. Parentheses also enclose cross-references to other parts of a book.

> Stevens writes that the demands of their offices turn the best university presidents into machines (43).

> Carmichael says that the argument Stevens makes is nonsense because (1) university presidents don't work as well as machines, (2) university presidents don't do any real work at all, and (3) universities would be better off if they were run by faculty committees.

Readers tend to find many parenthetical numbers distracting, as the numbers interrupt the flow of thought. If the numbers within parentheses were left out of the example above and the statements set off by commas alone, the passage would be more readable.

27d
[ ]

27d
Using Brackets

Use brackets to set off material within quoted matter that is not part of the quotation.

Samuel Eliot Morison has written, "This passage has attracted a good deal of scorn to the Florentine mariner [Verrazzano], but without justice."

In this sentence, a writer is quoting Morison. But Morison's sentence does not include the name of the "Florentine mariner." The writer adds the name—Verrazzano—but places it in brackets so readers will know the identity of the mariner Morison is talking about.

Sometimes material in brackets explains or corrects something that is quoted.

Vasco da Gama's man wrote in 1487, "The body of the church [it was not a church but a Hindu shrine] is as large as a monastery."

The brackets in this example correct a mistake made by one of the early sailors who went to India with Vasco da Gama. The material within the brackets is supplied by the writer of the essay.

Brackets are also used with you must change a quotation slightly to make it fit the style or grammar of your own sentence.

Full Quotation

I went back to the country and farmed a crop of tobacco with my dad that next year. For all the work I put in I didn't make half as much as I'd been making at the factory, so, after market closed, I wandered back to town and started looking for another job.

—ANN BANKS

Edited Quotation

Jim Wells came off the farm to work in a cigarette factory in North Carolina during the depression. He was fired because he hit a foreman who mistreated him, and, he said, "I went back to the country and farmed a crop of tobacco with my dad that next year [but] I didn't make half as much as I'd been making at the factory." The only thing he could do was to go back to the city and look for another job.

The bracketed word *but* eliminates the need for an ellipsis (three spaced periods), although several words have been cut out of the quotation. The brackets show that the writer has changed the quotation to fit the style of the paper that uses the material.

Brackets may enclose the word *sic* after a piece of correctly quoted information that a reader might believe had slipped into the text erroneously.

The dean said, "Those kids is [*sic*] going to get kicked out of school for saying I don't know no [*sic*] grammar."

Brackets are frequently used to enclose editorial notes, page numbers, or other information inserted in a text. In formal essays they should be used sparingly.

27e
Using the Slash

As a rule, use the slash only to divide lines of poetry written as a quotation within a sentence (see 26a).

Sophocles wrote of the uncertainty of human knowledge: "No man can judge that rough unknown or trust in second sight/For wisdom changes hands among the wise."

Occasionally the slash is used to show that something happened over a couple of calendar years.

The book sold well in 1976/77.

But it is usually better to write this:

The book sold well in 1976 and 1977.

The slash is sometimes used to substitute for the conjunction *or* or as a marker between the words *and* and *or* when the words suggest options.

The course was offered credit/noncredit.

The winner will be chosen by lot, and he/she will drive a new car home.

You can buy the toaster oven and/or the microwave.

Most writers, however, consider such usage awkward. It is usually better to rephrase the sentence.

Students who took the course received no grades. If they satisfied the requirements, they got credit; if they did not, they received no penalty.

27e

/

The winner, to be chosen by lot, will drive a new car home.

You can buy the toaster oven or the microwave, or both.

(Appropriate use of the pronouns *he, she, his,* and *her* is discussed more fully in Chapter 12, "Avoiding Bias.")

27f
Using Ellipses

If you wish to shorten a passage you are quoting, you may omit some of its words. To show readers that you have left out some words, use three spaced periods, called an **ellipsis.**

Full Quotation

In the nineteenth century, railroads, lacing their way across continents, reaching into the heart of every major city in Europe and America, and bringing a new romance to travel, added to the unity of nations and fueled the nationalist fires already set burning by the French Revolution and the wars of Napoleon.

Edited Quotation

In his account of nineteenth-century society, Wilkins credited railroad building with increasing nationalism when he wrote that "railroads . . . added to the unity of nations and fueled the nationalist fires already set burning by the French Revolution and the wars of Napoleon."

27f
. . .

Most writers do not use ellipses to indicate that words have been left out at the beginning or the end of a quotation. Academic writers occasionally use ellipses to show omissions at the beginning or at the end of quotations, but such usage is discouraged. The primary function of the ellipsis is to show that something has been left out of the middle of a quotation.

Ellipsis marks may be used at the end of a sentence if you mean to leave a thought hanging, either in your own prose or in something you are quoting. Such a usage suggests that you are not sure how the thought might be ended.

Oh God, I'm scared. I wish I could die right now with the feeling I have because I know Momma's going to make me mad and I'm going to make her mad, and me and Presley's gonna fight . . . . "Richard, you get in here and put your coat on. Get in here or I'll whip you."

—DICK GREGORY

The ellipsis should serve only as a means of shortening a quotation, never as a device for changing its fundamental meaning or for creating emphasis where none exists in the original.

■ Exercise 27.1

1. Write three sentences using dashes and three using parentheses. What difference, if any, do you find in the effects of using the two punctuation marks?
2. Go to the periodical reading room of your library and look at *Time, Newsweek, Sports Illustrated, Popular Mechanics,* or *The New York Times Magazine.* Find sentences that use parentheses and sentences that use the dash. Copy as many of them as you can find. What can you say about the ways these punctuation marks are used?
3. Write a paragraph in which you quote something and insert material within brackets in the quotation. Explain what you have done.

■ Exercise 27.2
Explain the use of the punctuation marks in color in each of the following examples. Is the punctuation appropriate to the meaning? What other punctuation might serve as an alternative?

1. An air-cooled engine requires no antifreeze in winter (an advantage), but it must be fairly small for the cooling to work (a disadvantage).
2. Diesel engines are fuel-efficient and durable—but they are expensive to manufacture.
3. The Ford Motor Company paid workers five dollars a day (people said Henry Ford was undermining capitalism by paying so much) to build the Model T on assembly lines before World War I.
4. The rotary gasoline engine (the first popular model sold in the United States was the Japanese Mazda) was smooth, quiet, and durable, but it burned 15 percent more fuel than conventional engines—a reason for its swift demise.
5. Mechanical automobile brakes operated with springs, levers, and

27f
. . .

the physical strength of the driver — a strength that might not be sufficient to stop a car hurtling down the highway at forty miles per hour.

27g
Using the Hyphen

Use the hyphen to divide a word at the end of a line only when such division is absolutely necessary. (The use of hyphens to form compound words is discussed in 28e.) Try to avoid breaking words at the ends of lines because such divisions slow your readers down. Never divide the last word on a page. Leave yourself wide margins and you will rarely have to divide a word.

When you must break a word, put a hyphen at the end of the first line only, not at the start of the next line. The general rule is to divide words only between syllables. If you are unsure about how to break a word into syllables, consult your dictionary (see 13b). The following pointers will help you to divide words correctly.

Never divide one-syllable words.

Incorrect

None of us at the dean's luncheon thought that the dean would arrive in tattered jeans and a torn undershirt.

His weird and uncontrollable laugh echoed down the corridor.

Never divide a word if the division leaves only one letter at the end of a line or only one or two letters at the beginning of a line. Avoid breaking such words as *hap·py, could·n't, read·er, o·pen, light·ly,* and *hat·ed.*

Incorrect

Naomi Lee Fong, who graduates today, never felt so happy in her life before.

Divide compound words into the words that make them up, or at the hyphen if the word contains a hyphen. Compound words such as *hard-working, rattlesnake, bookcases,* and *paperwork* should be broken only between the words that form them: *hard-working, rattle-snake, book-cases, paper-work*. Compound words that already have hyphens, such as *brother-in-law, self-denial, ex-convict,* and *anti-Semitic,* are broken after the hyphens only.

Incorrect

She loves being a detective, but she hates the paperwork.

I gave my old fishing rod to my brother-in-law, and he will sell it at his yard sale.

When two consonants come between vowels in a word you are divid-ing, make the split between the two consonants. Do not split the two consonants if the division does not reflect pronunciation. In the following words, for example, make the split where the dot appears:

ter·ror   run·ning
shel·ter   bril·liant

In a word like *respire,* however, you would have to divide the word after the prefix *re* and not between the *s* and the *p,* because the word is pronounced *re·spire* and not *res·pire.*

Avoid confusing word divisions. Sometimes part of a divided word forms a shorter word that can mislead your readers. In such cases, write the complete word or break the word where it will not cause confusion. The checklist shows some misleading divisions and some possible alterna-tives.

✓ CHECKLIST: CONFUSING WORD DIVISIONS

Divisions to avoid	Possible alternatives
a-toll	atoll
at-tire	attire
bar-row	barrow
fat-uous	fatuous
his-torian	histor-ian
im-pugn	impugn
mud-dled	muddled
pig-mentation	pigmen-tation, pigmenta-tion

**27g
hyphen**

PART
SIX

UNDERSTANDING
MECHANICS

CHAPTER

28

SPELLING

Spelling is one of the chief signs of literacy. If you misspell words, your readers may understand you, but they will be less likely to take your thoughts seriously. Frequent or even occasional misspellings in your writing can make people believe that you are careless or ignorant, and if that happens, you will have to work twice as hard to make them take you and your thoughts seriously.

The following checklist provides some suggestions to help you toward better spelling.

✓ CHECKLIST: SUGGESTIONS FOR IMPROVING SPELLING

1. Make yourself realize the importance of good spelling, and resolve to spell correctly.

2. Write down all the words you find you have misspelled. Writing each word over and over again when you realize you have made a mistake will help fix the correct spelling in your mind and in your fingers. Good spelling is a habit of both mind and hand.

3. Try to group your errors. Misspellings often fall into patterns — errors with prefixes, with suffixes, with plurals, and so on.

4. Pronounce words carefully. Many people misspell words because they pronounce them incorrectly.

5. Learn the rules that generally hold for spelling, and learn the exceptions to those rules. Most rules have only a few exceptions. When you have learned the exceptions, you will find that the rules themselves tend to stay in your mind.

6. Proofread your writing carefully. Misspellings creep into the prose of the best of writers when they are in a hurry, when they are thinking ahead to their next thought as they write, or when they do not wish to break their train of thought to look up a troublesome word.

7. Use your dictionary frequently when you proofread your work. Whenever you wonder about the correctness of your spelling of a word, look it up. Writing continually and using a dictionary continually are two excellent ways to become a good speller.

28a
Reading and Pronouncing Carefully

Some common words are frequently misspelled because people misread them or mispronounce them. Of course, pronunciations vary from region to region, and no list can include all mispronunciations that lead to spelling trouble. But if you study the following list, you can train your eye and your ear to spot the parts of common words that often cause spelling errors.

accidentally	NOT	accidently
arithmetic	NOT	arithemetic
athletics	NOT	atheletics
candidate	NOT	cannidate
corporation	NOT	coperation
disastrous	NOT	disasterous
drowned	NOT	drowneded
everybody	NOT	everbody
everything	NOT	everthing
February	NOT	Febuary
generally	NOT	genrally *or* generly
government	NOT	goverment
height	NOT	heighth
hundreds	NOT	hundereds
irrelevant	NOT	irrevelant
laboratory	NOT	labratory or labertory
library	NOT	liberry
lightning	NOT	lightening
literature	NOT	litrature or literture
mathematics	NOT	mathmatics
mischievous	NOT	mischievious
optimist	NOT	optomist
peremptory	NOT	preemptory
performance	NOT	preformance
perspiration	NOT	presperation
prescription	NOT	perscription
production	NOT	perduction
program	NOT	progrum
publicly	NOT	publically

re**pres**ent	NOT	re**pers**ent
stren**gth**	NOT	stre**nth**
stu**dious**	NOT	stud**jous**
tem**per**ature	NOT	tem**per**ture, tem**pra**ture, *or* tem**perchoor**
won**drous**	NOT	won**der**ous

Be especially careful of those words that sound nearly alike but have different meanings and different spellings (see also the Glossary of Usage).

Some common plurals may be misspelled because they are mispronounced. Misspelling is especially common in the plurals of words ending in *ist* or *est*. The plural of *scientist* is *scientists*. The final combination *ts* sounds like the *tz* in *Ritz* or the *ts* in *fights*. Because this *ts* is difficult for some people to pronounce, they often leave it off, thinking almost unconsciously that the *s* sound in *ist* or *est* is sufficient to make the plural. But the plurals of such words always require a final *s*. So remember:

The plural of *humanist* is *humanists*.

The plural of *nest* is *nests*.

The plural of *socialist* is *socialists*.

The plural of *biologist* is *biologists*.

The plural of *racist* is *racists*.

Other words with a difficult *s* sound in the final syllable sometimes trouble writers forming the plural, but the rule is the same: the final *s* is necessary to make the noun plural.

disc/discs, rasp/rasps, desk/desks

Since words like these are much less common, they give much less trouble than words ending in *est* and *ist*.

28b
Learning the Principles of Spelling

Some principles of English spelling are so generally true that learning them will help you be a better speller.

Distinguishing Between *ei* and *ie*

Consider the previous letter and the sound of the word when you are deciding between the combinations *ei* and *ie*. When these letters sound like the *ee* in *see*, usually place the *i* before *e* — except after *c*.

> believe, relieve, grief, chief, yield, wield
>
> receive, deceive, ceiling, conceit

But there are exceptions:

> species, seize, caffeine, codeine

When the sound is like *ay* in *bay* or *May*, the spelling is nearly always *ei*.

> neigh, feign, neighbor

As for most other words with different sounds, memorize the spellings:

> stein, weird, foreign, height, forfeit, pietism, sierra, pierce, pier, pie, pied, fiery, sieve

■ **Exercise 28.1** Some of the following words are misspelled. Spell them correctly. Put a check by each word in the list that is spelled correctly.

1. friendly
2. weight
3. sieve
4. beleif
5. beir
6. believing
7. ceiling
8. height
9. frieghten
10. wierd

■ **Exercise 28.2** Fill in the blanks in the following words with *ei* or *ie* to make the words correct. Explain the reasons for your choices.

1. s ___ zure	6. v ___ n	11. l ___ n
2. rec ___ pt	7. d ___ gn	12. p ___ ce
3. perc ___ vable	8. hyg ___ ne	13. s ___ ge
4. b ___ ge	9. th ___ f	14. conc ___ t
5. r ___ n	10. fr ___ ze	15. dec ___ t

Dropping e Before -ing

Before the suffix -ing, nearly always drop a final silent e from the root word.

> force/forcing, surprise/surprising, manage/managing, hope/hoping, scare/scaring, come/coming, pave/paving, become/becoming, fume/fuming

There are only a few exceptions to this rule:

> dye/dyeing (to avoid confusion with *dying*)
>
> shoe/shoeing (to avoid mispronunciation and confusion with *showing*)
>
> hoe/hoeing (to avoid mispronunciation)

Dropping e Before -ible

A final, silent e on a root word is always dropped before the suffix -ible.

> force/forcible

Dropping or Retaining e Before -able

Though the silent e of the root is usually dropped before the ending -able, the e is retained often enough to make this principle uncertain. It is best to memorize the words.
Drop e and add -able:

> observe/observable, advise/advisable, move/movable (*sometimes* moveable), argue/arguable, debate/debatable

Do not drop the e when adding -able:

manage/manageable, peace/peaceable, notice/noticeable, change/changeable, embrace/embraceable

Retaining or Changing y Before a Suffix

Keep the final *y* on the root word or change it to *i* according to the nature of the root and the nature of the suffix.

Keep a final *y* on the root word when you add *-ing*:

study/studying, rally/rallying, enjoy/enjoying, cry/crying, ready/readying, steady/steadying, lay/laying

When a final *y* follows a consonant in the root word, change the *y* to *i* before adding an ending other than *-ing*.

merry/merriment, merriest, merrier

happy/happier, happiness, happiest

rally/rallies, rallied, rallier

supply/supplier, supplies, supplied

pity/pitiless, pitiable, pitiful

mercy/merciful, merciless

kingly/kingliness

ugly/uglier, ugliest, ugliness

When a final *y* follows a vowel in the root word, keep the *y* when you add an *s* to make the plural of a noun or the third person singular of a verb.

valley/valleys, defray/defrays, delay/delays, dismay/dismays, enjoy/enjoys, toy/toys, ploy/ploys

To form the past tense of verbs ending in a final *y* preceded by a vowel, you usually keep the final *y* and add the suffix *-ed*.

play/played, dismay/dismayed, enjoy/enjoyed

But there are important exceptions:

pay/paid, say/said, lay/laid

**28b
spell**

■ **Exercise 28.3** Add the suffix indicated for each of the following words. Be sure to change the spelling of the root word when such a change is appropriate.

1. advance + ing
2. highboy + s
3. learn + able
4. horrify + ing
5. quote + able
6. sally + s
7. sense + ible
8. pray + ed
9. quality + s
10. solicit + ing

Adding a Suffix
Beginning with a Vowel to a Root Ending in a Consonant

Watch words formed when a suffix that begins with a vowel is added to a root that ends in a consonant. These suffixes are *-ing, -er, -est, -ed, -ence, -ance, -ible, -able,* and *-ened.*

With most words of one syllable ending in a consonant immediately preceded by a vowel, double the final consonant.

> grip/gripping, quip/quipped, stun/stunning, quit/quitting, plan/planned, sad/saddest, scar/scarring

If the root word ends with two consecutive consonants or with a consonant preceded by two consecutive vowels, do not double the final consonant before suffixes that begin with vowels.

> tight/tighter, stoop/stooping, straight/straightest, sing/singer, deep/deepened, creep/creeping, crawl/crawler

If the root word has more than one syllable, and if the accent of the root falls on the last syllable, usually double the final consonant.

> occur/occurrence, refer/referred, rebut/rebutting, concur/concurring

But if the final consonant of the root is preceded by a consonant or by two consecutive vowels, *or* if the accent shifts from the final syllable of the root when the suffix is added, don't double the final consonant.

> depart/departing
>
> refer/reference

repair/repairing

ferment/fermenting

This rule sounds so complicated that you may think it better to memorize the spellings of all these words rather than to memorize the rule. But give the rule a try; it does work!

Adding Standard Prefixes

Add most standard prefixes without changing the spelling of the prefix or the root word. Before root words beginning with vowels, prefixes ending in vowels sometimes have a hyphen added, although the hyphen is tending to disappear in such forms (see 28e).

appear/disappear

eminent/preeminent

operate/cooperate

usual/unusual

create/procreate

create/re-create (*to create again*)

creation/recreation (*a pastime or pleasurable activity*)

satisfy/dissatisfy

■ **Exercise 28.4** Use the rules you have learned to add the indicated suffixes to the root words below. Explain why you change some roots to add the suffix and why you leave other roots unchanged. The exercise will help you most if you discuss your choices with other members of the class.

1. attend + ance
2. din + ed
3. strip + ing
4. dine + ing
5. mar + ed
6. despair + ed
7. bob + ing
8. accept + ance
9. dip + er
10. map + ing
11. submit + ing
12. reckon + ed
13. detest + able
14. soon + est
15. omit + ed
16. silly + est
17. depend + ence
18. prefer + ing
19. mad + est
20. star + ing
21. confer + ence
22. hop + ed
23. disdain + ed
24. drown + ing
25. pretend + ed

28c
Learning the Regular and Irregular Plural Forms

Forming Regular Plurals

Form the plurals of most nouns simply by adding -s.

> grove/groves, boat/boats, cobra/cobras, bank/banks, scientist/scientists, moralist/moralists, gripe/gripes, gasp/gasps, disc/discs

Form the plurals of acronyms by adding -s to the acronym:

> It can be said that there have been two **FBIs** — the one before the death of J. Edgar Hoover and the one that came later on.

> Most nations believe that they cannot do without their **KGBs** and their **CIAs**.

A decade is usually indicated by -s added to the first year:

> The **1890s** are popularly called "The Gay Nineties" because of the extravagant pleasures of the rich during that decade.

Forming Plurals with -es

When the singular of a noun ends in -s, -x, -ch, or -sh, add -es to form the plural.

> kiss/kisses, Marx/the Marxes, Mr. Jones/the Joneses, church/churches, dish/dishes

A few words ending in a vowel and an x may change when the plural is formed.

> appendix/appendices, index/indices, vortex/vortices

But today -es is the preferred form for the plurals of these words:

> appendixes, indexes, vortexes

Retaining or Changing -y to Form a Plural

If a noun ends in -y preceded by a consonant, change the y to i and add -es to form the plural; if the final y is preceded by a vowel, keep the y and add -s to make the plural.

beauty/beauties, sally/sallies, glory/glories, city/cities, country/countries, destiny/destinies, crudity/crudities, ray/rays, boy/boys, joy/joys, valley/valleys

Forming the Plurals of Nouns Ending in -o

When a noun ends in -o in the singular, form the plural by adding -s or -es.
Fortunately, nouns that end in o in the singular are so rare that you can memorize them without much trouble.

hero/heroes, solo/solos, tomato/tomatoes, tyro/tyros, potato/potatoes, hypo/hypos, flamingo/flamingos *or* flamingoes, piano/pianos, manifesto/manifestos *or* manifestoes

Forming the Plurals of Nouns Ending in -f or -fe

To form the plurals of some nouns ending in -f, change the final f to v and add -es. If a silent e follows the f, also change the f to v.

leaf/leaves, hoof/hooves, beef/beeves, life/lives, wife/wives, self/selves

Here again modern practice favors the simpler form of plurals, merely adding a final s to some of these words:

hoof/hoofs, beef/beefs

Forming the Plurals of Hyphenated Words Beginning with a Noun

To form the plurals of many hyphenated words that begin with a noun, add s or es to the first noun.

mother-in-law/mothers-in-law, father-in-law/fathers-in-law, court-martial/courts-martial

Forming Irregular Plurals

Some nouns have irregular plurals that correspond to no rules and must be memorized individually. Fortunately, most of these nouns are familiar words we use every day.

child/children, man/men, woman/women, tooth/teeth

Forming the Plurals of Latin and Greek Words

Many Latin and Greek words have become part of the English language. To form the plurals of such words, drop the singular ending *-um* or *-on* and add *-a*.

> addendum/addenda, criterion/criteria, datum/data, medium/media, phenomenon/phenomena

Some writers now treat *data* as though it were singular, but the preferred practice is still to recognize that *data* is plural and takes a plural verb: "The data *are* clear on this point: the pass/fail course has become outdated by events."

Like *data*, the word *media* requires a plural verb.

Agenda, by contrast, is now fully accepted as a singular form.

A few English words with Latin roots ending in *-us* form their plurals by changing the *-us* to *-i*.

> alumnus/alumni, tumulus/tumuli, cumulus/cumuli, hippopotamus/hippopotami or hippopotamuses, calculus/calculi, cirrus/cirri

Even fewer words with Latin roots ending in *-a* form their plurals by changing the *-a* to *-ae*:

> alumna/alumnae

■ **Exercise 28.5** Form the plural of each of the following words. Check your plurals against those given in a dictionary when you have finished. (Chapter 13 discusses how to use a dictionary.)

1. mess	13. phlox	25. prophecy
2. harp	14. rest	26. symposium
3. disco	15. flamingo	27. rasp
4. arch	16. handful	28. fascist
5. potato	17. day	29. scientist
6. hello	18. valley	30. musicologist
7. dodo	19. father-in-law	31. rest
8. grief	20. sheep	32. risk
9. fish	21. cow	33. critic
10. buffalo	22. garnish	34. soprano
11. elegy	23. harpist	35. locus
12. harpy	24. rabbi	

28d
Using Lists of Words to Improve Spelling

The following lists of words misspelled in student papers were compiled a few years ago by New York State. Of the more than 31,000 misspelled words gathered by English teachers throughout the country, 407 were misspelled more frequently than others. These words are arranged in the checklist in descending order of difficulty. Study the list carefully. It will help if you have someone read the words aloud to you so that you can try to spell them without looking at them.

✓ **CHECKLIST:** WORDS MOST FREQUENTLY MISSPELLED

WORDS MISSPELLED 100 TIMES OR MORE

believe	lose	receive
belief	losing	receiving
benefit	necessary	referring
benefited	unnecessary	separate
beneficial	occasion	separation
choose	occur	similar
chose	occurred	success
choice	occurring	succeed
definite	occurrence	succession
definitely	perform	than
definition	performance	then
define	personal	their
description	personnel	they're
describe	precede	there
environment	principle	too
exist	principal	two
existence	privilege	to
existent	professor	write
its	profession	writing
it's		writer

WORDS MISSPELLED 50 TO 99 TIMES

accommodate	affective	apparent
achieve	all right*	argument
achievement	among	arguing
acquire	analyze	began
affect	analysis	begin

 * Although some dictionaries accept the spelling *alright*, most list it as nonstandard usage. Most college teachers regard *alright* as a misspelling.

WORDS MISSPELLED 50 TO 99 TIMES (continued)

beginner
beginning
busy
business
category
comparative
conscience
conscientious
conscious
consistent
consistency
control
controlled
controlling
controversy
controversial
criticism
criticize
decision
decided
disastrous
embarrass
equipped
equipment
excellent
excellence
experience
explanation
fascinate
forty

fourth
grammar
grammatically
height
imagine
imaginary
imagination
immediate
immediately
intelligence
intelligent
interest
interpretation
interpret
led
loneliness
lonely
marriage
Negro
Negroes
noticeable
noticing
origin
original
passed
past
possess
possession
prefer
preferred

prejudice
prevalent
probably
proceed
procedure
prominent
psychology
psychoanalysis
psychopathic
psychosomatic
pursue
realize
really
repetition
rhythm
sense
shining
studying
surprise
thorough
tries
tried
useful
useless
using
varies
various
weather
whether

WORDS MISSPELLED 40 TO 49 TIMES

accept
acceptance
acceptable
accepting
accident
accidentally
acquaint
acquaintance

across
aggressive
appear
appearance
article
athlete
athletic

attended
attendant
attendance
challenge
character
characteristic
characterized
coming

WORDS MISSPELLED 40 TO 49 TIMES (continued)

convenience
convenient

difference
different

disappoint

discipline
disciple

dominant
predominant

effect

exaggerate

foreign
foreigners

fundamental
fundamentally

government
governor

hero
heroine
heroic
heroes

humor
humorist
humorous

hypocrisy
hypocrite

incident
incidentally
independent
independence

liveliest
livelihood
liveliness
lives

mere

operate

opinion

opportunity

paid

particular

philosophy

planned

pleasant

possible

practical

prepare

quantity

quiet

recommend

ridicule
ridiculous

speech

sponsor

summary
summed

suppose

technique

transferred

unusual
usually

villain

woman

28d
spell

WORDS MISSPELLED 30 TO 39 TIMES

advice
advise

approach
approaches

author
authority
authoritative

basis
basically

before

careless
careful

carrying
carried
carries
carrier

conceive

conceivable

condemn

consider
considerably

continuous

curiosity
curious

dependent

desirability
desire

efficient
efficiency

entertain

extremely

familiar

finally

friendliness
friend

fulfill

further

happiness

hindrance

influential
influence

knowledge

laboratory

maintenance

ninety

oppose
opponent

optimism

WORDS MISSPELLED 30 TO 39 TIMES (continued)

parallel	relieve	therefore
permanent	religion	together
permit	response	undoubtedly
physical	satire	weird
piece	significance	where
propaganda	suppress	whose
propagate	temperament	you're

WORDS MISSPELLED 20 TO 29 TIMES

accompanying	completely	hear
accompanies	counselor	here
accompanied	counsel	huge
accompaniment	council	hungry
accomplish	curriculum	hungrily
accustom	dealt	hunger
actually	despair	ignorance
actuality	disease	ignorant
actual	divide	indispensable
adolescence	divine	intellect
adolescent	especially	interfere
against	excitable	interference
amateur	exercise	interrupt
amount	expense	involve
appreciate	experiment	irrelevant
appreciation	fallacy	laborer
approximate	fantasy	laboriously
arouse	fantasies	labor
arousing	favorite	laid
attack	fictitious	later
attitude	field	leisure
boundary	financier	leisurely
Britain	financially	length
Britannica	forward	lengthening
capital	guarantee	license
capitalism	guaranteed	likeness
certain	guidance	likely
certainly	guiding	likelihood
chief		luxury
clothes		magazine

WORDS MISSPELLED 20 TO 29 TIMES (continued)

magnificent	phase	source
magnificence	playwright	story
maneuver	politician	stories
mathematics	political	straight
meant	primitive	strength
mechanics	regard	strict
medicine	relative	substantial
medical	remember	subtle
medieval	reminisce	suspense
miniature	represent	symbol
mischief	roommate	synonymous
moral	sacrifice	tendency
morale	safety	themselves
morally	satisfy	them
narrative	satisfied	theory
naturally	scene	theories
noble	schedule	those
obstacle	seize	thought
omit	sentence	tragedy
peace	sergeant	tremendous
perceive	several	vacuum
persistent	shepherd	view
persuade	simply	whole
pertain	simple	yield
	sophomore	

28e
Using Hyphens

Hyphens are used to form compound words and to avoid confusion. Hyphens relate both to spelling and to style, and in using hyphens writers often have several options. For example, you could write *life-style* or *life style* or *lifestyle* and be correct in each case. A dictionary is the best help when you are unsure about using a hyphen.

The points below explain the most regular uses of hyphens.

Joining Two Nouns

Often in modern American English, a hyphen will join two nouns to make one compound word. Scientists speak of a *kilogram-meter* as a measure of force, and personnel managers speak of a *clerk-typist,* an employee who does general office work plus typing. The hyphen lets us know that the two nouns work together as one.

As compound nouns that once were new constructions come into general use, their hyphens tend to disappear. The nouns come to be written as one word, such as *housefly, firelight, firefight,* and *thunder-shower.*

Linking Nouns and Other Parts of Speech

A noun can be linked with an adjective or an adverb to form a compound word.

accident-prone	clear-out
by-product	first-rate

Designating Relations by Marriage

Use a hyphen to name people related to you by marriage rather than by birth.

brother-in-law	mother-in-law
sister-in-law	father-in-law

Linking Modifiers to Avoid Confusion

Hyphens often help us sort out modifiers that come before the word they modify. If we say "He was a hard running back," we might mean that he was hard and that he was also a running back. If we say "He was a hard-running back," we mean that he ran hard. If we say "She was a quick thinking person," we might mean that she was quick and that she was also thinking. If we say "She was a quick-thinking person," we mean that she thought rapidly.

Notice that the hyphenated words in these examples employ adverbs (*hard, quick*) that do not end in *-ly.* When adverbs end in *-ly,* they do not require a hyphen if they modify an adjective that in turn modifies a noun.

They explored the **newly discovered** territories.

They endured his **clumsily arrogant** bragging.

Modifiers that are hyphenated when they are placed *before* the word they modify are usually not hyphenated when they are placed *after* the word they modify.

He was a crisis-and-confrontation politician.

His politics were a mix of crisis and confrontation.

It was a bad-mannered reply.

The reply was bad mannered.

Attaching Prefixes

Hyphens are used to attach prefixes to some words. Often, for example, a hyphen joins a prefix and a capitalized word.

un-American, pre-Colombian, anti-Semitic

Prefixes are attached to a few words with hyphens even though the main word is not capitalized.

ex-husband, all-conference

The prefix *self-* is usually joined to a word by a hyphen.

self-interest, self-control, self-centered

Most prefixes, however, are not attached by hyphens. The prefix is simply joined to the stem with no punctuation:

antisocial   nonjudgmental

atypical   preliterate

Some proper nouns that are joined to make an adjective are hyphenated.

the Franco-Prussian war, the Sino-Japanese agreement, a Mexican-American heritage

Some numbers are hyphenated:

three-fourths of a gallon, twenty-five

■ **Exercise 28.6** Rewrite the following sentences to correct misspellings. Hyphenate words when necessary.

1. He beleived that the badly damaged plane could land safly.
2. The love them today leave them tomorrow philosophy is probly on the decline becaus people now unnerstan it's hypocricy.
3. His nervous laff was a hinderence to his carreer.
4. She remained an optomist though her experence told her that optomists often have trouble acommodating themselves to a pityless city.
5. He had a tendancy to miss classes as a sophmore, and his teachers were bad mannered enough to take attendence.

■ **Exercise 28.7** Add hyphens only where they are needed in the following words and phrases. Defend your choices.

1. an off color remark
2. narrow minded
3. preChristian
4. self motivated
5. her mother in law

CAPITALIZATION

Capital letters give readers signals about sentence patterns, names, titles, and pronouns. Most rules for use of capitals have been fixed by custom, but some rules are more flexible than others. A standard dictionary is a good guide to capitalization. Names that should always be capitalized are entered with capitals; all others are entered in lowercase (or small) letters. (Remember that capitalizing a word means that only the first letter in the word is capitalized; all other letters in the word appear in lowercase.)

29a
Capitalizing the First Word of a Sentence

The capital letter at the beginning of a sentence signals the reader that a new unit of thought is about to begin. The capital letter at the beginning of a sentence works with the punctuation mark at the end of the previous sentence to make reading easier.

> Because robots greatly reduce human error, the products they manufacture are of a much more uniform quality. But because they reduce human employment, robots risk eliminating part of the market for which their products are destined.

In sentence fragments used for special effects, capitalize the first word.

> But aside from good hair grooming, they are oblivious to everything but each other. Everybody gives them a once-over. Disgusting! Amusing! How touching!
>
> —Tom Wolfe

Why did she lie under oath on the witness stand to defend her husband? Because she knew he was innocent? No, because she knew he was guilty.

Some writers who ask a series of questions by using fragments do not capitalize the first word of each fragment.

How many individuals can we count in society? how many actions? how many opinions?

—RALPH WALDO EMERSON

The more common practice is to capitalize the first word in each fragment that answers a question.

And what are the fundamentals? Reading? Writing? Of course not!

—SLOAN WILSON

Most writers do not capitalize the first word of an independent clause immediately following a colon:

If a person suffer much from sea-sickness, let him weigh it heavily in the balance. I speak from experience: it is no trifling evil, cured in a week.

—CHARLES DARWIN

But some writers do capitalize the first word after a colon:

The answer is another question: How many days must go by before millions of people notice they are not eating?

—*The New York Times*

The first word in an independent clause following a semicolon is never capitalized unless it is a proper noun (see 29b below).

All in all, however, outside support counted for little; the men of the village did the work themselves.

—OSCAR HANDLIN

29b
Capitalizing Proper Nouns and Their Abbreviations

Proper nouns are the names of specific people or things, names that set off the individual from the species. Proper nouns include names like *Jane* (instead of the common noun *person*), *France* (instead of the common noun *country*), and *Empire State Building* (instead of the common noun *building*).

The following are all proper nouns.

Names and Nicknames of People

Wolfgang Amadeus Mozart, Ernest Hemingway, Jim Ed Rice, Ella Fitzgerald, John F. Kennedy, Sandra O'Connor, U. S. Grant, Gore Vidal, Joan Didion, the North Carolina Tarheels

Names of Places

France, the U.S.A., the USSR, Tennessee, the Panama Canal, Back Bay, the Mississippi Delta, the North Shore, the Irunia Restaurant, the Sierra Nevada, the Great Lakes

Official Names of Organizations

Phi Beta Kappa, the U.S. Department of Defense, The Authors' Guild of America, the University of Notre Dame, Cumberland College, Ford Motor Company, the Roman Catholic Church, the American Red Cross, the Boy Scouts of America, the NCAA, the NAACP

Days of the Week, Months, Special Days

Monday, July, Veterans Day, Christmas, Labor Day, Halloween, Yom Kippur, Earth Day, Pearl Harbor Day

Ethnic Groups, Nationalities, and Their Languages

Greeks, Chinese, Americans, Arabs, Turks; Greek, Chinese, English, Arabic, Turkish

The words *blacks* and *whites* generally are not capitalized when they are used to refer to ethnic groups, but many writers follow individual choice in this matter. The older and now less favored word *Negro* is capitalized.

29b
cap

Members of Religious Bodies and Their Sacred Books and Names

Jews, Christians, Baptists, Holy Bible, God, Allah, Hindus, Jesus Christ, Holy Spirit, the Koran, the Torah, Pentecostals, Christian Scientists

Many religious terms such as *sacrament, altar, priests, rabbi, preacher,* and *holy water* are not capitalized. The word *Bible* is capitalized (though *biblical* is not), but it is never capitalized when it is used as a metaphor for an essential book, as in this sentence: "His book *Winning at Stud Poker* was for many years the *bible* of gamblers."

Pronoun references to a deity worshiped by people in the present are sometimes capitalized, although some writers use capitals only to prevent confusion.

Allah, so Muslims believe, sent Mohammed to deliver **His** word to the world.

God helped Abraham carry out **His** law.

In each of the sentences above, the capitalization of the pronoun *His* helps avoid confusion. If the pronoun were not capitalized, readers might not be able to tell if it referred to Allah or Mohammed in the first sentence, or if the law mentioned in the second sentence was God's or Abraham's.

God acts for his own purposes and according to his own wisdom.

In this sentence the pronoun *his* is not capitalized, since no confusion would result. You may choose to capitalize the pronoun if you wish.

Pronoun references to deities no longer worshiped are not capitalized.

Jupiter, the Roman god of thunder and lightning, led a tempestuous love life that often got **him** into deep trouble with **his** wife, Juno.

Sometimes words not ordinarily capitalized do take capitals when they are used as parts of proper names.

My **aunt** is arriving this afternoon.
My **Aunt Lou** tells fantastic stories that I think she makes up.

I have to go to the **bank** before we leave.

The **Cambridge Bank** is on the corner.

I graduated from **high school** in 1951.
I went to **Lenoir City High School.**

Such appellations as *Mother, Father, Cousin, Brother,* and *Sister* may replace proper names in speech and writing. If you intend to refer to a specific individual, capitalize the word.

I still miss **Mother,** although she has been dead for over a decade.

He supposed that **Grandfather** would come to his aid again, as he had so many times in the past.

But most of the time these words are not capitalized, since they do not replace a proper name. Whether you capitalize such words depends on your intention.

I asked my **mother** to wake me at 5:00 A.M.

Some titles that may be capitalized before a proper name are often not capitalized when they are used after the name.

Everyone knew that **Governor** Grover Cleveland of New York was the most likely candidate for the Democratic nomination.

The most likely candidate for the Democratic nomination was Grover Cleveland, **governor** of the state of New York.

Writers and editors do not agree on the capitalization of titles. *President of the United States,* or the *President* (meaning the chief executive of the United States), is frequently but not always capitalized. Practice varies with other titles also. Some writers say, "I will speak to the *Governor* about your wish to give him a new Cadillac for his personal use." Others say, "The *governor* of this state received a Cadillac last week from an old political friend and business associate." Most writers say, "The *president* of this university has seventeen honorary degrees." Others will say, "The *President* of this university would rather have a winning football team than seventeen honorary degrees."

In general, editors and writers are tending to capitalize less, but it is still important to be consistent. If you write "the *President* of the *University,"* you should also write "the *Chair* of the *History Department.*" If you write "The *president* of the *university,*" you should also write "the *chair* of the *history department.*" And, of course, if you say "the *President* of the

29c

cap

University" in one place, you must capitalize in the same way whenever you write "the President of the University."

When proper names describe or identify common nouns, the nouns that follow are generally not capitalized.

> Sanka brand, Russian history, French fries, Pennsylvania-Dutch shoofly pie, English literature

Use capitals for abbreviations made from capitalized words or for words formed from the initial letters of words in a proper name. (These words, called acronyms, are discussed in 30e. With some few exceptions (*U.S.A., M.B.A., Ph.D.*), do not use periods between the letters.

> WAC, FBI, NOW, UNESCO, ANZAC, NCAA, SWAT

Abbreviations used as parts of proper names usually take capitals.

> T. S. Eliot; Sammy Davis, Jr.; George Sheehan, M.D.

Words derived from capitalized words generally keep the capitals of the original words.

> Reaganomics, Miltonic, Hollywoodiana

29c
Capitalizing Titles of Literary and Art Works

Capitalize the major words of the title of any piece of writing and of any work of art or architecture. Do not capitalize the articles (*a, an,* and *the*) or prepositions and conjunctions of fewer than five letters unless they begin the title. Capitalize the first word after a colon or semicolon in a title.

> *Pride and Prejudice (book)*
> *The Taming of the Shrew (play)*
> the *Eiffel Tower (architecture)*
> the *Titanic (ship)*
> the *Mona Lisa (painting)*
> "Beating the Market: How to Get Rich on Stocks" *(magazine article)*
> "On Old Age" *(essay)*
> *Two Years Before the Mast (book)*

Note that the preposition *Before* in the last title is capitalized. The general rule is that a preposition or conjunction of five letters or more is capitalized.

✓ **CHECKLIST: APPROPRIATE USE OF CAPITALS**

This checklist highlights appropriate uses for capitals; the numbers in color refer to the appropriate sections in the text.

Sentence conventions 29a, 29d

After periods, the pronoun *I*, quotations, after colons
> They laughed. The child grinned.
> When I finally spoke, I whispered.
> She said, "Let me check your blood pressure."
> This is clear: The (*or* the) lake is unfit for swimming.

<u>BUT</u>:
> They laughed; the child grinned.
> Did she ask who arrived?
> He said that fear can blind judgments.

People 29b

General George Patton
Justice Thurgood Marshall
D. K. Rivera, **M.D.**
Chancellor Joseph Murphy
The Governor (*or* governor) waved to the crowd.
Uncle Kwok; hearing Uncle (*or* uncle) speak
<u>BUT</u>: the general, the judge, a doctor, the chancellor, a governor, my uncle

Geographical locations 29b

Zimbabwe, Rhodesia
Pike's Peak
Tennessee
Main Street
Lake Placid
<u>BUT</u>: a new country, a historical mountain, this state, the street, a lake

Areas, regions, directions 29b

the Middle East
the West Coast
Northwest Territory
in the South
<u>BUT</u>: an eastern route, turn south, the territory, a midwesterner

Historical events, names, movements, and writings 29b, 29c

World War II
the Louisiana Purchase
Modernism
the Bill of Rights
Moby Dick
"To Autumn"

Continued

29c

cap

✓ CHECKLIST: APPROPRIATE USE OF CAPITALS

BUT: a war, a bill, a philosophy, a document, amendments, laws, a novel, that event, the book

Institutions, groups, and organizations 29b

Democratic Party
Boston Red Sox
the High School of Music and Art
University of Maryland
the Knights of Columbus
Bank Leumi
McGraw-Hill Publishing Company
USN
BUT: political party, team, a high school, this university, the organization, our bank, the company, the navy

Academic subjects 29b

English, Chinese, Indian religions
Mathematics 13
BUT: language, theology, mathematics, psychology, history, senior class

Religion, race, nationality, sacred things 29b

Judaism, Catholics
Old Testament
Almighty God
Allah
Caucasian, Negro, black or Black
Pakistani
BUT: my religion, a race of people

Days, months, holidays 29b

Tuesday
June
Labor Day
BUT: tomorrow, this month, spring, summer, fall, winter

Plants, animals, games, illnesses 29b

African violet, Queen Anne's lace
Siamese cat
Monopoly
Addison's anemia
BUT: elm tree, rose, kiwi, baseball, measles, pneumonia

29d
Capitalizing First Words of Dialogue

When you include spoken dialogue in quotation marks, capitalize the first word.

> "You're going to kill us both!" she shouted.
> "Calm down," he shouted back. "I spent just thirty minutes learning to drive this motorcycle, and we're already doing a hundred miles an hour."
> "Help!" she said.

Indirect quotations and questions require no capitals for words attributed to a speaker or writer.

> She said that jazz was one of the many contributions of blacks to world culture.

> He asked me which I liked better, bluegrass music without drums and electrically amplified instruments, or the more modern country music that is akin to soft rock.

Many authors in earlier centuries and some writers today—especially poets—have used capitals in eccentric ways. If you are quoting a text directly, reproduce the capitalization used in the source, whether or not it is correct by today's standards.

> Sun and moon run together in one of Pyramus's speeches, "Sweet Moon, I thank thee for thy sunny Beams."
>
> —ELIZABETH SEWELL

29e
Capitalizing Consistently and Carefully

Use capitals consistently when you have a reason for doing so, but avoid them when they are not necessary.

Some inexperienced writers are tempted to use capitals for emphasis, and they capitalize too much. Unnecessary capitals may confuse readers or irritate them. In modern prose, the tendency is to use lowercase whenever possible.

The Department of Agriculture and the Department of the Interior have often had conflicts because of overlapping jurisdictions. Both departments have responsibility for the American land. The secretary in charge of each department usually wants to increase his own power. The Congress must sometimes step in and arbitrate the disputes between the two. But a strong secretary of agriculture or a greedy secretary of the interior can quickly undo any compromise made between the departments.

In this paragraph the noun *department* is not capitalized when it stands alone, nor is *secretary* when it designates an office rather than a title preceding a name:

Secretary Lyng
Secretary of Agriculture Lyng
Richard E. Lyng, secretary of agriculture in the Reagan administration

■ **Exercise 29.1** Follow the directions in each item below, and write full-sentence responses. Observe the conventions of proper capitalization.

1. Name the professor in your school whose lectures you find most interesting.
2. Name the city and state (or city and country) where you were born.
3. Name a supermarket at which you or your family members buy groceries.
4. What is your favorite season of the year?
5. In what direction must you walk or ride to get to campus?
6. In what region of the country did you grow up?
7. What two academic subjects do you enjoy most?
8. Name a book you enjoyed reading recently.
9. What is your favorite TV show?
10. Name your favorite holiday.
11. What is your favorite flower?
12. What was the name of your high school? (Use the words *high school* immediately after the name of the institution.)

■ **Exercise 29.2** Fill in the correct capital or lowercase letters in the blanks below. Explain your choices.

1. __ hen __ overnor Blankenship stood on the steps of the state __ apitol __ uilding and said to the __ resident of the __ nited __ tates, "__ he states in the __ outh need more of the __ overnment's support," my neighbors on Main __ treet applauded wildly.

2. __ t the __ an __ iego __ oo last summer, I disliked the __ onkeys and the __ pes because they looked so much like little men and women in a cage, but I was fascinated by the reptile house, where I saw the __ frican __ ock __ ython as well as the __ ndian __ obras and the __ oa __ onstrictor.

3. __ ake __ ociology 320, a __ ourse in the __ ociology of __ eligion, where you learn to understand some of the strengths of __ rotestantism, __ udaism, and __ oman __ atholicism.

■ **Exercise 29.3** Rewrite the following sentences, using capital and lowercase letters correctly.

1. during Summer i like to visit the Ski Resorts in vermont, where few visitors disturb my meditations among the Fir Trees and the Maples that dot the Landscape.

2. when I was a child, thanksgiving day was one of the best holidays, not only because the family always got together for a huge dinner but also because thanksgiving came on thursday, and at Belmont high school, we were given both thursday and friday off.

3. in your sophomore course in english literature next fall, you may read at least one novel by daniel defoe, whose book *robinson crusoe* is sometimes called the first novel in the english language.

4. when we had our accident, we were taken to memorial hospital on greeley parkway, where a doctor named thomas babington examined us and told us there was nothing wrong with us.

5. later, when i discovered that i had a fractured skull and that my brother had a broken leg, we sued the hospital, but the hospital claimed that dr. babington was only visiting the emergency room that day and was not an employee of memorial hospital at all.

CHAPTER

30

NUMBERS AND ABBREVIATIONS

Variations in the styles of authors and in the demands of editors make it difficult to fix rules for figures and abbreviations. In some newspapers and some magazines, the use of figures to express numbers may be common. In books, figures and abbreviations are less common, at least in the body of a text. In footnotes, bibliographies, scientific or technical reports, letters, charts, tables, and graphs, figures and abbreviations must be used no matter what the publication.

You should use figures sparingly for numbers in standard essays, and you should use abbreviations for words only when convention allows. Spell out most abbreviations when you use them the first time in an essay.

30a
Spelling Out Numbers

In general, spell out numbers up to one hundred and round numbers over one hundred. But when spelled-out numbers would take a great deal of space, use figures, even in the body of an essay.

six cartons   BUT   181 cartons

twenty-four dollars   BUT $23.88

forty thousand children   BUT   39,658 children

three million chickens   BUT   4,623 chickens

If you must begin a sentence with a number, spell the number out.

30b
Using Figures

Use figures for statistical comparisons, for quantitative information, and for dates, times of day, and addresses.

In writing about some subjects, numbers are so frequent that you should write them as figures.

> The original plan for the house called for a dining room that would be 18 × 25 and a living room that would be 30 × 34 with plate-glass windows at each end.

Dates that include the year usually appear as figures, but some writers prefer to spell them out.

October 9, 1893	The ninth of October 1893
9 October 1893	October ninth (**NOT** October 9th)
the 1960s	the nineteen-sixties
1929–1930	from 1929 to 1930

The time of day followed by the abbreviation **A.M.** or **P.M.** is always expressed in figures.

> 6:00 **A.M.**, 6 **A.M.**, 8:15 **P.M.**
>
> six o'clock in the morning
>
> a quarter past eight in the evening

Street and highway numbers almost always appear as figures except when a house number and the number of a street come together in an address. Then one of the numbers is written out.

1 Park Avenue	850 Fifteenth Street
Apartment 6J	State Highway 2
Interstate 80	

30c
Spelling Out Words

In formal essay writing, spell out most words rather than abbreviate them.

Spell out unfamiliar abbreviations

Common titles such as *Mr., Ms., Mrs.,* and *Dr.* are abbreviated even in formal prose. Other abbreviations may cut down readability, however, since a general audience may be unfamiliar with them or may not recognize them at all. But in some technical writing such as memos or reports intended for a limited audience, you may use abbreviations that are standard to that audience.

> **Not:** Dr. Ruth Smith and SOL Dean Th. Luciano discussed the std. rules about hab. corp. proceedings in the pol. cts. as they might apply to studs. arrested on DWI charges in the commercial dist. alg. Mass. Ave.

> **But:** Dr. Ruth Smith and School of Law Dean Thomas Luciano discussed the standard rules about habeas corpus proceedings in the police courts as they might apply to students arrested on charges of driving while intoxicated in the commercial district along Massachusetts Avenue.

If you use the name of an agency or an organization frequently in an essay or a report, you may abbreviate it to make the repetition less tedious. Write out the name of the agency or the organization the first time you use it and give the abbreviation in parentheses.

> The Student Nonviolent Coordinating Committee (SNCC) was far to the left of other civil rights organizations, and its leaders often mocked the "conservatism" of Dr. Martin Luther King, Jr. SNCC quickly burned itself out and disappeared, but some scholars now give the organization much credit for some of the progress made in civil rights during those hard years.

Spell out the names of countries, cities, boroughs, and states and the words *Avenue, Boulevard, Highway, Street, River,* and *Mountains* and words like them used as parts of proper names when they appear in the body of your prose.

> The Catskill Mountains of New York flank the Hudson River to the west.

Veterans Highway crosses Deer Park Avenue.

Cherokee Boulevard in Knoxville, Tennessee, runs by the Tennessee River.

Spell out the names of months and days of the week, and spell out people's names.

In September and October Charles visits the botanical gardens every Sunday.

Avoid the ampersand

Use an ampersand only if it is part of an official name.

Loneliness and poverty often accompany old age.

The stock index published by Standard & Poors is one of the most important economic documents in America.

The pistol was a Smith & Wesson.

Spell out parts of publications, company names

Spell out the words *pages, chapter, volume,* and *edition,* the names of courses of study, and words such as *company, brothers,* and *incorporated* unless they are abbreviated in official titles.

Chapter 16 presents new developments in open-heart surgery.

The eleventh edition of the Encyclopedia Britannica has thousands of pages without one typographical error.

You may use abbreviations for *page, chapter,* and *edition* in footnotes, endnotes, and bibliographical references (see 34c, d, and f).

Use the abbreviation *Inc., Corp., Co.,* or *Bros.* only when it is part of the official title of a company.

His brothers formed a toy company called Kidstuff, Inc., and later changed the name to Goldstein Bros.

Avoid the use of etc.

It is almost always better to name the items you intend to blanket under the abbreviation *etc.* than to use the abbreviation as a catchall. If you don't want to make a long list, use *and so on, and so forth, for example,* or *such as.*

This garden is good for planting lettuce, broccoli, spinach, radishes, onions, and other cool-weather vegetables.

OR

This garden is good for planting cool-weather vegetables — broccoli and spinach, for example.

OR

This garden is good for planting vegetables such as lettuce and broccoli.

When you do use *etc.*, do not put the conjunction *and* before it. The abbreviation *etc.* stands for the Latin *et cetera* or *et caetera*, which means "and the rest," so the *and* is included in the abbreviation itself.

30d
Abbreviating Familiar Titles

Use abbreviations for familiar titles that appear before or after a person's name. Commonly abbreviated titles that always precede the person's name include *Mr., Mrs., Ms., Dr., St., the Rev., the Hon., Sen., Rep.,* and *Fr.*

Fr. Louis joined our monastery twenty years ago.

Mrs. Jean Bascom designed the brick walkway in front of our building.

Dr. Epstein and Dr. Kwang consulted on the operation.

The Rev. Dr. Karl Barth visited Gettysburg, Pennsylvania, shortly before he died.

Mr. Roger Jackson will marry Ms. Joan Wilkerson.

Many women prefer the title *Ms.* instead of *Miss* or *Mrs.* (see Chapter 12). Strictly speaking, *Ms.* is not an abbreviation, since it does not stand for a word. But it is used in the same way *Mr.* and *Mrs.* are used — before a name. The title *Miss* is not an abbreviation, so it is not followed by a period. It always precedes the name.

Some abbreviations are always used after a proper name. Usually they indicate academic or professional degrees or honors. Note that a comma is placed between the name and the abbreviation and that a space follows the comma.

Kai-y Hsu, Ph.D.

Maria Tiante, M.D.

Elaine Leff, C.P.A., LL.D.

Michael Bartlett, Esq.

But spell out titles used without proper names:

Mr. Carew asked if she had seen the doctor.

Notice that when an abbreviation ends a sentence, the period at the end of the abbreviation itself will serve as the period of the sentence. If a question mark or an exclamation point ends the sentence, you must place such a punctuation mark *after* the period in the abbreviation:

When he was in the seventh grade, we called him "Stinky," but now he is William Percival Abernathy, Ph.D.!

Is it true that he now wants to be called Stanley Martin, Esq.?

30e
Using Common Acronyms

Abbreviate the names of agencies, groups, people, places, or objects commonly referred to by capitalized initials. *Most* of these abbreviations do not use periods; some do. Follow standard practice, and consult a dictionary if you have any doubts.

CIA **OR** C.I.A.

JFK **OR** J.F.K.

U.S. government **OR** US government

Washington, D.C. **OR** Washington, DC

Many government agencies are regularly referred to by their acronyms or abbreviations, especially in publications that mention them frequently. Often these abbreviations are so well known that they do not require any explanation.

The FBI entered the case immediately, since under the Lindbergh Act kidnapping is a federal crime.

Both the Secretary of Defense and high officials in NASA worry about Soviet military technology in space.

30f
Using Other Common Abbreviations

Abbreviate words typically used with times, dates, and figures.

6 P.M.   OR   6:00 P.M.   A.D. 1066

9:45 AM   OR   9:45 A.M.   6000 rpm

498 B.C.

Note that in common practice, the abbreviation A.D. is written before the number indicating the year, and the abbreviation B.C. is written after the year number.

30g
Avoiding Latin Abbreviations

Use English translations rather than Latin abbreviations.

compare	cf.
for example	e.g.
and others	et al.
and so on, and so forth, and the rest	etc.
in the same place	ibid.
that is	i.e.

Although new documentation systems for research papers use a minimum of abbreviations, you may come across these abbreviations in your own reading. A list of the most familiar abbreviations appears on pages 462–463.

30f/g
no/ab

■ **Exercise 30.1** Rewrite the following sentences, using numbers and abbreviations properly.

1. Dr. Muscatel's house was on 2d. Ave. near the warehouse of the Ledbetter bros.
2. He got up early every a.m. and stayed in his office in the p.m. until the last patient had left.
3. You could call him in the middle of the night, & the dr. would come to your house in 20 minutes.
4. When you saw him on the st., he always seemed deep in thought.
5. 1936 was the year he moved here, & FDR was Pres. of the USA.

31

ITALICS

To emphasize or set off certain words and phrases, printers use *italics,* a typeface in which the characters slant to the right. Since most typewriters lack an italic face, and since it is impossible to make italics in handwriting, writers preparing manuscripts underline the words that a printer would set in italics.

Handwritten

> *Katharine Hepburn gives one of her best performances in <u>The African Queen</u>.*

Typed

```
Katharine Hepburn gives one of her best
performances in The African Queen.
```

Printed

Katharine Hepburn gives one of her best performances in *The African Queen.*

31a
Italicizing Titles

In manuscript underline titles of books, magazines, journals, newspapers, plays, films, works of art, long poems, pamphlets, and musical works.

Joan Didion, a former editor of <u>Vogue</u> and <u>The National Review</u>, received glowing reviews in <u>The New York Times</u> for her novel <u>A Book of Common Prayer</u>.

In most titles, *a*, *an*, or *the* as a first word is capitalized and underlined. If titles of newspapers and magazines include the name of a city, you may decide whether to underline that name. You may write "the Los Angeles Times" or "<u>The Los Angeles Times</u>." Writers often do not underline or use italics for the initial *the* in the title of a periodical. But no hard-and-fast rule exists here. In most titles other than those of periodicals, *a*, *an*, or *the* as a first word is usually italicized and capitalized.

Picasso's *Guernica* captures the anguish and despair of violence.

Plays by Shakespeare provide details and story lines for Verdi's opera *Falstaff*, the musical comedy *Kiss Me, Kate* by Cole Porter, and Franco Zeffirelli's film *Romeo and Juliet*.

Edwin Newman's book *A Civil Tongue* is an amusing essay on modern language.

This book is titled *The McGraw-Hill College Handbook*.

Special Cases

Some publishers of newspapers, books, and magazines have special rules for the use of italics. They often use quotation marks to save money in setting type or to conform to a preferred format. Usually such publishers give their writers a style manual to ensure consistency. *The New Yorker*, for example, italicizes newspaper titles but places the titles of books, musical works, films, and plays in quotation marks. Most newspapers use quotation marks where formal writing requires italics.

Nelson Gidding did the adaptation of the Shirley Jackson novel "The Haunting of Hill House."

—*The New Yorker*

On our way, dodging snowflakes, we picked up the Sunday *Times* to see what had happened to the world.

—*The New Yorker*

As readers of "Crazy in Berlin" and "Little Big Man" ought to know, you can never tell what to expect from a novel by Thomas Berger.

— CHRISTOPHER LEHMANN-HAUPT (in *The New York Times*)

In most writing, quotation marks indicate only the titles of short works — essays, newspaper and magazine articles and columns, short stories, television and radio programs, short poems, songs, chapters or other subdivisions in books, and unpublished dissertations and theses (see 26c).

Elizabeth Cullinan's "Only Human" appears in a collection of her stories called *Yellow Roses*.

Exceptions

In referring to the Bible or other sacred books such as the Koran, to court cases, or to government documents, use neither italics nor quotation marks.

The Book of Ecclesiastes provides some of the most haunting phrases in the Bible.

In Brown vs. Topeka Board of Education, the United States Supreme Court handed down a far-reaching interpretation of the Constitution.

Do not underline the title of your paper on the title page. When titles of books appear on the jacket, the binding, or the title page, they are not italicized. The titles of articles are not italicized or placed in quotes when they appear in the title position in a journal or a book.

31b
Italicizing Foreign Terms

Underline most foreign words and phrases.

They are wise to remember, however, one thing. He is Sinatra. The boss. *Il Padrone.*

— GAY TALESE

Chota hasari — the little breakfast — consists of a cup of tea at five-thirty or six in the morning, with possibly some fruit or toast served with it. At eleven or at midday a heavier meal is eaten, *chapatis* — thin unleavened wheat cakes — and curry, with *dal* — a kind of lentil soup — and curds and sweets of some sort.

—SANTHA RAMA RAU

Memphis, in fact, was definitely the mecca, yardstick and *summum bonum.*

—TERRY SOUTHERN

Many foreign words have become so common in English that everyone accepts them as part of the language, and they require no underlining or italics — words like rigor mortis (Latin), pasta (Italian), sombrero (Spanish), bête noire (French), and festschrift (German). In the sentence by Terry Southern above, a city in Saudi Arabia — Mecca — has given its name as a common noun meaning any place where large numbers of people go to have some uplifting experience.

Some foreign words are still borderline, and some writers underline them while others do not — words like *ex nihilo* (Latin for "from nothing"), *imprimatur* (Latin for "Let it be printed"), and *Weltanschauung* (German for "world view"). Often the preference of the writer or the need for a special effect dictates the decision to underline or not.

Dictionaries offer some help. By labeling as *French* a phrase like *mise-en-scène,* for example, a dictionary guides your decision to underline. Some dictionaries have special sections headed "Foreign Words." Others italicize foreign words when they appear. But writers must use their own judgment about the borderline words. Here it is good to consider your audience and to try to imagine the expectations that readers may bring to your work.

31c
Italicizing Words Used as Words

Underline (to indicate italics) words or phrases you use as words rather than for the meaning they convey.

> The use of the word *glide* at the end of the last stanza is effective and gives just the amount of emphasis required at the end of the poem.
>
> — CLEANTH BROOKS AND ROBERT PENN WARREN

> And if the word *integration* means anything, this is what it means: that we, with love, shall force our brothers to see themselves as they are, to cease fleeing from reality and begin changing it.
>
> — JAMES BALDWIN

Letters used alone also require underlining to show italics.

> The word *bookkeeper* has three sets of double letters: double *o*, double *k*, and double *e*.

Some writers use quotation marks to show that words are being used as words.

> When I was in graduate school in the late fifties, "criticism" was still a fighting word.
>
> — GERALD GRAFF

31d
Italicizing the Names of Ships and Vehicles

Underline the names of ships, and those of air and space vehicles as well.

> I packed my valise, and took passage on an ancient tub called the *Paul Jones* for New Orleans.
>
> — MARK TWAIN

Lindbergh had flown his tiny plane, *The Spirit of St. Louis,* from San Diego to New York, with one stop at St. Louis, in the elapsed time of twenty-one hours, clipping five hours from the transcontinental record.

—WILLIAM L. SHIRER

31e
Using Italics for Emphasis

Use italics for emphasis only occasionally. Too many italicized words will tire your readers; their eyes may leap over the underlined or italicized words — the very opposite effect from what you intended. Too much emphasis may mean no emphasis at all.

Weak: You don't *mean* that your *teacher* told the whole *class* that *he* did not know the answer *himself?*

Revised: It was your teacher, then, who astonished the class by not knowing the answer?

An occasional word in italics helps you emphasize a point:

That advertisers exploit women's subordination rather than cause it can be clearly seen now that *male* fashions and toiletries have become big business.

—ELLEN WILLIS

It now seems clear that we are not going to improve instruction by finding *the* method or methods that are good for all peoples.

—K. PATRICIA CROSS

In written dialogue, writers may use italics to emphasize words to show the rhythms of speech used by characters.

The lady, however, regarded it very placidly. "I shouldn't have gone if she *had* asked me."

—HENRY JAMES

31e
ital

As they turned to him, Blackburn said: "Can *you* give *me* a few minutes, Dr. Howe?" His eyes sparkled at the little audacity he had committed, the slightly impudent play with hierarchy.

—LIONEL TRILLING

■ **Exercise 31.1** Underline any words or phrases that require italics in the following sentences.

1. An advertisement in the San Diego Evening Tribune announced a cruise on the Queen Elizabeth II, but after I read Katherine Anne Porter's novel Ship of Fools, a vacation on the sea did not interest me.

2. Time reported that Da Vinci's painting The Last Supper had deteriorated seriously from pollution and neglect.

3. The word hopefully is common nowadays, but many people who take writing seriously object to it because they think the words I hope or we hope or it is hoped usually express the meaning more clearly.

4. By the time the police discovered the body, rigor mortis had set in, and Inspector Michaelson told reporters from the Times and the Globe that death had taken place about twelve hours before.

5. Russell Baker's column Observer appears in the New York Times several days a week.

■ **Exercise 31.2** Rewrite the following sentences to eliminate excessive emphasis. You may change the wording. You may also change the order of the sentences.

1. Mr. Watt promised that this was *absolutely* the last time that he or *any other* member of his department would even *mention* digging a coal mine in Yellowstone National Park.

2. Who could *possibly* have known that the landing gear *was* defective and that the pilot was *drunk*?

3. The crew of the space shuttle *firmly* believed that the *engineering problems of the flight were less serious than the psychological problems of living so close together under such a demanding* routine.

4. *Anyone* desiring to change sections *must* file a form with the registrar *before* Friday afternoon.

5. Do you *really* like *country* music?

PART SEVEN
WRITING A RESEARCH PAPER

PART EIGHT
OTHER WRITING TASKS

BOOK THREE

SPECIAL WRITING TASKS

PART
SEVEN

WRITING
A RESEARCH
PAPER

CHAPTER

32

STARTING A RESEARCH PROJECT: LOCATING SOURCES

Research projects rely on careful investigation of varied sources in the library and elsewhere. These sources include not just the obvious books, periodicals, and reference items but also films, plays, concerts, television programs, videotapes, audiotapes, records, computer programs, microfilm, and microfiche. Anything that can provide accurate information efficiently is a tool in the researcher's hands. Thus research often involves interviews; a reporter digging into corruption among city officials, for example, needs firsthand contact with municipal leaders and their aides. Often research involves telephone calls and casual conversations with your friends, teachers, or other experts who can help set you on the path to information quickly.

The chapters in this part of the handbook focus on a paper about short stories by Willa Cather. This paper draws on the documentation methods established by the Modern Language Association of America (MLA) and recommended for research in literature and the humanities. Because the conventions of writing about research can vary from discipline to discipline, we also present excerpts from a paper on a scientific topic, the phenomenon of black holes. This paper draws on the documentation methods established by the American Psychological Association (APA) and recommended for research in the social sciences. The more you know about the conventions of the various disciplines, the easier it will be for you to investigate sources and to present your findings for different courses of study.

Thinking through a research paper is much like thinking through any other written composition, even though research papers differ in content and format from other kinds of papers. The planning guidelines set forth in these chapters should help you to produce a successful paper.

32a
Choosing a Topic

Choose a subject that interests you, and develop a limited topic by doing prewriting exercises and using the library. Discuss the topic with friends or your instructor.

Select a general subject that fits both your own interests and your assignment. Think about various topics within that general area; then discuss them with people you know. Try brainstorming, jotting down ideas in an informal list, asking yourself questions about your subject, writing nonstop, or developing a subject tree (illustrated in 1a).

Prewriting exercises will help you explore what you already know about the subject and identify areas you would like to know more about. See, for example, how developing an informal list helped the writer of the paper on Cather to narrow diffuse ideas to a topic of more manageable proportions.

**32a
sources**

Informal List

Willa Cather
novel My Antonia my favorite in high school
  English
realistic picture of life on the frontier
hard existence for women
good descriptive detail
simple writing style, deep feelings though
hard to leave behind your family and move
  West
read one of Cather's short stories,
  "Sculptor's Funeral"
good short story writer: picture of the
  hard life for the artist on the Western
  plains
maybe read some other stories by Cather?
women as central characters? difference of
  effects of hard life on men and women?

```
making a new life in a new territory you're
  not prepared for
dangers of famine, weather, Indians
Where and how was Cather educated?
What was her life like as a writer?
What did other writers think of her work?
  book reviews?
Cather's view of her art? What was she
  trying to achieve in her stories and
  novels?
```

Once you have a preliminary idea for your paper, browse through the library. Check the card catalog, general reference books, and periodical indexes to see what other people have written on your topic. Preliminary reading in books and magazines helps you decide on the suitability of your topic and limit and sharpen its focus. This early exploring of books and magazines also will help you develop your topic and organize your later research.

How narrow a topic must you choose? The answer to that question depends on your interests, the nature of the assignment, the required length of the paper, the number and quality of available library materials, and the time you have to do your assignment. But try to narrow your topic as much as possible, because narrow topics allow you to use enough specific examples and details to keep readers interested. In the following examples, note how students narrowed their topics until they reached promising starting points for their papers.

Literature

Short stories
↓
Willa Cather's short stories
↓
The theme of isolation in Cather's short stories
↓
The theme of isolation in two stories by Cather

Astronomy

Current questions about the universe
↓
Black holes
↓
How black holes might be located in space
↓
Various techniques used in the search for black holes

As you do preliminary research, you may discover that you need to limit your topic further. Carefully limiting your topic will help you exclude many fruitless areas before you investigate them. For instance, the writer of the paper on Cather's stories (pp. 477–509) would have wasted time researching Cather's later novels, her views on naturalism in fiction, or the ups and downs of her reputation among critics.

When you think that you have a workable topic, talk about it with your instructor or with friends before you begin serious research. At this point, discussions with people whose judgment you trust can help you test your ideas and can lead to reshaping that may save time and work later on.

32b sources

■ **Exercise 32.1*** Choose three of the general subjects below, and limit each subject to produce at least one topic suitable for a research paper. (You may wish to choose one of these narrowed-down topics for your own library paper. Exercises marked with an asterisk [*] in this chapter and in Chapters 33 through 35 — that is, Exercises 32.1, 32.2, 32.3, 32.4, 33.1, 33.2, 33.3, 35.2, 35.4, 35.5 — are designed to help you with your own research project.)

1. black educators
2. mental illness
3. Vincent van Gogh
4. alcohol use in America
5. preschool education
6. urban novels
7. women corporate leaders
8. the history of the theater
9. cowboys
10. political essays
11. exercise
12. Carl Sandburg's poetry
13. jazz
14. existentialism
15. computers
16. mass transportation
17. dinosaurs
18. surrogate mothers
19. illegal aliens
20. one-act plays

32b
Learning About Libraries

Learn about the various libraries available to you. As you consider an appropriately narrow topic, check the library facilities on your campus and in the surrounding community.

If your college has only one library, that may simplify your life, but it may also limit your resources. Most large universities have several specialized libraries scattered across the campus. Your school may have both an undergraduate library and a graduate or a main library; it may have a science library and various other special collections. Many cities have large public libraries, and in cities that have several colleges, students in one school often can use the libraries of all the others.

The concept of the library is changing rapidly because new technologies to preserve information are competing with books and periodicals for shelf space. Many libraries collect phonograph records, films, audio- and videotapes, photographs, and microfilm or microfiche. *Microfilm* is a film on which printed materials are photographed, greatly reduced in size. *Microfiche* is a sheet of microfilm that can accommodate and preserve many pages of printed text in reduced form. Many libraries are now beginning to store information on compact disks that can be retrieved by computer.

32c
sources

Once you have chosen your topic and have put an initial limit on it, you should talk with a reference librarian who can tell you what resources are available for your research. Librarians enjoy helping people, and you can save time if you let them help you. Most librarians know not only the resources available in their own libraries, but also those you can consult elsewhere in the region. Ask for help at the very beginning. And as you write, ask for help whenever you need it.

32c
Making a Preliminary Bibliography

Find out what has been written about your subject and make a preliminary bibliography by using the library catalog, indexes to periodicals, reference books, and other sources.

Using the Library Catalog

A library catalog shows all the books owned by your library. Most libraries use *card catalogs*. Some libraries use bound volumes. Modern automation makes catalogs available on microfilm, microfiche, computers, compact disks, or a combination of these forms. Learn your library's catalog system as soon as you can; your librarian will help you use it efficiently.

If your library provides a card catalog, these cards are arranged alphabetically in the drawers, usually located near the circulation desk. At large schools with several libraries, each library has a card catalog. You may also find a union catalog in the main library listing all the holdings of the school's libraries, including the names of the libraries where the books can be found.

In the card catalog of your library, you will find that every book is listed on at least three cards: a *subject* card, a *title* card, and an *author* card. If it covers several subjects, the same book may be listed on several subject cards.

Author Entry: Catalog from Automated Library System

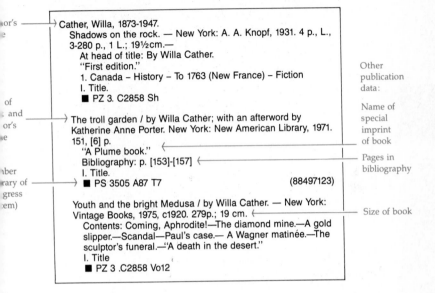

Title Entry: Catalog from Automated Library System

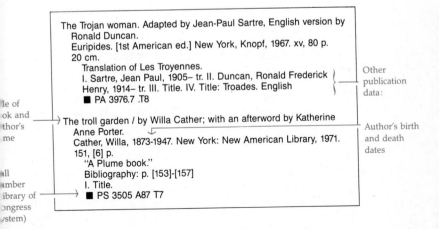

Card Catalog Entries

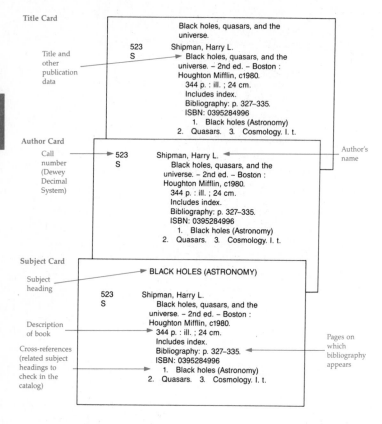

Title Card

Title and other publication data

Black holes, quasars, and the universe.

523
S
Shipman, Harry L.
Black holes, quasars, and the universe. – 2nd ed. – Boston : Houghton Mifflin, c1980.
344 p. : ill. ; 24 cm.
Includes index.
Bibliography: p. 327–335.
ISBN: 0395284996
1. Black holes (Astronomy)
2. Quasars. 3. Cosmology. I. t.

Author Card

Call number (Dewey Decimal System)

523
S
Shipman, Harry L.
Black holes, quasars, and the universe. – 2nd ed. – Boston : Houghton Mifflin, c1980.
344 p. : ill. ; 24 cm.
Includes index.
Bibliography: p. 327–335.
ISBN: 0395284996
1. Black holes (Astronomy)
2. Quasars. 3. Cosmology. I. t.

Author's name

Subject Card

Subject heading

Description of book

Cross-references (related subject headings to check in the catalog)

BLACK HOLES (ASTRONOMY)

523
S
Shipman, Harry L.
Black holes, quasars, and the universe. – 2nd ed. – Boston : Houghton Mifflin, c1980.
344 p. : ill. ; 24 cm.
Includes index.
Bibliography: p. 327–335.
ISBN: 0395284996
1. Black holes (Astronomy)
2. Quasars. 3. Cosmology. I. t.

Pages on which bibliography appears

32c sources

Libraries use a number system to organize books. To find a book, you need the *call number,* which appears in the catalog entry and on the spine of the book. Many libraries use the Library of Congress classification system. Others use the older Dewey Decimal System or a combination of the two. Whatever catalog system a library uses will be displayed on charts near the catalog and the circulation desk.

As soon as you pick a topic, find the subject section of the catalog and list the books related to that topic. You will probably notice that some authors seem to be experts in the field you are exploring. They may have written other books and articles, even though these titles were not listed in the subject catalog that you inspected during your preliminary research. Look them up in the author cards.

Even at this early stage, you should list each promising source on a separate 3×5 bibliography card. Record full publishing data for all your sources. The data you will need include the author's full name, the title of the book, its date and city of publication, and the publisher's name. (See the sample bibliography card, below.) Copy the names of editors and translators as well as volume numbers, names and numbers of series, and names of special imprints if any of this information appears in the catalog entry. When you get the book, you should check the data carefully against the information on the title page. Copying down full publishing data at this stage accomplishes two valuable tasks. First, it assures you that your notes are accurately and fully documented. Second, it saves you the trouble of going back to reference materials to copy data for your reference list after you have finished your research (see 34c and 34d).

**32c
sources**

Always include the call number at the bottom of your card. You must have this number, whether you search for the book in the stacks or fill out a slip asking someone to find the book for you. The call number identifies not only the book you want but also the general area in the library where you can find other books related to your topic. If you can go into the stacks in your library, check the shelves near the books you have found in the catalog. Look through them, and if they seem useful, jot down the titles and call numbers on bibliography cards so that you can go back to them later.

Sample bibliography card: book

Shipman, Harry L.
Black Holes, Quasars and the Universe.
2nd ed. Boston: Houghton Mifflin, 1980

523
S

Sample bibliography card: periodical

Daum, Bernard. "Willa Cather's Waste Land."
<u>South Atlantic Quarterly</u>.
Vol. 48
1949
pages 589-601

Using Indexes to Periodicals

General indexes to periodical literature list journal articles. A good index usually lists articles by year of publication, under various subject headings; some indexes list works by their authors' names as well. Some indexes also provide abstracts. An **abstract** summarizes the article, usually in a short paragraph, without criticizing it. Because this summary tells you much more than the title, it may save you considerable time.

Make bibliography cards for any articles that you think might relate to your subject. The data you record for periodicals include the name of the author, the title of the article, the title of the journal, the volume number of the journal, the year of publication, and the page numbers on which the article appears. Look at the formats for periodical entries on pages 443–445 and pages 458–460 before you prepare bibliography cards for periodicals; these formats show some of the other data you may need when you set up your reference list.

The periodical indexes have their own notation systems, and most of these formats do not match those required for documentation in your research papers. Unless you copy down data in the correct format on your bibliography cards, you may have trouble developing appropriate citations in your paper. You usually must check the article itself for information missing from the entry in the index—the author's first name, for example. Index entries also include information not required in footnotes or endnotes, so do not use an index entry as a model for your bibliography card.

The Readers' Guide to Periodical Literature (1900–)

The Readers' Guide is the best-known general guide to many popular periodicals. It is issued regularly (about every month) in paper covers throughout the year, and annual volumes appear in hard covers, fully indexed. Entries in *The Readers' Guide* are arranged by subject and by author. There is a helpful page of suggestions about how to use each volume, as well as a key to abbreviations used in the index.

Sample subject and author entries appear below. Marginal notations explain the parts of the entries.

32c sources

Subject Entry

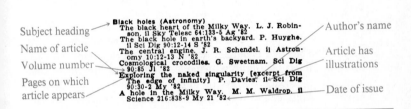

Author Entry

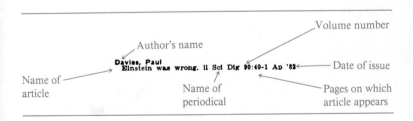

Other indexes

☐ *Access* (1975–) bills itself as "the supplementary index to periodicals," meaning that it indexes periodicals not included in *The Readers' Guide* and other general indexes. Even so, *Access* limits itself to the kind of periodical that you might find in a large magazine store.

□ *America: History and Life* (1964–), an especially useful index for the research writer investigating any topic dealing with American (including Canadian) history and culture, includes not only citations to articles but also abstracts.

□ *The British Humanities Index* (1962–), a British version of *The Readers' Guide,* indexes periodicals published in Great Britain and has a much broader range than its American counterpart because it includes scholarly and professional journals. It succeeds the *Subject Index to Periodicals,* published by the Library Association.

□ *Essay and General Literature Index* (1900–) lists essays and articles in essay collections in the humanities and social sciences.

□ *Humanities Index* (1974–) this includes entries from more than 250 periodicals in archeology, classics, language, literature, history, philosophy, religion, the performing arts, and folklore, arranged by author and subject. Book reviews appear in a separate section at the end.

□ *MLA International Bibliography of Books and Articles on the Modern Languages and Literatures,* an annual five-volume bibliography issued by the Modern Language Association, offers a classified list and index by subject of selections on modern languages, literatures, folklore, and linguistics. It draws on hundreds of books and periodicals as well as films, sound recordings, microfilms, and other machine-readable materials. Here is a typical entry, with marginal notes explaining the parts of the entry.

Entry: MLA Index

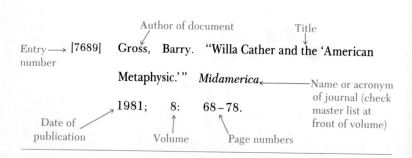

☐ *The New York Times Index* (1913–), an indispensable resource, includes all stories that have appeared in *The New York Times,* giving the date of each story, the page and column number of the paper, and an abstract of the entry. Cross-references are numerous.

☐ *Psychological Abstracts* (1927–). Abstracts of thousands of articles in psychology published every year make this volume an excellent tool for any topic with a psychological dimension.

☐ *Public Affairs Information Service Bulletin* (PAIS) (1915–), listing articles by subject, is a rich resource for almost any topic dealing with politics, economics, international relations, city planning, or other aspects of social or political life.

☐ *Social Sciences Index* (1974–) covers periodicals in the fields of anthropology, criminology, economics, law, political science, psychology, and sociology, among other areas of interest to social scientists. Here, too, a separate section of book reviews appears in each issue. From 1965 to 1974, the *Humanities Index* and the *Social Sciences Index* were published as the *Social Sciences and Humanities Index.* From 1907 to 1965 the name of the combined index was the *International Index.*

Other indexes to periodical literature deal with specialized fields and include citations to specialized journals. Some articles they list may help you in the later stages of your research, after you have summarized the information about your topic and have developed a general idea of what you want to say about it. Among the specialized indexes are the following:

Applied Science and Technology Index (1913–)

Art Index (1929–)

Arts and Humanities Citation Index (1978–)

Biography Index (1947–)

Biological and Agricultural Index (1964–)

Business Periodicals Index (1953–)

Current Index to Journals in Education (1969–)

Education Index (1929–)

Film Literature Index (1973–)

Index to U.S. Government Periodicals (1974–)

Music Index (1949–)

Social Sciences Citation Index (1973–)

Be sure to ask for help from your reference librarian.

Most periodicals publish their own annual indexes. When you work in a special field, consult the indexes of journals published in that field for articles useful in your research.

Using Standard Reference Books

You must do much more than merely repeat information you find in encyclopedias and dictionaries when you write a research paper. But it is always a good idea to use such reference works for background information and perhaps for inspiration to guide you to other ways to explore your topic. The reference section of your library will have several encyclopedias. Here are a few standard works you may wish to consult.

32c

sources

General encyclopedias

> *Collier's Encyclopedia*
> *Dictionary of American History*, 8 vols.
> *Encyclopaedia Britannica*
> *Encyclopaedia Judaica*, 16 vols.
> *Encyclopaedia of Religion and Ethics*, 13 vols.
> *Encyclopedia Americana*
> *Encyclopedia Canadiana*, 10 vols.
> *Encyclopedia of World Art*, 15 vols.
> *The Golden Bough: A Study in Magic and Religion*, edited by Sir James
>   G. Frazer, 13 vols.
> *Harvard Dictionary of Music*
> *The International Encyclopedia of Film*
> *International Encyclopedia of the Social Sciences*, 19 vols.
> *The McGraw-Hill Dictionary of Art*
> *The McGraw-Hill Encyclopedia of Science and Technology*, 15 vols.
> *New Catholic Encyclopedia*, 15 vols.
> *The New Columbia Desk Encyclopedia*
> *The New Grove Dictionary of Music and Musicians*, 20 vols.
> *The New York Times Film Reviews* (1913–)
> *The Oxford Classical Dictionary*, 2d ed.
> *The Oxford Dictionary of the Christian Church*

Literary research materials

When you write research papers for literature courses, you have a large body of research materials to draw from, including several outstanding works.

> ☐ *The Oxford Companion to American Literature*, 4th edition, edited by James D. Hart, offers biographies of American writers and sum-

maries of literary works written in English by Americans. This volume pays little attention to literature not written by U.S. authors, and it ignores Latin American writers.

☐ *The Oxford Companion to English Literature,* 4th edition, edited by Sir Paul Harvey, presents biographies of British writers and summaries of their important works; it also gives writers' biographies and summarizes plots of European literatary works considered influential in Britain and America.

☐ *The Oxford History of English Literature* comes in twelve volumes, each covering a period of literature and written by a distinguished specialist in that field.

☐ *The Year's Work in English Studies,* published in London annually since 1920, contains graceful, well-written summaries of books and articles published each year in the entire field of English literature.

☐ *Contemporary Authors* (1962 –) is a multivolume series giving short biographies and publication information for twentieth-century writers.

☐ *Contemporary Literary Criticism* (1976 –), another multivolume series, presents excerpts from reviews written by prominent critics of contemporary literature. The series has recently expanded to include film criticism.

☐ *The Harvard Guide to Contemporary American Writing,* edited by Daniel Hoffmann, 1979, surveys the works of the most prominent recent American writers.

**32c
sources**

Doing a Computer Search

Automated libraries now can store extensive information on sources and make the information quickly available to researchers. Using electronic reference lists, or **databases,** you can examine bibliographical information, as well as abstracts, cross-references, or summaries from hundreds of different sources. Good databases currently are available on the natural, applied, and social sciences, and you can save time by consulting one suited to your topic.

A successful electronic search starts with key words, or **descriptors,** which signal an area of interest and allow the computer to call up the articles. You need to match the key words for your topic with the words the database uses to call up information. Lists of key words accompany most databases. You should choose the most precise and specific descriptors that you can. A descriptor that is too general invariably produces an overly extensive list that will contain many selections you will not be able to use. When your key word does not trigger enough information from the database, your librarian can help you select more useful terms.

Sample printout

32c
sources

```
File 47:MAGAZINE INDEX –1959–MARCH 1970, 1973–86/SEP
(COPR. IAC) FMT 9 = $3.50

    Set   Items   Description
    ---   -----   -----------
?ss black( )hole? and astronomy

    S1   11064   BLACK
    S2    1093   HOLE?                                  ⎞   Number of entries
    S3     234   BLACK (W) HOLE?                        ⎬── for descriptors
    S4    2530   ASTRONOMY                              ⎠
    S5     126   BLACK ( ) HOLE? AND ASTRONOMY   ◄────  Target set
?ss s5/1986: 1987

           126   S5  ◄───────────────────  Limit "S5" (i.e., descriptor
    S6   75855   PY = 1986 : PY = 1987              Black holes and Astronomy)
    S7       3   S5/1986: 1987  ◄──────────  by dates 1986 and 1987
?type 7/5/all  ◄─────────────  Type out entries
```

```
7/5/1
2090944   DATABASE: MI File 47  ◄── Entry
    Falling into a black hole.  ◄──────── Title of article        Volume,
    Thomsen, Dietrick E.  ◄──────── Author's name                 page, and
    Science News   v130   p40(1)   July 19 1986  ◄── date
    CODEN: SCNEB  ◄──────── Code name for journal Science News
    NAMED PEOPLE: Gaskell, Martin—research  ◄── People named in article
    DESCRIPTORS: black holes (astronomy)—observations; quasars—observations
```

Name of journal

Abbreviation for "code name"

```
7/5/2
2086156   DATABASE: MI File 47  ◄───────────────── Entry
    Through a lens, darkly: the most massive object ever discovered. (black
hole gravitational lens)
    Discover   v7   p6(2)   July   1986
    illustration; chart  ◄──────── Features of article
    CAPTIONS: black hole gravitational lens.
    DESCRIPTORS: Black holes (Astronomy)—observations; Gravitational lenses
    —observations;   Gravitational   lens   effect—research;   Astronomy—
    Observations
                                              Key words
7/5/3
2041048   DATABASE: MI File 47  ◄──────── Entry
    Galactic center update.
    Killian, Anita
    Sky and Telescope   v71   p255(1)   March   1986
    CODEN: SKTEA
    illustration; chart
    CAPTIONS: Galactic center.
    DESCRIPTORS: Galaxies—research; Milky Way—observations; Black holes
(Astronomy)—research
```

   With most databases you will be able to print out the titles the computer produces. Before you do, examine the number of citations and the format in which they will appear. You may want to narrow your descriptors further or develop new combinations. You can command the computer to provide simple bibliographical data only, or you can request abstracts of articles as well as other relevant material. Ask only for what you need.

The student researching black holes used the *Magazine Index*, a popular database index available at many libraries. Using *astronomy* as a descriptor, he learned that more than 2,500 entries were available, far too many to be useful. The descriptor *black holes and astronomy*, on the other hand, had 126 entries, focusing the list on more relevant titles. The student then chose to limit the list further by requesting all items published in 1989 or 1990. Narrowing the search in this way produced just three titles, which the student asked the computer to name. Narrowing the search by dates, however, is not the only method of creating a manageable list of sources from the database. The student could have used one of these descriptors: *black holes and astronomy and evidence* or *black holes and astronomy and evidence or existence of,* among other possibilities.

32c sources

Marginal notes explain the entries in the sample printout shown at left on p. 412.

Using Bibliographies and Notes

Look carefully at the scholarly books and articles you consult to find useful bibliographies and notes. References to other books and articles often lead to new and useful sources of information.

In a 1984 collection, *Critical Essays on Willa Cather* by John J. Murphy, the student writing on Cather discovered a three-page list of sources after one of the essays. There she found a reference to a piece by Dayton Kohler in a 1947 issue of *College English*. Kohler's point about the effects of the barren landscape of the West on the human spirit helped the writer shape some of her ideas on Cather's stories.

■ **Exercise 32.2*** For any topic you narrowed down in Exercise 32.1 (p. 401), make a list of five indexes that you might use to help you locate articles in periodicals. Use the reference section of your library.

■ **Exercise 32.3*** If your library can do a computer search, make a list of key words relevant to your topic and check the list against the database descriptions. Print out a limited, focused list of sources.

■ **Exercise 32.4*** For any topic you narrowed down in Exercise 32.1, develop at least ten bibliography cards for books, periodicals, and other sources. Be sure to follow either the format suggested by your instructor or the format described in 32c as you copy the required data.

CHAPTER

33

PLANNING TO WRITE FROM SOURCES

Up to this point in your research project, you've concentrated on selecting and narrowing a topic suitable for research and on identifying appropriate libraries, reference tools, and other materials for investigation. Your main tasks now are to shape your thoughts about your topic by exploring some sources and taking notes. You should also develop a flexible plan for your paper. As you read and evaluate what you have read, your topic may change focus or emphasis, and your plan, too, will change. Reading, note taking, and planning will help you produce a well-written paper.

33a
Developing a Thesis and a Rough Plan

After prewriting and after limiting your topic, explore some of your resources for information about it. Your purpose at this stage is to develop your ideas about the topic.

Doing research is more than simply gathering information—it is developing something of your own to say about what you have read. Don't worry about the number of people who have already written about your topic. Some careful thought about your resources at this stage will stimulate your own original ideas. As your thoughts take shape, put together a hypothesis and a rough plan. Both will help you concentrate on the topic you expect to develop in your paper.

A **hypothesis** is a debatable assumption that you have to prove. A hypothesis is an educated guess. After some early exploration of your topic you should state tentatively what conclusion you expect your research to support. All researchers start with a hypothesis; it guides their investigations, helping them find appropriate sources and rule out others. For the paper on Cather, a sample of the early hypothesis and the topic from which it originated appears at the top of the next page.

Topic	Hypothesis
The theme of isolation in Cather's stories	In Cather's stories, characters isolated from familiar surroundings are severely affected physically and spiritually.

The student writing on Cather noted a remark one critic made about how the American West affected the lives of characters in Cather's novels, especially characters moving to the West from more "civilized" eastern societies. Was this true about characters in the short stories as well? As the student read Cather's stories and comments about them in secondary sources (see pp. 417–419), she could identify details that seemed to show the effects of separation on the body and spirit of central characters. Her hypothesis reflects the connection she sees between isolation from familiar worlds and its effects on people.

33a plan

As you continue reading and exploring, your hypothesis — even your topic itself — may change markedly. Other investigators may have disproved your idea. You may find that what seemed like promising sources offer little or no help. You may discover a new area of thought that reshapes your thinking and pushes you into new territory. At this stage your hypothesis is tentative, as is your plan for the research paper itself. As your reading continues and your hypothesis becomes more precise, you will refine your thoughts and develop a carefully worded thesis for your paper. In the paper on Cather you can see how the hypothesis changed as the writer thought about the topic during the course of her research (see 35a).

Your tentative plan and your thesis will help you eliminate from your reading list any books and articles that you cannot use.

The tentative thesis statement and the rough plan that follows might well have guided the writer of the paper on Cather.

Plan: Write about the effects of isolation in Willa Cather's short stories.

Tentative thesis: Cather's stories " 'A Death in the Desert' " and "A Wagner Matinee" deal with the theme of isolation.

1. Effects on characters' spirits
2. Effects on their appearance
3. How music is important

These preparatory steps bring the topic into focus for note taking and outlining. Of course, as you continue to read, you will make many changes, both in the thesis and in the rough plan.

■ **Exercise 33.1*** Do some preliminary reading to shape your ideas about the topic that you chose in Exercise 32.1. Then develop a tentative thesis and rough plan to guide your research.

33b
Using Primary and Secondary Sources

Read your sources with care, and take careful notes. Most of the sources you will use for a brief research paper will be *secondary*, although you should try to use *primary* sources whenever possible. **Primary sources** include works of literature, such as novels and poems; historical documents, such as diaries, letters, journals, speeches, and autobiographies; and interviews, private conversations, observations, and experiments. **Secondary sources** analyze and comment on other source material. The student writing about Willa Cather could use as a primary source one of Cather's short stories or novels or any of her other published works; as secondary sources, the student could use books or articles written about Cather or her fiction. Among the sources used for this paper, " 'A Death in the Desert' " and "A Wagner Matinee" are primary sources. Secondary sources include "Willa Cather and Her Music," and *Willa Cather: A Critical Introduction.*

Write your notes on 3×5 cards. Put only one idea on each card. Limiting your notes in this way will make it easier for you to organize your materials later (see 33c). Some students prefer larger index cards, but big cards make it tempting to copy down more information and more quotations than you need. Quote directly on your note cards only if you think you may use the quotation in your paper. Summarize or paraphrase many of your sources. Summarizing and paraphrasing force you to absorb the thoughts of your source and to express them in your own words rather than merely repeat them.

A **summary** is a sharply condensed version of an original source, in your own words. A summary usually states the thesis briefly and gives the main idea of the original. Your purpose in a summary is to condense important information and to eliminate unessential points.

A **paraphrase** is a much fuller summary; it may cite some of the evidence and use some of the words in the original source. A good paraphrase follows the line of reasoning in the original source and the sequence of ideas as well. In both paraphrases and summaries, you must acknowledge your sources.

Do not waste time copying down a long quotation or writing a paraphrase or a summary on a note card. Instead, make a signal card. On a **signal card,** note the page numbers where the information appears and record your thoughts about how a quotation might be used in your paper. Of course, you can't keep library books forever; so when you write signal cards, you should be ready to write your paper. If you think you may not have the book handy when you do write, copy down the material you need, either as a direct quotation or as a paraphrase. Because copying long direct quotations by hand leads to errors, you must proofread such passages with great care.

Copying machines are available in most libraries, and you can copy a page or two from a book or a periodical. (Such copying is strictly regulated by federal copyright laws, and your library may have regulations about the use of copying machines.) Remember that copying the source on a machine is no substitute for reading it. If you are going to use the source in your paper, you must read it carefully and make it part of your own thinking.

Often when you are taking notes, ideas about what you are summarizing, paraphrasing, or copying will occur to you. Be sure your notes distinguish your words and ideas from those of your source. In your paper you will have to identify the sources of all the ideas you have borrowed. If you do not make clear in your notes just whose ideas are whose, you may find yourself committing plagiarism (see 34g). Use parentheses, asterisks, arrows, or some other means to identify your own thoughts in your notes. Also, be careful to note page breaks when a quotation continues to another page. Only a small piece of what you record on a note card may appear in the final draft of your paper, and you must be able to report the exact page reference for the quotation you use.

Below is an excerpt from pages 280–281 of Sharon O'Brien's *Willa Cather: The Emerging Voice* (New York: Oxford University Press, 1987) on Cather's "A Wagner Matinee." Various types of note cards prepared from the excerpt follow it. Note that the writer has identified the source at the top of each card in an abbreviated form. (Full bibliographical data will appear on the writer's bibliography cards; see 32c.)

Source

In "A Wagner Matinee," for example, Cather integrates a family story into her fiction: Georgianna and her husband measure off their quarter section of land by tying a cotton handkerchief to a wagon wheel and counting off the revolutions, as had Cather's Aunt Franc and her husband George Cather when they first arrived in Nebraska in the 1880s.[8] In the grim portrayal of Georgianna's Nebraska farm, Cather also drew on her own memories of the difficult transition from Virginia to Nebraska, using her memories of her grandparents' farmhouse in describing Georgianna's bleak environment. Her portrayal of the gifted woman starving for music amid the "silence of the plains" also owes something to her own experience of aesthetic deprivation in Nebraska, a feeling intensified retrospectively when she discovered what her prairie education lacked. As she told Will Owen

Jones, the distaste she had felt for Nebraska was because she had been only half nourished there.[9] "The Sculptor's Funeral" also had real-life sources: Cather's witnessing an artist's funeral in Pittsburgh and, on another occasion, seeing the return of a Nebraska boy—in his coffin—to Red Cloud.

But there were dangers in turning from admiration to memory: the risk of punishment and retribution Cather had associated with self-exposure in her first college stories. After "A Wagner Matinee" appeared in *Everybody's Magazine* in 1904, a year before *The Troll Garden,* Cather faced a Nebraska uprising. The resulting controversy over the story was the "nearest she had come to personal disgrace," she told Viola Roseboro' later.[10] Like "The Sculptor's Funeral" and Hamlin Garland's *Main-Travelled Roads,* "A Wagner Matinee" portrays the Midwest as a harsh, oppressive, and repressive environment. Family members were particularly insulted by the supposed portrait of Aunt Franc in Georgianna and informed Cather that it wasn't "nice" to say such things in print. Friends and neighbors found the grim depiction of Nebraska unfair, and Cather was even attacked in her hometown paper by her old friend and colleague Will Owen Jones. "If the writers of fiction who use western Nebraska as material would look up now and then and not keep their eyes and noses in the cattle yards," he complained in the *Journal,* "they might be more agreeable company" (*WWC,* p. 254).

In the quotation card below, the exact words of the source are in quotation marks. An arrow distinguishes the writer's thought from that of the source. The summary card highlights the points in the passage that

Quotation Card

O'Brien, <u>Cather</u>, p. 281
"Her portrayal of the gifted woman starving for music amid the 'silence of the plains' also owes something to her own experience of aesthetic deprivation in Nebraska, a feeling intensified retrospectively when she discovered what her prairie education lacked."
→ Compare with Gerber and Stouck. This seems to be a major concern of Cather's—artist's survival on the frontier.

Summary Card

O'Brien, <u>Cather</u>, p. 281
Cather's own experiences contribute to the grim picture of Aunt Georgianna's Nebraska farm. Cather's own sense of artistic loss and weakness in education influences portrait of talented woman hungering for music on the plains.

33b
plan

concern the writer of the research paper. Note the many details omitted from the source. On the paraphrase card the notes closely follow the line of reasoning of the original, although the writer has used her own words to restate O'Brien's point. The few words in quotation marks are exact words from the source. Here too an arrow sets off the writer's own thoughts from the ideas in the original.

Paraphrase Card

O'Brien, <u>Cather</u>, p. 281
In "A Wagner Matinee" Cather drew on personal experiences such as measuring off land in Nebraska in the 1880s. Remembering her move from Virginia and the farmhouse of her grandparents in Nebraska, Cather portrayed "Georgianna's bleak environment." The picture of Georgianna and her lack of music on the silent plains relies on Cather's "own experience of aesthetic deprivation in Nebraska" and her sense of what she missed in her prairie education.
→ Where does phrase "silence of the plains" come from? Check stories, also sources at notes 8 and 9.

■ **Exercise 33.2*** Take notes as you read and consult the various sources you have selected for your research. Use the note cards on pages 418 to 419 as models.

33c
Organizing Notes

Read and organize your notes carefully, and use them to help you focus your ideas and develop your plan. Your early thesis statement and rough plan will guide your reading and note taking and will shape your thoughts about the topic. Your thoughts, in turn, will suggest changes in your thesis and plan. Don't worry if your thesis and plan change many times as you develop your outline, rough drafts, and final draft. Following a preliminary plan too rigidly keeps you from making the major changes in emphasis and organization that later reading and thinking often suggest.

If you have done your research carefully, you will have many note cards on which you have collected quotations, paraphrases, statistical information, and other data from your sources. Only one idea should appear on each card. Now you have to read your notes over carefully and organize them so that you can develop your paper.

In reading through your note cards, you should find that your material falls naturally into subject groups. The headings in your rough plan were your guide for taking and organizing notes from the beginning. By now you have probably clustered related data from various sources around the general headings. Yet as you reread your note cards, you will think of new major headings that bear on your topic and discover some old main headings that do not. You will also think of subheadings that flesh out the main headings.

At this point, you are ready to prepare a formal outline or to write a first draft. First, collect all your note cards, put them in order, and number them consecutively. Now you can prepare a summary guide that tells you, by number, where each note card fits into your plan. Excerpts from the summary guide developed for the paper on Cather are at the top of the next page.

This kind of guide helps you arrange the note cards according to tentative headings. And because the cards are numbered and each card includes the author's name and the title of the book or the article, you can keep track of your sources as you go along.

This system allows you to experiment. You can group and regroup related data and ideas and shift the order of subject groups around before

TOPIC SUMMARY GUIDE

Headings	Note cards
Music connections	3, 4, 6, 9, 22, 26, 30, 31
Artistic deprivation	1, 7, 12, 13, 14, 28
Physical strain of prairie life	2, 18, 32, 36, 37
Imagery of West	5, 24, 25, 46, 53
Imagery of "civilized" life	19, 59, 63, 64, 65, 68

**33c
plan**

you make any final decisions. This experimentation also can help you develop your plan by suggesting more effective headings and subheadings.

■ **Exercise 33.3*** Continue reading about your topic and taking notes. Using the rough plan you formulated in Exercise 33.1, develop a more detailed plan.

CHAPTER

34

CITING AND DOCUMENTING SOURCES

A research paper requires a thoughtful balance between your own language and the words and sentences you borrow from other sources. Intelligent use of source material is the heart of research writing. As a general rule of thumb, use quotations only when you feel that the original wording will add significantly to your point. Students are often tempted to quote lengthy passages, but this is not a good practice unless you have a clear, specific purpose for doing so. A lengthy passage can be tedious if the reader does not see why you didn't summarize it. Select quotations carefully and always keep them as short as possible.

To write a paper that does more than simply restate the ideas of others, you must interpret and evaluate source materials, provide commentary to clarify points, and assert your own conclusions. And you must acknowledge every source you use. You need to choose an appropriate and accepted method for citing and documenting materials you use in your paper.

34a
Integrating Material

Integrating source material smoothly into your writing takes thought and care. The thesis of your paper will determine the points you make, but you will be supporting those points with ideas drawn from sources and written in a language and style that may be quite different from your own.

Following the methods you used to record your data (see 33b), you could quote the source directly, or you could summarize, or paraphrase it. Suppose you wanted to use part of this passage, which appears at the end of the short story "A Wagner Matinee" by Willa Cather. The passage is about Aunt Georgiana, the main character.

The concert was over; the people filed out of the hall chattering and laughing, glad to relax and find the living level again, but my kinswoman made no effort to rise. The harpist slipped its green felt cover over his instrument; the flute players shook the water from their mouthpieces; the men of the orchestra went out one by one, leaving the stage to the chairs and music stands, empty as a winter cornfield. I spoke to my aunt. She burst into tears and sobbed pleadingly. "I don't want to go, Clark, I don't want to go!"

I understood. For her, just outside the door of the concert hall, lay the black pond with the cattle-tracked bluffs; the tall, unpainted house, with weather-curled boards; naked as a tower, the crookbacked ash seedlings where the dishcloths hung to dry; the gaunt, molting turkeys picking up refuse about the kitchen door.

—WILLA CATHER

34a cite

One option is to quote the source exactly. Depending on your purpose, you could quote a sentence or two to make your point, or you could present a longer quotation in block form, perhaps reproducing an entire paragraph. Either way, you must separate your ideas from those of your source. At the same time, you should blend your own words with the words of the writer you are quoting to produce a smooth and pleasing sentence. Later in this chapter you will learn the mechanics of documenting your sources in a variety of citation systems. Here we are concentrating on how to make smooth connections between your prose and the prose of your source.

Quotation from source

In the last lines of "A Wagner Matinee" we can see the horrible tragedy of the transplanted artist as Clark's aunt faces her life back home. Clark explains that "just outside the door of the concert hall, lay . . . the tall, unpainted house, with weather-curled boards" and "the gaunt, molting turkeys picking up refuse about the kitchen door" (115). It is the refuse of Aunt Georgiana's existence.

The writer uses her source to support the point she's making, the tragedy of the transplanted artist. Quotation marks are placed around each phrase copied from the source. The sentence that includes the quotation starting with "just outside the concert hall" follows smoothly from the sentence before it. The tag "Clark explains that" helps the writer integrate the quoted material with her own writing. The writer uses the conjunction *and* to connect two parts of Cather's sentence that are separated in the original. The spaced periods, called **ellipses** (27f), shorten the quotation. Note how the writer comments on the quotation with her own thoughtful observation: the turkeys' refuse is the refuse of Aunt Georgiana's existence. The parenthetical reference "(115)" is to the page number on which the quotation appears in Cather's story. Full documentation appears in the list of works cited (see 34c and 34d).

**34a
cite**

Quotation from source

The final overwhelming images of the story show the utter horror of the transplanted artist:

> For her, just outside the door of the concert hall, lay the black pond with the cattle-tracked bluffs; the tall, unpainted house, with weather-curled boards; naked as a tower, the crook-backed ash seedlings where the dishcloths hung to dry; the gaunt, molting turkeys picking up refuse about the kitchen door.

The block form sets off a long quotation from the source. No quotation marks are used for block quotes of four typed lines or more. The quotation supports the point the writer makes in the introductory sentence, which justifies the use of the long passage by calling attention to the "overwhelming images." Readers will read to see why the writer finds it overwhelming.

Summary

Cather leaves us with a grim picture of the life awaiting Aunt Georgiana after

she leaves the concert hall and returns to
her bleak homestead on the Nebraska
frontier.

Paraphrase

We see a stark, ugly world awaiting
Aunt Georgiana. When she returns to her
Nebraska homestead after the concert hall,
she must face "the black pond"
surrounded by cliffs, a weatherbeaten
farmhouse, small ash trees "where the
dishcloths hung to dry," and thin, bony
turkeys pecking at garbage outside the
kitchen (115).

**34a
cite**

In the paraphrase, which follows the original line of reasoning more closely than the summary, the writer uses quotation marks around the phrases from the original.

You must use your judgment about when to use quotation marks for individual words or for brief phrases borrowed from another source. Notice that the words *concert hall* appear in the original story, but in the summary and the paraphrase these words are not enclosed within quotation marks. A good general rule is that when you use three or more consecutive words from another source, you need quotation marks. The rule is a good one to keep in mind. It will make you think about what you are doing and will help you avoid the unconscious plagiarism that can get you into just as much trouble as the deliberate act (see 34g).

■ **Exercise 34.1** Select a passage from a magazine article or a book and write a paragraph in which you incorporate elements from the passage into your own writing by following the directions below. Use appropriate citations. Make a copy of the passage to show your instructor.

1. Write a brief summary of the passage as part of a paragraph that might appear in a draft of your paper.
2. Write a short paragraph in which you quote a few lines exactly from the passage.
3. Write a short paragraph in which you paraphrase the passage.

Commenting on Source Material

Although summaries of sources are important elements in most research
papers, you should provide more than summaries alone. Readers expect
you to guide them by explaining, interpreting, and evaluating source
materials. You build paragraphs from summaries, paraphrases, or quotations by giving your own thoughts on your topic.

Extensive research will shape your thoughts and opinions, and as you
continue examining different sources, you will formulate new ideas or
modify existing ones. Some of your sources may provide conflicting data.
Others may simply disagree in their interpretation of facts or even in their
definitions of key terms. Still others may offer opinions that challenge
what you have read elsewhere. Readers of your paper need your help in
sorting out the contradictions and in separating the important ideas from
the routine and the facts from the speculations.

Commenting on source material is not easy; there are no exact rules
to follow. A sensitive researcher learns from experience just when to shed
light on a complex point and when to interpret or challenge an important
idea. You should respect your sources, of course, but you should not be
intimidated by them. In citing authorities it is right to question their
conclusions, to lay them alongside conclusions drawn by others, or to use
them as springboards for your own conclusions. The following examples
demonstrate how a writer can integrate source material while providing
useful commentary on it.

Cather's debut into fame was noted in volumes concerning
American fiction, the first being Grant Overton's *The Women Who
Make Our Novels,* issued late in 1918. A literary reporter rather than
critic, Overton compiled information about all American female novelists of importance or popularity; but he did not prognosticate which
of them, if any, might continue to be read fifty years hence. The order
of his chapters was accidental and therefore meaningless; Willa
Cather is sandwiched between one Grace S. Richmond, whose books
were said to sell "faster than the books of any other American
writer," and Clara Louise Burnham, author of "twenty-six books
which have sold a half million copies." The thirteen pages Overton
granted Cather are devoted largely to a biographical sketch (not
always noted for accuracy) and to a summary of her achievement,
drawn from reviews; these cover her work from *Alexander's Bridge,*
which might have been written by Mrs. Wharton, through the indisputably personal triumph of *My Antonia.* Overton's judgments, re-
flecting a cross section of others' evaluations, emphasize the significance of Cather's early western experience, her controlled
accessibility to it, her fidelity to character, and the esthetic delight
furnished by her method.

—PHILIP GERBER

Much more than a summary appears here. Certainly we learn the essence of Overton's entry on Cather and two of her contemporaries. But Gerber's comments and evaluations guide our perceptions. Note how he judges Overton's credentials as a writer about Cather, how he calls the order of chapters in *The Women Who Make Our Novels* meaningless, and how he questions the biographical accuracy in Overton's sketch of Cather. A reader unfamiliar with Overton has not only a summary of his work but also an assessment of it from Gerber's perspective.

34a cite

> Two of the shorter pieces in *The Troll Garden,* "A Wagner Matinee" and "The Sculptor's Funeral," take firm grip on the fatality of deprivation which was an inherent part of Miss Cather's native Nebraska material. "A Wagner Matinee" is a bleakly effective *récit,* holding in concentration the terrible spiritual toll taken by frontier life, especially upon women. An old aunt of the narrator, grizzled and deformed, comes to visit her nephew in New York; she had been a music teacher at the Boston Conservatory, and marriage had taken her to a Nebraska homestead fifty miles from a railroad, to live at first in a dugout in a hillside. He takes her to a concert. At the *Tannhauser* overture, she clutches his coat sleeve. "Then it was I first realized that for her this broke a silence of thirty years; the inconceivable silence of the plains. . . ."
>
> —DOROTHY VAN GHENT

Van Ghent's purpose is to summarize the main action of "A Wagner Matinee," but she provides her own interpretations as well. She classifies the story as a *récit* — a term usually reserved for short novels with simple narrative lines.

■ **Exercise 34.2** Read the following passage from the book *Sociology* by Paul Horton and Chester Hunt. Write a paragraph or two in which you integrate quoted or paraphrased material from the passage. Provide commentary on the quotes or paraphrases by offering your own clarifications, interpretations, or judgments.

Stereotypes. A *stereotype* is *a group-shared image of another group or category of people.* Stereotypes can be positive (the kindly, dedicated family doctor), negative (the unprincipled, opportunistic politician), or mixed (the dedicated, fussy, sexless old-maid teacher). Stereotypes are applied indiscriminately to all members of the stereotyped group, without allowance for individual differences. Stereotypes are never entirely untrue, for they must bear *some* resemblance to the characteristics of the persons stereotyped or they would not be recognized. But stereotypes are always distorted, in that they exaggerate and universalize *some* of the characteristics of *some* of the members of the stereotyped group.

Just how stereotypes begin is not known. Once the stereotype has become a part of the culture, it is maintained by *selective perception* (noting only the confirming incidents or cases and failing to note or remember the exceptions), *selective interpretation* (interpreting observations in terms of the stereotype: e.g., Jews are "pushy" while gentiles are "ambitious"), *selective identification* ("they look like school teachers . . ."), and *selective exception* ("he really doesn't act at all Jewish"). All these processes involve a reminder of the stereotype, so that even exceptions and incorrect identifications serve to feed and sustain the stereotype.

—PAUL B. HORTON AND CHESTER L. HUNT

34b
Using Various Formats for Documenting Sources

You have already considered the importance of acknowledging information borrowed from others. Researchers often use other people's words and ideas but they always name the sources from whom they borrow.

The format for presenting information on the sources you use for research may vary, depending on the discipline in which you are doing research. Most up-to-date documentation systems require *internal* (or *parenthetical*) citation. With internal citation, sources are enclosed in parentheses and are named directly in the text of the paper instead of in footnotes. This system also requires a list of references or works cited.

Because academic disciplines vary in the precise forms they require for documentation, you must follow the specific format that your instructor requests. Two of the most popular formats are those recommended by the Modern Language Association of America (MLA) in its 1984 *MLA Handbook for Writers of Research Papers* and in its counterpart for scholars, *The MLA Style Manual* (1985), and by the 1983 version of the *Publication Manual of the American Psychological Association* (APA). This chapter focuses on these formats. In addition, you will see how to use other parenthetical documentation systems as well as footnotes or endnotes. Your instructor may require the documentation format recommended in the University of Chicago Press's *Chicago Manual of Style* or in Kate L. Turabian's *Manual for Writers of Term Papers, Theses, and Dissertations*. Many other manuals for researchers are also available.

34c
Using the MLA Format

Most research papers in the humanities use the MLA format. The main features of this format include parenthetical citations directly in the text, a list of works cited, and, when necessary, explanatory endnotes.

Using Parenthetical References

**34c
cite**

The MLA system uses an abbreviated format for documentation within the text. (A list of works cited, to be discussed shortly, supplies full publishing data.)

A citation in the text typically includes:

☐ The author's last name.

☐ The location of the material you borrowed. Usually the page numbers alone are enough; in a multivolume source, give the volume number as well. For literary works, you may want to give the act, scene, line, chapter, book, or stanza.

Remember: Complete bibliographical information must appear in your list of works cited at the end of the paper. The following model will help you write your own sentences to indicate your sources.

The complete entry for Van Ghent's book appears in the list of works cited on page 509. (The full text from which the quotation in this model internal documentation is taken appears on p. 427.)

The key to successful parenthetical documentation is your complete list of works cited at the end of the paper. Every reference you make in your text must correspond to an entry on that list. Information you provide in the parenthetical documentation must match the information on your list of works cited.

Try to be concise and unobtrusive with your parenthetical references. Place them where pauses occur naturally in your sentences and as close as possible to the information you are identifying.

What you include in parentheses and what you include in the accompanying text will reflect your individual style as a writer. Feel free to experiment with different formats for references, remembering that what you include in your text determines what you include in the parenthetical documentation. If you use the author's name in a sentence, do not put that name in parentheses. If you do not name the author in your sentence, name him or her in parentheses.

We cannot show all the stylistic possibilities for internal documentation, but the following examples illustrate the simplest options. Wherever possible, these examples correspond to examples presented in later sections (Preparing a List of Works Cited, p. 437, and Preparing Footnotes and Endnotes, p. 454).

Model Internal Documentation: MLA Format

34c cite

Cather's ''A Wagner Matinee'' shows ''the terrible spiritual toll taken by frontier life, especially upon women'' (Van Ghent 11).

no comma or period here

quotation ends here

space only; no punctuation

author's last name only

open parentheses

period at end of sentence

close parentheses

page number from text

Parts of single-volume books or articles

Van Ghent believes that "A Wagner Matinee" is a story about "the terrible spiritual toll taken by frontier life, especially upon women" (11).

"A Wagner Matinee," as Van Ghent points out, "is a bleakly effective récit, holding in concentration the terrible spiritual toll taken by frontier life, especially upon women" (11).

In Cather's short story we see how life on the frontier imposes itself on a woman's spirit (Van Ghent 11).

It may be true that some of Cather's
writing shows "the fatality of
deprivation" (Van Ghent 11), but
certainly a story like "A Wagner Matinee"
also is a tribute to the power of art in
human life.

Van Ghent highlights the bleak, deprived
life of Aunt Georgiana (11).

**34c
cite**

To cite an entire work rather than a part of it, name the author in your
text and avoid a parenthetical reference.

Dorothy Van Ghent comments on all of
Cather's novels.

An interesting collection of Greek and
Roman myths appears in the volume by Mark
Morford and Robert Lenardon.

Clifford Morgan, Richard King, and Nancy
Robinson have provided a basic text for
beginning students of psychology.

Albert Baugh and his colleagues trace the
growth and development of English
literature from the Middle Ages to the
twentieth century.

Multivolume works

Sir Thomas Browne's <u>Pseudodoxia Epidemica</u>
was "no hasty compilation, but was the
product of many years of patient thought,
reading, observation, and experiment"
(2:vii).

The number before the colon in parentheses refers to the volume; the number after the colon refers to the page number. (The "vii" tells you that the quotation comes from the preface; pagination in the preface or other front matter in a book is generally in lowercase roman numbers.)

> Modern readers may be mystified by the
> range of classical allusions in the
> <u>Pseudodoxia Epidemica</u> (Browne, vol. 2).

**34c
cite**

This parenthetical reference is to an entire volume of a multivolume work and not to any particular part of that volume. Here you use a comma to separate the author's name from the volume number and you use the abbreviation for *volume.*

Works cited by title only

> Cather had already published <u>The Troll
> Garden</u> and <u>Song of the Lark</u>, but it was <u>My
> Antonia</u> that widened her reputation in
> 1918 ("Cather").

For parenthetical references to a work that appears in the list of works cited by title only, use a shortened version of the title. Omit the page number if the article is brief; otherwise include the page number after the title.

Works by a corporate author

> In 1980 the Commission on the Humanities
> recommended that "the humanities,
> sciences, and technology need to be
> substantially connected" (21), but we
> have made little progress toward that
> goal.

The reference is to *The Humanities in American Life.*

Two or more works by the same author

Bacon condemned Plato as "an obstacle to science" (Farrington, <u>Philosophy</u> 35).

Benjamin Farrington points out that Aristotle's father, Nicomachus, a physician, probably trained his son in medicine (<u>Aristotle</u> 15).

The title, or a shortened form of it, is necessary in the parenthetical reference to a work by an author who appears more than once on your list of works cited. A comma follows the author's name if you use it in the parenthetical reference. If you put the author's name in the text, give only the title and the page reference, as in the second example above. Two of Farrington's books, *The Philosophy of Francis Bacon* and *Aristotle: Founder of Scientific Philosophy,* would appear in the list of works cited in this case.

Literary works

In the opening sentence of <u>Lord Jim,</u> Conrad shows us the physical power of his hero (3; ch. 1).

Marlowe says that what set Brown apart from other scoundrels "was the arrogant temper of his misdeeds and a vehement scorn for mankind at large and for his victims in particular" (Conrad 352–53; ch. 38).

For classical literary works in several editions, readers find it useful to have more than just page numbers in a reference. Chapter, book, or act and scene numbers make it easier to find materials in any copy of a novel or play. In the parenthetical reference, cite the page number first, then use a semicolon, and then give any other useful information, such as chapter, book, or act and scene numbers. Use accepted abbreviations.

More than one work in a single reference

```
Several critics refer to the place of music
in Cather's art (Giannone; Brennan; Van
Ghent 20-21).
```

Use semicolons to separate works when you cite more than one work in a single parenthetical reference. The first two entries ("Giannone" and "Brennan") are to complete articles; the last entry ("Van Ghent 20–21") is to specific pages in Van Ghent's article. Because a reference that is too long will distract your readers, you may want to use a footnote or endnote to cite multiple sources, as described in 34f.

**34c
cite**

Indirect sources

```
Wolfe was upset at an anonymous criticism
of his play The Mountains. He told his
teacher at Harvard, George Pierce Baker,
that "if I knew who wrote that, I would no
longer be responsible for my actions"
(qtd. in Turnball 54).
```

You should take material from original sources whenever you can. But when the original is unavailable and you have only an indirect source (for example, a published account of someone's spoken comments), use the abbreviation "qtd. in" in your parenthetical reference, right before your citation. Your list of works cited would include a reference like this:

```
Turnball, Andrew. Thomas Wolfe. New York:
     Scribner's, 1967.
```

You might choose to document your original source in a footnote or an endnote, as described in 34f.

Plays, concerts, films, and television programs

```
Linda Lavin's performance in Broadway
Bound by Neil Simon pleased most of the
New York drama critics.
```

In <u>Heartbreak Ridge</u> Clint Eastwood
continues to impress his audiences with
his skills as an actor and a director.

■ **Exercise 34.3** Write a sentence that summarizes, paraphrases, or quotes a portion of each selection below. Within your sentence, provide documentation for the source according to the MLA guidelines. Publishing data appear in parentheses; you will not have to use all the information, however.

34c
cite

1. "When Shakespeare came to London from Stratford-on-Avon, the new poetry, which was to crown the last decades of the sixteenth century and the beginning of the seventeenth, was already established. Its arrival had been announced in 1579 by the publication of Spenser's *The Shepherd's Calendar.*" (The selection is from *Shakespeare's Songs and Poems,* edited by Edward Hubler. The quotation is from pages xii–xiii. The book was published in 1959 by McGraw-Hill in New York.)

2. "Every summer, one of the nation's longest-running and most hotly contested photo competitions takes place at the offices of Sierra Club Books in San Francisco. Between 50,000 and 100,000 color transparencies are submitted for publication in the four Wilderness calendars, and the flood of entries keeps a small army of freelance photo editors and clerks busy from July to November." (The selection is from an article called "Wilderness Pin-Ups by Sierra Club" by Catherine Kouts in *Publishers Weekly,* vol. 225, no. 17, April 27, 1984, p. 41.)

3. "The Greeks' most important legacy is not, as we would like to think, democracy; it is their mythology. Even though in the second century A.D. a mysterious voice was heard exclaiming "great Pan is dead," the Greek gods and many obscure and irrational stories about them lived on in the imaginations of artists and writers, no matter how often or in how many different ways Christians and philosophers tried to dismiss the myths as frivolous or harmful. And even in the twentieth century, when man has acquired greater power than ever before to alter the natural world, the old myths continue to haunt us, not just in the form of nymphs and shepherds on vases or garden statuary, but in many common assumptions about the shape of human experience. The notions — now presumably obsolete — that a man should be active and aggressive, a woman passive and subject to control by the men in her family, are expressed in virtually every Greek myth, even the ones in which the women seek to gain control of their own lives. That the most important phase of a woman's life is the period immediately preceding her marriage (or remarriage) is preserved in the

plot of many novels, as is the notion that virginity, or at least celibacy, offers a woman a kind of freedom that she is no longer entitled to when she becomes involved with a man." (The selection is from p. 207 of an article called "Women in Greek Myths" by Mary R. Lefkowitz. The article appears on pp. 207–19 of the Spring 1985 *American Scholar,* vol. 54, no. 2. *The American Scholar* is a journal that numbers pages continuously throughout the annual volume and is published in Washington, D.C., by Phi Beta Kappa.)

34c
cite

Using Explanatory Notes

When you use parenthetical references in your research paper, you can use footnotes or endnotes to provide additional information that you do not want to include in the text of your paper.

You can provide evaluative comments on your sources or other relevant information that does not fit neatly in your text. Or you can use an explanatory note to list a number of citations. (The preparation of footnotes and endnotes that cite sources is discussed in 34f.)

Indicate notes by a raised number in your text. Put your explanatory notes before your list of works cited on a separate page under the heading "Notes."

Notes to explain

Earlier, when Clark received the letter from Howard announcing Aunt Georgiana's arrival, Clark says that her name called up her figure, "at once pathetic and grotesque" (107).[1]

[1]Cather's family and friends objected to her portrait of Nebraska life when this story first appeared in <u>Everybody's Magazine</u>. A good friend, Will Jones, complained that strangers would always associate Nebraska with Aunt Georgiana's terrible shape, her false teeth, and her

```
yellow skin. Cather denied that she wanted
to disparage her homeland but admitted
that her family felt insulted: "They had
already told her that it was not nice to
tell such things" (Woodress 117).
```

The writer uses a parenthetical reference to cite the page, "(107)," from which she quotes the words "at once pathetic and grotesque." She uses the note to explain information that does not belong in the text itself. In addition, she cites a reference to a critical piece about Cather.

Note to cite multiple sources

```
    Music is a very important element in
much of Cather's fiction.²

    ²Giannone; Brennan, "Willa Cather";
Brennan, "Music"; Gerber 71-73; Bloom
and Bloom 123; Daiches 8; Van Ghent
20-21.
```

The note permits the writer to cite several sources. The inclusion of seven references in a parenthetical citation in the text itself would distract readers.

Preparing a List of Works Cited

You must provide a list of works cited for readers of your research paper. A **list of works cited** is an alphabetical list of books, articles, and other sources (such as films, interviews, or dramatic productions) that you consulted in doing your research. All the citations in your paper will be keyed to this list of research materials. (If you use print materials only, your list will be called a **bibliography.**)

If you make bibliography cards carefully (as disscussed in 33b), you can produce a list of works cited without much trouble. Each card will have all the data you need when you prepare your list for the final draft of your paper.

The following models show you how to document the usual kinds of sources for your research. If you cite some special sources (cartoons, computer programs, musical compositions, and works of art, for example), you should consult the *MLA Handbook* itself.

Books and reference works

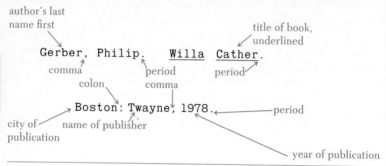

Model Entry (MLA) in a List of Works Cited: A Book with One Author

author's last name first

title of book, underlined

Gerber, Philip. Willa Cather.

comma   period   period

colon   comma

Boston: Twayne, 1978.   period

city of publication   name of publisher

year of publication

The periods set off three major divisions in the entry: the author's name, the title, and the publishing data. Note that the MLA style does not include the abbreviation for the state after the city. If the entry requires more than one line, indent the second line and all other lines five spaces.

Sometimes other facts are required, as in the following sample:

McCray, Curtis L. "Kaptain Kronkite: The
    Myth of the Eternal Frame."
    Television: The Critical View. Ed.
    Horace Newcomb. 2nd ed. New York:
    Oxford UP, 1979. 319-33.

McCray is the author of an essay in the second edition of a book edited by Newcomb. Newcomb collected a number of essays and prepared them for publication, hence his designation as editor (Ed.) of the book. The book is in its second edition (2nd ed.), which means that one earlier version exists but that the researcher used the more recent book. Note the short form *Oxford UP* for *Oxford University Press.* Short forms are acceptable.

An Anthology

Wolfe, Don M., ed. American Scene: New
    Voices. New York: Stuart, 1963.

The abbreviation *ed.* says that Wolfe is the editor of this collection. If the author is a compiler (of a bibliography, for example) or a translator, use *comp.* or *trans.* after the name.

A Book by Two or More Authors. The abbreviation *ed.* here stands for *edition.* An arabic number (with an appropriate suffix to show that the number is ordinal) indicates the edition number. The abbreviation **et al.** is short for the Latin *et alii,* meaning "and others"; when a work has more than three authors, *et al.* replaces the names of all authors but the first.

34c cite

Morford, Mark P. O., and Robert J.
       Lenardon. <u>Classical Mythology</u>. New
       York: Longman, 1971.
Morgan, Clifford T., Richard A. King, and
       Nancy M. Robinson. <u>Introduction to</u>
       <u>Psychology</u>. 6th ed. New York: McGraw,
       1979.
Baugh, Albert C., et al. <u>A Literary History</u>
       <u>of England</u>. New York: Appleton, 1948.

Two or More Books by the Same Author. When you list more than one book by the same author, give the author's name in the first entry only. For each succeeding entry, instead of the author's name type four hyphens and a period, then skip a space and type the title. The hyphens always stand for the author's name exactly as it appears in the entry that comes directly before. (Brooks' name is repeated in the third entry because hyphens would have referred to his name only; he is one of two authors of *Understanding Poetry.*) If the author is an editor, a compiler, or a translator, use a comma after the hyphens and write in the correct abbreviation— *ed., comp.,* or *trans.*—before the title. All works listed for the same author appear alphabetically by title.

Brooks, Cleanth. <u>Fundamentals of Good</u>
       <u>Writing: A Handbook of Modern</u>
       <u>Rhetoric</u>. New York: Harcourt, 1950.
- - - -. <u>The Hidden God: Studies in</u>
       <u>Hemingway, Faulkner, Yeats, Eliot,</u>
       <u>and Warren</u>. New Haven: Yale UP, 1963.

Brooks, Cleanth, and Robert Penn Warren,
    eds. <u>Understanding Poetry</u>. 3rd ed.
    New York: Holt, 1960.

Farrington, Benjamin. <u>Aristotle: Founder
    of Scientific Philosophy</u>. New York:
    Praeger, 1969.

----. <u>The Philosophy of Francis Bacon</u>.
    Chicago: U of Chicago P, 1964.

**34c
cite**

A Book with Corporate Authorship

Commission on the Humanities. <u>The
    Humanities in American Life: Report
    of the Commission on the Humanities</u>.
    Berkeley: U of California P, 1980.

A Book with no Author's Name on the Title Page. The entry begins
with the title; in the list of works cited, alphabetize the entry by the first
word other than an article.

<u>Greece: 1974</u>. Athens: National Tourist
    Organization of Greece, 1973.

A Selection from an Anthology. Page numbers indicate where the
essay being cited appears in the longer work.

Sewell, Elizabeth. "Bacon, Vico,
    Coleridge, and the Poetic Method."
    <u>Giambattista Vico: An International
    Symposium</u>. Ed. Giorgio Tagliacozzo
    and Hayden V. White. Baltimore: Johns
    Hopkins P, 1969. 125-36.

A Preface, an Introduction, a Foreword, or an Afterword. The
name of the writer of the preface, introduction, foreword, or afterword
begins the entry, followed by the name of the part you are citing. Quotation marks or underlining is unnecessary. When the writer of the piece

differs from the author of the book, use the word *By* after the title and cite the author's full name, first name first. If the writer of the piece is the same person who wrote the book, use only the last name after the word *By*. In the first entry, Blackmur wrote the introduction; James wrote the prefaces. In the second entry, the writer of the preface is also the author of the book.

```
Blackmur, Richard P. Introduction. The Art
     of the Novel: Critical Prefaces. By
     Henry James. New York: Scribner's,
     1962. vii-xxxix.
Fowles, John. Preface. Islands. By Fowles.
     Boston: Little, 1978. 1-2.
```

34c
cite

A Work in More Than One Volume.   The first entry says that the work is in four volumes and that the researcher used them all. The second entry says that only the second volume was used.

```
Browne, Thomas. The Works of Sir Thomas
     Browne. Ed. Geoffrey Keynes. 4 vols.
     London: Faber, 1928.
Browne, Thomas. The Works of Sir Thomas
     Browne. Ed. Geoffrey Keynes. Vol. 2.
     London: Faber, 1928. 4 vols.
```

An Edited Book.   Harris prepared this work of Buck's for publication. The entry indicates that citations in the text of the paper are to Buck's writing. If the citations are to the editor (his introductory comments, for example), his name would begin the entry. See the entry for Blackmur above.

```
Buck, Pearl. China as I See It. Ed.
     Theodore F. Harris. New York: Day,
     1970.
```

A Translation.   If your citations are to the translator's comments, and not to the translation itself, use the translator's name to begin the entry. See the entry for Blackmur above.

Maffei, Paolo. <u>Beyond the Moon</u>. Trans. D.
    J. K. O'Connell. Cambridge: MIT P,
    1978.

A Publisher's Imprint. An imprint is the name a publisher sometimes gives to a special group of books to be published under that name.
Doubleday, for example, uses the imprint Anchor; Avon uses Camelot;
New American Library uses Mentor. When a publisher's imprint appears
on the title page, give the imprint name before the publisher's name. Use a
hyphen between them.

Farrington, Benjamin. <u>The Philosophy of
    Francis Bacon</u>. Chicago: Phoenix-U of
    Chicago P, 1964.

A Republished Book. The original edition appeared in 1959; the
writer of the paper used the edition republished by Bantam in 1966.

Knowles, John. <u>A Separate Peace</u>. 1959. New
    York: Bantam, 1966.

Reference Books. Material from a well-known reference work such
as the *Encyclopaedia Britannica* does not require full publication data, but
you should note the year of publication. The title in quotation marks is the
entry word for the topic in the encyclopedia.

"Kindergarten."<u>Encyclopaedia Britannica:
    Macropaedia</u>. 1974 ed.

For a signed article in an encyclopedia, include the author's name. Sometimes only initials appear after the article; in that case check the list of
initials in the index or in some other volume of the encyclopedia to find
out the author's full name.

Moore, Norman. "Hodgkin, Thomas, M.D."
    <u>Dictionary of National Biography</u>.
    1908.

Naylor, John Henry. "Peninsular War."
        <u>Encyclopaedia Britannica:</u>
        <u>Macropaedia</u>. 1974 ed.

Pamphlets, Bulletins, and Public Documents. For a work by a government, the name of the government comes first, then the name of the agency.

United States. Congressional Budget
        Office. <u>Proposition 13: Its Impact on</u>
        <u>the Nation's Economy, Federal</u>
        <u>Revenues, and Federal Expenditures</u>.
        Washington: GPO, 1978.
National Academy of Sciences. Committee on
        Water, Division of Earth Sciences.
        <u>Alternatives in Water Management</u>.
        National Research Council Publication
        No. 1408. Washington: National
        Academy of Sciences, 1969.

A Work in a Series. Neither underlined nor in quotation marks, the name of the series appears after the title of the book.

<u>Swimming Medicine IV</u>. International Series
        on Sports Sciences 6. Baltimore:
        University Park P, 1978.

Journals, magazines, and newspapers

The author's name, the title, and the publishing data are also the main divisions in the entry for a journal article. Note the titles both of the article and of the journal in which the work appears.

An Article in a Journal that Numbers Pages Separately in each Issue of an Annual Volume. If each issue in a volume is numbered,

Model Entry (MLA) in a List of Works Cited: An Article in a Journal with Pages Numbered Continuously Throughout the Annual Volume

author's last name first   period

comma

open quotation marks for title of article

**34c
cite**

Baum, Bernard. ''Willa Cather's Waste

period

close quotation marks

Land.'' The South Atlantic Quarterly 48

title of journal, underlined

volume number

(1949): 589-601.

year of publication, in parentheses

colon

period

pages on which the article appears

include the issue number in the citation. Write the volume number, then a period, then the issue number. If the journal uses only issue numbers, treat them like volume numbers.

Jewell, Walter. "The Contribution of
    Administrative Leadership to Academic
    Excellence." WPA: Writing Program
    Administration 3.3 (1980): 9-13.

An Article in a Monthly or Bimonthly Magazine

Arnold, Marilyn. "Willa Cather's
    Nostalgia: A Study in Ambivalence."
    Research Studies Mar. 1981: 23-24.

An Article in a Weekly or Biweekly Magazine

Jones, Howard Mumford. "The Novels of
     Willa Cather." <u>The Saturday Review of</u>
     <u>Literature</u> 6 Aug. 1938: 3-4, 16.

An Unsigned Article in a Magazine

"Return of the Sweatshops--They Flourish
     Anew." <u>U.S. News & World Report</u> 14
     Jan. 1980: 73-74.

**34c
cite**

An Article in a Daily Newspaper. For the readers' convenience in locating the article, the section designnaion *A* appears along with the page reference, 13. If an edition is named on the masthead, specify the edition (*natl. ed.* or *late ed.*, for example) after the date. Use a comma between the date and the edition.

Clark, F. Atherton. "Metric Lengths Make
     Computation Easier." <u>San Antonio</u>
     <u>Express</u> 31 July 1978: A13.

Special works

Unpublished Dissertations and Theses

Eisenberg, Nora. "The Far Side of
     Language: The Search for Expression
     in the Novels of Virginia Woolf."
     Diss. Columbia UP, 1977.

Book Reviews

Fleming, Peter J. "Nobel Lady." Rev. of
     <u>Pearl S. Buck: A Biography</u>, by T. F.
     Harris. <u>Catholic World</u> Dec. 1969:
     138-39.

Recordings. The entry starts with the composer, followed by the title of the work. The major performers appear after the word *with*. *Cond.* is an abbreviation for *Conductor* and *Orch.* is an abbreviation for *Orchestra*. LDR-73002 is the catalog number.

**34c
cite**

Verdi, Giuseppe. <u>La Traviata</u>. With Joan
    Sutherland, Luciano Pavarotti, and
    Matteo Manuguerra. Cond. Richard
    Bonynge. National Philharmonic Orch.
    and London Opera Chorus. London,
    LDR-73002, 1981.

Performances: Plays, Concerts, Films, Television or Radio Programs, Interviews. In the first entry the abbreviation *dir.* is for *director.* The date given is that of the performance cited.

Brown, Arvin, dir. <u>American Buffalo</u>. By
    David Mamet. With Al Pacino. Circle
    in the Square Downtown Theatre, New
    York. 14 Aug. 1981.

<u>The Mother</u>. Writ. Paddy Chayevsky. Dir.
    Delbert Mann. Philco Television
    Playhouse. NBC, 4 Apr. 1954.

Redford, Robert, dir. <u>Ordinary People</u>.
    With Donald Sutherland, Mary Tyler
    Moore, and Timothy Hutton. Paramount,
    1980.

Sills, Beverly. Telephone interview. 6
    Dec. 1981.

Thomas, Michael Tilson, cond. American
    Symphony Orch. Concert. Carnegie
    Hall, New York. 15 Feb. 1981.

Final list of works cited

Your list of works cited, placed at the end of your paper, must include data for all the materials you used. A list that also includes data for materials consulted but not cited is headed "Works Consulted." For a sample of a full "Works Cited" list, see pages 507–509.

✓ **CHECKLIST: PREPARING A LIST OF WORKS CITED**

1. Set up your list on a separate page at the end of your paper.
2. Type the title ("Works Cited," "Works Consulted," or "Bibliography") about one inch from the top of the page, and double-space before you type the first entry.
3. Arrange all your entries alphabetically according to the author's last name, but do not number them. The author's last name goes first, then the first and middle names.
4. See page 439 for listing two or more books by the same author.
5. List all entries without authors alphabetically according to the first important word in the title.
6. Do not separate books from periodicals. Strict alphabetical order guides the arrangement of entries. (For advanced research projects, writers sometimes separate primary from secondary sources.)
7. Start the first line of each entry at the left margin. Indent five spaces all the other lines within each entry. Double-space within entries and between them.

34c cite

Model: MLA Style List of Works Cited (Excerpt)

Works Cited

Bloom, Edward A., and Lillian D. Bloom.
     <u>Willa Cather's Gift of Sympathy</u>.
     Carbondale: Southern Illinois UP,
     1962.

Brennan, Joseph X. "Music and Willa
     Cather." <u>University Review</u> 31 (1965):
     257–64.

————. "Willa Cather and Music."
     <u>University Review</u> 31 (1965): 175–83.

"Cather." <u>World Scope Encyclopedia</u>.
     1955 ed.

Cather, Willa. <u>On Writing</u>. New York:
     Knopf, 1949.

■ **Exercise 34.4** Using the models in 34c, write correct entries for the following sources to be included in a list of works cited. (You may not need all the data that appear in each group.)

1. *Writing in the Arts and Sciences,* a 1981 textbook published by Winthrop Publishers, Inc., in Cambridge, Massachusetts. The authors, in the order that appears on the title page, are Elaine Maimon, Gerald L. Belcher, Gail W. Hearn, Barbara F. Nodine, and Finbarr W. O'Connor.
2. An article by Leo Seligsohn called "A Simple Service for Harry Chapin," in *Newsday,* a Garden City, New York, newspaper. The article appeared on Wednesday, July 22, 1981, on page 3.
3. A book by Stewart C. Easton called *Roger Bacon and His Search for a Universal Science,* published by Greenwood Press of Westport, Connecticut, in 1970.
4. In the quarterly journal *Sewanee Review,* an essay about Hart Crane, which was printed in the spring of 1981 and called "Two Views of *The Bridge.*" Malcolm Cowley is the author. The article appears on pages 191–205.
5. Volume 1 of the two-volume edition of *Joseph Conrad: Life and Letters,* edited by G. Jean-Aubry and published in 1927 by Doubleday in Garden City, New York.

■ **Exercise 34.5** Return to Exercise 32.4 and write a list of works cited, including any five sources.

34d
Using the APA Format

The *Publication Manual of the American Psychological Association* (APA) provides guidelines for writers of research papers in the social sciences and other academic areas. APA addresses its manual to writers aiming at publication in one of the many APA journals. It recommends that students writing papers in APA style follow supplementary guidelines established by their colleges. If you are told to use the APA *Publication Manual,* check with your teacher for further instructions. For example, APA manuscripts submitted for publication require an **abstract,** which is a short, comprehensive summary of the paper. Yet many undergraduate papers written in the APA format use an outline instead of an abstract.

Like the MLA format, APA format recommends short references documented within the text and a complete list of sources, called **references,** at the end of the paper. The APA parenthetical citation includes the author's last name and the year of publication.

Using Parenthetical References in the Text

Model Internal Documentation: APA Format

34d
cite

```
Scientists generally agree that a black hole is an
area in space with such a high density that
nothing can escape it (Cloud, 1978).
```
period

author's name   comma   date of publication

Here are some other examples:

```
This definition of black holes is one with
which Cloud (1978) would agree.

In 1978 Cloud pointed out that black holes
are definable, but many people still find
it difficult to believe that they exist.
```

Multiple Publications in One Year. If an author has published more than one work in a single year, after the date use an *a* for the first publication, a *b* for the second, and so on. These letters will also appear beside the dates in your reference list. T. G. R. Bower, for example, published two books in 1977. In alphabetical order by title, they are labeled 1977a and 1977b.

```
Bower (1977a,b) discusses the developing
child's perceptions.
```

Multiple Authors. The following examples show how to cite references with multiple authors. In the APA system, if a source has six authors or fewer, cite them all in the first reference. For two authors only, name them both each time you cite their material. For more than two but fewer than six, subsequent references use *et al.* after the first author's name. (As explained earlier, the abbreviation *et al.* is for the Latin phrase *et alii,* meaning "and others." Do not underline the abbreviation. Do not use a period after *et;* do use a period after *al.*) If your source has more than six authors, use *et al.* after the first name each time you cite the work. Use the date in each case.

**34d
cite**

Some psychologists see suicide attempts as a gamble (Lester & Lester, 1971).

An important study connects birth order and a child's need to conform (Becker, Lerner, & Carroll, 1966).

Conformity also relates to group pressure (Becker et al., 1966).

Page Citations. If you want to cite a specific part of your source, put the page number(s) you've taken your information from after the date. Use *p.* and *pp.* as the abbreviations.

A six-year-old child who could not speak, Isabelle was "apparently unaware of

---

Model Entry (APA) for a References Page: A Book with One Author

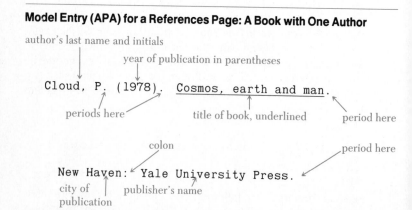

author's last name and initials

year of publication in parentheses

Cloud, P. (1978). Cosmos, earth and man.

periods here

title of book, underlined

period here

colon

period here

New Haven: Yale University Press.

city of publication

publisher's name

relationships of any kind" (Mason, 1942, p. 299).

Listing All Sources Cited

At the end of your paper, on a separate page headed "References," make a list of all the sources you cited.

A Book by Two or More Authors or Editors

34d cite

Lester, G., & Lester, D. (1971). <u>Suicide: The gamble with death</u>. Englewood Cliffs, NJ: Prentice-Hall.

Lewis, M., & Rosenblum, L. A. (Eds.). (1974). <u>The effect of the infant on its caregiver</u>. New York: Wiley.

Model Entry (APA) for a References Page: An Article in a Journal with Pages Numbered Consecutively Throughout the Annual Volume

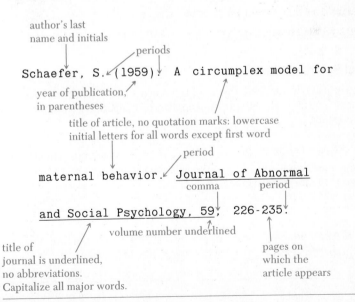

author's last
name and initials

periods

Schaefer, S. (1959). A circumplex model for

year of publication,
in parentheses

title of article, no quotation marks: lowercase
initial letters for all words except first word

period

maternal behavior. <u>Journal of Abnormal</u>

comma   period

<u>and Social Psychology, 59</u>, 226-235.

volume number underlined

title of
journal is underlined,
no abbreviations.
Capitalize all major words.

pages on
which the
article appears

An Article in a Journal That Numbers Pages Separately in Each Issue of an Annual Volume

```
Labouvie-Vief, G. (1980). Beyond formal
    operations: Uses and limits of pure
    logic in life-span development. Human
    Development, 23 (3), 141-161.
```

The number 23 after the title is the volume number. The number 3 in parentheses after the volume indicates the issue number.

An Article in a Monthly or Bimonthly Magazine or Daily Newspaper.
A comma separates the year of publication from the month. Use *pp.* to abbreviate *pages* only for magazine and newspaper entries, not for journals.

```
Shepard, Nathaniel, Jr. (1981, October
    11). Strong gun law sought in Chicago.
    New York Times, p. 38.

Tresemer, D. (1983, October). Fear of
    success: Popular but unproven.
    Psychology Today, pp. 82-85.
```

Final Reference List
Like the list of works cited, the list of references names all sources cited in the text. The list is alphabetical and appears on a separate page at the end of the paper.

■ **Exercise 34.6** Return to Exercise 34.3. Revise your parenthetical documentation according to the APA format and prepare a reference page for the three sources.

■ **Exercise 34.7** Return to Exercise 32.4. Select any five entries and prepare a reference page according to the APA format.

✓ **CHECKLIST:** PREPARING A REFERENCE LIST

1. Type the word *References* at the center of a separate page placed at the end of your paper. Number the page as you would other pages of your manuscript. Double-space between the word *References* and the first entry.
2. Arrange all entries in alphabetical order according to author's last name. Do not number entries. Do not separate books from periodicals.
3. Type the first line of each entry flush with the left margin. Indent two spaces all other lines within each entry. Double-space within entries and between them.

**34e
cite**

Model: APA reference list (excerpt)

```
            References
Cloud, P. (1978). Cosmos, earth, and man:
  A short history of the universe. New
  Haven: Yale University Press.
Dupress, A. K., & Hartman, L. (1979,
  October). Hunting for black holes.
  Natural History, pp. 30-37.
```

34e
Using Other Systems of Parenthetical References

Your instructor may recommend the number reference system or a full publication data system for citing sources in your paper.

The Number System

The number system requires an arabic number for each entry in the list of works cited; these numbers appear in the parenthetical citation, too. A comma separates the number of the entry from the relevant page number, and the entry number is often underlined, as you see below. With such a system, references included in the list of works cited may be arranged in any useful order, such as the order in which the writer cites the references in the text.

This definition of black holes is one with
which Cloud would agree (2, 37).

Full Publication Data in Parenthetical References

If you are required to give full parenthetical citation, use square brackets to replace the parentheses you would ordinarily use around city, publisher, and date. Full publication information in parenthetical references is rare; it distracts readers from the text and does not provide for a list of works cited, which readers always find useful. Occasionally, however, you will see this system in a bibliographical study or in a work that cites only a few references.

Cloud describes the shrinking of the
volume in a black hole to zero (Cosmos,
Earth and Man: A Short History of the
Universe [New Haven: Yale UP, 1978] 37).

34f
Using Footnotes or Endnotes

Many researchers use a system of notes to document their sources accurately. In such a system, notes provide full publishing information.

Footnotes appear at the bottom of the page, numbered consecutively throughout the paper. Endnotes are easier to set up because you number them consecutively and put them at the end of an essay. Footnotes and endnotes appear in both student papers and scholarly works.

Annotation must be clear and consistent. Your notes should make it easy for a reader to locate your sources, and they should be done consistently to avoid confusion. The following notes (based on the *MLA Handbook*) show the most common style used in academic publications. Each note corresponds to an entry in 34c or 34d. For each source, therefore, you can compare the format for a footnote (or an endnote) with the format for an entry in the list of works cited or on the reference page.

Books and Reference Works

Model Footnote Entry: A Book with One Author

34f
cite

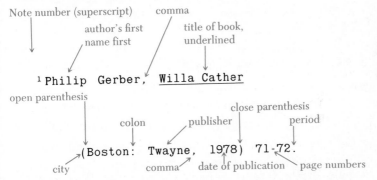

A comma separates the author's name from the title. Parentheses set off the publishing data from the rest of the reference, and, as in bibliographic entries, you can always use the short form of the publisher's name. A period completes the entry. Raised a half space above the line, the number of each note comes after a five-space indentation.

An Anthology

²Don M. Wolfe, ed., <u>American Scene: New Voices</u> (New York: Stuart, 1963) xi-xii.

A Book by Two or More Authors

³Mark P. O. Morford and Robert J. Lenardon, <u>Classical Mythology</u> (New York: Longman, 1971) 153-154.

⁴Clifford T. Morgan and Richard A. King, <u>Introduction to Psychology</u>, 2nd ed. (New York: McGraw, 1961) 10.

⁵Albert C. Baugh et al., <u>A Literary History of England</u> (New York: Appleton, 1948) 307.

⁶Clifford T. Morgan, Richard A. King, and Nancy M. Robinson, <u>Introduction to Psychology</u>, 6th ed. (New York: McGraw, 1979) 296.

A Book with Corporate Authorship

⁷Commission on the Humanities, <u>The Humanities in American Life: Report of the Commission on the Humanities</u> (Berkeley: U of California P, 1980) 21.

A Book with No Author's Name on the Title Page

⁸<u>Greece: 1974</u>. (Athens: National Tourist Organization of Greece, 1973) 141.

A Selection from an Anthology

⁹Elizabeth Sewell, "Bacon, Vico, Coleridge, and the Poetic Method," <u>Giambattista Vico: An International Symposium</u>, ed. Giorgio Tagliacozzo and Hayden V. White (Baltimore: Johns Hopkins P, 1969) 127–28.

A Preface, an Introduction, a Foreword, or an Afterword

¹⁰Richard P. Blackmur, Introduction, <u>The Art of the Novel: Critical Prefaces</u>, by Henry James (New York: Scribner's, 1962) xvii.

A Work in More Than One Volume The number 2 refers to the second volume. A colon and a space after it separate the volume number from the page number, here page 7. If you wanted to cite the entire volume, you would write "vol. 2" right after the space following the final parenthesis. A period would complete the entry.

¹¹Thomas Browne, <u>The Works of Sir Thomas Browne</u>, ed. Geoffrey Keynes, 4 vols. (London: Faber, 1928) 2:7.

An Edited Book

¹²Pearl Buck, <u>China as I See It</u>, ed. Theodore F. Harris (New York: Day, 1970) 15.

A Translation

¹³Paolo Maffei, <u>Beyond the Moon</u>, trans. D. J. K. O'Connell (Cambridge: MIT P, 1978) 19.

A Republished Book

¹⁴John Knowles, <u>A Separate Peace</u> (1959; New York: Bantam, 1966) 66.

A Work in a Series

¹⁵<u>Swimming Medicine IV</u>, International Series on Sports Sciences 6 (Baltimore: University Park P, 1978) 416.

Selections from Reference Books

¹⁶"Kindergarten," <u>Encyclopaedia Britannica: Macropaedia</u>, 1974 ed.

**34f
cite**

[17]Norman Moore, "Hodgkin, Thomas, M.D.," <u>Dictionary of National Biography</u> (1908).

[18]John Henry Naylor, "Peninsular War," <u>Encyclopaedia Britannica: Macropaedia</u>, 1974 ed.

Pamphlets, Bulletins, and Public Documents

[19]United States, Congressional Budget Office, <u>Proposition 13: Its Impact on the Nation's Economy, Federal Revenues, and Federal Expenditures</u> (Washington: GPO, 1978) 7–8.

[20]National Academy of Sciences, Committee on Water, Division of Earth Sciences, <u>Alternatives in Water Management</u>, National Research Council Publication No. 1408 (Washington: National Academy of Sciences, 1969) 3.

Journals, Magazines, and Newspapers

Model Footnote Entry: An Article in a Journal with Pages Numbered Continuously Throughout the Annual Volume

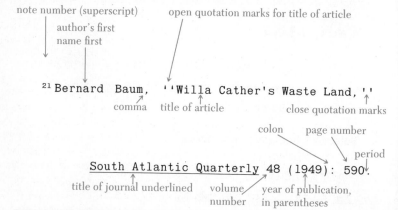

An Article in a Journal That Numbers Pages Separately in Each Issue of an Annual Volume

[22]Walter Jewell, "The Contribution of Administrative Leadership to Academic Excellence," <u>WPA: Writing Program Administration</u> 3.3 (1980): 9–13.

An Article in a Monthly or Bimonthly Periodical

[23]Marilyn Arnold, "Willa Cather's Nostalgia: A Study in Ambivalence," <u>Research Studies</u> Mar. 1981: 28.

An Article in a Weekly or Biweekly Magazine

[24]Howard Mumford Jones, "The Novels of Willa Cather," <u>The Saturday Review of Literature</u> 6 Aug. 1938: 4.

An Unsigned Article in a Magazine

[25]"Return of the Sweatshops--They Flourish Anew," <u>U.S. News & World Report</u> 14 Jan. 1980: 74.

An Article in a Daily Newspaper

[26]Atherton F. Clark, "Metric Lengths Make Computation Easier," <u>San Antonio Express</u> 31 July 1978: A13.

Special Works

Unpublished Dissertations and Theses

[27]Nora Eisenberg, "The Far Side of Language: The Search for Expression in the

Novels of Virginia Woolf," diss., Columbia UP, 1977, 29-30.

Book Reviews

[28]Peter J. Fleming, "Nobel Lady," rev. of <u>Pearl S. Buck: A Biography</u>, by T. F. Harris, <u>Catholic World</u> Dec. 1969: 139.

Recordings

[29]Giuseppe Verdi, <u>La Traviata</u>, with Joan Sutherland, Luciano Pavarotti, and Matteo Manuguerra, cond. Richard Bonynge, National Philharmonic Orch. and London Opera Chorus, London, LDR-73002, 1981.

Performances: Plays, Concerts, Films, Television or Radio Programs, Interviews

[30]Arvin Brown, dir., <u>American Buffalo</u>, by David Mamet, with Al Pacino, Circle in the Square Downtown Theatre, New York, 14 Aug. 1981.

[31]Michael Tilson Thomas, cond., American Symphony Orch. Concert, Carnegie Hall, New York, 15 Feb. 1981.

[32]Robert Redford, dir., <u>Ordinary People</u>, with Donald Sutherland, Mary Tyler Moore, and Timothy Hutton, Paramount, 1980.

[33]<u>The Mother</u>, writ. Paddy Chayevsky, dir. Delbert Mann, Philco Television Playhouse, NBC, 4 Apr. 1954.

[34]Telephone interview with Beverly Sills, director of the New York City Opera, 6 Dec. 1981.

Later References to the Same Source

Once you have provided full publishing data in a note, you can use a shortened form of citation in each later reference to your source. Generally, these references include only the author's last name and the page number. Although the *MLA Handbook* discourages the use of the Latin abbreviation *ibid.* (for *ibidem*, meaning "in the same place"), the form persists in academic writing. *Ibid.* indicates that the citation appears in exactly the same source as in the preceding note. Capitalize *ibid.* as the first word of the sentence in the note, but do not underline it, and always use a period after the abbreviation. The samples below of first and later citations show both styles.

34f cite

[1]Bernard Baum, "Willa Cather's Waste Land," <u>South Atlantic Quarterly</u> 48 (1949): 590.

[2]Philip Gerber, <u>Willa Cather</u> (Boston: Twayne, 1978) 71-72.

[3]Baum 593.

[4]Baum.

[5]Gerber 72.

[1]Bernard Baum, "Willa Cather's Waste Land," <u>South Atlantic Quarterly</u> 48 (1949): 590.

[2]Ibid. 592.

[3]Philip Gerber, <u>Willa Cather</u> (Boston: Twayne, 1978) 72.

[4]Ibid.

[5]Baum 592.

When you use two or more sources by the same author, the author's name alone in later references would be unclear. Avoid confusion by using a shortened form of the title along with the author's name, but be sure that readers can recognize the source easily.

[15]William Labov, "The Study of Language in Its Social Context," <u>Studium Generale</u> 23 (1970): 68.

[16]William Labov, <u>The Study of
Nonstandard English</u> (Urbana: NCTE, 1970)16.

[17]Labov, "Study of Language" 33.

[18]Labov, <u>Nonstandard English</u> 18.

Abbreviations

The Modern Language Association recommends that writers avoid using some Latin abbreviations that at one time were standard in research papers. You will encounter abbreviations often in your reading, however, and you should know what they mean. The following list includes familiar abbreviations for bibliographical citations, along with some of the short forms of Latin terms that you may encounter.

anon.	anonymous
bk., bks.	book(s)
c., ca.	circa ("about"), used with approximate dates
cf.	*confere* ("compare")
ch., chs., chaps.	chapter(s)
col., cols.	column(s)
diss.	dissertation
ed., eds.	edition(s) or editor(s)
et al.	*et alii* ("and others")
ff.	and the following pages, as in *pp. 85ff.*
ibid.	*ibidem* ("in the same place")
illus.	illustrated by, illustrator, illustration(s)
l., ll.	line(s)
loc. cit.	*loco citato* ("in the place cited")
ms, mss	manuscript(s)
n., nn.	note(s), as in *p. 24, n. 2* or *p. 24n*
n.d.	no date (of publication)
no., nos.	number(s)
n.p.	no place (of publication) or no publisher
n. pag.	no pagination
op. cit.	*opere citato* ("in the work cited")
p., pp.	page(s)
passim	throughout
pt., pts.	part(s)
q.v.	*quod vide* ("which see")
rev.	revision, revised, revised by; or review, reviewed by
rpt.	reprint, reprinted

sec., secs.   section(s)
trans.   translator, translated by, translation
univ.   university
vol., vols.   volume(s)

✓ CHECKLIST: PLACEMENT OF FOOTNOTES AND ENDNOTES

34f
cite

1. Number your notes consecutively throughout the paper, starting with 1. Do not use asterisks or other symbols instead of numbers. If you decide to add a note as an afterthought, renumber all subsequent notes; do not number the new note, for example, "5a." In the text, type the arabic number of the note a half space above the line after all punctuation (except a dash).

2. Note numbers always come in a logical place after a quotation or a paraphrase, and they should not distract the reader by breaking up a thought unit. Keep your notes as unobtrusive as possible.

3. For research papers that require notes, the MLA recommends that you use endnotes (instead of footnotes). Type endnotes on a separate page (or pages) after your last page of text, and use double spacing throughout. (Leave a one-inch space on top of the first page, then type the word *Notes;* double-space beneath it before you type the first note of your paper.) Place note numbers half a space above the line. Continue numbering the pages of endnotes as consecutive pages of your text.

4. If you use footnotes, leave enough space to type them at the bottom of each page. Leave four blank lines between the last line of your text and the first footnote. Indent five spaces before typing the note number (again raised above the line), and leave one space after it. Indent only the first line of each note; all other lines are flush with the left margin. Use single spacing between the lines in each note, double spacing between notes.

■ **Exercise 34.8** Write footnotes or endnotes according to the following instructions.

1. In note 1 cite pages 28 to 29 in Sidney Verba and Norman H. Nie's 1972 book *Participation in America,* published in New York by Harper & Row.

2. In note 2 cite page 1 of an article called "Joint Project with University Aims at Revitalizing High School" by Beverly T. Watkins in *The Chronicle of Higher Education* dated May 16, 1984. *The Chronicle* is a weekly newspaper.

3. In note 3 cite page 8, column 2, of the same article.

4. In note 4 cite the Verba and Nie book again, page 40.

5. In note 5 cite the Verba and Nie book again, same page as in note 4.

34g
Crediting Your Sources

You commit **plagiarism** whenever you present words or ideas taken from another person as if they were your own. The easiest way to avoid plagiarism is always to use quotation marks when you quote directly from a source, and always to acknowledge a source when you borrow or even allude to someone else's ideas and language, even though you may not have used that person's exact words. Sections 34c–f explain accepted methods of documentation and citation.

If you fail to follow these rules for borrowing from other writers, you may be guilty of plagiarism. The most obvious plagiarism is simply **copying,** either word for word or with a few words added or shifted around. Anyone who compares the source and the copy can recognize plagiarism instantly.

Mosaic plagiarism may result when a well-meaning, uninformed writer takes bad notes or when a dishonest one deliberately attempts to deceive. Here is an example in which the words are not copied entirely from the source. The writer may add words or sentences or even whole paragraphs. But anyone who reads the source and the plagiarism can tell that the latter entirely depends on the former:

Source

A territory is an area of space, whether of water or earth or air, which an animal or group of animals defends as an exclusive preserve. The word is also used to describe the inward compulsion in animate beings to possess and defend such a space. A territorial species of animals, therefore, is one in which all males, and sometimes females too, bear an inherent drive to gain and defend an exclusive property.

In most but not all territorial species, defense is directed only against fellow members of the kind. A squirrel does not regard a mouse as a trespasser. In most but not all territorial species — not in chameleons, for example — the female is sexually unresponsive to an unpropertied male. As a general pattern of behavior, in territorial species the competition between males which we formerly believed was one for the possession of females is in truth for possession of property.

—ROBERT ARDREY

Mosaic Plagiarism

Territory may be defined as an area of space, water, earth, or air, which animals defend as an exclusive preserve. The word *territory* also describes the inner compulsion in living beings to own and defend such a space. In a territorial species, males and some females are driven to gain and defend their exclusive property against fellow members of the species. The female of most territorial animals is not responsive sexually to a male without property, and the competition between males that we once believed was for the possession of females is really for possession of property.

Plagiarism is a very serious offense. The prose we write ourselves is so individual that when we write something in a striking way or express a new idea, we have produced something that always belongs to us. To call someone else's writing your own is wrong and foolish. The student who plagiarizes can expect a failing grade on the paper, and in many schools for the whole course. Plagiarism is an honors-code violation and is often grounds for expulsion.

**34g
cite**

✓ **CHECKLIST: AVOIDING PLAGIARISM**

1. Always keep your own notes and comments about a subject separate from the things you copy from other sources. Students sometimes commit plagiarism accidentally because their notes fail to distinguish between what is their own and what they have copied.
2. Always acknowledge your sources. Here is how the writer of the mosaic plagiarism on page 464 could have avoided it by acknowledging the source of those thoughts, Robert Ardrey:

    Ardrey defines territory as an area "whether of water or earth or air" which animals see as theirs exclusively and which they are driven by an "inward compulsion" to defend against members of their own species. A female in a territorial species is "sexually unresponsive to an unpropertied male." Ardrey believes that males do not compete for females. Instead, "the competition. . . is in truth for possession of property" (3).

3. Always use quotation marks when you are quoting directly, even if you choose to quote only a short phrase or clause.
4. Even when you are not quoting directly from a source, always be sure to attribute striking ideas to the person who first thought of them.
5. You need not attritbute information that is common knowledge. If you say that World War II ended in 1945, do not cite the source of your statement, since it is common knowledge. But if you do not know whether information is common knowledge or not, consult your teacher or an expert in the field.

CHAPTER

35

DEVELOPING, WRITING, AND REVISING THE RESEARCH PAPER

By this time you are ready to prepare your paper. You have investigated sources and taken careful notes. You can see relations between ideas. You note contradictions and differences of opinion. Your ideas form and re-form; your hypothesis changes; you read further to explore a point you missed or to check on a point you're not sure of.

You need to think carefully about your thesis now. Your reading and other research should focus your thoughts and allow you to state your point clearly and accurately. You may find that a formal outline helps you organize your paper. A formal outline provides an orderly visual scheme of the paragraphs with main and subordinated points clearly related. From your outline you can write first and final drafts. You will need to revise your research paper several times, paying attention to all the special details of documentation as well as to the general concerns of manuscript preparation. The research paper included in this chapter is a model.

35a
Revising the Thesis

After studying your rough plan, your tentative thesis, and your notes (which you now have in order), reevaluate your thesis. Here are the thesis sentences that the writer developed for the Willa Cather paper:

Tentative	Revised 1	Revised 2
Willa Cather's stories are about isolation.	Cather's " 'A Death in the Desert' " and "A Wagner Matinee" show people who are isolated from familiar environments.	The central characters in Cather's stories " 'A Death in the Desert' " and "A Wagner Matinee" show the effects of an untamed country on people who go to live there from a stable, civilized world.

**35a
revise**

The thesis that appears in the final draft of the research paper is this:

Final draft

In two particular stories, " 'A Death in the Desert' " and "A Wagner Matinee," the central characters bear the burden of escape and isolation from familiar, stable traditions to a "new country."

■ **Exercise 35.1**   Look at the hypothesis (p. 415) for the paper on Willa Cather. Then examine the thesis statements as they developed for the paper. Comment on the evolution of the thesis. What was the writer's original hypothesis? How did it change? How does the thesis reflect the concerns of the hypothesis?

■ **Exercise 35.2***   Study your notes and make revisions in your thesis sentence as required.

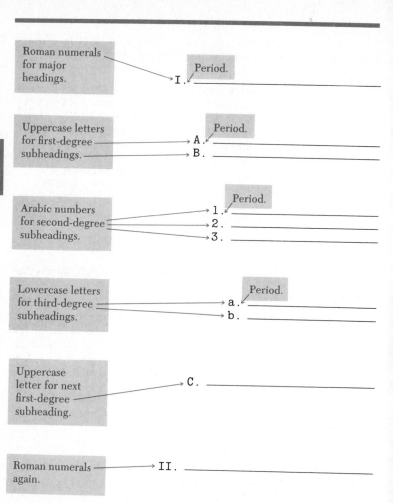

Roman numerals for major headings.

I. _____ Period.

Uppercase letters for first-degree subheadings.

A. _____ Period.
B. _____

Arabic numbers for second-degree subheadings.

1. _____ Period.
2. _____
3. _____

Lowercase letters for third-degree subheadings.

a. _____ Period.
b. _____

Uppercase letter for next first-degree subheading.

C. _____

Roman numerals again.

II. _____

35b
revise

35b
Writing a Formal Outline

Your instructor may require a formal outline, or you may find an outline useful in your efforts to refine your plan. A formal outline gives you an orderly visual scheme of your ideas. As you set down these ideas, use roman numerals for the most important points, capital letters for the next most important points, arabic numbers for supporting points under lettered points, and lowercase letters for the smallest items you include in the outline. Further subordination is possible, but you will rarely need to use as many as four levels. For most papers, two or three levels of subordination will do. The scheme is shown at the top of the opposite page.

Once you have grouped large related ideas in your notes, label them with accurate, mutually exclusive, logically arranged headings. Follow your rough plan, but concentrate on making headings sufficient in number and breadth to cover the topic properly.

35b
revise

As you look over these headings, you may see a need for some changes in organization. Make whatever changes you need to shape your ideas, and then fill in supporting information under each major heading. Watch for and delete any overlap or repetition of ideas. Watch for proper sequence of ideas.

All outlines follow the same format, but you can write them as topic outlines or sentence outlines. In a **topic outline,** you write out points as brief capsules of meaning. Each item must communicate an idea, of course, but the items need not be full sentences. In a **sentence outline,** each point appears as a complete grammatical statement, with a subject and a predicate. The sentence outline requires more effort: it asks you to name what you are going to talk about and also to indicate what you are going to say about it. For this reason, a sentence outline may be more productive, but a topic outline can be just as helpful if you think it through just as carefully.

Two rules govern the construction of every formal outline:

1. *Every entry requiring division must be divided into at least two parts.* When you divide a topic, you must have two or more subheadings under it. If you can come up with only one subpart, incorporate it into the main heading; it belongs there. In short, a *I* requires a *II*; an *A* requires a *B*; a *1* requires a *2*; an *a* requires a *b*.
2. *Main headings must be parallel in form, and subheadings under each main heading must be parallel in form.*

For a paper on black holes, a student prepared the topic outline on pages 470–471. The sentence outline on pages 478–479 shows you the skeleton of the Cather paper on pages 477–509. Study the outlines carefully and use them as models for form and style.

The rules will help you to construct a clear and useful outline. But remember that you should never be bound to your outline as you write. Feel free to use the ideas that come to all writers, ideas they did not have when they planned their work. In fact, you may prepare the formal outline

Thesis: Although the search for black holes goes on, they are, by definition, almost impossible to find.

I. Black holes vs. ordinary stars
  A. Definition of black holes
  B. Contrary forces on ordinary stars
    1. Expansion from nuclear burning
    2. Compression from gravity
  C. Theory of formation of black holes
    1. Crush of atoms
    2. Lack of light

II. Beginnings in the search for black holes
  A. Problems in finding them
    1. Their invisibility
    2. Their infinitesimal size
    3. Their place in theories of the universe
  B. Discovery of pulsars, or neutron stars

III. Russian work on black holes
  A. Idea of binary relationship
  B. Method of search
    1. Examination of star catalogs
    2. Theory of stars' X-ray emission
IV. Continuation of search among binaries
  A. <u>Uhuru</u> satellite and X-ray detection
  B. X-ray star called V861 Sco
  C. Doubts resulting from inadequate instruments
V. The continuing hunt for black holes

after you write the paper. Every essay that has a logic and structure can be outlined; so you should be able to outline your essay, once you have completed it. Then the outline will help you check that you have constructed a logical and clear piece of prose, that you have put everything in its proper place, and that you have developed a thesis in a thoughtful and well-written series of paragraphs leading to a conclusion.

■ **Exercise 35.3**   Discuss the strengths and weaknesses in the following outline. Look especially at the relation of the thesis to the points in the outline; look at the main headings and subordinate points; look at the form of the outline, including divisions and the use of numbers and letters.

```
                    Outline
Thesis: A study of liberal arts and
        sciences is valuable for
        students seeking careers in
        business.
   I. Exclusion of liberal arts and
      science courses from business
      curricula
      A. Need for specialized business
         courses for job training
  II. An understanding of people
      A. Value of psychology and
         sociology
         1. In a study of personality
            and group dynamics
      B. Value of natural sciences in
         seeing problems and in stating
         and in finding solutions to
         them
      C. Insights into human character
         from literature
         1. Complete personality studies
            from fiction
         2. Opportunities to share
            thoughts of pressured
            characters
```

III. Recognition by businesses today of
     capabilities developing from
     employees' varied educational
     backgrounds
     A. Strong qualities of character
     B. Ability to deal with future
        technologies
 IV. Transmission of humanity's
     cherished values

■ **Exercise 35.4*** As your instructor directs, prepare a formal outline for your research paper. Use a *topic* or a *sentence* outline according to your instructor's wishes.

35c
Writing the First Draft

Using your rough plan, your formal outline, and your note cards, write a rough draft of your research paper. This is not final copy, and the point is not to say everything perfectly but simply to flesh out what you have to say. Once you have paragraphs drafted, use them to adjust and refine the rough plan or your formal outline.

At this stage you will have a rough draft but a nearly final outline. Your outline should now be a guide to the next draft, although as new ideas come to you in the process of creating that draft, you may need to refine the outline further. Throughout the writing process, the outline enables you to check the logic of your progress from one point to the next. The outline also helps you check the accuracy and the consistency of your argument.

As you write your draft, you will be drawing on your note cards. Review 34a, on integrating source material into your own writing. Be sure to acknowledge all sources, using the citation and documentation system your instructor requires. Use the checklist below as a guide.

✓ **CHECKLIST:** QUESTIONS TO ANSWER AS YOU REVISE
YOUR RESEARCH PAPER

1. Is my thesis clear? Does it state accurately the intent of the paper?
2. Have I done more than simply summarize other sources? Have I made appropriate commentary on source materials?
3. Do my source materials—quotations, summaries, paraphrases—support my points throughout?
4. Do my ideas follow logically? Are transitions clear?
5. Are all sources cited? Have I always indicated my source of ideas even when paraphrasing or summarizing? Are citations unobtrusive and correctly written?
6. Are sources listed with full publication data on a separate page at the end of my paper?

35d
revise

35d
Editing the First Draft and Preparing the Final Version

Take the time to polish your prose, checking also carefully for clarity of language and ideas and for conciseness; also check paragraph and sentence structure, grammar, spelling, and mechanics. Check the accuracy of quotations, paraphrases, and summaries. Avoid plagiarism by citing sources clearly and consistently (see 34c and 34d). Most instructors ask that you type long papers, and you should follow the guidelines for manuscript preparation (3d) carefully. Handwritten research papers are hard to produce neatly because of their length and are difficult to read. If, with your instructor's permission, you choose to write your final copy in longhand, take special pains to produce a neat, clear manuscript.

Number all pages consecutively in the upper right corner, starting with page 1 of the text. Some writers type their last name before the page number in case pages are misplaced. Do not use a period, hyphen, or the word *page* (or the abbreviation *p.*) with the page number. Remember that endnotes and the list of works cited count in the total pagination of your paper. Do not paginate the title page or cover sheet. The outline is paginated with lowercase roman numerals (i, ii, iii).

✓ CHECKLIST: FORMAT FOR FINAL COPY

Final copy for a research paper or a term paper usually includes, in this order:

1. A title page. The *MLA Handbook* suggests that the author's name, the class, the date, and so on should appear on the first page of the paper, an inch down from the top and an inch from the right. The title is centered, four spaces above the text of the paper. But when formal outlines are required, many instructors prefer a title page. (A sample title page appears on p. 477.) APA recommends a cover sheet.

2. A formal outline.

3. The body of the essay.

4. Endnotes. (If your instructor requires footnotes, place them at the bottoms of pages. If you use parenthetical documentation, endnotes or footnotes will be minimal.)

5. The list of works cited.

**35e
revise**

35e
Sample Research Paper

The research paper that follows illustrates many of the suggestions made in this chapter. The paper on Willa Cather uses the MLA system of citing sources in the text. Examine the paper and the explanatory comments and use it as a model whenever you encounter problems in setting up research papers of your own.

(To show the APA citation format, we have provided references from a research paper on black holes.)

■ **Exercise 35.5*** After reading the sample paper and following the guidelines in 35c, prepare the final copy of your research paper. Observe any requirements made by your instructor.

(t-a) Title: one-third down, double-spaced.

(t-b) Cather used double quotation marks around the title of the story to show her debt to Robert Browning's poem "A Death in the Desert," which gave Cather her title. The title of the story, then, is written as a quote within a quote.

(t-c) Leave two inches before typing the next line.

(t-d) The writer's name, the instructor's name, the course and section number, and the date the paper is submitted, all double-spaced.

(t-a)   Isolation and Escape
                       in
(t-b)   Cather's " 'A Death in the Desert' "
                      and
               "A Wagner Matinee"

(t-c)

                       by
(t-d)   Shirley Hawkins
                Mr. C. Prager
          English 101, Section 4
              April 7, 1990

Thesis: The central characters in Willa
Cather's stories " 'A Death in the
Desert' " and "A Wagner Matinee"
show the effects of an untamed
country on people from a stable,
civilized world.

I. The main characters show the physical
burden of living in the barren West.

   A. In " 'A Death in the Desert' "
Katharine Gaylord, self-isolated
in the Cheyenne of her youth, is
dying of tuberculosis.

   B. In "A Wagner Matinee" Aunt
Georgiana is a wreck after thirty
years on the Nebraska frontier.

II. The characters are also burdened by
the toll on their spirits.

   A. Wyoming is for Katharine a
spiritual desert.

      1. She misses her former life as a
famous singer.

      2. The emptiness of the desert
intrudes on the room she
modeled after music studios in
the East.

      3. She will never return to art.

      4. Her death separates her from
art no more surely than did her
life.

    B. Georgiana's spirit also suffers the deprivations of frontier life.

        1. In a world of worries about survival she had little opportunity to enjoy the music she has loved so much.

        2. When she returns to Boston, the prairie world is always painfully close.

III. Cather uses music to identify the pain of separation from civilization and life in a primitive setting.

    A. For Katharine Gaylord music symbolizes the swift passage of her own life.

        1. Both life and artistic achievement are too brief.

        2. In a new sonata she recognizes her own personal tragedy of isolation from music.

    B. The music Aunt Georgiana hears echoes her particular condition.

        1. The overture to <u>Tannhäuser</u> reflects her own struggle between art and the frontier.

        2. Other selections echo the opposing forces in her life.

IV. Cather acknowledged that the theme of escape ran through her work.

(1-a) **Title is centered two inches from the top of the page.**

(1-b) *qtd. in Woodress:* **the source of the quote from Fisher is** *Willa Cather* **by James Woodress (listed among works cited, p. 509). As Fisher's original article was not available, the writer used a secondary source.**

(1-c) *Gerber, preface:* **the quote appears in the preface, which is unpaginated in Gerber's book (listed among works cited, on p. 507).**

(1-d) **The thesis clearly states the topic. The introduction builds to the thesis. Here is an earlier draft of the introduction.**

Dorothy Canfield Fisher was a friend of Willa Cather's from college days at the University of Nebraska. She wrote an essay on Cather's works for the New York *Herald Tribune* in 1933. She said: "the one real subject of all her books is the effect a new country—our new country—has on the people transplanted to it from the traditions of a stable, complex civilization" (qtd. in Woodress 247). Fisher was answering complaints by critics about disconnectedness in Cather's novels. But even in Cather's short stories, you can see that Fisher is right. The central characters in the stories generally are hurt by their escape from familiar places to a new one.

Isolation and Escape in
Cather's " 'A Death in the Desert' "
and "A Wagner Matinee"

In a 1933 essay for the New York
Herald Tribune Dorothy Canfield
Fisher wrote about her friend from
college days at the University of
Nebraska. "I offer you a hypothesis
about Willa Cather's work: the one
real subject of all her books is the
effect a new country--our new
country--has on the people
transplanted to it from the traditions
of a stable, complex civilization"
(1-b) (qtd. in Woodress 247). Fisher was
addressing complaints by contemporary
critics who saw disconnectedness in
Cather's writing, and Fisher wanted to
show that novels like A Lost Lady and
Shadows on the Rock had a common bond
(1-c) (Gerber, preface). But even in
Cather's first collection of short
stories, The Troll Garden, published
in 1905, readers can see that Fisher's
(1-d) comment is valid. In two particular
stories, " 'A Death in the Desert' "
and "A Wagner Matinee," the central

(2-a) The writer's last name and the page number appear near the top of all pages; margins are 1 to 1½ inches.

(2-b) The words *character* and *story* and the repeated reference to separation connect the paragraphs. The first sentence of this paragraph corresponds to the major heading I in the outline. The rest of this paragraph and the next develop subhead I.A in the outline.

(2-c) The summary gives only essential details to help readers who may not know the story.

(2-d) The quote blends with the writer's own prose. The parenthetical citation indicates that the quoted words appear on page 72 of the collection *The Troll Garden,* abbreviated here as *TG.* The title is required along with Cather's name because the list of works cited contains other works by Cather.

(2-a)

characters bear the burden of escape
and isolation from familiar, stable
traditions in a "new country."

(2-b)

    The physical appearance of the
main character in each story shows
the strain of the separation she lived
through. When we first see her in
" 'A Death in the Desert,' " Katherine

(2-c) Gaylord, a former singer, is dying of
lung disease in Cheyenne, Wyoming,
the home of her youth. In the past she
had lived in New York and Chicago and
had traveled throughout Europe with
the brilliant yet selfish composer
Adriance Hilgarde, a man she loved
deeply without his knowing it.

    Now Everett Hilgarde, Adriance's
brother and an almost exact look-
alike for the famous musician,
observes Katharine, who is being
destroyed by her long illness. Her
loose-fitting gown could not hide

(2-d) "the sharp outlines of her emaciated
body, but the stamp of her disease
was there; simple and ugly and
obtrusive, a pitiless fact that could
not be disguised or evaded" (Cather,
TG 72). She has stooped shoulders;
she sways unevenly when she walks; and
her face is "older, sadder, softer"

(3-a) **The writer has paraphrased from the words Katharine Gaylord speaks in the story. Here is the original source:**

Formerly, when it was not *if* I should ever sing Brunnhilde, but quite simply when I *should* sing Brunnhilde, I was always starving myself and thinking what I might drink and what I might now. But broken music boxes may drink whatsoever they list, and no one cares whether they lose their figure.

(3-b) **The writer interprets the quotes she has presented.**

(3-c) **Corresponding to subhead II.B of the outline, this paragraph briefly summarizes important plot elements in "A Wagner Matinee." Note the smooth integration of a quote from the story in the opening sentence.**

(3-d) **The page number alone is enough in parentheses here. Readers know that the discussion is still about "A Wagner Matinee."**

(3-e) **The superscript 1 corresponds to reference note 1 on page 13.**

(72) than when Everett saw her a long time ago. Self-exiled in the

(3-a) Gaylords' house, Katharine refers to herself as a broken music box (81).

(3-b) Her physical decay reflects her separation from the lively world of art she once knew.

(3-c)   In "A Wagner Matinee" Aunt Georgiana, a former music teacher at the Boston Conservatory, returns to Boston--"the place longed for hungrily half a lifetime" (Cather, TG 110). For thirty years she had tended a ranch on the desolate Nebraska frontier. Her nephew Clark, who spent some of his boyhood years on the farm with her and his uncle Howard, notes

(3-d) her "misshapen figure" (108), her "soiled linen duster," and her stooped shoulders "now almost bent together over her sunken chest.... She wore ill-fitting false teeth, and her skin was as yellow as a Mongolian's from constant exposure to a pitiless wind and to the alkaline water which hardens the most transparent cuticle into a sort of flexible leather"

(3-e) (109).[1] Earlier, when Clark received the letter from Howard announcing Aunt Georgiana's arrival, Clark

(4-a) The opening sentence corresponds to the major heading II in the outline. The subhead A identifies the character to be discussed here. Second-level subheads 1, 2, 3, and 4 correspond to details introduced and expanded upon in succeeding paragraphs.

(4-b) The quotation card for this source appears below. Note that in the paper the writer quotes only the most relevant point.

Kohler, "WC," 9.
"To a generation coming to maturity between wars Miss Cather already seemed a little old-fashioned. It was true that she did not always flatter the West, and her stories were filled with images of the waste that its barren loneliness imposed upon the human spirit."
* Good statement to support Fisher's point -- tough new world's effect on the spirit.

(4-c) Since the sentence identifies Porter as the source, only the page number is required as documentation. Readers can check the list of works cited for full publishing data.

said that her name called up her figure, "at once pathetic and grotesque" (107). Clark himself knows about the pains of that frontier life; when he thinks of corn-husking days on the ranch, he says, "I felt the knuckles of my thumb...as though they were raw again" (107).

(4-a)   But Cather's stories show more than just the effects of the untamed West on a person's body. They also show "the waste that its barren (4-b) loneliness impose[s] upon the human spirit" (Kohler 9). It is true that for Katharine Gaylord, life in the West has not caused her bodily pain. Still, her physical condition is a symbol of the barren life the former artist must live now as she is dying of tuberculosis. As Katherine Anne Porter says in her 1952 Afterword to The Troll Garden, "Wyoming is for her not only an earthly desert but one of the heart, the mind, the spirit" (4-c) (151). Forced to leave the life of musical fame that she once had, she is very unhappy, her brother says, dying "like a rat in a hole, out of her own world, and she can't fall back into ours" (Cather, TG 69).

(5-a) **This paragraph develops the second-level subhead II.A.1 and II.A.2.**

(5-b) **The writer interprets and evaluates Cather's image.**

(5-c) **Here is the signal card that the writer made and, below it, the quote from "A Wagner Matinee."**

Cather, "Wagner Matinee," 74-75.
Quote about Everett talking with Katharine – as
desert suddenly glares through window -- good
to show contrast between two worlds tugging
at Katharine.

(5-d) **Note the writer's interpretation. Here is the paragraph from the short story:**

"I remember," Everett said seriously, twirling the pencil between his fingers and looking, as he sat with his head thrown back, out under the red window blind which was raised just a little, and as it swung back and forth in the wind revealed the glaring panorama of the desert—a blinding stretch of yellow, flat as the sea in dead calm, splotched here and there with deep purple shadows; and, beyond, the ragged-blue outline of the mountains and the peaks of snow, white as the white clouds.

(5-e) **This paragraph develops points II.A.3 and II.A.4 in the outline.**

(5-a) We can see how much that former life meant to her and how deeply she misses it. It is easier to die in the West, she maintains: "to go East would be dying twice" (70). It is not that Wyoming is a new land for her-- she grew up there as a child--but it

(5-b) is a land now alien to her spiritual needs. With a brilliant image Cather shows the conflicting forces of past and present in Katherine's life. In the Wyoming house, the music room makes Everett feel that he has stepped into a familiar New York studio almost exactly like his brother's, "so individual and poignantly reminiscent here in Wyoming" (71). As he sits chatting with Katharine, a window

(5-c) blind swinging in the wind reveals "the glaring panorama of the desert--a blinding stretch of yellow, flat as the sea in dead calm" (75).

(5-d) Blinding, yellow, flat, dead: so is Katharine's life away from the East, even in the studio room she has tried so hard to make like Adriance's.

(5-e) Only Everett with his tales of city life and, finally (at Everett's prompting), a letter from Adriance with a copy of a new sonata he has

(6-a) **The writer has paraphrased Bloom and Bloom:**

This avowed hostility between the artist and society gave her the subject for an undergraduate theme, which was published in the *State Journal,* on Thomas Carlyle's fierce withdrawal from social concerns. Later, in " 'A Death in the Desert,' " she further alluded to the alienation as a "long warfare" so futile and enervating that it can only distract the artist's attention from his singular purpose.

(6-b) **The opening sentence places the issues of frontier life and artistic fulfillment in a larger critical context and provides a thoughtful bridge to the discussion of "A Wagner Matinee." The parenthetical documentation identifies three critics who have called attention to the issue emphasized here. Full documentation is given in the list of works cited.**

(6-c) **The point here matches the first-level subhead II.B in the outline.**

(6-d) **Brief details of the plot explain Aunt Georgiana's reactions in Boston.**

just written cheer Katharine up somewhat. But it is very clear from her regular conversations with Everett that her desperate longing for the art she once knew and her own fate not to achieve it are the great ironies of the story. When the singer dies, Cather writes, "the madness of art (6-a) was over for Katharine" (86). As Bloom and Bloom have noted (151), Cather was fascinated by the artist isolated from society. In the portrait of Katharine Gaylord, we see that the singer's death separated her from art no more surely than the final years of her life.

(6-b)   Many critics note Cather's concern with the difficulties an artist has in leading a satisfying life on the harsh frontier (Gerber 44; Bloom and Bloom 8; Stouck 299). As (6-c) with Katharine Gaylord, "the fatality of deprivation" (Van Ghent 11) has a serious effect on Clark's Aunt Georgiana in "A Wagner Matinee." Yet Georgiana's circumstances are somewhat different from Katharine's. Passionate love, not illness, has removed her from the civilized world of Boston. (6-d) Against her family's wishes, she eloped with a shiftless village boy

(7-a) **This paragraph develops the second-level subhead II.B.2 in the outline.**

(7-b) **Compare the quotation with the paragraph from which it comes. The ellipsis indicates the omission of words that the writer felt were unnecessary for her point.**

The concert was over; the people filed out of the hall chattering and laughing, glad to relax and find the living level again, but my kinswoman made no effort to rise. The harpist slipped its green felt cover over his instrument; the flute players shook the water from their mouthpieces; the men of the orchestra went out one by one, leaving the stage to the chairs and music stands, empty as a winter cornfield.

(7-c) **The writer's evaluation here emphasizes the importance of the image and justifies the use of the long quotation.**

who was nine years younger than she
was. Howard led her to the Nebraska
homestead, which she did not leave
for many years. Their lives were
always threatened by roving bands of
Indians and insufficient supplies. A
little parlor organ and church singing
provided the only music she heard
during all that time. Clark recalls
that once, as he practiced at the
organ, she told him in a quivering
voice, "Don't love it so well, Clark,
or it may be taken from you" (Cather,
TG 110).

(7-a)   Unlike Katharine in her permanent
exile, Aunt Georgiana returns to her
former world of art. Clark takes her
to a performance of the symphony
orchestra. Here, too, Cather's images
weave together the civilized world
and the grim prairie. Clark wonders
how much of her ability to understand
music "had been dissolved in soapsuds
or worked into bread or milked in the
bottom of the pail" (114). At the end
of the concert, Aunt Georgiana sits
weeping as the musicians file out,
(7-b) "leaving the stage...empty as a winter
cornfield" (115). The final
(7-c) overwhelming image of the story shows

(8-a) This quotation occupies more than four typed lines and therefore is set off from the text. Introduced by a colon, the quotation starts on a new line indented ten spaces from the left margin. Quotation marks are not used and all lines are double-spaced. As the quotation is part of a single paragraph, no further paragraph indentation is necessary. When a quotation is set off, the parenthetical reference comes after the punctuation mark. (The options of quoting, paraphrasing, and summarizing the original source are discussed in 34a.)

(8-b) Note the pair of single quotation marks within the pair of double quotation marks to indicate a quote within a quote.

(8-c) The opening sentence corresponds to major heading III in the outline.

the utter horror of the transplanted
artist:

(8-a)
> For her, just outside the
> door of the concert hall,
> lay the black pond with the
> cattle-tracked bluffs; the
> tall unpainted house, with
> weather-curled boards; naked
> as a tower, the crook-backed
> ash seedlings where the
> dishcloths hung to dry; the
> gaunt, molting turkeys
> picking up refuse about the
> kitchen door. (115)

It is the refuse of Aunt Georgiana's
existence. Clark realizes that no
matter how painful a human life, the
soul always can be revived. Yet we
must wonder if, in fact, he did a
service for his aunt by reawakening
her to the joys she had missed for so
long. We understand, as Clark does at
(8-b)
the end, when she "burst into tears
and sobbed pleadingly. 'I don't want
to go, Clark, I don't want to go!' "
(115). Yet, of course, go she must.

(8-c)
> It is obvious that Katharine and
> Georgiana are both very much involved
> in music, and in the two stories,
> music helps Cather show how dramatic
> the separation from civilized society

(9-a) **The superscript 2 corresponds to the reference note on page 505.**

(9-b) **The citation indicates a paraphrase. Although the writer's language is original, she nonetheless acknowledges the source of her ideas. Merely changing Brennan's words does not change the fact that the ideas are his.**

It seems likely, too, that she subscribed to a prevalent nineteenth-century view (one prevalent even yet, for that matter) that music is the supreme act, that the musical experience — in its sensuous immediacy, its emotional intensity and profound spiritual appeal — is the most rapturous, most transcendent, the most certainly ineffable of all aesthetic experiences. In Willa Cather's fiction, at any rate, it is the musical moment which is generally employed to characterize a transcendent rhapsodic emotion that drenches the soul in its intensity but eludes all precise definition.

(9-c) **The opening sentence corresponds to outline point III.A. The rest of the paragraph develops outline points III.A.1 and III.A.2.**

(9-d) **The writer interprets the meaning of the image and relates it to the thesis of the paper.**

(9-a) can be for a person isolated in a primitive setting. Music is a very important element in much of Cather's fiction.[2] Of all the arts, Cather saw music as the most dynamic form in our culture--even more dynamic than literature. Through the power of music Cather characterizes an emotion so powerful that it goes beyond ordinary limits to saturate the human soul

(9-b) (Brennan, "Music" 175).

(9-c)   Richard Giannone sees music for Katherine Gaylord in " 'A Death in the Desert' " as a symbol of how swiftly her life is passing. Though art is humanity's supreme effort, it is futile, finally, because life and artistic achievement are so brief (41). Transplanted now from the life of art, she realizes her dilemma as she listens to Adriance's composition. As Everett plays the piece, Katharine recognizes its great tragic themes. Adriance's achievement prods her own suffering. "This is my tragedy, as I lie here spent by the racecourse," she proclaims, "listening to the feet of the runners as they pass me. Ah, God! The swift feet of the runners!"

(9-d) (81). The feet of the runners are elements of that stable, complex

(10-a) **The opening sentence corresponds to III.B in the outline. The rest of the paragraph expands on III.B.1.**

world, to use Fisher's terms again, from which Katharine was transplanted. Adriance's music tells her of the "tragedy of the soul" and "the tragedy of effort and failure, the thing Keats called hell" (Cather, _TG_ 81). It is, of course, Katharine's own failure that she recognizes in the sonata.

(10-a)   In "A Wagner Matinee" the musical selections at the concert echo the themes of the story. The first piece Aunt Georgiana hears is the overture to _Tannhäuser_, one of Wagner's early operas. The overture starts with the Pilgrims' Chorus, the solemn chanting of travelers on their way to Rome (Ewen 673). Giannone says that the motif in this chorus "represents the ecstasy of sacred yearnings" (43). Then the Venusberg motif begins, the music of the sensual, tempting, yet disturbing world of Venus and her followers. Giannone sees this as a contrasting world of profane longings. He points out that in the overture to _Tannhäuser_, Wagner presents the "struggle between the sacred and profane in man" (43). For Aunt Georgiana, the sacred is her

(11-a) This paragraph develops point III.B.2 in the outline.

(11-b) The conclusion reminds readers of the introduction and the important point made by Fisher. This paragraph is not simply a restatement of the introductory paragraph. The writer provides interesting background information as she explains Cather's own reaction to her friend's criticism. The conclusion builds further credibility for the thesis of the paper. The writer is implying that even Cather might acknowledge that the two stories treated the lives of women transplanted to a new country from stable societies.

(11-c) The citation "Cather" refers to an encyclopedia entry in the list of works cited.

higher yearning for art and music;
the profane is the dry prairie in an
unfriendly world. The terrible tragedy
here, Giannone suggests, is that "in
the tug between 'the inconceivable
silence of the plains' and 'the little
parlor organ,' silence won" (43).

(11-a)   Other selections that Aunt
Georgiana hears at the matinee,
including excerpts from The Flying
Dutchman and Tristan and Isolde,
similarly reflect the battle between
the opposing forces that she so fully
embodies. The last piece, Siegfried's
funeral march from the Ring cycle,
signals the defeat of Wagner's hero,
just as it predicts Aunt Georgiana's
defeat--her return to Nebraska after
the concert ends. Unlike many of
Wagner's operas, "A Wagner Matinee"
does not end in glory or victory,
with good overpowering evil. Art does
not win here, nor do sacred
yearnings. Nothing redeems Aunt
Georgiana's fate (Giannone 45).

(11-b)   By 1933, when Dorothy Canfield
Fisher was writing her essay for the
Tribune, Cather was highly sensitive
to comments by critics. Honored for
literary accomplishments with the
(11-c) Prix Femina Americain ("Cather"),

(12-a) Here the writer draws upon another primary source to make an important point. Note again the smooth integration of source material.

(12-b) The conclusion highlights major points made throughout the research paper.

she nonetheless was attacked by many of her contemporaries (Murphy and Synnott 12-14). After she read a prepublication copy of Fisher's essay, Cather sent her friend a telegram asking her to give up the project. As for Fisher's idea that Cather's fiction deals with the effects of a new country on people removed to it from a civilized world, Cather unhappily "summarized this thesis in one word, 'escape' " (Woodress 247). Yet she recognized that this theme ran through her work. Just a few years

(12-a) later she would write in a letter to <u>The Commonweal</u>, "What has art ever been but escape?" ("On Writing" 18). In " 'A Death in the Desert' " and "A Wagner Matinee" Cather explores the complex theme of escape by showing

(12-b) artistic women transplanted from civilized societies into hostile worlds.

(13-a) These notes correspond to the superscripts that appear on pages 3 and 9 of the research paper. Notes generally go on a separate page at the end of the text with the word *Notes* centered one inch from the top. Notes are double-spaced and indented five spaces from the left margin. If more than one line is required, subsequent lines are flush with the left margin. Some instructors require the notes to be placed at the bottom of the page on which the matching numeral appears in the text. See 34f.

(13-b) Note the format of the multiple references. The writer separates the references with semicolons. No page numbers follow the first three references because in each case the writer is referring to the whole piece.

Notes

(13-a)

[1]Cather's family and friends objected to her portrait of Nebraska life when this story first appeared in _Everybody's Magazine_. A good friend, Will Jones, complained that strangers would always associate Nebraska with Aunt Georgiana's terrible shape, her false teeth, and her yellow skin. Cather denied that she wanted to disparage her homeland but admitted that her family felt insulted: "They had already told her that it was not nice to tell such things" (Woodress 117).

(13-b)

[2]Giannone; Brennan, "Willa Cather"; Brennan, "Music"; Gerber 71-73; Bloom and Bloom 123; Daiches 8; Van Ghent 20-21.

Entries are listed alphabetically by author's last name or, as with unsigned works, by the first main word of the title. Books and articles are not separated.

(14-a) A book with two authors. *UP* stands for *University Press.*

(14-b) Four hyphens followed by a period indicate a piece by the author of the previous piece. Both selections here are journal articles with pages numbered consecutively throughout the annual volume. The articles are listed alphabetically by the first word of the title.

(14-c) An article in an encyclopedia.

(14-d) A republished book. The date of the original edition is 1905; the date of the current edition is 1971. Also, this NAL book has a special imprint, Plume, which precedes the publisher's name.

(14-e) Standard reference to a book with one author.

(14-f) An entry for an encyclopedia in only one edition. Ewen wrote the particular entry and the rest of the book as well. He is author of the article and author of the encyclopedia. Hence, his name appears in two places.

Works Cited

(14-a) Bloom, Edward A., and Lillian D.
        Bloom. <u>Willa Cather's Gift of
        Sympathy</u>. Carbondale: Southern
        Illinois UP, 1962.

Brennan, Joseph X. "Music and Willa
        Cather." <u>University Review</u> 31
        (1965): 257-264.

(14-b) ----."Willa Cather and Music."
        <u>University Review</u> 31 (1965):
        175-183.

(14-c) "Cather." <u>World Scope Encyclopedia</u>.
        1955 ed.

Cather, Willa. <u>On Writing</u>. New York:
        Knopf, 1949.

(14-d) ----.<u>The Troll Garden</u>. 1905. New York.
        Plume-NAL, 1971.

(14-e) Daiches, David. <u>Willa Cather: A
        Critical Introduction</u>. Ithaca:
        Cornell UP, 1959.

(14-f) Ewen, David. "Tannhauser." <u>The New
        Encyclopedia of the Opera</u>, by
        Ewen. New York: Hill, 1971.

Gerber, Philip L. <u>Willa Cather</u>.
        Boston: Twayne, 1975.

Giannone, Richard. <u>Music in Willa
        Cather's Fiction</u>. Lincoln: U of
        Nebraska P, 1968.

(15-a) Murphy's complete book is *not* cited in the text of the paper and hence might seem out of place here. However, since the writer of the paper used *two* articles from this anthology, she lists the collection itself and then cites the articles with *cross-references* to this main entry. See 15-c below.

(15-b) Murphy's name is spelled out here as well as in the previous entry. The first entry is a book published under his name alone. If the list included other books by Murphy alone, four hyphens and a period would appear in place of his name in the second and subsequent entries (as in 14-b). The four hyphens, however, stand for only the name or names of authors in the preceding entry. Since the authors of "The Recognition of Willa Cather's Art" are Murphy *and* Synnott, both names are listed.

(15-c) A cross-reference. "Murphy 1–28" refers readers to *Critical Essays on Willa Cather,* the main entry for Murphy. The numbers 1–28 identify the pages on which this essay is found.

(15-d) Porter's Afterword, published in 1952, appears in the volume of *The Troll Garden* already cited under Cather's name. The cross-reference "Cather, *Troll Garden*" is used instead of "Cather" because another book by Cather appears in the list.

(15-e) Another cross-reference to Murphy.

(15-f) A book in a series. When the title page indicates that the book is part of a series, put the series name (without quotations or underlining) and number before the publishing data.

Kohler, Dayton. "Willa Cather:
    1876–1947." <u>College English</u> 9
    (1947): 8–18.

(15-a) Murphy, John J., ed. <u>Critical Essays
    on Willa Cather</u>. Boston: Hall,
    1984.

(15-b) Murphy, John J., and Kevin A. Synnott.
    "The Recognition of Willa
(15-c) Cather's Art." Murphy 1–28.

(15-d) Porter, Katherine Anne. Afterword.
    1952. Cather, <u>Troll Garden</u>,
    134–151.

(15-e) Stouck, David. 1905. "Willa Cather's
    Last Four Books." Murphy
    290–304.

(15-f) Van Ghent, Dorothy. <u>Willa Cather</u>. U
    of Minnesota Pamphlets on
    American Writers 36. Minneapolis:
    U of Minnesota P, 1964.

Woodress, James. <u>Willa Cather</u>. 1970.
    Lincoln: Bison-U of Nebraska P,
    1975.

Sample References Page: APA Format

References

Cloud, P. (1978). <u>Cosmos, earth and man: A short history of the universe</u>. New Haven: Yale University Press.

Dupree, A. K., & Hartman, L. (1979, October). Hunting for black holes. <u>Natural History</u>, pp. 30–37.

Jastrow, R. (1979). <u>Red giants and white dwarfs</u>. New York: Warner.

Schwarzschild, Karl. (1985). In <u>Encyclopaedia Britannica Micropaedia</u> (Vol. 10, p. 548). New York: Encyclopaedia Britannica.

Thomson, D. (1979, July 14). V861 Sco's UV flare. <u>Science News</u>, p. 25.

Thorne, K. S. (1977). The search for black holes. In <u>Cosmology + 1</u> (pp. 66–70). San Francisco: Freeman.

PART
EIGHT

OTHER
WRITING
TASKS

511

36

WRITING LOGICAL ARGUMENTS

We argue to persuade others to accept a point of view. In ordinary speech, the word *argument* is often associated with anger and conflict. But in writing, and especially in research papers, **argument** means a conflict of opinions, not of people. The writer of an argumentative paper strives by reason and logic to persuade readers to accept the writer's point of view or conclusion. A good argument is one that is carefully stated and well supported by evidence; it makes friends, not enemies.

36a
Differentiating Between Argument and Persuasion

Persuasion includes any means by which we get people to do what we want them to do. You can persuade some people to buy a certain brand of beer by showing them funny commercials featuring the beer. You can persuade others to give money to help the homeless by showing them photographs of homeless people living in the streets. You may persuade your parents to lend you the family car for the weekend because you want to go to a party.

Persuasion includes argument. An argument is a carefully reasoned conclusion derived from evidence. We make arguments to prove that our point of view is more logical than others. We argue that our interpretation of *Hamlet* or of a short story or novel is the correct one, and we quote from the text to support our conclusion. You want your readers to think through your argument and agree with you. The primary appeal of argument is to reason, to judgment. You evaluate evidence and draw conclusions that seem to be inescapable or at least extremely probable.

The parts of an argument are tightly connected. These logical connections can be built on two kinds of reasoning: *inductive* and *deductive*. Inductive reasoning moves from particular examples to general truths.

Statistics show that cigarette smokers are ten times more likely than non-smokers to get lung cancer. The examination of thousands of specific events leads to a general truth: cigarette smoking is dangerous to health. Deductive reasoning moves from a general truth we know to a conclusion about a specific instance. Deductive reasoning may start with a general truth that has been proved by induction. Cigarette smoking is dangerous to health; therefore, if you smoke cigarettes, you will probably not live as long as a nonsmoker.

36b
Using Inductive Reasoning

The most common way to reason is by induction: we have specific experiences and move from them to general conclusions about what they prove or mean.

    Some conclusions require rigorous study to substantiate. Arguments about medical research, for example, often stand on years of experiments. We conclude that cigarette smoking causes lung cancer because the disease is common among heavy cigarette smokers and relatively uncommon among nonsmokers. But we do not know what agent in cigarette smoke causes the cancer, and we cannot observe the smoke acting to make a cancer. Our conclusion is based on *statistics,* a number of instances that seem to have meaning when we construct a generalization that explains them. Some conclusions can be drawn from only one instance. If you accidentally burn yourself with a lighted match, you conclude that matches should be handled with care. You do not have to burn yourself over and over again. The same is true if you slip on an icy sidewalk. You do not have to fall again and again to prove to yourself that ice can be dangerous.

    Here an argument based on induction is presented by Jane Brody, nutrition expert for *The New York Times,* in writing about cholesterol:

> In a famous study of 12,000 middle-aged men in seven developed countries, Dr. Ancel Keys and his coworkers from the University of Minnesota found that the people of east Finland had the highest death rate from diseases of the coronary arteries—220 per 10,000 men in a five-year period—the highest percentage of saturated animal fats in their diet (22 percent of total calories were saturated fats, mostly from cheese, butter, and milk), and the highest blood cholesterol levels. The United States was not far behind in coronary deaths (185 per 10,000) and blood cholesterol levels.

But in Mediterranean countries like Greece and Italy, where the fat is mostly of vegetable origin and therefore unsaturated and lacking cholesterol, early death from coronary heart disease was far less common. And in Japan, where only 10 percent of the diet is fat and most of that is polyunsaturated fat from vegetable sources (only 3 percent of total calories is saturated fat), the cholesterol levels were very low and the death rate from coronary artery disease was only 20 per 10,000.

—JANE BRODY

The conclusion to which this assembled evidence points is that a diet high in cholesterol leads to heart attacks. Here is induction in action.

Inductive arguments begin as people study issues and raise questions that are not easily answered. Often people develop hypotheses or theories to explain the facts and then study the evidence inductively to see if they are true. That is what nutrition experts did in the studies Jane Brody cites.

Inductive argument always involves a gathering of facts and the drawing of a conclusion from those facts. Here are some simple examples:

**36a/b
argue**

Fact	Conclusion
More than one thousand people were vaccinated against smallpox during a great epidemic that swept our state early in the century. Not one of those people got the disease. Not one of the people who did get the disease had been vaccinated.	Vaccinations against smallpox prevented the disease.
My next-door neighbor got into a fight last week with the mail carrier because he said the mail carrier made too much noise walking up on the porch to deliver the mail. The same neighbor was arrested at a high school basketball game Tuesday night because he started a fight with an official over a foul call. He threatened to fight the trash haulers because they made so much noise with his garbage cans, and the paper boy refused to deliver papers anymore after my neighbor yelled at him for being late.	My neighbor has a bad temper.

Charles Darwin, the nineteenth-century naturalist, always asked questions as he studied facts. He wondered, for example, how certain plants that grew in ponds and marshes came to be spread across the oceans so that the same varieties grew thousands of miles apart. In his travels he noticed that the types of marsh grass that grew along the shores of North America also grew along the coasts of Europe, yet the animals in these widely separated regions differed considerably. Darwin could understand why aquatic plants (seaweed and so on) might have a wide range. But how did plants with roots in the soil spread around the earth? To solve the problem he made an **inference.**

When we infer, we use some previous experience or knowledge to make sense of something we observe. If someone smiles at us, we infer friendly feelings because when people have smiled at us in the past, they have been showing friendly feelings. If we wake up in the night and hear a drumming of water on the roof, we infer that it is raining, though we cannot see the rain fall. We have heard rain fall on our roof before, and we recognize the sound when we hear it. If we see fire trucks roaring down the street, their sirens wailing and all the firemen looking grim, we assume there is a fire somewhere. Inference is not certainty. A smile may mask evil intent; some practical joker may have turned a hose on our roof; the firemen may be going out for coffee. But none of these possibilities is as likely as the expectation we have as a result of our experience. A smile is probably a sign of friendship; water drumming on the roof is probably rain; and the fire trucks screaming down the street are probably going to a fire. Darwin considered the problem of the wide dispersion of certain plants and constructed an argument to answer this question: How is it that the same varieties of plants grow so many thousands of miles apart?

**36a/b
argue**

> With respect to plants, it has long been known what enormous ranges many fresh-water and even marsh species have, both over continents and to the most remote oceanic islands. This is strikingly illustrated, according to Alph. de Candolle [a French botanist], in those large groups of terrestrial plants, which have very few aquatic members; for the latter seem immediately to acquire, as if in consequence, a wide range. I think favourable means of dispersal explain this fact. I have before mentioned that earth occasionally adheres in some quantity to the feet and beaks of birds. Wading birds, which frequent the muddy edges of ponds, if suddenly flushed, would be the most likely to have muddy feet. Birds of this order wander more than those of any other; and they are occasionally found on the most remote and barren islands of the open ocean; they would not be likely to alight on the surface of the sea, so that any dirt on their feet would not be washed off; and when gaining the land, they would be sure to fly to their natural fresh-water haunts. I do not believe that botanists are aware

how charged the mud of ponds is with seeds; I have tried several little experiments, but will here give only the most striking case: I took in February three tablespoonfuls of mud from three different points, beneath water, on the edge of a little pond: this mud when dried weighed only 6¾ ounces; I kept it covered up in my study for six months, pulling up and counting each plant as it grew; the plants were of many different kinds, and were altogether 537 in number; and yet the viscid mud was all contained in a breakfast cup! Considering these facts, I think it would be an inexplicable circumstance if water-birds did not transport the seeds of fresh-water plants to unstocked ponds and streams, situated at very distant points. The same agency may have come into play with the eggs of some of the smaller fresh-water animals.

— CHARLES DARWIN

Forming Plausible Conclusions

Darwin's conclusion is plausible. To say that a conclusion is *plausible* is to say that we can believe it even if we cannot prove it by observation. Most argumentation is based on plausible reasoning rather than on direct observation. When we can observe something directly, we do not have to argue about it.

Induction builds on facts and arrives at an explanation that tries to account for everything we know. But we may lack the key observation that will prove our conclusion beyond all doubt. We can only infer a conclusion. Scientists often make observations of several facts (they usually call these facts *phenomena*) and try to explain them in a logical way. They arrive at a *theory* that explains the facts — an inference, a conclusion that seems to arise naturally from what they know.

An inductive argument proceeds from the gathering of facts and the explanation of how these facts are related. That is, an inductive argument involves analyzing facts and deciding which of them are causes and which of them are effects. Sometimes that analysis leads to an obvious conclusion: cigarette smoking causes lung cancer. But sometimes the conclusions are not so obvious. When a fifty-five-mile-an-hour speed limit was imposed on American highways after the fuel crisis of 1973, traffic fatalities dropped dramatically. Did the lowered speed limit cause this drop? Or did the completion of the American interstate highway system, which occurred about the same time, cause the drop? One must study the issue and gather many data before one can make a compelling argument on either side.

Weighing the Plausibilities

Inductive arguments may lead to a clearly plausible point of view. For many centuries, no one knew what caused typhoid fever. Once scientists observed under the microscope that the blood of everyone who had typhoid fever contained certain bacteria that were not seen in the blood of people free of the disease, the most plausible inference was that those bacteria caused the disease.

But often in the arguments you make in college papers, in position papers in business or professional life, and in writing about public issues, you discover many plausible sides to an argument. Arguments that have only one side are rarely interesting. So you must assemble the facts and decide what you want to argue. Your decision may depend on how you interpret those facts, or it may depend on what you value in those facts. In either case, you must gather as many facts as you can to be certain that you are being fair to the evidence and let readers know that you know what you are talking about.

✓ **CHECKLIST: INDUCTIVE REASONING**

1. What question do you want to ask of the data?
2. Do you have enough specific facts to suggest an answer to the question?
3. How are these facts related to one another?
4. What answer takes into account the most evidence?
5. Can you suggest other plausible answers to your question?
6. What evidence opposes your answer?

**36a/b
argue**

■ **Exercise 36.1**   Construct a brief argument from the following group of statements to answer the question "Should the library of Sourmash State University be kept open on Friday nights?" Assume that each statement is true; consequently you can use each statement in your argument.

The administration of Sourmash State University wants to close the school library at 6:00 P.M. on Fridays. Accounts figure that it costs an average of $984.62 for heat, lights, and personnel to keep the library open from 6:00 P.M. until 11:00 P.M. Closing the library will mean a saving of about $10,000 every ten weeks, or about $30,000 during the academic year. An average of five readers and one professor use the library on Friday night. On the average, ten books were checked out of the library on each of the last ten Fridays that the library was open. "We are trying to save money so student tuitions will not rise," President Vessie Reins told the faculty in explaining the decision to shut the library. One of the students who use the library every Friday night is senior Helen Walden. Her novel *Late Hours* won the Pulitzer Prize last year and has been translated into seventeen languages. The one professor who uses the library on Friday nights is Judith Franklin, of the Women's Studies Program. She has completed three volumes of a projected six-volume history of American women writers. Critic and activist Helen Garfield Black says that Franklin's literary history of women writers will change the way literature is taught in American universities for the next century. Should the administration close the library on Friday nights?

36c
Using Deductive Arguments

A deductive argument is an application of a general truth to a specific case so that a conclusion may be drawn. A general truth is supposedly accepted by everyone likely to be interested in the argument. Deductive reasoning proceeds through a syllogism. In a **syllogism**, the general truth includes the specific case and is the cause of the conclusion. The general truth is called the *major premise,* the specific case is called the *minor premise,* and the conclusion shows what the major premise proves about the minor premise. Here is a standard syllogism:

> MAJOR PREMISE: All men are mortal.
> MINOR PREMISE: Socrates is a man.
> CONCLUSION: Socrates will die.

The general truth accepted by everyone is that all men are mortal. That is, all men will eventually die. No one who reads the argument can deny that assumption. The specific case here is a statement joining Socrates to the general truth by remarking that he is an individual member of the class of beings called men. The conclusion then follows. You can always rephrase a syllogism to use the word "because" or "since" in the statements you make in conclusions derived from the general truth.

> All men are mortal; since Socrates is a man, he is mortal.

Constructing a Syllogism

When we reason deductively, we begin with a general truth and use it to give meaning to a fact. The major premise is always a broad generalization; the minor premise is always a statement somehow included within the major premise. The conclusion follows necessarily because of the relation of the major premise and the minor premise. Here are more syllogisms based on deductive reasoning:

> MAJOR PREMISE: This textbook is revised every three years.
> MINOR PREMISE: Three years have passed since the last edition of this textbook appeared.
> CONCLUSION: A new edition of this textbook will appear this year.

> MAJOR PREMISE: Rain nearly always falls soon after the barometer falls rapidly when the air is warm and moist.
> MINOR PREMISE: The barometer is falling fast, and the air is muggy and hot.
> CONCLUSION: It is going to rain.

> MAJOR PREMISE: Medical research has proved that excessive drinking of alcohol damages the heart, the digestive tract, and other organs of the body, and that heavy drinking is often associated with cancer, insomnia, psychological depression, high blood pressure, and the breakdown of the immune system.
> MINOR PREMISE: My Aunt Mabel drinks a quart of whiskey a night.
> CONCLUSION: Aunt Mabel will probably not live to a healthy old age.

36c
argue

> MAJOR PREMISE: The ability to write well is a great advantage to business and professional people.
> MINOR PREMISE: I write well.
> CONCLUSION: I have an advantage if I go into business or professional life.

These syllogisms are not quite so solid as the one about Socrates. Socrates has to be mortal because all men eventually die. But Aunt Mabel may live to be ninety-five, and the ability to write well does not guarantee success in business or professional life. When we reason about most subjects to make an argument, the syllogisms we use may not fall together with the certainty of a good key turning a lock. If the major premise is not true, the syllogism will not be true. If the major premise is flawed or not accepted by others, the syllogism built on it will not be convincing.

> MAJOR PREMISE: Nonsmokers will never die.
> MINOR PREMISE: My cousin Horace is a nonsmoker.
> CONCLUSION: Horace will never die.

All people eventually die, whether they smoke cigarettes or not. Although Cousin Horace may live longer than a chain smoker, he will eventually die.

MAJOR PREMISE: First-rate rock composers are much more creative than classical-music composers.
MINOR PREMISE: John Lennon was a first-rate rock composer.
CONCLUSION: John Lennon was more creative than Beethoven.

The syllogism might stand among people who accept the major premise. But lovers of classical music, especially lovers of Beethoven, would reject the conclusion because they reject the supposed general truth from which the conclusion is drawn. Lovers of the Beatles might accept the syllogism, but it would not convince those on the other side.

Constructing an Argument with Syllogisms

You may find several syllogisms in the same argument. The following paragraph contains two syllogisms:

36c
argue

> In the Declaration of Independence, Thomas Jefferson wrote that people established government and entrusted it with power to pre-serve their rights to life, liberty, and the pursuit of happiness. A government can legitimately exercise those powers that the people consent to yield to it. The government of King George III of England had not protected those rights; it had, instead, violated them by tak-ing the lives of Americans, by attempting to destroy their liberty, and by making it impossible for them to pursue happiness. Americans did not consent to those actions. Therefore, Jefferson argued, the En-glish government was not a legitimate government; and since it was not a legitimate government, Americans owed it no allegiance. Since they did not owe allegiance to the English government, Americans had a right to abolish it and establish another government in its place.

Here are the syllogisms:

MAJOR PREMISE: Governments, which were established by the people to preserve their rights to life, liberty, and the pur-suit of happiness, may legitimately exercise those powers to which the people have consented.
MINOR PREMISE: The government of King George III had taken ac-tions to which the American people had not con-sented.
CONCLUSION: King George's government was not legitimate.

MAJOR PREMISE: People have a right to abolish a government that is not legitimate.
MINOR PREMISE: King George's government was not legitimate.
CONCLUSION: Americans had a right to abolish King George's government.

■ **Exercise 36.2** Construct syllogisms from the arguments in the following paragraphs:

1. Universities exist to further the intellectual life of their students and faculty and society at large. The intellectual life is not cheap. It costs money for faculty, money for the buildings where classes are conducted, money for libraries, and money to keep those libraries open at night. Judith Franklin furthers the intellectual life of society every Friday night when she works in the library. The university should support her by keeping the library open so she can work. She is doing what Sourmash University exists to do.

2. Lightning can kill. Bike riders sometimes believe that they are protected from lightning because they are on rubber tires. They think that the rubber protects them by preventing the lightning from running through them into the ground. But that belief is a superstition. Lightning can strike bikers. It kills some cyclists every year. So when a thunderstorm blows up and you are on your bike, seek shelter at once.

3. You can do thousands of things with computers — word processing, complicated math, architectural modeling, graphic design, and more. The more elaborate your computer, the more you can do with it. But the more elaborate your computer, the more it will cost. Most students use their computers only for word processing. Therefore, if you are going to use your computer only to write papers, avoid buying an expensive and elaborate computer.

**36c
argue**

■ **Exercise 36.3** Study the following syllogisms. Which of them are good syllogisms, and which are bad? What is wrong with the bad ones?

1. MAJOR PREMISE: Good teachers always give students good grades.
   MINOR PREMISE: I got a bad grade in my writing class.
   CONCLUSION: I had a bad teacher.

2. MAJOR PREMISE: Professional athletes make a lot of money.
   MINOR PREMISE: I love basketball.
   CONCLUSION: I should spend all my time practicing so I can become a professional basketball player.

3. MAJOR PREMISE: Taxes are necessary to support state and federal governments.
   MINOR PREMISE: Taxes on cigarettes provide a substantial proportion of government revenue.
   CONCLUSION: We should encourage people to smoke cigarettes.

4. MAJOR PREMISE: Sunburns cause skin cancer.
MINOR PREMISE: My skin is very sensitive.
CONCLUSION: I should avoid sunburn.

Making Assumptions

In making a deductive argument, often we do not spell out the entire syllogism. We assume that the major premise is clear to readers even if we do not state it. We assume that they accept it. Sometimes we call an unexpressed major premise an **assumption**. Here are some examples:

> Professor Churl promised us that half our grade would depend on our research paper. We all worked night and day on those papers. I spent every night for three weeks in the library working on mine. But then he said that the term papers were all so good that he would have to give everyone in the class an A if he kept his word. So he counted the term papers as only one-tenth of the grade and said the other nine-tenths would come from the midterm and the final.

Here is the syllogism with the major premise stated:

MAJOR PREMISE: Professors who break their promises to students are unfair.
MINOR PREMISE: Professor Churl broke his promise.
CONCLUSION: Professor Churl was unfair.

Many American students make a spelling mistake when they form the plurals of words ending in -*est* and -*ist* — words such as *guest, nest, humanist, scientist,* and *colonist*. They do not add a final *s*. The plurals of these words are *guests, nests, humanists, scientists,* and *colonists*. The error seems to come about because these students fail to form the plural forms of these words correctly when they speak. It is difficult to make the *s* sound after -*ist*, so many Americans pronounce the singular and the plural the same way. Therefore they spell them the same way. The rule is simple: To make the plural of all words ending in -*est* or -*ist*, add the letter *s*.

MAJOR PREMISE: Mispronunciations may cause misspellings.
MINOR PREMISE: Students often mispronounce words such as *guests, nests, humanists, scientists,* and *colonists*.
CONCLUSION: The mispronunciation causes these plurals to be spelled without the final *s*, as if they were singular nouns.

✓ CHECKLIST: DEDUCTIVE ARGUMENTS

1. Can you locate the syllogisms in your argument?
2. Can you locate incomplete syllogisms in your argument?
3. Will your major premises be accepted by your readers?
4. Will your assumptions in your incomplete syllogisms be accepted by your readers?
5. Does each minor premise truly fit its major premise or assumption?
6. Do your conclusions follow logically from your major premise and your minor premise?

■ **Exercise 36.4** Find the implied major premise in each syllogism embedded in the following paragraphs.

36c
argue

1. Sylvester Pecks has been campaigning to be elected governor of the state, telling us that he won the Congressional Medal of Honor in Vietnam. He has limped to the platform again and again to tell us how he was wounded in the leg holding his position against overwhelming enemy attack. But now it turns out that he spent the entire Vietnam war in Switzerland acting as a security guard for a girls' school. The headmaster of that school has come forward to tell us that Mr. Pecks broke his leg when he fell through a kitchen window one night as he was making off with steaks from the school's refrigerator. The headmaster has produced medical records from a Swiss hospital to support his claim. Do not vote for Sylvester Pecks.

2. Rattlesnakes abound in the Wyoming countryside around Independence Rock, one of the great landmarks along the old overland trail followed by the pioneers on their way to California and Oregon. Climbing up Independence Rock is a great adventure, and from the top you can see for miles across the rolling prairie. But be sure you wear tall boots as you walk through the high grass around the rock, and be careful where you put your hands.

3. A recent survey revealed that the average American watches seven hours of television a day. If the average American spent half that much time reading, we would have one of the most knowledgeable citizen bodies in the world. As it is, Americans, entertained by television and neglecting their books, are woefully ignorant of simple facts necessary to understand the world. Another recent survey disclosed that one-third of the students in a large American university could not locate the continent of Europe on a map of the world. Almost half of all Americans claim that they have never read a book through in their lives. Because they watch television

and do not read, Americans run the risk of being unable to make policy decisions that may help them survive as a nation.

■ **Exercise 36.5** Write a paragraph in which you imply a major premise to support an argument.

36d
Arguing from Authority, Testimony, and Personal Experience

Arguing from Authority

If you should write a paper arguing that the characters in Shakespeare's *A Midsummer Night's Dream* are not profound, you may quote Shakespearean scholar David Young, who has written on that subject and reached a similar conclusion. Young is an authority who strengthens your case because he is known to have studied Shakespeare and to have written a great deal about the plays, especially about the comedies.

Never be afraid to ask for help on a paper. People who have become authorities in their fields usually enjoy talking with students. Are you writing a paper about changes taking place in the Soviet Union or in other countries of Eastern Europe where communist regimes held power for so long? There is probably a professor on your campus who teaches Russian history and who can talk to you about events in the Soviet Union and other countries in Eastern Europe. Go talk to that person. He or she can become an authority for your paper.

Any time you quote facts from a book or cite an author's opinion to support your own in an argument paper, you are arguing from authority. (The use of quotations and citations of sources is discussed in 34c). When you do research, you know enough to be on the lookout for evidence that can give authority to the assertions you make in a paper. But even when you do random reading or when you listen to lectures in other disciplines or watch TV or go to the movies, keep your eyes open for materials you can use in your paper.

The following paragraphs present an argument from authority. The historian David McCullough has investigated the recurring attacks of asthma that afflicted young Theodore Roosevelt, later president of the

United States. What causes asthma? McCullough believes the disease is at least partly *psychomatic*, that is, caused by the mental state of the victim rather than by germs, viruses, or some other physical entity. (The nickname "Teedie" in the selection was given young Theodore Roosevelt by his family, and McCullough uses it to indicate the child.)

> In 1864, or two years after the infant Teedie's asthma had begun, a highly important work was published in Philadelphia, a book of 256 pages titled *On Asthma*. The author was an English physician, Henry Hyde Salter, a very keen observer who as the father of an asthmatic child had "experienced the horrors" of the disease. . . . Salter had found no abnormalities in the lungs of his asthmatic patients, no trace of the disease in either the respiratory or circulatory system, and hence concluded that the trouble lay in the nervous system. Asthma, a disease of "the direst suffering," a disease "about whose pathology more various and discrepant ideas prevail than any other," was "essentially a *nervous* disease."
>
> Sudden "mental emotion," Salter said, could both bring on an attack and abruptly end one. He did not know why, only what he had observed. He reported on a patient whose attack ceased the moment he saw a fire outside the window and another who had his asthma stop when put on a fast horse. Still other patients found that as soon as they neared the doctor's office, their asthma vanished, "suddenly and without any apparent cause except the mental perturbation at being within the precincts of the physician." The onset of an attack, he noted, was frequently preceded by a spell of depression or "heaviness" (what Teedie called feeling "doleful"), and twenty years in advance of what might be regarded as the first studies in the psychosomatic side of asthma he reported on a small boy who "found his disease a convenient immunity from correction."
>
> "Don't scold me," he would say, if he had incurred his father's displeasure, "or I shall have the asthma." And so he would; his fears were as correct as they were convenient.

—DAVID MCCULLOUGH

36d argue

Arguing from Testimony

When we argue from testimony, we say that something happened to us and that this happening proves a point that we wish to make or that it proves our entire argument. Your personal experience may support an argument only if the experience has given you enough information to support generalizations that will help the case you are trying to make. If you have not learned from your experience, your argument may be weakened by inadequate support.

Disneyland has been criticized for giving a sanitized version of American history, for trivializing internal relations and national differences, and for taking all the frightening moments out of fairy tales. But I visited Disneyland with my two children last summer, and we loved it. Yes, it is a form of escapism. But why else do we go to an amusement park? Only a new form of puritanism requires us to be serious every moment about everything. Sometimes we have to relax. And I can't think of a time when I have been happier than I was sitting with my seven-year-old and my five-year-old in Dumbo, the Flying Elephant, circling round and round, suspended over the crowds by the strong steel arms of a friendly Disneyland machine that rotated us in the friendly sunshine.

36e

argue

36e
Building a Good Argument

Choose a limited topic

Avoid arguments that are so broad that you can write only a series of assertions. You must gather enough information to know what you are talking about. Topics too broad require more knowledge than you can gather during the term.

You cannot argue in only a few pages that the American government is spending too much money for defense unless you are an expert on the federal budget, particularly on military spending. But you can argue in a brief paper that military spending involves a lot of waste — *if* you can gather evidence of that waste. You can get this information from magazine articles and newspaper stories and from budget hearings recorded in the *Congressional Record*. Many of these sources will be in your school library.

Your argument must be limited enough to state clearly. Your readers must know what you want to prove. Otherwise your argument will be useless.

Choose a topic that lends itself to debate

A strong argument starts with a limited topic that lends itself to debate. If people can take sides on the issue, it's probably a good topic — provided it is limited enough to allow you to know it thoroughly and argue it convincingly. To test a topic for argument, you might ask if anyone cares to debate it.

Shakespeare wrote some interesting plays.	No. Few people would disagree with this topic.
Radio stations should not be allowed by the federal government to play rock music with lyrics that glorify drugs or casual sex.	Yes. Many people think that something should be done to protect young children from such music; others think that a prohibition against such music would violate the First Amendment of the Constitution, with its guarantee of free speech.
Private persons should not be allowed to own pistols.	Yes. Many people, citing the number of murders committed with pistols, think that private ownership of such weapons should be banned. Many others believe that such a ban would restrict the freedom of law-abiding gun owners.
We should find a cure for AIDS.	No. AIDS is one of the epidemic diseases of our age, and whether we should seek a cure is not a subject of serious debate.
AIDS victims should be quarantined.	Yes. Many people believe AIDS victims should be kept away from society to protect those who do not have the disease. Others argue that the disease cannot be transferred by casual social contact and that quarantine of its victims would be cruel and inhuman.

**36e
argue**

Controversy is not essential for good argument. People do not have to be passionate about the subject. But the topic must be debatable. Often controversial topics (such as abortion, welfare, and legalizing drugs) have been argued so much that fresh insights are hard to come by. Do not argue an issue unless you have something fresh to say about it.

Matters of taste are seldom debatable. It is difficult to argue that a movie or a novel or a short story or a play is good or bad. People often disagree; what seems to be trash to one critic may seem like a masterpiece to another. Many people love the novel *Moby Dick;* others find it boring. Horror movies scare some people almost out of their wits; they strike others as silly.

You can argue that a movie or something you read contradicts itself or that it presents stereotypes or that it glorifies violence; you can argue that a movie is complicated, that it addresses this or that issue in society, that it strives for this or that effect. But the simple argument that the movie — or whatever — is "good" or "bad" will carry little weight.

■ **Exercise 36.6** Which of the following statements would make good arguments? Which cannot be argued in a college paper seven or eight pages long? Write a short paragraph explaining your response to each suggested argument.

1. William Faulkner used descriptions of light in his novels to help emphasize the moods of his characters.
2. Mark Twain's novel *Huckleberry Finn* contains much that can injure the feelings of modern African Americans.
3. The movie *Star Wars* was the most brilliant film ever produced by Hollywood.
4. The movie *Star Wars* uses clichés developed in Hollywood Westerns, but it makes them interesting by transposing them to outer space.
5. Everyone who drives to school would be happier if there were more free parking spaces.

■ **Exercise 36.7** Here are suggested topics for argument papers. Which are debatable and which are not?

1. The law should ban smoking in all public places.
2. War is one of the great sources of misery in our time.
3. Women in the army should take part in combat.
4. The president of the United States holds great responsibility.
5. A constitutional amendment should outlaw any desecration of the American flag.

Consider contrary evidence

The facts rarely line up neatly on one side of any debatable issue. Debatable topics are debatable *because* they have at least two sides. Evidence can be interpreted in different ways. If you are to be fair-minded and reasonable, you must consider the opposing arguments. It is unfair to misquote or misrepresent the opposition. You must think out the opposing point of view as carefully as you can and be sure you represent it correctly.

In dealing with contrary evidence, you have three options:

1. You can argue that the contrary evidence is invalid because it has been misinterpreted by your opponents and that it therefore does not damage your position.

> It is true that keeping the library open on Friday nights costs the university nearly a thousand dollars a week. People who want to close the library argue that all that money will be saved if we take this step. But they have forgotten that when the building is closed, we must pay the salary of a security guard. They have forgotten that even when the building is closed, the lights must be kept on for security, and the heat remains on to protect the books from dampness. They have forgotten that library personnel on duty at night are students working their way through college and that to cut off their pay might be to exclude them from higher education.

2. You can concede the contrary evidence but argue that your point of view is still superior.

36e
argue

> I do concede that only a handful of people use the library on Friday nights. Although those who want to close the library overestimate the money they would save, I concede that they would indeed save some money. But why does a university exist? It exists to promote the life of the mind, to expand the intellect and the imagination, to produce knowledge. By keeping the library open on Friday nights, the university confirms these purposes to the handful of people who work there. The books two of these people have written confirm the purposes of the university to the thousands of people who read those books. Through these writers, the university reaches out to readers who can never enter the campus.
>
> The student union is also open on Friday nights. I have checked into the costs of operating the union on those nights. They amount to some six thousand dollars an evening. I am not opposed to keeping the union open on Friday nights. But I do say that a university that saves a little money by closing its library while it keeps open its poolrooms, its bowling alleys, its subsidized soda fountains, and its movie auditorium is selling its soul to the accountants and losing its fundamental purpose.

3. You can change your mind.

> I once believed in legalizing marijuana. Smoking the weed made people feel good. It seemed to have no harmful effects, and it was not addictive, like alcohol or nicotine. Users said that marijuana did not

impair vision or judgment, so drivers high on marijuana could operate cars and trucks in perfect safety. But now a considerable body of
research has been built up to prove that marijuana *does* have harmful
effects. Smoking marijuana is just as hard on the lungs as smoking
tobacco. It does appear to be addictive. And marijuana has been
implicated in several private-plane crashes, automobile wrecks, and,
recently, train wrecks. It is not the harmless pleasure it once appeared
to be, and I now think there are powerful reasons *not* to legalize the
drug.

Use a courteous tone when you argue

Too often, writers of argument papers believe that they can win their
argument only by assaulting and insulting everyone who disagrees with
them. Fair-minded readers quickly reject writers who argue as though
they were at a shouting match. You should learn to argue by friendly
persuasion.

36e

argue

It is the fashion today to argue that Machiavelli's *The Prince* is a work
of genius and to condemn the critics who have condemned Machiavelli through the centuries. No doubt Machiavelli was a brilliant observer of the sixteenth century and understood the tactics of the
petty princes who ruled the Italian city-states. They were immoral
men, and Machiavelli described their immorality in elaborate detail.
Much of the criticism that has been leveled against Machiavelli
through the years should be directed against those princes. He considered himself to be a sort of reporter, describing in great detail how
they grasped power and held on to it. One can even argue that like the
Christian thinkers of the Middle Ages, Machiavelli believed that
human beings were selfish and ignorant, slaves of a flawed human
nature.

But despite the brilliance of his observations and the blame that
can be placed on the rulers he observed, Machiavelli himself can still
be chilling. No particle of sympathy for the victims of those princes
penetrates his stately prose. He seems to be above concern for the
suffering of the innocent. He was passionately dedicated to building
an Italian state strong enough to repel the French, German, and
Spanish invaders. But nothing in his writings indicates dedication to
human rights or even awareness that human beings have rights. No
matter how highly we praise his genius, we must recognize that something is lacking in his spirit.

The tone of the preceding paragraphs does not insult those who have
said that Machiavelli was a genius and that he has been judged too harshly

by later writers. It makes an argument based on evidence and treats those who have expressed different views gently.

Avoid fallacious reasoning

Fallacious reasoning may appear at first to be logical, but on examination the fallacies or errors in reasoning appear. Readers who catch you in fallacious reasoning will not be likely to take your work seriously.

36f
Avoiding Common Fallacies

Certain common errors in reasoning appear again and again in arguments we see in political debate, in advertising, in editorial writing, and indeed in almost every public forum. Learn to recognize the common fallacies and to avoid them in your own writing. Here are some common fallacies.

36f
argue

Improper reasoning from cause to effect

The mere fact that happening *B* occurred after happening *A* is not proof that *A* caused *B*. You must make a stronger connection than mere sequence to establish cause and effect. Many superstitions arise because people make connections between events that have no real relation except that one happened after the other.

> A black cat walked across my path last night, and when I got home, I discovered that my house had been robbed. The black cat brought me bad luck.

> Since radio, TV, and the movies began emphasizing stories about crime, crime has steadily increased; therefore, radio, TV, and the movies have been responsible for the increase in the crime rate.

Crime increases for many reasons. We might make the argument if we interviewed several convicted criminals who said they had been motivated by the broadcast media and the movies to commit crimes. Or if we could discover a rash of crimes identical to some crime that had been shown in a TV story or in a movie, we might have some indication that that medium increased the crime rate. But the mere fact that the crime rate rose after such stories became popular in the media is not evidence that the media caused the crimes. We might also discover that the crime rate had increased since TV started broadcasting more basketball games. Would you argue that basketball broadcasts had increased crime?

Generalizing from too little information

When we engage in inductive reasoning, we gather facts and arrive at generalizations. If you don't gather enough facts, you may make a faulty generalization.

> In many of his novels, William Faulkner wrote about terrible happenings in the American South. Therefore Faulkner must have hated the South.

> In his novel *The Turn of the Screw*, Henry James wrote about two ghosts who attempted to corrupt two little children. Therefore James believed in ghosts.

> I was in Paris last summer, and a French police officer was very rude to me when I asked him how to find the Louvre Museum. "You are standing next to it," he said. All the French are rude.

> My Uncle Herbert smokes two packs of cigarettes a day and is eighty-five years old. Therefore all the talk about the dangers of cigarette smoking is a lie.

36f
argue

Inappropriate and unfair either/or reasoning

This sort of fallacy rests on the demand that we accept one of two extreme positions.

> Either we must stop our children from listening to rock music or civilization will crumble.

> Either you buy the new supercharged TurboLemon convertible when our sale ends or you will never have such an opportunity again in your life.

> Either people must understand Shakespeare or they cannot consider themselves educated.

Straw men and the ad hominem argument

The term *straw man* denotes a weak argument that one attributes to one's opponent for the sole purpose of refuting it. This strategy is designed to make readers (or hearers) think the opponent's position is so indefensible that no sensible person could possibly hold it. Often the attack on the straw man is a variation of the either/or fallacy.

Statement: In the United States, prayer in public schools offers many difficulties. It is difficult for sincerely religious people to keep from trying to influence others to accept their point of view. Prayers may easily become sermons. Different people use different forms of prayer. Christians customarily pray with their eyes closed; Jews pray with their eyes open; Americans of some other faiths pray by chanting. Children of various religious backgrounds are forced by law to go to school. But they should not be forced to worship God in a way that contradicts their own beliefs or the beliefs of their parents. The United States is the most religious of all the industrial countries, and we may suggest that religion has flourished here because it has not been forced on anyone. We would do well to ponder this question: Is religion helped by being prescribed by law, no matter how inoffensive the form may seem to those who prescribe it?

Reply: My opponent has questioned the value of prayer in the public schools. Only an atheist would do such a thing. He does not believe in God. He denies that we owe reverence to our Creator. He has blasphemed the Almighty by saying that little children should not pray to Him. It is his kind that will destroy this country, for if we forsake God, God will forsake us. I do not say that he is a Communist, but I say that he is playing into the hands of the Communists by denying God just as they deny God. If you vote for my opponent, my beloved friends, you are voting against religion.

36f
argue

The straw man is related to another fallacy that you should avoid: the *argumentum ad hominem*, or the "attack on the person." The writer (or speaker) avoids the central issue of the opponent's argument and instead attacks the opponent's character.

My opponent spent an hour last night explaining his economic policies to the nation on television. He advanced columns of figures about jobs and about workers and employment and inflation. He gave us a six-point program that he said would reduce inflation, increase employment, strengthen the dollar, and control the federal deficit. These items were very interesting, but I could not think about them very much because as the cameras zoomed in on him, I realized that he dyes his hair. Now I ask you, what kind of man dyes his hair? Can you believe in such a man? Would any of you women out there marry a man who dyes his hair? People who dye their hair are lying about themselves. And my friends, a man who lies about himself will lie about the budget of the United States. Look at me! I am totally bald. I have an honest, pure-bald head. Look at me, and see a man who believes in the truth. Look at my opponent and see a man who lies about his hair and his age and about anything else that will help him get elected president of the United States.

Begging the question and the red herring

Begging the question occurs in deductive reasoning. The person who begs the question states the major premise in such a way that it is a conclusion, without allowing an argument to decide the merits of the case.

He could not be lying because he is president of the Campus Society for Moral Uplift.

Here is how this statement would be set up in a syllogism.

MAJOR PREMISE:	The president of the Campus Society for Moral Uplift cannot tell a lie.
MINOR PREMISE:	He is president of the Campus Society for Moral Uplift.
CONCLUSION:	Therefore he cannot tell a lie.

If we accept the major premise, we have no argument. But if the president of the Campus Society for Moral Uplift was charged with lying, the argument should turn on the evidence. Does the evidence show that he told the truth or not? The major premise is false.

Begging the question often goes hand in hand with another fallacy, that of the red herring. A **red herring** is any issue introduced into an argument that distracts attention from the main issue. People often introduce a red herring when they think they are about to lose an argument. The original red herring was a smoked salt fish with a strong taste and smell. Sometimes during fox hunts, when farmers wanted to keep riders from galloping across their crops and ruining them, they would drag a red herring through the grass before the dogs came along. The smell of the herring would make the dogs lose the scent of the fox, and the farmers' fields were saved because the dogs became confused and often ran in circles.

That rugged-looking cowboy smokes a famous cigarette in beautiful magazine ads that show stunning color photographs of the American West. You can almost smell the fresh air and feel the glory of space in those ads. You can look at that beautiful scene and that handsome face and know that cigarettes are not nearly as bad for your health as the surgeon general claims they are.

The advertisers of cigarettes know that medical evidence is solidly against smoking. So they present red herrings, beautiful ads that feature people doing athletic or robust things while they smoke. The ads distract attention from the central issue—whether people should smoke or not.

■ **Exercise 36.8** Read the following sentences and identify the logical fallacies.

1. Anyone who claims that Americans have the right to burn the flag hates the United States.
2. Forty years ago, when my opponent was a freshman in college, he plagiarized a term paper and had to withdraw from school for a year. That proves he is a dishonest person and does not deserve your vote.
3. If you do not read Plato and Aristotle, you are contributing to the moral laxity of our times.
4. Anyone who thinks Stephen King writes serious novels is a fool.
5. I cannot write about this book because I dislike it so much.
6. I would not want my daughter to be a soldier because it is not ladylike to carry a gun.
7. Religious people are ignorant.
8. Morals have fallen in America because of television.
9. Athletes in TV commercials drink beer; so I will drink beer, too.
10. Writing cannot be taught; so I will not take a writing course.

**36f
argue**

✓ CHECKLIST: MAKING ARGUMENTS

1. Is your argument worth making?
2. Does anyone dispute your argument?
3. Can you make your argument in the space you have available?
4. Can you develop your argument by reasoning, or can you only assert your opinions?
5. Can you identify the inductions you have made in your argument?
6. Can you identify the syllogisms in your argument?
7. Have you considered contrary arguments?
8. Have you been courteous to your opponents?
9. Can you find any logical fallacies in your argument?
10. Is your conclusion supported by your evidence?

CHAPTER
37

WRITING ABOUT
LITERATURE

Many of your English courses will require you to write about novels, short stories, poems, or plays that you read on your own or that you study and discuss in class. An essay on a literary subject shows your understanding of the work you have read. Such an essay is always critical in the sense that it states your position on, attitude toward, or opinion of the work and provides details to support your point.

Literature falls into **genres**, or types. Short stories form a genre within literature. Other genres include plays, poetry, novels, and essays. Screenplays represent a new literary genre.

37a
Analyzing the Assignment

Your teacher may have a specific goal in asking you to write about a piece of literature. For example, your assignment may be to write about sound images in *The Tempest*, to analyze the theme of Melville's story "Bartleby the Scrivener," to compare two love sonnets by Keats, or to trace the development of a character in a novel. Or your teacher may give a general assignment—to write about a specific literary work or to choose a work on your own and write about it. In these last two cases you have to define the terms of the assignment yourself.

The student whose paper appears at the end of this chapter received this assignment: "Read 'in Just-' by E. E. Cummings and write an essay of about two or three typed pages that explains the meaning of the poem." The class was studying poetry and had read and discussed some of Cummings' other poems. The text of "in Just-" appears on page 547.

Both specific and open-ended writing assignments about literature almost always require **analysis**. When you analyze something, you scrutinize its parts in order to understand the whole. You look closely at the words and sentences, the motivations and the actions of the characters, the events of the narrative, and the writer's techniques, among other elements. Analysis often involves **interpretation**, an explanation of what you think the work means, and **evaluation**, your opinion and judgment of the literary work. Analysis and interpretation lead to evaluation. You should base your judgments on thorough analysis and careful interpretation.

37b
Reading Actively

Don't write until you've read the work carefully several times. You cannot write a good paper about a work that you have read only once. When you read a text several times, you will begin to notice things that deepen your appreciation and enlarge your understanding of it. That detailed knowledge is a resource that will enable you to write a good paper.

Read actively. If you own the book, underline words and phrases and make notes to yourself in the margin. Some students of literature make their own indexes on the blank pages at the back of a book, especially in longer works. They copy a key phrase and the number of the page on which the phrase appears. Later, when they think and write about the work, they can find important passages easily.

To read literature actively is to ask questions. Stimulate your mind by posing questions about literary selections and seeking answers to them as you read. When you examine some of the approaches to writing about literature in 37e, you will find questions that will help you understand a novel, short story, poem, or play. Not all the questions will apply to every work. But if you keep them in mind as you read, you will become a more attentive reader, and you will see things in the literature that will help you write about it.

Appendix A, "Study Techniques," suggests other ways to read actively.

37a/b/c
lit

37c
Developing an Appropriate Thesis

Follow the guidelines for prewriting in Chapter 1 as you prepare to write an essay about a piece of literature. Do brainstorming, make an informal list, or use a rough outline. Keep returning to the literary text as you shape your ideas.

Develop a tentative thesis for your paper. Before you begin writing your thesis statement, look at your assignment again. You may be able to use some of its language in your thesis. For example, if your assignment is "Explain how Iago convinces Othello of Desdemona's guilt," your thesis might be "Iago convinces Othello of Desdemona's guilt by means of carefully developed circumstantial evidence."

See the research paper on Willa Cather in Chapter 35. Willa Cather wrote about harsh and grim life on the Great Plains and how that life deprived people of certain kinds of culture and beauty. You can see how the writer of this paper developed that theme in two of Cather's short stories. This research paper goes beyond a mere summary of the plot.

To develop such themes, you must study a text, think about it, read it again and again, and write down various ideas that you may try out as paper topics. These ideas may become an informal outline built around a central thesis. You may have to write a draft before your most important idea becomes clear; then you will have to write at least one more draft to develop it.

Use the guidelines in 2c as you formulate your thesis. Remember that your thesis should be flexible and probably will change as you write successive drafts. As with other kinds of writing, the thesis should state a concrete position that you can argue about. Both your topic and your opinion about it should be stated clearly.

The student who wrote about Cummings' poem developed his thesis in three stages:

**37c
lit**

Tentative thesis	**Revised thesis 1**	**Revised thesis 2**
Cummings' "in Just-" is about a group of children who respond to the whistle of the balloon man on a spring afternoon.	In the poem "in Just-" Cummings paints a child's world in the child's own terms.	In the poem "in Just-" E. E. Cummings presents a child's world filled with childhood's delights and dangers.

The tentative thesis is not a thesis at all. It is a summary of the action. It makes no arguable point. The first revised thesis does make an assertion, but it is too broad and not well focused. The second revised thesis makes an arguable assertion that is sufficiently limited for a brief literary paper. For the final draft (pp. 548–555) the student revised the thesis again.

When you get to a final draft, you must be sure to keep your paper focused on one leading idea. In the paper about Willa Cather in Chapter 35, the writer is not concerned about how Cather got from her birthplace in Virginia to Nebraska. Nor is the writer concerned about the many nineteenth-century stories about artistic young women dying of tuberculosis. These are interesting subjects. They might make interesting topics for other papers. But this paper is about the effect of the vast spaces of the Great Plains and the hardships of life there on two people with a great love of music and the culture that music reflects. The writer would have spoiled the effect if she had been distracted by these other ideas and had neglected her central theme.

37d
Considering Audience and Purpose

Your audience for a paper on a literary subject is usually your instructor. In most cases your instructor is familiar with the work he or she has asked you to write about and does not need a detailed plot summary.

Unless your assignment explicitly requires you to do so, avoid writing an extensive plot summary. Of course, you may have to refer to elements in the plot to make your point. But your instructor does not want to read a paper that tells her something she already knows quite well. She wants to see your mind at work. She wants you to think about the piece and to develop ideas that your reading has stimulated in your mind. Write your essay as if both of you know the work and you want to tell her some things you have learned about it.

Your purpose in writing will influence the outcome of your paper. If you are writing an essay with limits defined by your teacher—about two pages (500–750 words), for example—make your point quickly and offer supporting detail and no more. If the assignment is due within a few sessions, you should avoid an overly ambitious plan that draws upon extensive use of secondary sources and other library materials. For brief literary essays most teachers expect you to develop ideas from the primary text itself. If you have been given a substantial amount of time to carry out the assignment, library research is probably a requirement. Chapters 32 through 35 present a research paper on a literary topic and show you how the paper was developed.

37d/e
lit

37e
Considering Approaches to Literary Analysis

You may take any of a variety of approaches when you write about literature and you may ask several kinds of questions as you think about your assignment.

Writing About the Characters
- ☐ Who are the most important characters in the work?
- ☐ How are they related to each other?
- ☐ How do they relate to each other?
- ☐ Does one character dominate the work, or do several characters share the action equally?
- ☐ What exactly do the characters do? Do they talk more than they act?

☐ Do the characters' actions match their talk, or do they talk one way and act another?

☐ What do the actions and the talk reveal about the characters?

☐ What makes you sympathize with or like one or more of the characters?

☐ What makes you unsympathetic toward or dislike one or more of the characters?

☐ What moral values do the characters have?

☐ How do the characters judge their own situation?

Writing About the Plot and/or the Setting

The **plot** is the action of a work; the **setting** is the place and time of the action. Writing about the plot means analyzing the relation of one event to another or the effects of the action on the characters or the effects of the characters on the action. Writing about the setting means trying to present your sense of why the author chose to create the scene as he or she did. The setting involves not only a specific location but also a broader environment of history and geography. You can raise many questions about plot and setting.

☐ How has the author arranged and connected the events?

☐ Are the events told in the order in which they occur or in some other order?

☐ How does a single important event relate to other events?

☐ Where does the action of the work take place?

☐ Is there any significance to the setting where the action takes place?

☐ What period or periods of time does the work embrace?

☐ Why do you suppose the writer set the work in that time?

☐ What surprises you in the work?

☐ Why are you surprised?

Writing About the Structure of the Work

How has the author put the pieces together? How do the various chapters or stanzas or acts relate to each other? What particular chapter or stanza or act stands out for any reason? Why does it stand out? How is the work similar to or different from works in the same literary category, or genre? All poems belong to the genre of poetry, but the structure of a poem by E. E. Cummings is very different from the structure of a poem by John Keats or Thomas Hardy. And, despite similarities, one poem by Cummings is very different from other poems by Cummings. How does the author meet or challenge your expectations for the genre?

Writing About the Tone of the Work

The **tone** is the author's attitude toward the subject. How does the author feel about the characters and their actions, and how does the author make you feel about them? Is the tone impartial, serious, mocking, condemning, playful? What accounts for the author's attitude toward the subject? Why do you think the author wrote the work? Considering tone usually means considering the speaker, or **narrator**, the person through whose eyes and lips we learn about the events. All narrators have a **point of view**, or perspective. What is the narrator's point of view? Is the story told by a third-person narrator, someone who is not a character in the piece? Or is it told by a first-person narrator? Does the third-person narrator follow one character exclusively, or does the point of view shift from character to character? How much does the narrator know about the characters he or she describes? Are his or her perceptions reliable? How does the narrator's knowledge affect what we as readers know about the action of the work? You never should assume that the narrator in any work is the same as the author of the work. What is the relation between the narrator and the author?

37e
lit

Writing About Language and Style

The **language** comprises the words the writer uses. **Style** includes language as well as sentence structure, usage, and diction. Imagery, figurative language, and symbolism (see Chapter 10 and 37f) contribute to style. Some questions to ask about language and style are:

- □ Are the words informal, colloquial, formal?
- □ What kinds of words does the author seem to like?
- □ Which words does the author repeat frequently?
- □ Which words seem to have special meaning for the author?
- □ Where and how has the author used sensory language?
- □ Are the images original?
- □ Can you identify a pattern in the uses of imagery?
- □ How do figurative expressions contribute to the style and meaning of the work?
- □ Does something in the work appear to stand for something else? That is, does some word, some action, some description or character make you think of something beyond it?
- □ How are the sentences structured—are they simple or complex, long or short?
- □ Which sentences do you like and why?
- □ What special qualities of style do you notice?

✓ CHECKLIST: APPROACHES TO LITERARY ANALYSIS

In analyzing a work of literature you may concentrate on any of the following elements:

1. The characters.
2. The plot and/or the setting.
3. The structure of the work.
4. The tone of the work.
5. The language and style of the work.

■ **Exercise 37.1**   Read "A Rose for Emily," by William Faulkner. Answer in brief paragraphs the following questions about the story.

1. Who is the narrator in the story?
2. Where and when does the story take place?
3. How long a time does the story cover?
4. How old is the narrator?
5. How does Faulkner prepare us for the surprise ending?
6. How is Miss Emily Grierson related to her town?
7. What does Miss Emily say in the story?
8. What do you notice about the style of the work?

37f
lit

37f
Key Literary Devices and Terms

Writers often use certain literary devices to help them tell stories with more effect. Often these devices help integrate the whole piece for the reader and perhaps reveal an unexpected meaning that makes the text more vivid and more memorable. When you recognize such devices and know their names, you can write about them more effectively and make your papers about literature more interesting. Here are some common literary devices.

Climax

The **climax** of a literary work is that point toward which the entire piece seems to be directed. Usually literary works end shortly after the climax. The problems are resolved or made clear; some point of understanding is reached; the major action of the story takes place.

The climax of Faulkner's "A Rose for Emily" is the point at which the astonished citizens of Miss Emily's little town break into a room of her house after her funeral and discover the corpse of Homer Barron lying in the bed and a strand of Miss Emily's "iron-gray" hair lying on the pillow beside the corpse.

Being able to identify the climax will help you see more clearly all the devices the author is using to keep you reading to see how everything turns out, and to see the relation of the various parts of the work to the whole.

Irony

A writer or speaker who uses **irony** means something different from the literal meaning of the words. Sometimes the writer means something entirely opposite from the words in the text. The most famous bit of irony in English is Jonathan Swift's "A Modest Proposal." Swift, enraged by the exploitation of Ireland by England in the eighteenth century, was especially concerned about the neglect of poor Irish children while members of the English upper classes lived in luxury. He wrote:

37f
lit

> I have been assured by a very knowing American of my acquaintance in London, that a young healthy child well nursed is at a year old a most delicious, nourishing and wholesome food, whether stewed, roasted, baked, or boiled, and I make no doubt that it will equally serve in a fricassee, or a ragout.

Swift was not serious about serving little Irish children up for food. But he was serious in his belief that the rich, especially the rich English lords of Ireland, were treating the poor like animals.

Dramatic Irony

Dramatic irony comes from characters in plays, poems, or stories who present or encounter a reality that is the opposite of appearances.

Shakespeare often uses dramatic irony in his plays. Macbeth is told that he will not die until Birnham Wood comes to Dunsinane Castle. He thinks he is secure because he does not believe a forest like Birnham Wood can move; but then Macduff's soldiers cut branches from the trees of Birnham Wood and use them as camouflage to disguise their movements, and so Birnham Wood comes to Dunsinane—and Macbeth is defeated and killed. Dramatic irony is common in all forms of literature.

In all irony, the audience must know that it is irony. In well-done ironic pieces, we know throughout that we are reading something not meant to be taken literally. Inexperienced writers may fail because they know they are writing with irony but do not give their readers any clues. Therefore the readers take their words literally.

Hyperbole

Hyperbole is exaggeration so extravagant that no reasonable person would take it for literal truth.

> The father of this pleasant grandfather, of the neighbourhood of Mount Pleasant, was a horny-skinned, two-legged, money-getting species of spider, who spun webs to catch unwary flies, and retired into holes until they were entrapped. The name of this old pagan's God was Compound Interest. He lived for it, married it, died of it. Meeting with a heavy loss in an honest little enterprise in which all the loss was intended to have been on the other side, he broke something — something necessary to his existence; therefore it couldn't have been his heart — and made an end of his career.
>
> — CHARLES DICKENS, *Bleak House*

37f
lit

Dickens here amuses himself by going back into the genealogy of the Smallweed family, people he does not like in his novel *Bleak House.* He wants to show us that the entire family of Smallweeds was greedy, heartless, and cruel.

Understatement

Like exaggeration, **understatement** often pops up in ordinary speech, especially in humorous statements intended to defuse a tense situation. Your roommate comes home and starts throwing books against the wall one by one and screaming at the top of his voice because he received a grade of C— on a paper that he was certain would get an A. You say, "I believe you're upset."

Here is Mark Twain, in *The Innocents Abroad,* describing a celebration of the Fourth of July on an American ship in the Mediterranean during one of his trips to Europe:

> The speeches were bad — execrable, almost without exception. In fact, without *any* exception, but one. Capt. Duncan made a good speech; he made the only good speech of the evening. He said:
> "LADIES AND GENTLEMEN:— May we all live to a green old age, and be prosperous and happy. Steward, bring up another basket of champagne."
> It was regarded as a very able effort.

"It was regarded as a very able effort" expresses the enormous relief of the passengers that they were about to be treated to champagne rather than a long speech.

Allusion

When writers make **allusions** they refer to something indirectly without precisely identifying it. It may be a literary work, a historical event, a work of art, a person, or something else. In writing papers about literature, you should be especially interested in allusions to other written works:

> Methought I saw my late espousèd saint
>   Brought to me like Alcestis from the grave
> Whom Jove's great son to her glad husband gave,
> Rescued from death by force, though pale and faint.
>
> —JOHN MILTON, "ON HIS DEAD WIFE"

At the beginning of this famous sonnet, Milton alludes to the classical myth of Alcestis, the wife of King Admetus of Thessaly. She sacrificed her life to save her husband, and later Zeus (or Jove, as the Romans called him) permitted Hercules to go down into the realm of the dead and bring her back to her husband. Milton also alluded frequently to the Bible.

An allusion can often be used as the topic of a paper about literature because the allusion may provide a key to understanding the work. In poetry particularly, an allusion may give the key to the entire work.

37f
lit

Symbols and Images

Fiction writers, dramatists, and poets sometimes use language that makes us think both of the literal truth they are describing and of something beyond that truth. Use of symbols may intensify the meaning of the literary work.

To find images and symbols in literature, you must read the text carefully and look closely at individual words to see what special meanings the writer may have poured into them. Look especially at words that are frequently repeated.

> Still falls the Rain—
> Dark as the world of man, black as our loss—
> Blind as the nineteen hundred and forty nails
> Upon the Cross.
>
> —EDITH SITWELL, "STILL FALLS THE RAIN"

The English poet Edith Sitwell wrote these lines about the German air raids over London in 1940, early in World War II. We may see in the image of the cross the suffering of innocent humankind from war throughout the 1,940 years since Christ.

✓ CHECKLIST: COMMON LITERARY DEVICES

Climax	The point toward which the entire piece is directed.
Irony	The use of words to express a meaning opposed to the literal meaning.
Dramatic irony	The use of characters who present or encounter a reality that is the opposite of appearances.
Hyperbole	Exaggeration so extravagant that no one would mistake it for the literal truth.
Understatement	A moderate statement in ironic contrast to what the situation warrants.
Allusion	An incidental, indirect reference to someone or something.
Symbols and images	Language that suggests or stands for something beyond its literal meaning.

37g
lit

■ **Exercise 37.2**   Read the poems "Richard Cory," by Edwin Arlington Robinson; "Ozymandias," by Percy Bysshe Shelley; and "Death and Co.," by Sylvia Plath. See how many literary devices you can find in each poem.

37g
Writing About Literature: A Sample Paper

Use your prewriting to guide you as you develop the first and later drafts of your essay on a literary topic. Be prepared to revise your thesis as your ideas take shape. Return often to the work you are writing about.

Write your essay as you would an essay on any topic. Write an introduction followed by paragraphs that support your points with specific details. Make your conclusion a natural ending.

One further point: Write about your literary topic in the present tense: "Cummings *uses* words and images that a child would use"; "But beneath this simple world *is* a much more complex one"; "the poet only *raises* the questions but *provides* no definite answers."

The following essay about a literary subject was written in response to the assignment asking for an analysis of E. E. Cummings' poem "in Just-." The full text of the poem appears below.

in Just-
spring   when the world is mud-
luscious the little
lame balloonman

whistles   far   and wee

and eddieandbill come
running from marbles and
piracies and it's
spring

when the world is puddle-wonderful

the queer
old balloonman whistles
far   and   wee
and bettyandisbel come dancing

from hop-scotch and jump-rope and

it's
spring
and
    the

        goat-footed

balloonMan   whistles
far
and
wee

**37g
lit**

✓ CHECKLIST: QUESTIONS TO ANSWER AS YOU WRITE YOUR ESSAY ABOUT LITERATURE

1. Did I examine the assignment carefully?
2. Did I read and reread the literary work actively so that I understand it well?
3. Did I do prewriting to develop my ideas on the work?
4. Did I state my thesis as a hypothesis that I can argue intelligently?
5. Did I offer specific details to support my thesis?
6. Did I quote accurately? Did I enclose in quotation marks any exact words that I used from the literary work?
7. Did I avoid extensive plot summaries?
8. Did I demonstrate my understanding of the work by analyzing it carefully? Did I address literary terms and devices, where appropriate?
9. Did I consider my audience and purpose?
10. Did I revise my essay carefully?

(1-a) The short introduction states the thesis succinctly. Compare this final thesis with the tentative and revised theses on p. 538.

(1-b) The writer analyzes the language and draws details from the poem. Note the quotation marks enclosing words quoted from the poem and the slash indicating the end of one line and the beginning of the next. See 27e.

Delights and Dangers of Childhood

(1-a)   E. E. Cummings' poems show an inventive, playful use of words and sentence structure to force readers to consider common ideas and feelings in a new context. The poem "in Just-" presents an entirely familiar world of children at play in the spring. Yet the poet's unusual use of language shows us the subtle dangers lurking about the delights and pleasures we all associate with childhood.

(1-b)   Cummings uses words and images that reflect a child's perception of the world. He calls the world "mud-luscious" and "puddle-wonderful." With those phrases we can feel a child's delight at springtime. The games abandoned at the balloonman's call-- "marbles and / piracies" and "hop-scotch and jump-rope"-- accurately show us children at play. Cummings runs the names of the children together on the page so that we hear them just as children would say them, "eddieandbill" and "bettyandisbel." In addition the

(2-a) Note that the writer offers no summary of the poem, as none is needed to understand this essay, but does express his own thinking about the poem.

(2-b) "But" and "this simple world" connect this paragraph with the preceding one.

(2-c) By explaining the allusion to the satyrs, the writer enriches our understanding of the poem.

(2-d) The writer comments on structure. Any phrase repeated in a short poem demands consideration. The writer makes an interesting point about the phrase "far and wee."

(2-a) balloonman "whistles far and wee," a child's excited expression certainly. The words "it's spring" are repeated twice, again to show the innocent excitement of youngsters outdoors after the spring rain.

(2-b) But beneath this simple world is a much more complex one. The balloonman has a peculiar, ominous power over the children. They stop everything, running and dancing to see him. On one level, of course, it is not surprising for children to greet a neighborhood visitor who sells balloons. Yet Cummings calls him "lame," "queer," and "goat-footed."

(2-c) In Greek mythology, the satyrs, creatures who enjoyed wild merrymaking, were humanlike gods with goats' features. By alluding to the satyrs, the poet implies something sinister.

(2-d) The phrase for the sound of the balloonman's whistle, "far and wee," which is used three times in this poem of twenty-four very short lines, also suggests something unusual, even dangerous. Why "far"? Will the sound transport the children far away? Can children far away hear it?

(3-a) Again, an explanation of an allusion puts the poem in a broader context.

(3-b) The writer offers his view of the theme of the poem. Clearly he reached this conclusion after considering many elements of the poem, such as language, style, character, and setting.

(3-c) Analyzing a key phrase, and relating it to the structure of the poem, is a good strategy here.

(3-a) Although Cummings' piper is more contemporary--he uses a whistle instead of a flute--the poet certainly is alluding here to the Pied Piper of Hamelin, who enchanted all the children with his magic flute and lured them away from their town.

(3-b) In a sense, then, the poem may be viewed as a story of the loss of innocence awaiting children as they grow up. In a secure world of play there are no troubles. But evil and danger are imminent, maybe even necessary for passage into adulthood.

(3-c) These ideas help call attention to the phrase "in Just- / spring." (Cummings probably used an uppercase letter for the j in Just for emphasis. The only other capital letter in the poem is for the word Man in BalloonMan, when the word appears for the third time. Even the children's names are set in lowercase letters.)

Does the word Just mean "only," suggesting that spring alone, the season of growth and renewal, is the time of joy in a child's life? Or is the message darker, perhaps even ironic? If spring is "just,"

(4-a) The questions are interesting, especially in light of the writer's conclusion: "the poet raises the questions but provides no definite answers."

meaning fair or honorable, where is
the justice in children (or their
childhoods) being stolen away? Perhaps
Cummings is saying that spring is not
just at all, that its delights are
merely seductions. What makes the
poem so compelling and provocative is
that the poet raises the questions

(4-a) but provides no definite answers.

CHAPTER

38

WRITING
AN ESSAY
EXAM

Most college courses require students to write a midterm and a final examination and perhaps other exams as well. The pressure of time during an examination makes this kind of writing especially challenging, but essay examinations call for the same skills demanded by other kinds of writing. Here are some points to note.

38a
Reviewing Notes

If you have taken adequate notes on lectures and assigned readings, preparing for the exam should not be overwhelming (see Appendix A). Read the notes you have written in the margins of your text and in your notebooks. Underline key words and phrases. Develop outlines. Your goal should be to highlight the major concepts and details the exam is likely to cover.

38b
Anticipating Questions

Imagine that you are the teacher and write out the questions that you would give. Merely writing questions down helps you organize your mind to answer them. You will often be surprised at how close you can come to the questions that appear on the examination.

38c
Reading Questions and Outlining Responses

When the examination is before you, read it through carefully and spend a minute or two thinking about it. You may find that a later question reminds you of information that is useful for an earlier question. Be sure you understand exactly what each question is asking you to do. A great many students go wrong on exams because they read the questions hastily and misunderstand them.

Next jot down a few words to help guide your answer. They will provide a brief outline for you to use in developing your answer, and they will nearly always stimulate your mind to think more clearly about the question. The two or three minutes you spend reading the question and writing down words to help you answer it will save you much time in the actual writing. Suppose you have a question such as this:

> What were the major causes of World War I? Which of these causes do you think was most important in the conflict that broke out in the summer of 1914? Justify your opinion.

38a,b,c
essay

Look at the question carefully: it is really *two* questions. The first one requires you to name several causes of World War I. The second requires you to make a choice among the causes you have named, and then to give reasons for your answer.

Once you understand the question, you are ready to start jotting down words and phrases to help form your answer. You begin by asking yourself who took part in the war as it developed in the summer of 1914 — information you should remember readily if you have taken careful notes from your lectures and your reading. You remember that Germany and Austria-Hungary stood on one side and that against those two powers stood Serbia, Russia, Belgium, France, and Great Britain. Then you write phrases like these:

> Russia vs. Austria-Hungary in the Balkans/Sarajevo
> Germany vs. France and England; Alsace-Lorraine/naval race
> Germany vs. Russia; Germans fear Russians; Schlieffen Plan
> Neutral Belgium in the way of German army
> Most important cause: German fear of Russia

With these notes before you, you can then begin to write.

38d
Justifying Opinions with Concrete Details

Many responses to essay questions are so vague and general that teachers wonder whether the students who wrote them ever came to class. A good answer mentions names, dates, facts, and specific details. A good answer also carries an argument and makes a point—just as any other good piece of writing does.

A good beginning for the answer to the question about World War I might read something like this:

38d,e
essay

> In the summer of 1914, Europe was an arena of peoples who hated each other. The Germans hated the English because the English had a great empire and they themselves had little. The English hated the Germans because, since 1896, the Germans had been building a huge navy under the goading of the German Kaiser, Wilhelm II. The British believed that this German navy was to be used against them, and when the Kaiser sided with Britain's enemies in the Boer War, the British people saw their darkest suspicions confirmed.
>
> The French hated the Germans because the Germans had annexed the French territories of Alsace and Lorraine after the Franco-Prussian War of 1870–1871; the French wanted their land back and spoke continually of "revenge." The Germans heard that talk about revenge and hated the French for not adjusting to the new reality of Europe, which in the German view meant German domination of the continent.

The writer establishes the theory that national hatreds were a major cause of World War I by giving specific reasons for each country's hatred of another country, including appropriate names and dates.

38e
Reviewing and Improving Your Answer

Once you have written your response, read it over. Though you cannot rewrite it, you can often improve it by making minor corrections and additions. Look for ways to strengthen general statements by making them more specific. Simply adding a name, a date, or a factual detail may transform a vague claim into a specific reference that will demonstrate knowledge of the subject.

Vague: Though others flew before them, the Wright brothers are credited as the first to fly.

Specific: Because their powered flights of December 17, 1903, were recorded by witnesses and photographs, the Wright brothers are credited as the first to fly.

Vague: Time is an interesting concept in Faulkner's "A Rose for Emily."

Specific: In Faulkner's "A Rose for Emily" we have a narrator who seems to be older than Miss Emily Grierson and lives longer than she does. Who is this narrator? How is the narrator related to time?

Vague: John Donne's poem "Death Be Not Proud" ends up being hopeful.

Specific: John Donne's poem "Death Be Not Proud" addresses Death as a person and exalts human nature by condemning the traditional claim that Death finally triumphs over humankind.

**38d,e
essay**

✓ CHECKLIST: TAKING AN ESSAY EXAM

1. Have you read the exam all the way through?
2. Do you understand every question?
3. Have you made a few brief notes on each question?
4. Does your answer have an argument?
5. Is your answer specific?
6. Does your answer take in all parts of the question?

CHAPTER

39

BUSINESS WRITING

Whenever you send out a business letter, a job application, a memo, or a résumé, you can expect to be judged on the form of what you have written as well as on the content. If you misspell words, type over errors without first removing them, or leave smudges and stains on what you send out, you can expect readers to conclude that you are sloppy and careless in your work. If you do not use the standard business forms, readers will assume you do not know how to use them. If you do not communicate information in a clear and structured way, readers will think you are disorganized. But if your business correspondence is written clearly, directly, and neatly, your business audience will be inclined to take you seriously.

39a
Following Accepted Standards for a Business Letter

When the block style is followed, the major parts of the letter are set flush with the left margin. Do not indent for paragraphs. Indicate paragraphs by leaving a line of space between the last line of one paragraph and the first line of the next.

Letterhead stationery

If you are writing for a business firm or a professional organization, you will probably use stationery with a printed letterhead at the top. The letterhead will give the name of the firm, its address, and often some sort of advertising slogan. You begin such letters with the date, written a couple of spaces under the letterhead. You may center the date, or you may move it to the right or left side of the page.

Space down three or four lines, and write the name and address of the person to whom you are sending the letter. The address of the recipient of your letter is called the *inside address.* Space down another couple of lines and write the salutation. Skip a line, and begin your first paragraph. Do not indent the paragraph. At the end of the paragraph, skip another line and begin the next paragraph.

When you have finished the letter, skip a couple of lines and write the complimentary close, again starting flush with the left margin. Space down four lines and type your name. If you have a title, write it just under

International Automobile
3821 Oceanside Drive
Bancroft, Idaho 83217
Telephone: 208-489-0199
Dealers in Antique Car Replacement Parts

July 29, 1991

Ms. Lenore P. Raven, President
Nevermore Antique Car Restorations, Inc.
35 Oak Street
Belmont, Massachusetts 02178

Dear Ms. Raven:

Thank you for your letter of July 14
inquiring about parts for the standard
six-cylinder 1948 Chevrolet Fleetmaster
engine. I am happy to tell you that we do
carry pistons, rods, and crankshafts for
that engine. I am enclosing a price list
for the various parts. Shipping charges
are included in the prices. We ship by
United Parcel Service on the day orders
are received. We can arrange overnight
delivery at an additional charge.

We accept payment by Visa, MasterCard, or
American Express, or money order or
certified check.

Thank you for thinking of International
Automobile.

Yours sincerely,

Roderick Usher

Roderick Usher
President and General Manager

Enclosure

your typed name. Sign your name with a pen in the space between the complimentary close and your typed name.

If you enclose anything with the letter, space down another two lines and write "Enclosure" or "Enclosures" flush with the left margin.

A sample business letter on letterhead stationery, typed in block form, is shown on page 561.

Stationery without a letterhead

If you write to a business or to an institution, type your letter on unlined, sturdy bond paper, 8½ × 11 inches. Type your own address at the center of the top of the page. Put the date under your address. Make the other parts of the letter the same as you would if you were using letterhead stationery.

```
                          28 Horseshoe Lane
                          Fair Hills, New York 10020
                          March 15, 1990

Mr. Basil Carmine
Ajax Industrial Chemicals
3939 Gentilly Boulevard
New Orleans, Louisiana 70126

Dear Mr. Carmine:

Last week I bought a fifty-gallon drum of
your industrial-strength floor cleanser
for my automotive repair business.
According to your full-page advertisement
in last week's Mechanic's Companion, your
cleanser, sold under the brand name Wipe
Out, is guaranteed to remove every trace of
oil and grease from the floor of a garage.

I carefully followed your directions in
applying the cleanser. I put on rubber
gloves and spread the powder over all the
grease and oil stains on the floor of my
establishment. I then hosed down the
powder with water. You can imagine my
astonishment when your cleanser began to
boil violently and to give off thick red
fumes that forced us to evacuate the
building.
```

When we were finally able to reenter the building the next day, we discovered that Wipe Out had not only removed the oil and grease stains but had also eaten large holes in the concrete floor underneath the stains.

I have discussed the situation with my lawyer, Rosalyn Eastwick, of Eastwick, Burns, and Tavern, and she has advised me to ask you to pay for repairs on my building. To that end, I am having several reputable contractors give me estimates on these costs. I shall forward these estimates to you.

If you are unwilling to pay for these repairs, we shall have no recourse but to sue you and your firm under state and federal laws regulating interstate commerce and false and misleading advertising.

I hope that a lawsuit will not be necessary. And I look forward to your reply.

Yours sincerely,

Glenda Ruby

Glenda Ruby
President, Southside Garage, Inc.

Modified Block Style

In the block format, every line of the letter except the heading begins flush with the left margin. This format is common in business writing because it is efficient. Word processing programs on computers can be set up to produce the block format automatically, and the writer can move swiftly through the letter.

Some businesses prefer the modified block format. The only difference here is that the complimentary close is centered and the first letter of the typed name of the letter writer is placed four lines directly under the first letter of the typed complimentary close.

Address and Salutation

Give the title of the addressee (the person to whom you are writing) and use an appropriate salutation. The title may appear immediately after the name, or it can be put beneath the name.

> Ms. Glenda Ruby
> President, Southside Garage, Inc.
> 28 Horseshoe Lane
> Fair Hills, New York 10020

> Ms. Glenda Ruby, President
> Southside Garage, Inc.

Never abbreviate titles. Do not write:

> Ms. Glenda Ruby, Pres.
> Southside Garage, Inc.

> Mr. Sylvan Glade, Asst. Mgr.
> Micawber Loan Company

Instead, write:

> Ms. Glenda Ruby, President

> Mr. Sylvan Glade, Assistant Manager

Some titles ordinarily are placed before the name in the inside address, and some of these titles can be abbreviated:

> Dr. Ishmael Romer
> Dean Ivy Wallace
> Bishop Bernard Law
> The Rev. Hiram Welch
> Captain Jennifer Jones
> Sister Mary Annunciata

The salutation, always followed by a colon in a business letter, greets the person who receives the letter. It is placed flush with the left margin, below the inside address, and separated from the inside address by a double space.

Use the addressee's last name in the salutation. Do not address the person by his or her first name unless you are very good friends. Never address by first name a person you have not met or one you know only slightly.

Always say "Dear _____." Do not say "Hi," "Hi there," "Greetings," or anything else that attempts to be cute. The conventions of business writing require the traditional salutation.

Use *Messrs.* (the abbreviated plural of the French *Monsieur*) when you address more than one man. When the addressees are two or more women, use *Mmes.* (the abbreviation of *Mesdames*).

Here are some sample salutations acceptable to most people:

Dear Ms. Ruby:
Dear Dr. Farnsworth:
Dear Messrs. Doolittle and Kreisburg:
Dear Mmes. Cohen and Grey:
Dear Miss Williams:

39a business

To avoid unnecessary reference to marital status, many writers favor *Ms.* as a title for women (see 30d). This usage has won wide acceptance, and many women prefer it. However, *Miss* and *Mrs.* are still acceptable, and you should use one of these forms of address if you know that the person you are addressing prefers it. Note whether she has indicated any preference by the way she has typed her name on any letter she has written to you or on the envelope. If she has supplied no clue, use *Ms.*

In writing to business organizations or to someone whose name you do not know, use one of the following kinds of salutation:

Dear Registrar:
Dear American Express:
Dear Sir or Madam:
Dear Sir:
Dear Madam:
Gentlemen:
Mesdames:
Dear Colleagues:
To whom it may concern:

A good dictionary will provide correct forms of addresses and salutations in the special cases of elected government officials, religious leaders, military personnel, and so on.

The Body of the Letter

Get to the point quickly and let your reader know what you want.

Business letters are like college papers: they should have a thesis. You write a letter to get the recipient to do something or to believe something. You do not write a business letter to ramble on about all sorts of things that may be on your mind. You may write a business letter to apply for a job, to report on something you have done, to request information, to complain, to apologize, to ask advice, to give information, to develop a plan, or for many other reasons. You should make your purpose clear within the first two sentences of your letter.

Dear Mr. Armstrong:

As president of the Environmental Coalition, I am sending you this letter by certified mail to inform you that we are suing you in federal court to shut down your factory on the Hiwassee River. I have written you several times on this matter, but you have not responded. In the meantime, the pollutants from your factory have gone on killing fish by the thousands. So we have no recourse but to sue, and we have taken the first steps to get our suit before the court. You will be hearing from the court and from our lawyers shortly.

Dear Dr. Farnsworth:

I would like to apply for the job of dental hygienist that you have advertised in today's *Morning Bugle.* I worked as a hygienist for ten years in Dallas, Texas, before my wife was transferred here by her business. I am enclosing my résumé, and I would welcome an opportunity to talk with you about the position.

Business people do not have time to study a letter in search of the writer's meaning. They want to know right away what the writer wants of them. You should express that purpose as quickly and as directly as possible. Practice getting to the point as quickly as you can.

Use a simple and direct style

Many people think that a good business letter must be bland and impersonal or that the writer must use complicated language to impress the recipient. Less frequently, they think they must use slang or other informal language to attract attention. In fact, a business letter should be simple and direct, without jargon and without inappropriate informality.

Unnatural Voice: I want to take this opportunity to inform you of the important fact that I am most seriously interested in the announcement of the accounting job that you advertised last week.

Too Informal: The accounting job you guys are offering in the latest *Daily Snort* sounds like a real grabber. Count me in. I look forward to pressing the flesh and to throwing all the facts on the table.

Natural: I want to apply for the accounting job you announced in today's *Times-Standard*.

Unnecessarily Complex: In your recent communication dated March 16, you asked us to enumerate, categorize, and prioritize the need-based scholarship applicants eligible for financial aid under Title 6 of the Federal Grants Act of 1987. We are able to report that we have now enumerated, categorized, and prioritized the need-based scholarship applicants eligible for financial aid under Title 6 of the Federal Grants Act of 1987.

Simple and Direct: In your letter of March 16, you asked us to count the students who need financial aid, to classify them according to the sort of help they need, and to decide which of them should have preference. We have done what you asked. Here are our findings.

39a business

Be brief

Whenever possible, keep a business letter to one page. Longer letters burden the people who must read them. They often obscure your meaning. Since business letters almost always ask for some action on the part of the recipient, you may feel that you have to argue your case at length. Sometimes you do indeed have to write a longer letter. But it is usually much better to make your request clearly, briefly give reasons for your request, and close quickly as possible. Readers of business letters appreciate brevity and clarity.

Let the recipient know clearly what you want

Close the body of your letter by saying clearly what you want the recipient to do next. You may be ordering merchandise; you may be asking for information; you may be requesting agreement; you may be asking for a proposal; you may be asking how a complaint will be met; you may be asking for a response to a report. Many other reasons move people to write business letters. Now and then you may not want a response to the letter. You may, for example, acknowledge receipt of a report and thank the writer for her hard work in putting together information you have requested. You do not expect the recipient to respond to a thank-you note. But much of the time you will expect a response to your letter, and you should spell out clearly what sort of response you expect. Do you want the person to telephone you? Do you want to meet with the person? Do you want a report? Do you want a replacement for faulty merchandise?

Dunham Engineering
31 Pine Crest Industrial Park
Atlanta, Georgia 30375

November 21, 1991

Mr. Michael Elia, President
Rocky Mountain Scenic Railroad, Inc.
1313 Grand View Street
Boulder, Colorado 80832

Dear Mr. Elia:

I want to arrange a day-long scenic excursion on your railroad for approximately a thousand people on Saturday, May 6, 1992. At that time, the National Association of Subdivision Engineers will be having its annual convention in Denver. We are sure to have at least a thousand who would enjoy such a trip. We would like to leave around 9:00 A.M. and to return to Boulder around three-thirty or three o'clock in the afternoon. We would like to charter our own train, and we would like to stop for a picnic lunch in the middle of the day.

Please let me know if your line is available for such a trip, and, if it is, quote me your group rates. Please tell me also if you are able to provide the lunch or if we should arrange to have it catered by another firm.

Many people have spoken to me of the beauty of your rail route and the courtesy of your service. I look forward to an enjoyable day on your line.

Yours sincerely,

David Dunham

David Dunham
President

Here is a model outline of a typical business letter like the one on the opposite page:

1. In the first sentence, give the purpose of the letter.
2. Tell the recipient what you want.
3. Give brief reasons for what you want.
4. Tell what the recipient can do next.
5. Close the letter.

Closing the Letter

Avoid clichés

You should always maintain a courteous and businesslike tone in your letters, but you can avoid some of the clichés of letter writing. Don't end your letters with a worn-out expression of gratitude such as "Thank you for your time," "Thank you for your consideration of this request," or "I await the courtesy of a reply." If you write in a friendly tone, you can close the letter immediately after you have stated your business and no one will accuse you of discourtesy. If you want to thank your recipient for something specific, you can do that. The writer of the preceding letter closed with a friendly expression of expectation. You can often close with a pleasant word about future relations. But avoid formula closings.

39a
business

At the end of your letter, include the complimentary close, a handwritten signature, and your typed name (and title, if appropriate).
Letters usually close with one of the endings below. A capital letter always starts the first word of the complimentary close; a comma always follows the complimentary close.

Yours truly,	Sincerely,
Very truly yours,	Sincerely yours,
Yours very truly,	Yours sincerely,
Cordially,	Cordially yours,
Respectfully,	Respectfully yours,
Regards,	Best regards,

The signature appears in a four-line space between the complimentary close and the typed name of the writer. Most writers avoid adding a professional title (such as attorney-at-law) or a degree (such as Ph.D.) after their typed name. However, to indicate their official capacity, writers who have a business title sometimes use it.

Sincerely yours,   Very truly yours,

Carolyn Garfield   W. Prescott Blast
Marketing Manager   Dean of the Faculty

39b
Addressing the Envelope

Address the envelope to include all essential information required for postal delivery. The address centered on the envelope is the same as the inside address; the return address in the upper left of the envelope includes the sender's name and address. Write out all words according to standard practice (see 30c) except for official post office abbreviations for names of states.

```
Julie Holden
3200 Lake View Drive
State College, PA 16801


          Ms. Delores Smith
          Personnel Manager
          Farm Journal, Inc.
          230 West Washington Square
          Philadelphia, PA 19105
```

Fold 8½ × 11 stationery in thirds so that it fits a standard 4 × 9½ envelope. Fold the bottom third up, then the top third down, leaving about a quarter inch between the top edge of the paper and the bottom fold so that your recipient can open the letter easily. For smaller business envelopes, fold standard paper in half from the bottom up; then fold the paper in thirds, left side first, right side over left.

39c
Writing a Memo

Modern business runs on **memos**, short communications exchanged within an office or between offices in the same firm. As the name indicates, a *memo* refers usually to something that should be remembered by people on the staff. Most conferences in a well-run business result in a memo that records what was decided. Supervisors in such businesses use memos to make announcements. Memos are usually kept on file. They are often used to trace the development of policy.

A good memo has many of the qualities of the business letter. But since the memo usually goes out to several people — perhaps hundreds of people — at once, it usually lacks some of the more personal conventions of letters.

Use the correct heading

A memo begins with a date in the upper right corner of the page. But instead of the salutation "Dear Ms. Adams," the memo begins with a general address, usually preceded by "To" followed by a colon.

The recipients are assumed to be within the organization; so the memo does not include an inside address other than the classification of the people who are to receive the memo.

The memo does not have a complimentary close, and it usually does not have a signature. Instead, the name of the writer of the memo appears after "From" followed by a colon. The writer's initials are then written by hand next to the name. The writer's title may or may not appear on the memo.

A good memo announces the subject on a third line after the word *subject* followed by a colon. Here are some standard headings for memos:

```
To: All the staff
From: RCM  RCM
Subject: Midterm grades

To: All coaches
From: Jack Booster, president of the
university  JB
Subject: The upcoming NCAA investigation
of our athletic program

To: Department supervisors
From: Michele Johnson, Affirmative Action
Officer  MJ
Subject: Affirmative Action guidelines
```

Limit each memo to one page, and treat only one subject.

Like a good business letter, a good memo should be brief and to the point. It should treat only one subject. It should be clear. If some response is required, the expected response should be spelled out. The memo does not have a complimentary close or a signature at the bottom. Here is a sample memo:

July 29, 1991

To: All members of the staff
From: LB
Subject: Dental care

We have recently made arrangements with the North Slope Community Health Group for complete dental care for employees of the company and their families. Your cost will be a $5.00 monthly fee that will be added to the medical insurance deduction in your paycheck. The company will defray all other costs for each employee enrolled in the dental plan.

The enclosed brochure from the North Slope Community Health Group will answer many of your questions about the plan. If you have further questions, please call Dr. Jerry Pullem at North Slope at 524-7529.

You must enroll in the plan by September 30. If you wish to enroll, please sign the enclosed form and return it to me. Your payroll deduction will begin with your October paycheck.

If you do not wish to enroll, you need not do anything.

39d
Writing a Letter to Accompany a Résumé

When you send your résumé (described in 39e) to a prospective employer, enclose a letter that catches attention by its careful statement of your qualifications. Among the scores of responses a personnel director receives after a job is advertised, your letter must stand out if you are to receive the consideration you want. Yet your letter must not violate the conventions of courtesy and restraint that have developed in business correspondence over the centuries. You are best served if you present your strongest qualifications clearly, briefly, and carefully.

A job-application letter usually accompanies a full résumé, which gives the applicant's educational background, work experience, and other interests. Your letter should show that you bring special talents to the position. Make your letter specific. Don't be satisfied with saying "I have had much valuable experience that will help me do this job." Spell out what that experience has been.

The letter reproduced below is forceful and concise. Note that each paragraph serves a specific function. The first states the writer's purpose

---

Route 2, Box 9
Manheim, Pennsylvania 17545
February 22, 1991

Ms. Delores Smith
Personnel Manager
Farm Journal, Inc.
230 West Washington Square
Philadelphia, Pennsylvania 19105

Dear Ms. Smith:

I would like very much to become an editorial assistant at Farm Journal. My four years of education at the Pennsylvania State University and my twenty years' experience as the daughter of a farming couple have given me the knowledge and background necessary to do this job.

Like many of your readers, I was born and raised on a farm. I have planted corn, mowed hay with a tractor, delivered calves, and built fences. I share with your readers an appreciation of farm life and an understanding of many of the problems of the independent farmer.

As you will see on my résumé, I am graduating from the university in June with a bachelor of arts degree and a double major in English and sociology. I have studied the problems of writing, editing, and producing a magazine. In my classes I have practiced and refined my knowledge of writing and editing. Now I would like to apply what I have learned.

I will be in Philadelphia for a week starting March 25. If we could arrange for an interview on the morning of March 27, I would be most grateful. I will call you before that day to see if it is convenient or to see if we can make an appointment at another time.

I look forward very much to meeting you.

Sincerely,

Julie Holden

Julie Holden

Encl.

in sending the letter. The second describes how the writer's background would help her do the job well. The third paragraph explains how the writer's education has prepared her for this job. The last paragraph asks for an interview. Everything is to the point.

39e
Preparing a Résumé

A standard résumé presents your education, your work experience, your interests, and other pertinent personal data. Formats for résumés vary.

Some are in the form of paragraphs, giving full information about past experience relevant to the job for which the writer is applying. Others are brief summaries. All good résumés include the information potential employers need to know about their workers. As the sample shows, you should type your résumé and lay it out attractively. Because a brief résumé helps a prospective employer evaluate your record quickly, you should try to keep your presentation to a single page. Do not inflate your résumé with unnecessary details in an effort to make it seem more impressive than it really is. If you are just starting a career, no one will expect you to be rich in experience and skills.

☐ **Personal data.** Give your name, current address, home address (if it is different from your current address), zip code, and telephone number with the area code. Mention any special abilities, such as fluency with languages other than English or experience in using business machines or computers. Mention any travels that might be relevant to the job.

☐ **Career objective.** Express your interest in a specific kind of position by stating your immediate and perhaps also your long-range objectives realistically.

☐ **Education.** List the schools you attended, beginning with high school. Start with your most recent school and work backward. Give your dates of attendance and the degrees you received, and include any honors or awards you won, your major, and any courses you think qualify you especially for the job you are seeking.

☐ **Experience.** List the jobs you have held, the dates of your employment, the names of your supervisors, and a brief description of your duties. Again, start with the most recent job and work backward.

☐ **Special interests.** To reveal details about yourself as an individual, you may wish to include information about hobbies, about membership in clubs and organizations, about volunteer work, or about any special talents you have. Be sure to mention any interests that might be useful in the job you are applying for.

☐ **References.** Give the names, addresses, and telephone numbers of people who will attest to your character and skill as a student and a worker. (Be sure to ask permission from anyone you list as a reference, and be sure to select people who know you well and will write or speak strongly in your behalf.) People you use as references should write directly to the prospective employer. You may send copies of letters that you have received in the past, commending you for your work, and sometimes you may send letters of recommendation that you have solicited from various people. But some employers tend to disregard such letters, preferring instead those written directly to the employer in your behalf.

Julie Holden

<u>Current address</u>   <u>Home address</u>
8200 Beaver Avenue   R.D. 2, Box 9
State College, PA   Manheim, PA
16801   17545
Tel.: (814) 998-0004   Tel.: (717) 777-7888

<u>Career objective</u>
A position of responsibility on the
editorial staff of a magazine or
publishing firm.

<u>Education</u>
1987–1991   The Pennsylvania State
                         University, bachelor of
                         arts in English (June
                         1991).
                         <u>Grade point average</u>:
                         3.25 of 4.0.
                         <u>Honors</u>: Dean's List.
                         <u>Major courses</u>: Article
                         Writing, News Writing
                         and Reporting,
                         Techniques of Fiction,
                         Technical Writing,
                         Advanced Technical
                         Writing and Editing,
                         Magazine Journalism,
                         Problems of Style,
                         Nonfiction Writing; also
                         Sociology, Rural Social
                         Psychology, Intergroup
                         Relations, Rural
                         Community Services.

1984–1987   Central High School,
                         Manheim, Pennsylvania
                         Academic diploma (1987)

<u>Experience</u>
Summers of 1989   Employed as a clerical
and 1990   assistant at Central
                         High School under the
                         supervision of Mr.

Horace K. Williams
Manheim, Pennsylvania.
Duties included
microfilming
confidential permanent
records, typing, and
filing.

Summers of 1987
and 1988

Worked as a farmhand on
the Schwarzmuller Dairy
Farm under the
supervision of Mr.
Robert Wilkes, Manheim,
Pennsylvania. Duties
included field work
(operating tractors and
implements) and barn
work (feeding and
cleaning).

<u>Special
interests</u>

Painting, photography,
gardening, macramé.

<u>References</u>
Professor Bernard Krimm
Department of English
The Pennsylvania State University
University Park, PA 16802
Phone: (814) 987-4994

Professor Carolyn Eckhardt
Department of English
The Pennsylvania State University
University Park, PA 16802
Phone: (814) 987-2268

Mr. Horace K. Williams
Guidance Counselor
Central High School
Manheim, PA 17545
Phone: (717) 998-8768

STUDY TECHNIQUES

Develop your study skills by applying techniques for improving your comprehension and retention of what you read. Learn to take useful notes when you read and when you listen to lectures. Studying is an active, continual process that requires planning, repetition, and *writing* to help you remember and use information.

Planning a Reasonable Study Schedule

Develop a realistic weekly plan for studying. Consider all the demands on your time — eating, sleeping, attending classes, doing homework, exercising, socializing, commuting, watching TV — and set aside time for studying. Some students make a weekly chart of their activities. If you do block in regular activities and study time on a calendar, leave a number of free periods so that you have time for relaxing and for making adjustments. When exams or special projects come up, for example, you'll need blocks of time over several days, even weeks, to complete work on time. Try to avoid cramming for tests, because the stress it produces prevents deep learning and memory. If you must cram, try to outline the major points you need to cover and concentrate on learning the central ideas and facts.

Active Reading

You can improve your ability to learn and retain material by approaching your reading with a clear plan and by taking various kinds of notes.

Survey the text before you read it

Surveying — looking at the text for information without reading every word — gives you an outline of the material so you can focus on what you are about to read. When you survey a book, look for chapter titles and subtitles, headings and subheadings, charts, graphs, illustrations, and words in boldface or italics. Skim the opening and closing paragraphs of a chapter or of chapter sections. Surveying of this kind can give you the sense of a book very quickly.

Make up questions so that you can read with a purpose

Once you have looked through the material, jot down some questions about it. Writing will help make things stick in your mind, and your written questions will provide a good short review. It is always better to write your own questions, but if there are questions at the end of a chapter, let them guide your reading.

Keeping questions in mind as you read will get you actively involved in the material at hand. Your reading now has a purpose: you are trying to find answers to your questions.

Summarize rather than underline

Learn how to make summaries. When you read, try to summarize every paragraph by composing a simple, short sentence. Put the author's thoughts into your own words. Don't try to duplicate the style of the book or article you are reading. Putting somebody else's ideas into your own words is a good way of making sure you truly know those ideas.

Underlining has several disadvantages. Obviously, you cannot underline in a library book. If you underline material, you will have to own the book. Underlining is also a passive approach. When students come back to passages they have underlined, they often cannot remember why they underlined them in the first place. Most people underline too much, and the result is boring and confusing. Underlining is never as effective as writing a short summary sentence for each paragraph or each page. A summary sentence ensures that you will reconsider the thoughts in the book, translate them into your own words, and put them on paper.

**App A
study**

Read in a variety of sources

You can also help retain information by looking for the same topic or closely related information in another source. Your teacher may require you to buy one or more books for the course, and you should read these books and make notes about them. But it is also an excellent idea to look up the topics in some of the many reference books available in the library. Try an encyclopedia, various dictionaries, and other reference books your librarian may help you find. (Many of these reference books are listed in 32c of this handbook.)

When you read the same information presented in slightly different ways, you will find that each source has some detail the others do not have. Variety in your learning can be a wonderful help in remembering. If you have taken careful notes on the various things you have read, you should remember more easily.

Analyze what you read

Another required skill is the ability to analyze, to tell what things mean, to discover how they fit with other things you know. Here again, writing will help you to study. Many teachers advise students to keep a notebook in which they jot down their notes from sources on one page and their thoughts about those notes on a facing page. If you ask yourself questions about the things you put down, you will develop your analytical powers. Pay attention to your own feelings. Do you like a book? Make yourself set down reasons why you like it. Do you dislike a book? Again, write down the reasons for your preference. Whether you feel interested, bored, repelled, or excited, ask yourself what there is in the book (or movie or whatever else you may be studying) that arouses such feelings. Then write your reasons down. You do not have to like a work of literature or art or history merely because someone else does. But you should be able to justify your opinions to others and to yourself. As you get into the habit of writing down these justifications, you will find your analytical ability steadily improving.

Look up and learn unfamiliar words

With the aid of a dictionary, keep a written record of new words; write them on index cards or in a notebook. Include correct spelling, pronunciation clues, clear definitions that you write yourself, and a phrase or a sentence using the word properly. Arrange the words in related groups to help yourself study (business words, economics words, psychology words, literature words, and so on). Incorporate any new words into your speaking and writing vocabulary. Here is an example:

```
       puerile ( PYOO ar il )
juvenile in a bad sense. People who are
puerile are not just children; they are
childish. He was puerile when he re-
fused to let her name appear before his
on the program for the play.
```

**App A
study**

Review your notes and your reading assignments

Immediately after you finish reading, and at convenient intervals thereafter, look over the questions, notes, summaries, or outlines you have created from your reading. Don't try to read every word of the original material in the book or article every time you review. Skim over it. You will learn better from many rapid readings than from one or two slow readings. Skimming will help you get the shape of the material in your mind. As you study your own notes, you will recall many of the supporting details.

Use your written work to help you complete your assignments. It often helps if you close the book, put away your notes, and try to jot down from memory a rough outline of what you are studying. The more ways you can write about material you are learning, the more effectively you will learn it.

Taking Notes

Learn to write good notes on your lectures

Taking good notes requires practice. Some students tape-record lectures so they can listen again to what the teacher has said. But even if you have a tape recorder and the teacher is willing to be recorded, good notes can still help you understand and remember the lecture.

Never try to write down everything you hear in the lecture as it is going on. Unless you know shorthand, you cannot write as fast as a person speaks, and while you are struggling to get a sentence down, the lecturer will have gone on to another point. In your haste, you may garble both what has been said and what is being said.

Your best bet is to write down words, phrases, and short sentences. Use these jottings to stimulate your memory later on. As soon as possible after the lecture is over, take your notes to a quiet place and try to write down as much of the lecture as you can remember. If you do this regularly, you probably will find yourself remembering more and more of each lecture.

Once you have written up your notes, compare what you have with the notes taken by another member of the class. If four or five of you get together to share your notes, you will each acquire an amazingly complete set, and in your discussions of gaps and confusions, you will further your learning.

Don't try to sit for hours without a break. Get up every forty-five minutes or so and walk around the room and stretch. Then sit back down quickly and go to work again. Taking a break will relax your body and perhaps stimulate your mind to some new thought that you can use when you start studying again.

App A study

Compare Notes with Classmates

Use a separate notebook for each class

For the sake of good order, don't keep your notes for all of your courses in one notebook. You can keep track of your notes much more easily by using a separate notebook for each course. At graduation, you will have an orderly record of your college education.

WRITING WITH A WORD PROCESSOR

By all means learn to use computers and word processing programs before you leave college. The computer has become a standard medium of communication. Word processing programs enable you to make sweeping revisions or small changes with relative ease. They are fun to use, and they often give writers a sense of control over their work which they lacked when they were doing everything with a pencil, or even with a typewriter.

Choose a word processing program that you can learn easily and that someone you know is using successfully. Manuals are notorious for poor writing. If you cannot understand the manual, you can always consult a friend who knows the program.

Learn to compose at a keyboard. It is a much faster and more convenient way of writing than longhand. If you are going to use a computer, you must be able to use a keyboard. A little practice will show you that composing at a keyboard will make you much more productive.

Computers eliminate much of the physical labor of writing, but you still have to work hard. No computer can think for you or tell you what you ought to say. But the computer, a good word processing program, and a printer will make some of your choices easier. Revision becomes much easier, and as we have said so frequently, revision is the heart of writing. A computer is useful to a writer in a variety of ways: you can use it to take notes, to store data, and to create outlines as well as to write and revise your papers.

Taking Notes

You can make many of your notes with a computer and a word processor. Bookstands that hold books open and upright beside the keyboard are available in all office-supply shops and in many campus bookstores. If you can use a keyboard at all, you can type much more quickly and with much less fatigue than you can write in longhand. You are also likely to take notes more accurately with a keyboard, especially if you learn how to touch-type.

Taking notes on a computer gives you several advantages. You can find them quickly by using the search command on your word processing program. For example, suppose you are reading stories by the writer Peter Taylor for a literature paper on his work and you notice how often he mentions mirrors. You think you might mention that detail, perhaps even make a paper out of it. But you don't yet know. So you make this note:

> The person in the mirror now eyed him curiously, even incredulously, and momentarily he resented the intrusion of this third, unfamiliar person on the scene, a person who, so to speak, ought still to have been asleep beside his wife back there in the family's guest room.
> —"At the Drug Store," *The Collected Stories of Peter Taylor*
>
> (New York: Penguin Books, 1986), p. 117

You might want to add a thought of your own about the use of the mirror in this passage. (In making notes, you may make a file in which you put the full bibliographical information for every source you consult. If in that file you have the full information for *The Collected Stories of Peter Taylor,* you need only write "Taylor" and a page number with your note on mirrors.)

When you have made several dozen notes, you may want to recover all those places where Taylor mentions a mirror. All you have to do is command your word processor to search for the word *mirror.* It is a much faster process than keeping notes on 3×5 cards and having to shuffle through them when you sit down to work on your paper.

All good word processing programs have another feature you can use in your writing. By using only a few keystrokes, you can copy any of your notes from your note file into the body of the paper you are writing. If you wanted to quote the passage above from Peter Taylor, you would not have to type it again. You could move it quickly from your note file to the essay you are writing. Not only is the process much easier than typing the note all over again; it also cuts down your chances of making a copying error.

In taking notes with a computer, you should avoid the temptation to take too many notes or to copy too much **verbatim** (word for word) from the source. You should summarize most information, perhaps using only sentence fragments or abbreviated sentences. So, for the quotation above, you might write:

Taylor, mirrors, p. 117, *Collected Stories*

Then your computer file serves as an annotated index of your sources. Seeing the word *mirrors* on your computer, you can pick up the book of short stories and turn quickly to the passage. It is always good to

App B
wp

take notes and to make comments on the notes you take. Your thoughts as you write the note should also go into your computer file, marked in some clear way that allows you to distinguish between what you are thinking and what you are seeing in the source.

Avoid taking so many notes that doing the research becomes a substitute for writing the paper. Many writers, both experienced and inexperienced, take so many notes and do so much research that they never get around to writing the paper.

You can set up a separate computer file for each set of notes — a file for English literature, another for history, another for chemistry, and so on. You can set up a bibliography file, listing the various books and articles you use in a research project. You can make a directory that might, for example, combine all the files of notes made in various English courses you have taken in college. You can add files and notes throughout your formal education and afterward.

Creating Outlines

The same features that make a word processing program a good note file can also help you in outlining a paper.

You can construct an outline on your word processor and then move the various parts around easily to achieve a more effective organization.

As you work, you can gradually fill in your outline, using sample sentences and paragraphs that you can later fit into your paper. You can try out introductions and conclusions to see which of them best express your purposes.

If you have consulted several sources, you can often put your paper together by transferring notes from your note file to the place where you think they ought to fit in your outline. You can try different arrangements and experiment with different organizations.

App B wp

You can save the various versions of your expanded outlines, print them out, and compare them to see which seems to suit your purposes best.

Some word processing programs now have built-in outlining functions, and some outlining programs with special functions are on the market. These outliners allow you to put your final paper together easily from an extended outline merely by pressing a few function keys. But by using the search and copy functions of any program, you can use it as an outliner.

If you use the computer to outline and to arrange your notes in organized blocks, you will see more clearly that writing is seldom a linear process in which one sits down and starts writing a paper from the beginning and goes straight through to the end. Writing is nearly always a process by which we bring chunks of material together and then blend them into a whole.

Writing the Paper

Revise your work carefully

When you have used a computer for a while, you will learn to revise on the screen, inserting here, deleting there. But you should always print your work out and read it on paper, at least for the final run-through. Read with a pencil in hand to mark those places where you want to revise.

Be sure to give special attention to two errors common in word processing. One is deleting too much; the other is not deleting enough.

Often a writer will produce a sentence like this:

Mr. Harrington, who has been convicted of car theft, said that his criminal record had nothing to do with his present effort to become city fire inspector, since cars had nothing to do with city buildings.

The writer, looking at this long sentence, naturally thought of ways of shortening it. And so he deleted some words. But as people often do in using computers, he deleted too much.

Mr. Harrington, of car theft, said that his criminal record had nothing to do with his present effort to become city fire inspector, since cars had nothing to do with city buildings.

He had to insert a word he had accidentally deleted:

App B
wp

Mr. Harrington, convicted of car theft, said that his criminal record had nothing to do with his present effort to become city fire inspector, since cars had nothing to do with city buildings.

Another error is failure to delete enough. A writer wrote this:

Custer seemed to think that a dramatic victory over the Sioux Indians in 1876 would make him a national hero and might make him president in the election later that year.

In looking at his sentence, he decided to revise and came up with this:

Custer seemed to think that a slaughtering the Sioux Indians would make him a national hero and might make him president in the election later that year.

The writer has decided to make Custer's intentions more vivid by changing "a dramatic victory over" to "slaughtering." So he has deleted and inserted. But he has not deleted the article *a*, thus leaving the sentence confused. It should be this:

> Custer seemed to think that slaughtering the Sioux Indians would make him a national hero and might make him president in the election later that year.

Computers allow you to move groups of words or, indeed, whole pages from one part of your essay to another by using a few function keys. You can try out a great many forms for the information you present. But be sure that you make the parts you move fit into their new spot. Read your work over again to be sure that you have not moved something without proper regard for the new context or that you have not left a noticeable hole in the place where the moved text was originally located. Working on a computer grants marvelous efficiency to the writing process. But it does not take away the requirement of any writer to read the text again and again and again to see that everything hangs together as it should.

Keep your successive drafts, on either backup disks or printouts or both. You may decide that you want to return to an earlier version of a sentence or a paragraph.

Use the computer to check on stylistic mannerisms or tedious repetitions

All writers have certain words or expressions they like and therefore tend to use too often. If you think you have used some stylistic mannerism too frequently, use the search function on the word processing program to see how many times you have used it in your paper. For example, you may like the word *doggedly*. Search your paper to see how many times you have used it. If you have used it more than once, you should probably find a synonym.

App B
wp

Sometimes, especially in a long paper, you may repeat information unnecessarily. If you write a paper about southern literature, you might mention Peter Taylor as someone whose writing has little to do with the agrarian tradition of much southern writing. Suppose you are writing and think you may have said that earlier. It's easy to search for "Taylor" in your preceding text to see if you have given the information before.

You can use parts of this handbook more effectively by searching in your writing for words that you were warned against in these pages. Are you afraid that you have used needless intensifiers such as *absolutely*, *definitely*, and *incredibly*? Search for them on the computer and decide if you want to eliminate them. Do you think you may have overused modifiers such as *very*, *rather*, and *really*? Search for them on the computer, and see if you can eliminate them where they turn up.

Physical Format

Be courteous to your readers

Computers make life easier for writers but sometimes harder for readers. Be sure you do not let technology burden your readers. You can be courteous in the kind of printer you use for your final drafts and in the way you manage computer paper.

Computer printers are of three main types. Laser printers are fast, and they have the clearest typeface. Letter-quality printers are heavy and slow, but they also have an excellent typeface, comparable to that of a good electric typewriter. Dot-matrix printers are perhaps the most common and reliable printers generally available. They make characters out of combinations of little dots; the dots are pressed onto the paper by tiny wires pushed through an inked ribbon, and the effect is like the appearance of the lights that form letters and numbers within a square on a scoreboard.

Dot-matrix type has improved dramatically over the years, but some models still make characters that are difficult to read. If you use a dot-matrix printer, be sure that it makes letters with true descenders. That is, the *g, p, q,* and *y* should have tails that come below the baseline of the rest of the type. The dots should also be close enough together to make legible letters. Before you use or buy a dot-matrix printer, look at a document that printer has produced. Can you read the document without being distracted by the type? If you have any doubts, find another printer.

Beware of printers that work with thermal-sensitive paper. These printers are often advertised as needing no ribbon; they make an impression by applying great heat to treated paper. Such printers are fast and quiet. But often the type fades quickly as chemical changes take place in the paper. You can write something on thermal-sensitive paper and discover in a few months that you have nothing but blank sheets in your file! (Always be careful around any kind of dot-matrix printer; in operation, the printing head is extremely hot and can cause severe burns.)

Be sure the ribbon on your printer is dark enough to provide legible copy. The ribbons on dot-matrix printers wear out rapidly. A faint, scarcely legible type in dot matrix can make life even more difficult for a hard-pressed teacher.

Computer paper is usually fed into the printer on a continuous roll. A perforated strip on each side allows a tractor feed to roll the paper line by line into the printer so that the paper does not wrinkle or twist on the roller. When you hand in your paper, be sure to tear off the perforated strip that has been used by the tractor feed. Be sure, too, to separate the pages. Don't hand in a continuous roll of printed pages! Teachers become justifiably annoyed if they have to separate individual sheets and put a student's work together before they can read and grade it.

Computer paper is notoriously poor in quality. But nearly all computer printers will accept ordinary white bond paper. You must feed bond paper into most printers one sheet at a time. This process is slower than continuous-feed printing, but the greatly improved appearance justifies the extra effort.

When you format a document, be sure to consider your readers

When we format a document, we lay out a page by adjusting the margins, setting material (including page numbers) at the head and the foot of each page, determining the positions of the subheads, deciding whether the page will be single- or double-spaced, and setting the number of lines of type that will appear on a page.

In word processing, as in typing, take care to provide good margins —usually an inch and a half on the left side and at least an inch at the top, the right side, and the bottom. A little practice with your computer and your word processing program should make it easy for you to set these margins.

Always number your pages. Word processing programs can set numbers at the top or the bottom of each page, and they can center the number or set it on the right or left side. It's usually a good idea to number pages at the top.

You can also set headers and footers. A **header** is a line of type that goes across the top of every page; a **footer** is a line of type that goes across the bottom of every page. Headers and footers should be separated from the body of the text by one line of space if the text is single-spaced and by two lines of space if the text is double-spaced.

Page numbers are usually set as headers or footers. You can add other information as well—the title of your paper, your last name, the date. It's generally good to keep headers and footers simple so they will not distract from the body of the text.

Be sure that you do not end with a subhead at the bottom of the page. When you prepare the computer to paginate, you must tell it how many lines to put on a page. If you double-space on 8½ × 11 paper, you will usually have a header with a page number and about 27 lines of text. Sometimes the page will end with a subhead, and the material that the subhead introduces will not begin until the next page. This arrangement can be confusing to readers, and it makes your work look sloppy. With a little practice, you can learn to insert blank lines to make the computer move your heading to the top of the next page, where it belongs. Every time you repaginate your text after inserting or deleting material, you should check through your work to be sure that you have not pulled or pushed a subhead to the bottom of a page.

Don't overuse the variety of types your computer may offer you. With some printers, the temptation is great to use as many of the available

**App B
wp**

typefaces as possible. Avoid eccentric typefaces. Boldface and italic are the only special typefaces you need for most work. Never turn in papers written in a script or gothic typeface.

With most word processing programs, you can justify the right margin. Unless your word processing program and your printer will do proportional spacing, it's always better to leave your right margin unjustified.

Housekeeping Chores

Use the dictionaries that come with many word processing programs Many word processing programs come with dictionaries that allow you to check the spellings of words in your text. These dictionaries are usually smaller than standard desk dictionaries. Most collegiate desk dictionaries list about 150,000 words; a dictionary on a word processing program usually has around 50,000 words. Geographical, biographical, and specialized names are not usually included in a computer dictionary. But you can add words to the dictionary. Computer dictionaries also do not define words; they only list words with their correct spelling. You must be sure that you are using the word in the right sense; the computer program probably will not tell you what the word means.

The computer dictionary, often called a *spell checker*, is usually activated when one or more function keys are pressed while the cursor is on the word whose spelling you wish to examine. The computer will usually give you a message telling you whether the word is in the computer's dictionary. If it *is* in the dictionary, you may assume that you have spelled it correctly. If it is *not* in the dictionary as you have spelled it, either you have misspelled it or the computer dictionary does not include it. You might get a message, for example, that the word *dilettante* is not in your computer's dictionary. But on consulting your desk dictionary, you discover that you have spelled the word correctly! So you should never depend on the computer dictionary alone; use it in conjunction with a good desk dictionary.

Computer dictionaries can be a great help in ensuring the accuracy of spelling. But you have to use them. If you have any doubt about your spelling of a word, check it with the computer dictionary. And if your spelling is not listed in the computer dictionary, look it up in a desk dictionary.

Some dictionary programs can be set to work as you are typing. A quiet buzzer sounds each time you type a word not in the computer's dictionary. Such a function not only helps you with your spelling but also warns you against typographical errors. The computer will buzz if you misspell the word *believe* by writing "beleive." It will also buzz if you reverse letters in the word *the* so that you get "teh." The computer dictionary can become a valuable aid in proofreading.

Back up all your work and print out copies whenever you can

Computer data are stored by means of electric impulses that are translated onto disks by much the same sort of process that allows us to make tape recordings. Small disks, measuring either 3½ inches or 5¼ inches across, are called *floppies* and can be carried around and used in various compatible computers. Hard disks with vast storage capacities are sealed and fixed in the computer and are not intended to be moved from computer to computer.

All these disks are extremely fragile. Floppies can be ruined if they are placed too close to the speakers of a stereo set or even too close to the video monitor of the computer itself. Floppies are also sensitive to dust, to cracker crumbs, to fingerprints, to spilled coffee, and to anything else that touches the magnetic surface. Hard disks are sealed against dust and may give good service for several thousand hours. But all hard disks fail eventually. The failure comes suddenly, without warning. The hard disk simply fails to record data or to give data back to the computer screen.

Once a disk is ruined, the data you have put on it—a copy of your research paper, for example—may be gone forever. And even if you can retrieve the data by some of the technology now available, the process is time-consuming and sometimes expensive.

So you should always make backup copies of your work. That means that you should copy the work on one disk to another and keep the two disks in separate places so that if something happens to one, you will not lose your data. If you are using a hard disk, back your work up on floppies. If your computer fails, you can take your floppies to another compatible computer and go back to work with a minimum of lost time and with no lost data. Whenever you can do so, it's a good idea to print your work out at the end of a session with the computer. Printing the work out takes more time than making a backup disk. If you have a printed copy of your work, you may suffer the inconvenience of having to type it over again to store it on a disk. But at least you have your work.

**App B
wp**

GLOSSARY OF USAGE

Although the meanings of words often change through the years, clear communication is enhanced when these changes take place slowly and meanings are kept as constant as possible. The following words and expressions are often misused or used in nontraditional ways. Studying this list will help you improve your vocabulary and your precision in the use of words.

Accept/Except *Accept* is a verb meaning "to receive willingly." *Except* is a preposition meaning "but."

Please *accept* my apologies.
Everyone *except* Carlos saw the film.

Advice/Advise *Advice* is a noun; *advise* is a verb. The *c* in *advice* is pronounced like the *c* in *certain;* the *s* in *advise* is pronounced like the last *s* in *surprise.*

I took his *advice* about buying stock, and I lost a fortune.
I *advise* you to disregard his stock tips.

Affect/Effect The verb *affect* means "to impress, to move, to change."
The noun *effect* means "result."
The verb *effect* means "to make, to accomplish."
The noun *affect,* meaning a feeling or an emotion, is used in psychology.

Inflation *affects* our sense of security.
Inflation is one of the many *effects* of war.
Inflation has *effected* many changes in the way we spend money.
To study *affect,* psychologists probe the unconscious.

Ain't *Ain't* is an eighteenth-century contraction that has become a sign of illiteracy and ignorance; it should not be used in formal writing or speech.

All/All of; More/More of; Some/Some of Except before some pronouns, the *of* in these constructions can usually be eliminated.

All of us wish you well. [The pronoun *us* requires the *of* before it here.]
All France rejoiced.
Some students cut class.

All right/Alright The spelling *alright* is an alternate, but many educated readers still think it is incorrect in standard written English.

I told him it was *all right* to miss class tomorrow.

All together/Altogether *All together* expresses unity or common location; *altogether* means "completely," often in a tone of ironic understatement.

At the Imitators-of-Elvis national competition, it was *altogether* startling to see a swarm of untalented, loud young men with their rhinestones, their dyed and greased hair, and their pretensions, gathered *all together* on a single stage.

Allusion/Illusion   *Allusion* means an indirect reference to something; *illusion* means a fantasy that may be confused with reality.

He wrote to her of an "empty house," an *allusion* to their abandoned love affair.

They nourished the *illusion* that they could learn to write well without working hard.

Almost/Most   *Almost,* an adverb, means "nearly"; *most,* an adjective, means "the greater part of." Do not use *most* when you mean *almost.*

He wrote her about *almost* [NOT *most*] everything he did.

He told her about *most* things he did.

Among/Between   *Between* is usually said to express a relation of two nouns; *among* is supposed to express a relation involving more than two:

The distance *between* Boston and Knoxville is a thousand miles.

The desire to quit smoking is common *among* people who have smoked for a long time.

But throughout the history of English, *between* has sometimes been used with more than two nouns. It often has the sense of "within":

He covered the space *between* the four corners of his yard with concrete.

Between is sometimes used for more than two when each noun is considered individually:

The treaty that was signed was *between* the United States, Israel, and Egypt. [Each country signed the treaty individually.]

Between usually expresses a more precise relation, and *among* is more general.

Gloss usage

Amount/Number   Things measured in *amounts* usually cannot be thought of as having any individual identity, things measured in *numbers* can be sorted out and counted separately.

The *amount* of oil left underground in America is a matter of dispute.

But the *number* of oil companies losing money is tiny.

Anxious/Eager   Careful writers distinguish between these two words when they are used to describe feelings about something that is going to happen. *Anxious* means fearful; *eager* signals strong interest or desire.

I am *anxious* when I visit the doctor.

I am *eager* to get out of the hospital.

Any more/Anymore   *Anymore* is an adverb. *Any more* may be an adjective and a pronoun as in the sentence "I can't stand any more." Or it can be an adverb and an adjective, as in the sentence "I don't want any more peanut butter."

Anymore is always used after a negation: "I don't enjoy dancing *anymore.*"

Anyone/Any one; Anybody/Any body; Everyone/Every one; Everybody/Every body   Observe the difference between the indefinite pronouns *anyone,* *anybody, everyone,* and *everybody* and the noun *body* modified by the adjectives *any* and *every.*

> *Anybody* can make a mistake.
>
> A good murder mystery accounts for *every body* that turns up in the story.
>
> The Scots always thought that *any one* of them was worth three of the enemy.
>
> *Anyone* can see that this book is complicated.

Apt/Liable/Likely   *Apt* means that someone has a special talent for doing something. *Liable* means having legal responsibility. *Likely* conveys a general expectation or consequence.

> The president is an *apt* negotiator.
>
> If my singing breaks your chandelier, I am *liable* for damages.
>
> People who picnic in the woods are *likely* to get poison ivy.

As   Do not use *as* as a synonym for *since, when, while,* or *because.*

> UNCLEAR: I told him that he should visit Alcatraz *as* he was going to San Francisco.
>
> BETTER: I told him that he should visit Alcatraz *since* he was going to San Francisco.
>
> UNCLEAR: *As* I complained about the meal, the cook said he didn't like to eat there himself.
>
> BETTER: *When* I complained about the meal, the cook said he didn't like to eat there himself.
>
> UNCLEAR: *As* American Indians fought as individuals and not in organized groups, no wagon train in the history of the West ever had to circle up and fight off a mass attack by an Indian tribe.
>
> BETTER: *Because* American Indians fought as individuals and not in organized groups, no wagon train in the history of the West ever had to circle up and fight off a mass attack by an Indian tribe.

Gloss usage

As/Like   In formal writing, avoid the use of *like* as a conjunction. Although this usage is becoming more common even among the educated, it still irritates so many people that you would be wise to avoid it.

> NOT: He sneezed *like* he had a cold.
>
> BUT: He sneezed *as if* he had a cold.

Like is perfectly acceptable as a comparative preposition.

> He rode his horse *like* a cavalry soldier.
>
> The peas were *like* bullets.
>
> At the closing bell, the children scattered from the school *like* leaves before the wind.

It is unnecessary to substitute *as* for *like* any time *like* is followed by a noun unless the noun is the subject of a dependent clause.

> She enjoyed tropical fruits *like* pineapples, bananas, oranges, and mangoes.
>
> They did the assignments uncomplainingly, *as* they would have done nothing, uncomplainingly, if I had assigned them nothing.

At Avoid the use of *at* as a false particle to complete the notion of *where*.
Where is Carmichael?
NOT: Where is Carmichael at?

Awful/Awfully Use *awful* and *awfully* only to convey the emotion of terror
or wonder.
The vampire flew out the window with an *awful* shriek.
Careful writers avoid the use of *awful* and *awfully* when they mean *very* or
extremely.

A while/Awhile *A while* is an article and a noun:
Many authors are unable to write anything else for *a while* after they
publish their first novel.
Awhile is an adverb:
Stay *awhile* with me.

Because Avoid expressions like this one: "*The reason is because* I don't
have the time."
Write: "The reason is that I don't have the time."

Being as/Being that These terms should not be used as synonyms for *since*
or *because*.
NOT: *Being as* the mountain was there, we had to climb it.
BUT: *Because* the mountain was there, we had to climb it.

Beside/Besides *Beside* means "next to" or "apart from." *Besides* means
"in addition to" or "except for."
The ski slope was *beside* the lodge.
She was *beside* herself with joy.
Besides a bicycle, he needed a tent and a pack.

Gloss usage

Better Avoid using *better* in expressions of quantity.
Crossing the continent by train took more than [NOT better than]
four days.

But that/But what Avoid writing these phrases when you mean *that* in
expressions of doubt.
NOT: I have no doubt *but that* you can learn to write well.
BUT: I have no doubt *that* you can learn to write well.
NOT: I doubt *but what* any country music singer and writer has ever
had the genius of Hank Williams.
BUT: I doubt *that* any country music singer and writer has ever had
the genius of Hank Williams.

Can't hardly This is a double negative that is ungrammatical and self-
contradictory.
NOT: I can't hardly understand algebra.
BUT: I can hardly understand algebra.
I can't understand algebra.

Case/Instance/Line These words are often used in expressions that can be
revised, made more clear, or shortened.

NOT: In Murdock's case, I had to decide if he was telling the truth.
BUT: I had to decide if Murdock was telling the truth.
NOT: In that instance, Murdock lied.
BUT: Murdock lied.
    Murdock lied then, but he told the truth the rest of the time.
NOT: Along that line, Murdock lied.
BUT: Murdock lied when he said he was allergic to cats.

In many sentences, the use of *in that instance* or *along that line* or some other similar phrase keeps writers from being specific and keeps their prose from being lively.

Censor/Censure To *censor* is to keep a part or all of a piece of writing, a film, or some other form of communication from reaching its intended audience. To *censure* is to scold or condemn someone. Sometimes the censure is a formal act; sometimes it is a personal expression.

The Argentine government *censors* newspapers.
The House of Representatives *censured* Congressman Larsonee for stealing from the Post Office.

Compare with/Compare to When you wish to stress either the similarities or the dissimilarities between two things, use *compare to;* when you wish to stress both similarities and differences, use *compare with*.

She compared his singing to the croaking of a wounded frog.
Compared to driving a motorcycle, driving a sportscar is safer.
He compared Omaha with San Francisco.

The use of *compared with* means that he found some things alike in Omaha and San Francisco and some things that were not alike, and that he mentioned both the similarities and dissimilarities.

Complement/Compliment A *complement* is something added to something else to complete it. A *compliment* is an approving remark. *Complimentary* is an adjective referring to something freely given, as approval or a favor.

He considers sauerkraut a perfect *complement* to hot dogs.
She received many *compliments* on her speech.
All veterans received *complimentary* tickets.
His remarks were *complimentary*.

Contact Many writers and editors frown on the use of *contact* as a verb because it is weak, imprecise, and overused in common speech. You should not *contact* all the members of your club who have not paid their dues; you should *call, write, threaten,* or *speak to* them.

Convince/Persuade *Convince* usually means to win someone over by means of argument; *convince* should always take *that* with a clause. *Persuade* means to move to some form of action or change by argument or by some other means. *Persuade* is followed by *to*.

The experiment *convinced* him *that* light was subject to gravity.
I *persuaded* him *to* buy stock in the company.

Gloss usage

Could of/Should of/Would of These are ungrammatical forms of *could have, should have,* and *would have.* Avoid them and use the proper forms.

Differ from/Differ with *Differ from* expresses a lack of similarity; *differ with* expresses disagreement.

> The ancient Greeks *differed* less *from* the Persians than we often think.

> Aristotle *differed with* Plato on some important issues in philosophy.

Different from/Different than The idiom is *different from.* Careful writers avoid *different than.*

> The east coast of Florida is *different from* the west coast.

Disinterested/Uninterested To be *disinterested* is to be *impartial.* A disinterested party in a dispute has no selfish reason to favor one side over another. To be *uninterested* is to have no concern about something, to pay no attention, to be bored.

> We expect members of a jury to be *disinterested.*

> Most people nowadays are *uninterested* in philosophy.

Don't/Doesn't *Don't* can only be a contraction for *do not. Doesn't* is the contraction for *does not.*

> You *don't* know what you're talking about.

> He *doesn't* either.

Some American speakers say *he don't* and *she don't.* But such usage is nonstandard and should be avoided.

Due to/Because *Due to* is an overworked, wordy, and often confusing expression when it is used to show cause.

> **WORDY:** Due to the fact that I was hungry, I ate too much.

> **BETTER:** Because I was hungry, I ate too much.

Most writers accept the causative use of *due to* in short phrases, such as "His failure was *due to* laziness." But such constructions can be vague and confusing. Whose laziness? His or someone else's? The sentence does not tell us. What about a sentence like this one: Their divorce was due to infidelity. Whose infidelity? Were both partners unfaithful? Sentences that include an agent are almost always clearer and more vigorous.

> He failed because he was lazy.

> His unfaithfulness to her caused their divorce.

A good rule of thumb is to use *due to* only in expressions of time in infinitive constructions or in other contexts where the meaning is *scheduled.*

> The plane is *due to* arrive at five o'clock.

> He is *due to* receive a promotion this year.

Each and every Use one or the other but not both:

> Every cow came in at feeding time.

> Each bale has to be put in the barn loft.

Eager/Anxious *See* Anxious/Eager.

Gloss usage

Either . . . or/Neither . . . nor Always singular when followed by a singular noun or pronoun.

> *Neither* Kant *nor* Hegel enjoys much popularity today.
> When things get calm, *either* he *or* she starts a fight.

Either has an intensive use that *neither* does not, and when it is used as an intensive, *either* is always negative.

> She told him she wouldn't go *either.*

Eminent/Imminent/Immanent *Eminent* means "exalted," "celebrated," "well known." *Imminent* means "about to happen" or "about to come." *Immanent* refers to something invisible spread everywhere through the visible world.

> Many *eminent* Victorians were melancholy and disturbed.
> In August 1939 they sensed that war was *imminent.*
> Medieval Christians believed that God's power was *immanent* through the universe.

Enthused/Enthusiastic Most writers and editors prefer the word *enthusiastic.*

> The Secretary of the Interior was *enthusiastic* about the plans to build a high-rise condominium in Yosemite National Park.

Etc. This is a Latin abbreviation for *et cetera,* meaning "and others" or "and other things." Since the *and* is included in the abbreviation, you should not write "and etc." In a series, a comma comes before *etc.* just as it would come before the coordinating conjunction that closes the series.

Everyone/Every one *See* Anyone/Any one.

Except/Accept *See* Accept/Except.

Expect Avoid the use of *expect* as a synonym for *suppose* or *presume.*

> I *suppose* that he lost money on the horses.

Farther/Further *Farther* is used for geographical distances. *Further* means "in addition" when geography is not involved.

> Ten miles *farther* on is a hotel.
> He said *further* that he was annoyed with the play, the actors, and the stage.
> The Department of State hired a new public relations expert so that *further* disasters could be more carefully explained to the press.

Fewer/Less *See* Amount/Number.

Fewer is the adjective for groups or collections whose parts can be counted individually; *less* is used for things in bulk not commonly considered collections of individual entities.

> *Fewer* people were at commencement this year.
> Your argument has *less* substance than you think.

Flaunt/Flout *Flaunt* means to wave, to show publicly. It connotes a delight tinged with pride and even arrogance. *Flout* means to scorn or to defy, especially in a public way, seemingly without care for the consequences.

He *flaunted* his wealth by wearing overalls lined with mink.
He *flouted* the traffic laws by speeding, driving on the wrong side of the road, and running through a red light.

Former/Latter   These words can refer only to one of two persons or things — in sequence, named first, named last.

John saw *Star Wars* and *The Empire Strikes Back*. He liked the former better than the latter.

If you are speaking of three or more things, use *first* and *last*.

Guy's closest friends were Paul, Curtis, and Ricco. The first was Greek, the second was English, and the last was Italian.

Get   *Get* is one of the most flexible verbs in English. But in formal writing, you should avoid some of its more colloquial uses, as in *get with it, get it all together, get-up-and-go, get it, get me,* and *that gets me.*

Good/Well   *Good* is an adjective; *well* is an adverb except when it refers to good health, in which case it is an adjective. Avoid confusing them.

I felt *good* after the doctor told me that I looked *well*.
She did *well* on the exam.

Half/Half a/A half of   Write *half, a half,* or *half a,* but not *a half a* or *a half of* or *half of.*

Half the baseball players went out on strike.
Half a loaf is better than none unless you are on a diet.
I want *a half*-dozen eggs to throw at the candidate.

Hanged/Hung   People are *hanged* by the neck until dead. Pictures and all other things that can be suspended are *hung*.

Hopefully   Since the 1960s, *hopefully* has come into common use as an adverb modifying an entire sentence. Adverbs usually modify only verbs, adjectives, or other adverbs, although there are exceptions to this practice. Many careful writers and speakers object to *hopefully* as a modifier of an entire sentence because it does not tell who has the hope; it is usually uneconomical, and it may be confusing.

Hopefully Franklin will play poker tonight.

Will Franklin play poker with hope in his heart? Who has the hope, Franklin or the other players who hope to win his money? Or perhaps the hope is held by someone who yearns for Franklin to be out of the house this evening.

I *hope* Franklin is going to play poker tonight.
Franklin *hopes* to play poker tonight.
All his gambling friends *hope* that Franklin will play poker with them tonight.

If . . . then   Avoid the common redundancy that results when you use these words in tandem.

REDUNDANT: *If* I get my license, *then* I can drive a cab.
BETTER: If I get my license, I can drive a cab.
Once I get my license, I can drive a cab.

Gloss usage

Imply/Infer To *imply* means to suggest something without stating it directly; to *infer* means to draw a conclusion from evidence.

> By pouring hot coffee on his head, she *implied* that he should stop singing.
>
> When she dozed off in the middle of his declaration of love for her, he *inferred* that she was not going to marry him.

In/In to/Into *In* refers to a location inside something. *In to* refers to motion with a purpose. *Into* refers to movement from outside to inside or from separation to contact.

> Charles kept a snake *in* his room.
>
> The dorm supervisor came *in to* kill it.
>
> The snake escaped by crawling *into* the drain.
>
> The supervisor ran *into* the wall, and Charles got *into* trouble.

Incredible/Incredulous The *incredible* cannot be believed; the *incredulous* do not believe. Stories and events may be *incredible;* people are *incredulous.* Avoid using *incredible* and *incredibly* so loosely that your reader can tell that you were too lazy to think of a more precise and more vivid word.

> Our *incredible* journey began with a bomb threat and ended with a robbery.
>
> The audience was *incredulous* at his bizarre tale of why his shirt and trousers were torn.

Individual/Person Avoid the use of *individual* as a pompous synonym for *person*, and avoid using *individuals* when *people* will do. *Individual* as either a noun or an adjective should be used only to show a contrast between a person or a single entity and the group. Even then, *person* or one of its cognates may often be used.

> The Bill of Rights guarantees *individual* liberties.
>
> **OR:** The Bill of Rights guarantees *personal* liberties.
>
> The speech was directed to every *person* in the square.
>
> **BUT:** One of the oldest political questions is the relation between the *individual* and society.

Inside of/Outside of The *of* is unnecessary.

> He was *inside* the house watching the pro football game on television.
>
> She was *outside* the house mowing the lawn.

Irregardless This is a nonstandard form of *regardless.* The construction *irregardless* is a double negative, since both the prefix *ir-* and the suffix *-less* are negatives.

It's/Its *It's* is commonly the contraction for *it is;* sometimes it is a contraction for *it has.* *Its* is a possessive pronoun.

> *It's* clear that *its* paint is peeling.
>
> *It's* often been said that English spelling is difficult.

Kind/Kinds *Kind* is a singular form and must take singular verbs and modifiers.

Gloss usage

This kind of house *is* easy to build.

These kinds are better than those kinds.

Kind, sort, and *type* are often overused in writing. Try to do without them unless the classification they imply is necessary.

AWKWARD: She was a happy kind of person.

BETTER: She was a happy person.

Lie/Lay *Lie* means to recline; *lay* means to place. Part of the confusion in the way we use *lie* and *lay* comes because the principal parts of the verbs are confusing. Study the following sentences:

I am going to *lie* down to sleep.

He said he would *lay* the clothes carefully on the bed.

I often *lie* awake at night. [present]

He *lay* on his stomach for a long time and listened intently. [past]

He had *lain* there for an hour before he heard the horses. [past participle]

He will *lay* the bricks in a straight line. [present]

She *laid* her book on the steps and left it there. [past]

He had *laid* away money for years to prepare for his retirement. [past participle]

Literally *Literally* indicates that an expression often used in a figurative way is to be taken as true in this case.

Literally thousands of people gathered for the funeral.

The writer knows that *thousands* is sometimes used to mean merely "a great crowd." He wants people to know that if they counted the crowd at the funeral, they would number thousands.

Literally is often incorrectly used as an intensive adverb. Avoid this usage, which can sound misleading or even ridiculous.

He *literally* scared Grandpa to death.

His blood *literally* boiled.

Her eyes *literally* flashed fire.

Maybe/May be *Maybe* is an adverb, meaning "perhaps"; *may be* is a verb, meaning "is possible."

Maybe he can get a summer job selling dictionaries.

That *may be* a problem because he doesn't know how to use one.

Moral/Morale The noun *moral* means "lesson," especially a lesson about standards or one that is supposed to convey a general insight about life. It is most commonly used in the idiom *the moral of the story*.

The noun *morale* means "attitude" or "mental condition."

Morale dropped sharply among the students when they discovered that they would be penalized for misspelling words.

More important/More importantly The correct idiom is *more important,* not *more importantly.*

More important, if Jackson had not won the battle of New Orleans, the city might have remained in British hands.

Myself (Himself, Herself, etc.) All the pronouns ending with *-self* are best used as reflexives that intensify the stress on the noun or pronoun that serves as the antecedent.

"I cleaned the stables *myself,*" Hercules said.

Standing in the doorway was Count Dracula *himself* with a silver goblet in his hand.

We *ourselves* have often been guilty of the same fault.

In writing, avoid nonstandard usages like the following:

The quarrel was between him and *myself.*

John and *myself* shoed the horses.

These usages are correct:

The quarrel was between him and me.

John and I shoed the horses.

When you are unsure whether to use *I, me, she, her, he,* or *him* after a verb, you may be tempted to substitute one of the reflexive pronouns. Don't.

Nohow/Nowheres These words are nonstandard for *anyway, in no way, in any way, in any place,* and *in no place.* Don't use these words in writing.

Of/Have *See* Could of/Should of/Would of.

Off of Omit the *of.*

He knocked the hide *off* the ball.

She took the painting *off* the wall.

Parameter *Parameter* is a mathematical term used especially in computer science. It is often misused as a synonym for *perimeter,* or *limit,* especially in the plural:

The *parameters* of his biography of Theodore Roosevelt were set by Roosevelt's birth and death.

Parameter can be used correctly in speaking of computers:

The *parameters* were set to give the standard deviation from many distributions.

Parameter can sometimes be used correctly outside of mathematics to mean some constant whose value varies, allowing us to measure other variables by it:

Because religion is a *parameter* of human life in all times and places, its effects on the relation between family and society may readily be observed.

Plus Avoid using *plus* as a substitute for *and.*

NONSTANDARD: He had to walk the dog, wash the dishes, and take out the garbage, *plus* he had to write a book.

STANDARD: He had to walk the dog, wash the dishes, take out the garbage, and write his book.

Practicable/Practical *Practicable* is an adjective applied to things that can be done.

A tunnel under the English Channel is *practicable,* given today's machinery and engineering skills.

Practical means sensible.

> The English don't think such a tunnel is *practical.*

Previous to/Prior to Avoid these wordy and somewhat pompous substitutes for *before.*

Principal/Principle *Principal* is an adjective meaning first in importance or a noun referring to the highest office in an organization. *Principle* is a noun referring to a standard for life, thought, or morals, or else the underlying unity that joins distinct phenomena.

> The *principal* objection to our school's *principal* is that he had no *principles.*

Real/Really Avoid the use of *real* when you mean *very.*

> The cake was *very* good.

It is grammatically correct to use *really* for the adverb *very,* but *really* is overworked nowadays and should be given a rest, especially because it rarely adds anything worthwhile to a sentence. The overuse of *really* makes you sound insincere, as if you were trying to convince somebody of something without having any evidence at your command.

Reason is because This is a redundant expression.

> The reason he fell on the ice is *that* he cannot skate.

Relation/Relationship A short while ago *relationship* was most commonly used for *blood kin.* Now it has almost replaced *relation. Relationship* is called a *long variant* of *relation* by H. W. Fowler, a great authority on the English language. It says nothing that *relation* does not say, but often writers use it because it lets them imagine that they are saying much more than they are.

Respective The word is almost always unnecessary in constructions like the following, and you can usually leave it out.

> Charles and Robert brought in their *respective* assignments.

Set/Sit *Set* is usually a transitive verb, taking a direct object. Its principal parts are *set, set,* and *set.*

> DiMaggio *set* the standard of excellence in fielding.

It is occasionally intransitive.

> The concrete took a while to *set.*

Sit is always intransitive; it never takes a direct object except in the idiom *he sits his horse,* meaning that he sits *on* his horse — so some writers would argue that *horse* is not a true direct object. The principal parts of *sit* are *sit, sat,* and *sat.*

> The dog *sat* on command.

Shall/Will Not long ago, *shall* was the standard first-person future of the verb *to be* when a simple statement of fact was intended; *will* was the future for the second and third persons. But to say *I will, you shall, she shall,* or *they shall* implied a special determination to accomplish something.

I *shall* be forty-eight on my next birthday.

I *will* eat these cursed beets because they are good for me.

Now the distinction is blurred in the United States, although it is still observed in Britain. Most writers use *will* as the ordinary future tense for the first person.

We *will* come to New York next week.

Shall is still used in a few emphatic constructions in the second and third person.

They *shall* not pass.

You may take my life, but you *shall* not rob me of my dignity.

Some   Avoid the use of the adjective *some* in place of the adverb *somewhat*.

He felt *somewhat* better after a good night's sleep.

Somewheres   Don't use this nonstandard form for *somewhere*.

Sure   Avoid confusing the adjective *sure* with the adverb *surely*.

The hat she wore on the streetcar was *surely* bizarre.

Sure and/Sure to   *Sure and* is often used colloquially:

Be *sure and* get to the wedding on time.

In formal writing, *sure to* is preferred:

Be *sure to* get to the wedding on time.

That/Which   A few writers use *that* as a restrictive pronoun to introduce restrictive clauses and *which* to introduce nonrestrictive clauses.

The bull *that* escaped ran through my china shop, *which* was located on the square.

This distinction has never been so widely observed or respected that it can be considered a rule of grammar. The distinction offers no help for restrictive and nonrestrictive phrases or for *who* and *whom* clauses, which can be restrictive or nonrestrictive. The best rule is to set off the nonrestrictive elements with commas and to avoid setting off restrictive elements with commas.

Their/There/They're   *Their* is a possessive pronoun; *there* is an adverb of place; *they're* is a contraction of *they are*.

They gave *their* lives.

She was standing *there*.

They're reading more poetry than they once did.

This here/These here/That there/Them there   Avoid these nonstandard forms.

Try and/Try to   *Try to* is the preferred form.

Try to understand.

Use/Utilize   *Utilize* seldom says more than *use*, and simpler is almost always better.

We must learn how to *use* computers.

Gloss usage

Verbatim   Copying or reproducing word for word from a source.

Wait for/Wait on   People *wait on* tables or customers; they *wait for* those who are late.

> *Wait for* me.
> Steve *waited on* four tables at the diner.

Which/Who/Whose   *Which* is used for things, *who* and *whose* for people.

> The plane, *which* was late, brought the team home from California.
> My lost fountain pen was found by a man *who* had never seen one before, *whose* whole life had been spent with ballpoints.

But *whose* is increasingly being used for things in constructions where *of which* would be awkward.

> The cathedral, *whose* towers could be seen from miles away, seemed to shelter its city.

Some writers, however, would insist on this form:

> The cathedral, the towers of which could be seen from miles away, seemed to shelter its city.

GLOSSARY OF GRAMMATICAL TERMS

Grammar is the science of the English language; studying grammar helps us analyze and talk about everyday spoken and written communication. This handbook has not provided a comprehensive course in grammar but instead has offered a general introduction to the scientific study of our language (see Chapters 14–21). The terms and definitions below expand some of the concepts introduced earlier.

Absolute phrase　A phrase made up of a noun and a participle, extending the statement made by the sentence but not modifying any particular element in the sentence.

> The sun rose at six o'clock, *its red light throwing long shadows in the forest.*

When the participle is some form of the verb *to be,* it is often omitted.

> He flung the ball from center field, *his throw* [being] *like a bullet.*

Absolutes are common in modern English style; they allow compression of action and provide variety in sentences.

Abstract noun　A noun that does not call up a concrete memory involving sensual experience. Examples of abstract nouns are *relation, idea, thought, strength, matter, friendship, experience,* and *enmity.* An abstract noun refers to some quality *abstracted,* or drawn, from many different experiences, and it may be used to name many different kinds of experiences. In writing you should always be sure that abstract nouns do not dominate your prose. Abstract nouns require the help of concrete nouns if they are to make sense.

Acronym　A noun made of the initials of an organization and sometimes pronounceable as if it were a word. Common acronyms in recent history include FBI (Federal Bureau of Investigation), CREEP (Committee to Re-elect the President), SNCC (Students Nonviolent Co-ordinating Committee), and HEW (Department of Health, Education, and Welfare). The forms of acronyms usually do not change, but the possessive case and the plural are formed in the same way as those of other nouns.

> SNCC's first leader was Bob Moses.

Active voice　The voice of a verb used to report that the subject does something.

> The guitar player *sang* tenor.

The active voice always makes a stronger sentence than the passive voice.

Adjectival　Refers to any word or group of words (a phrase or a clause) that can be used as an adjective to modify a noun or pronoun. In the following examples, the adjectival words are in italics:

my book, *your* picture, *his* anger, *her* success
She painted the house *next door.*
The table *in the corner* belonged to me.
Writers *who write truly* always have readers.

Adjective Any word that modifies a noun or pronoun by describing some quality.

The *red* coat; the *blue* book

Adjectives can come before or after a noun:

The roof of the *old red* barn collapsed.
The barn — *old, weather-beaten,* and *abandoned* — finally collapsed in the last snow.

Adjectives can also come after a verb when they modify the subject. In this position they are *predicate adjectives.*

The barn was *red.*

Adjectives often have special forms in comparisons:

Her car is *big.*
Jack's car is *bigger.*
My car is the *biggest* of all, and I can't afford to drive it.
She bought an *expensive* meal at the Ritz.
She bought a *more expensive* meal at the Algonquin.
But she bought her *most expensive* meal at Tommy's Lunch, since it gave her food poisoning and put her in the hospital for a week.

Adjective clause A clause used to modify a noun or pronoun.

The car *that I drove then* appears in these old snapshots.

Adjective phrase A phrase such as a prepositional phrase that modifies a noun or pronoun.

He came to the end *of the road.*

Adverb A word used commonly to modify a verb, an adjective, or another adverb. Increasingly in modern English, adverbs are being used to modify whole sentences, though here the effect may be confusing. Adverbs tell us *when, where, why,* or *how.*

They left *yesterday.*
The sun was *insufferably* hot.
The *more frequently* used room deteriorated *more seriously.*
Happily, the car hit the wall before it could hit me.

Adverbial, adverbial clause, adverbial phrase A clause that acts as an adverb, usually modifying a verb in another clause but sometimes modifying an adjective or another adverb. Adverbial clauses often begin with words like *when, because, although, since, if, whether, after,* and *before.*

After he lost at Gettysburg, Lee knew he could not invade the North again.
We often think that women's fashions in the nineteenth century were dull *because we see them only in black-and-white photographs.*

An *adverbial* is a word sometimes used to describe a phrase or a clause that acts as an adverb. Sometimes nouns are pressed into service as adverbials.

Many Americans go to church *Sundays.*

We plan to go *home* for Thanksgiving.

Any phrase used as an adverb is an adverbial phrase. The most common adverbial phrase is the prepositional phrase.

You may find me *at home* this evening.

We groped around *in the dark.*

Agreement between pronouns and antecedents A matching in number and gender between pronouns and the nouns to which they refer.

Most *Americans* pay too little attention to *their* bodies.

Emma Bovary hated *her* dull life in *her* little town.

Flaubert created in her *his* greatest character.

Agreement between subjects and verbs A matching in number between subjects and verbs. A singular subject must take a singular verb; a plural subject must take a plural verb.

The *general* over all the armies *was* Eisenhower.

The *horses run* nearly every day at Suffolk Downs.

The greatest trouble in agreement between subjects and verbs usually comes in the third person singular, where *s* or *es* is added to the dictionary form of the verb.

She dances with grace and strength.

He yearns to return to the South.

The common contractions *don't* and *doesn't* give particular difficulty. Remember that *doesn't* is used in the third person singular in the present tense; *don't* is used in all other forms of the present tense:

It *doesn't* matter now.

They *don't* believe us.

She *doesn't* live here any more.

Appositive A noun or noun phrase that identifies another noun or pronoun, usually by naming it again in different words. Appositives usually come after the nouns they identify.

This is my brother *John.*

They loved Chinese food — *tofu, rice, and sweet-and-sour sauces.*

Clarence Penn, *the children's leader at the YMCA,* loved to lead hikes.

Notice that the appositives have the same relation to the rest of the sentence as the nouns they identify. You can leave out either the appositive or the noun identified by the appositive and have a grammatically complete sentence:

The children's leader at the YMCA loved to lead hikes.

Article The *indefinite articles* are *a* and *an;* the *definite* article is *the.* An article (sometimes called a *determiner*) sets off a noun or noun substitute in a sentence or phrase.

a broken toy

an unsettling thought

the treehouse

**Gloss
gram**

Auxiliary verb A verb used to help form the proper tense of another verb in a clause. Common auxiliary verbs are *am, is, are, was, be, been, were, have, has, had, shall, will, may, might, can, would, should, must,* and *ought.*

> He *had been* sleeping before the earthquake hit.
> Rock music *must* have some strange power over children.
> They *have* invited Norman to the party, but he *has* not yet accepted.
> She *should have been* studying but instead she *was* watching television.

Biased writing Writing that fosters stereotypes or that demeans, ignores, or patronizes people on the basis of gender, age, religion, country of origin, physical abilities, sexual preference, or any other human attribute.

Case An inflected form of a noun or pronoun that shows a grammatical relation to some other part of the sentence. English has only three cases: the *nominative* (or the subjective), the *possessive,* and the *objective.* Only pronouns change their form from the nominative in both the possessive and the objective case. Nouns commonly change their form only in the possessive.

To form the possessive of a singular noun, add *'s.* For nouns ending in *s,* some writers add only an apostrophe; others add *'s.*

> Erasmus/Erasmus', Dick/Dick's, Germany/Germany's

Some pronouns have different forms of all three cases.

Nominative	Possessive	Objective
I	my/mine	me
who	whose	whom
we	our/ours	them
they	their/theirs	them
he	his	him

Some pronouns have only two forms.

Nominative	Possessive	Objective
you	your	you
it	its	it
she	her/hers	her

Clause A group of words that includes a subject and a predicate. An independent clause may stand alone as a sentence; a dependent clause acts as a noun, an adjective, or an adverb for some element of another clause. Independent clauses are sometimes called *main clauses;* dependent clauses are sometimes called *subordinate clauses.*

> He thought his book was a failure *because it lost money.*

The independent clause (beginning with "He thought") can stand alone as a sentence; the dependent clause (in italics) acts as an adverb modifying the verb *was* in the independent clause.

Gloss gram

Clustering Tying together various related ideas; can be done by drawing a subject tree.

Collective noun A noun naming a group of people or things. In American English it is usually considered a grammatical singular.

The *team* was upset because of the penalty.

The *government* is the plaintiff in the case.

The *majority* is opposed to the measure.

Comma splice/Comma fault The misuse of a comma to join two independent clauses without the help of a coordinating conjunction. You can mend a comma splice by using a coordinating conjunction or by replacing the comma with a semicolon.

COMMA SPLICE: They gathered the wood, she built the fire.

REVISED: They gathered the wood; she built the fire.

They gathered the wood, and she built the fire.

Common noun A noun that is not specific enough to be capitalized within a sentence. Common nouns are words like *desk, typewriter, chair, aircraft, automobile, glue, cow,* and *football.*

Comparative degree See **Comparison.**

Comparison Adjectives and adverbs can make comparisons. They indicate degrees with different inflected forms.

The positive degree is the form that makes no comparison: *swift, quickly.*
The comparative degree compares no more than two things: a *swifter* boat, runs *more quickly.* Form the comparative degree by adding *-er* to the modifier or by using the word *more* before the uninflected form of the modifier.
The superlative degree compares three or more things: the *swiftest* boat, runs *most quickly.* Form the superlative degree by adding *-est* to the modifier or by using the word *most* before the uninflected form of the modifier. Exceptions exist, of course:

Positive	Comparative	Superlative
good	better	best
bad	worse	worst

Complement A word or group of words that extends the meaning of some other element in a clause.
A subjective complement usually follows the verb but adds something to the meaning of the subject. Subjective complements can be predicate nominatives or predicate adjectives:

PREDICATE NOMINATIVE: Her work was her *life.* [The noun *life* defines the subject, *work.*]

PREDICATE ADJECTIVE: Her work was *difficult.* [The adjective *difficult* modifies the subject, *work.*]

Both the predicate nominative and the predicate adjective are subjective complements.

Gloss gram

An objective complement follows immediately after the direct object of a verb or another object in the sentence and extends or provides the meaning of the object.

> I wrote a letter to my sister *Nancy.* [*Nancy* is the complement of the object of the preposition, *sister.*]
> The university named her *president* last week. [*President* is the complement of the direct object, *her.*]

Complete predicate The predicate, together with all the words that help make it a statement about the subject.

Complete subject The subject and the words that describe it.

Complex sentence A sentence with an independent clause and at least one dependent clause.

> If you want to write well, you must work hard.
> Because she worked hard, she received a promotion.
> Although he hates exercise, he ran six miles every morning.

Compound sentence A sentence with at least two independent clauses joined by a comma and a coordinating conjunction or by a semicolon or a colon.

> We faced strong opposition, but we won.
> She washed the clothes; he did the dishes.
> Their point was this: men and women should receive equal pay for equal work.

Compound subject Two or more subjects connected by a conjunction.

Compound-complex sentence A sentence that has at least two independent clauses and at least one dependent clause.

> The Russians declared war on Germany, and the Germans invaded Belgium because a Serbian killed an Austrian prince.

Conjugation A listing of the various forms of a verb to show tense, person, number, voice, and mood.

Conjunctions Words that join elements of sentences to one another. Coordinating conjunctions (*and, but, or, nor, for,* and sometimes *so* and *yet*) can join independent clauses. *And,* the most frequently used coordinating conjunction, can be used to join many different elements in a sentence, but all the elements joined by *and* must be grammatically equal. That is, you should not write a sentence like this one: "The house was large, old, and it had not been painted in years." Revise it: "The house was large, old, and weather-beaten."

Some conjunctions are called *subordinators* because they mark a dependent clause to come. Example: *although, after, because, when, before.* Some relative pronouns such as *that* and *which* act as conjunctions and introduce dependent clauses.

Some adverbs can act as conjunctions. These adverbs are words such as *however, nevertheless, moreover, indeed, in fact,* and *as a result.* These conjunctive adverbs are not strong enough to join two clauses without the help of a strong punctuation mark such as the semicolon, as in this sentence: "The sea voyage was long and difficult; however, Darwin seemed to enjoy it." Conjunctive adverbs may be used to begin a sentence to indicate a strong relation between that sentence and the one immediately before it.

Another way is not inevitable. Indeed, nothing in human life is inevitable except death.

Connotation The traditional collection of associations that surround the use of a word. If I say, "I *demand* an answer," the connotation is much less friendly than if I say, "I *request* an answer." If I say, "The orchestra *slogged through* Beethoven's Third Symphony," the impression is much less flattering to the orchestra than if I say, "The orchestra *marched* through Beethoven's Third."

Contraction A combination of two words with the help of an apostrophe. Contractions include forms such as *doesn't* for *does not, can't* for *cannot,* and *won't* for *will not.* Contractions are common in informal speech and writing; they are generally not used in formal writing. You may find contractions in a magazine article; you will probably not find them in a textbook.

Coordinating conjunction See **Conjunctions.**

Coordination A grammatical structure that joins sentence elements so that they are of equal importance.

They flew, but we drove.

The bird tumbled from its perch and did a flip.

Correlative conjunctions Conjunctions, used in pairs, that connect sentence elements of equal value. Examples: *both . . . and, either . . . or, neither . . . nor, not only . . . but also.*

Dangling modifier An adjectival element, often at the beginning of a sentence, which does not correctly modify the grammatical subject.

DANGLING MODIFIER: *Crushed by the debt on her credit cards,* it was difficult for her to understand that she was making $40,000 a year and was still broke.

REVISED: Crushed by the debt on her credit cards, she could hardly understand that she was making $40,000 a year and that she was still broke.

Declarative sentence A sentence that makes a statement. Some writers define a *declarative sentence* as a sentence that begins with the subject followed by a verb without any intervening phrases or clauses.

Declension A table of all the forms of a noun or pronoun, showing the various cases. In English, a declension includes the forms of the nominative, the possessive, and the objective in the singular and the plural.

Degree See **Comparison.**

Demonstrative adjective An adjective like *these, those, this,* or *that* which points out a noun or noun substitute.

**gloss
gram**

Demonstrative pronoun See **Pronoun.**

Denotation Primary meaning(s) of a word; the strict dictionary definition.

Dependent clause See **Clause.**

Determiner See **Article.**

Diagramming A pictorial method of showing relationships among various grammatical parts of a sentence.

Direct and indirect quotation In a *direct quotation,* the exact words of a source are given within quotation marks.

> The chair of the board said today, "I will not permit that no-good turkey of a president to dictate to this corporation."

In an *indirect quotation,* the sense of what has been said is given in a paraphrase; the exact words of the source are not used.

> The chair of the board declared that he would not allow the president to tell the corporation what to do.

Direct object See **Object.**

Discourse community A group with certain interests, knowledge, and expectations and with certain conventional ways of communicating with one another, such as baseball fans or biologists.

Double negative A substandard construction that makes a negative statement by using two negative forms. A double negative can be a single word such as the nonstandard *irregardless:* a word that has a negative form, *ir-,* at the beginning and another negative form, *-less,* at the end. A double negative is more commonly two negative words, as in this sentence: "I *don't* have *no* reason to go there." To correct the sentence, remove one of the negatives: "I *don't* have a reason to go there," or "I have *no* reason to go there." A common double negative is the phrase *can't hardly,* as in the sentence "I *can't hardly* do that assignment." The sentence should read, "I *can hardly* do that assignment."

Ellipsis An omission from within a direct quotation, marked off by three dots made with the period on the typewriter. You should mark an ellipsis by making a space after the last word you quote; setting a period after the space; making another space, another period, another space, a third period, and another space; and then typing the first word of the quotation beyond the omitted material.

A sentence from David McCullough's *Mornings on Horseback:*

> He must bide his time, maintain perfect decorum and silence, and so passive a role did not sit at all well with him.

The sentence quoted with an ellipsis:

> "He must bide his time, . . . and so passive a role did not sit at all well with him," McCullough said.

Notice that the comma after *time* is included before the ellipsis marks.

Elliptical elements Phrases or clauses that we understand although some words have been left out.

[what is] *More important,* we learned to write well.
They are older *than she* [is old].
We enjoyed France more than [we enjoyed] *Switzerland.*

Expletive The use of *there, here,* or *it* followed by a form of *to be.*
We saw that *there were* feathers beneath the fence.
"*Here are* footsteps in the mud!" she exclaimed.
It was only Lucinda the cat who had torn a pillow to shreds.
When *it* is used as an expletive, this pronoun is the grammatical subject of a clause, the *it* having no antecedent.
It is said that his grandfather did time in prison.
It was all a mystery, and we were baffled.

Expository writing Writing that presents, develops, and discusses ideas, rather than telling a story or describing how things look.

Finite verb A verb with a tense that reports action done in the past, present, or future. A subject must control a finite verb to make a clause. Nonfinite verbs are verbal forms without time in themselves, forms like *infinitives, participles,* and *gerunds.*

Fragment See **Sentence fragment.**

Free modifier A modifier, usually in the form of the present or past participle, serving as an adjective modifying the subject but appearing after the verb. Free modifiers may be multiplied almost infinitely without confusing the sentence:

> Hank Williams began his country music career as a young boy in Alabama, *playing* nightclubs called blood buckets, *writing* songs in cars between engagements, *drinking* too much whiskey, *making* his way painfully to the Grand Ole Opry and national fame.

Freewriting Writing nonstop for a stated time period, without any attention to coherence or organization.

Fused sentence See **Run-on sentence.**

Future perfect tense See **Tense.**

Future tense See **Tense.**

Gender Nouns and pronouns can have a masculine, feminine, or neuter *gender,* the name given to sexual reference in grammar. Many writers now make a special effort to use nouns that do not specify gender when both males and females may be included in the name: *police officer* rather than *policeman, chair* or *chairperson* rather than *chairman, flight attendant* rather than *stewardess.*

Genitive case Another name for possessive case. (See **Case.**)

Gerund A verbal (a nonfinite verb) in the form of the present participle (with the ending *-ing*). It is used as a noun.
Bicycling is my favorite exercise.

Helping verb See **Auxiliary verb.**

Gloss gram

Idiom A word or expression that conveys a meaning established by custom and usage rather than by the literal definition. According to American English idiom, *making out* with someone is different from *making up* with that person. If you say you are *burned out* at your job, you are saying something different from what you mean if you say you are *burned up* at your boss.

Imperative mood See **Mood.**

Indefinite pronoun A pronoun (such as *anybody* or *everybody*) that does not require an antecedent noun or pronoun, although it may refer to a noun or pronoun that comes after it in a sentence or a paragraph. (See **Pronoun.**)

Independent clause See **Clause.**

Indicative mood See **Mood.**

Indirect object A noun or pronoun placed before a direct object and used to show for whom or to whom the action is conveyed by the verb.

Indirect quotation See **Direct and indirect quotation.**

Infinitive A verbal (nonfinite verb) in the form of the simple present and usually marked by the infinitive marker *to.* Infinitives can be used as nouns or adjectives or adverbs.
> NOUN: *To die* may not be the worst thing one can do.
> ADJECTIVE: She believed she had many books *to write.*
> ADVERB: Most Americans are willing *to work.*

**gloss
gram**

Inflections The changes in nouns, pronouns, verbs, adjectives, and adverbs that make these words serve various functions in sentences. The inflections of nouns and pronouns are called *declensions,* the inflections of verbs are called *conjugations,* and the inflections of adverbs and adjectives are called *comparisons.* (See **Declension; Conjugation; Comparison.**)

Intensifiers Adjectives and adverbs that can be used to add emphasis to the words they modify. Some common intensifiers are *very, really, absolutely, definitely,* and *too.* Intensifiers are often unnecessary.

Intensive pronoun See **Pronoun.**

Interjection A part of speech used to express sudden or strong feeling.
> *Ouch!* That hurts!
> *Hey!* You can't do that to me!

Interrogative pronoun See **Pronoun.**

Intransitive verb A verb that reports an act or a state of being and does not take a direct object.
Intransitive verbs that join a subject with a subject complement are called *linking verbs.*
> Jack *ran* all the way home.

He *was* sick all that week.

She *had been* an architect in Missouri.

Inverted object   A direct object that comes before the subject in a sentence, used only occasionally for sentence variety.

Whiskey he drank by the barrel.

Inverted sentence   A sentence in which the subject comes after the verb. The most common inverted sentences begin with the adverb *there:*

There is something in what you say.

Ding, ding, ding went the bell.

Far, far away sounded the trumpets against the hills.

Irregular verb   A verb whose simple past and past participle are not formed with the addition of the suffix *-ed.* Irregular verbs are verbs such as *come/came/come; think/thought/thought;* and *sit/sat/sat.*

Linking verb   A verb that joins a subject to its complement. The most common linking verbs are forms of the verb *to be,* but all the verbs of sense are also linking verbs, so you should follow them with an adjective form:

I felt bad because he disliked my play.

The spring rain smelled good.

Main clause   See **Clause.**

Misplaced modifier   A modifier that is misplaced in the sentence so that it modifies the wrong thing.

Mrs. Hotchkiss, who loved Indian customs, served the Thanksgiving turkey in a sari and sandals.

Modifier   Any word or group of words used as an adjective or adverb to qualify another word or group of words. The *red* truck is set off from trucks that are not red, and the horse *in the field* is set off from horses not in the field.

Mood   The form of a verb that shows whether the writer or speaker thinks the action reported is true, false, or desirable.

The *indicative mood* reports actions that the writer assumes to be true:

Cat books now *crowd* the best-seller list.

The *subjunctive mood* reports actions that the writer assumes are untrue or at least uncertain:

If I *were* rich, I would do nothing but farm.

The subjunctive mood can report actions or states that may not be true but that the writer thinks are desirable:

Let justice roll down like waters and righteousness as a mighty stream.

The *imperative mood* expresses a command or a request for an action that the writer or speaker thinks is desirable.

Get out of here!

Bring the books with you when you come.

Nominative case   See **Case.**

Nonrestrictive modifier   A clause or phrase that adds to the description of

Gloss gram

the word it modifies without being essential to the core assertion of the sentence. Nonrestrictive modifiers are usually set off by commas from the word they modify.

Faulkner, *who never finished college,* became one of America's greatest writers.

He ran toward the sound of the train, *stumbling in the tall grass, laughing, longing to see the locomotive and the engineer.*

The DC-3, *one of the most durable aircraft ever built,* still flies the skies in some parts of the world.

Noun Nouns are names of persons, places, things, ideas, actions. Any word can be a noun if in a given context it can be a name. A sure test for a noun is whether it can have one of the articles — *a, an,* or *the* — placed before it. The plurals of nouns are usually formed with the additions of *-s* or *-es,* but there are exceptions: sheep/*sheep,* child/*children,* and man/*men.*

Common nouns name things according to a general class: *desk, street, tractor, welder. Proper nouns* name specific people, places, or things and are spelled with initial capital letters: *Italy, the Department of Agriculture, Abraham Lincoln. Abstract nouns* name entities that lack any specific associations with sense experience: *friendship, ambition, relationship, haste, details. Concrete nouns* name entities that we may recall from our own sense experience: *wood, house, computer, cigar, highway, truck stop, bulldozer. Collective nouns* name groups: *team, crew, church, synagogue, audience, department.*

The categories of nouns may overlap. The collective noun *community* is also an abstract noun, since the idea of community is abstracted from our observations of people acting together. *George Washington* is a proper noun, since the name refers to a specific person and is capitalized; but it is also a concrete noun, since the man George Washington was a person whom we can identify by his picture and by works that have been written about him.

Gloss gram

Noun clause A dependent clause used as a noun.

They told me *where we would meet in Athens.*

Number The form of a noun, verb, pronoun, or demonstrative adjective that indicates singular or plural.

Object A noun or noun substitute that receives the action reported by a verb, a preposition, or a verbal. (Verbals are infinitives, participles, and gerunds.) Objects usually come after the element that conveys action to them. A direct object receives the action of a verb (or a verbal) and generally follows the verb in a sentence.

Politicians must raise *money* to be elected. [direct object]

An indirect object is a noun or pronoun placed before a direct object and used to show for whom or to whom the action is conveyed by the verb.

He promised *me* a hot cup of coffee. [indirect object]

Infinitives and verbals may take objects too.

We hoped to give her the *victory.* [object of an infinitive]

Pushing *the couch*, she injured her back. [object of a verbal]
Prepositions always take objects.

They swam across the *river* together. [object of a preposition]

Object complement A word or group of words appearing after an object in a sentence and further defining that object.

He named his son *John*.

They called the storm a *hurricane*.

Objective case Properly speaking, we say that any noun or noun substitute is in the objective case when it is a direct object, an indirect object, or the object of a preposition or verbal. (See **Case**.)

Ordinal numbers Numbers such as *first*, *second*, and *third*, distinguished from the cardinal numbers — *one, two, three*, etc.

Parenthetical element An element not essential to the main assertion of the sentence. If a parenthetical element represents a large interruption of the flow of a sentence, that element is usually placed within parentheses or dashes. Nonrestrictive modifiers are sometimes called parenthetical, since their removal does not make the main assertion of the sentence unintelligible. Some words and expressions such as *incidentally* and *to be sure* are also considered parenthetical.

Herbert Hoover detested Franklin Roosevelt (Hoover would scarcely speak to him during Roosevelt's inaugural in 1932) and went on denouncing the New Deal for years.

He disliked the country — its loneliness appalled him — and he refused to visit it, even to ski or picnic or hike.

Participial phrase See **Phrase**.

Participle See **Past participle** and **Present participle**.

Parts of speech The names given to words to describe the role they play in communication. The eight parts of speech are noun, pronoun, verb, adjective, adverb, preposition, conjunction, and interjection.

Passive voice The form of a verb phrase that causes the subject of a clause to be acted upon. The passive is always made with some form of the verb *to be* and a past participle. (See **Active voice; Voice**.)

Lincoln *was elected* President in 1860.

The houses on the hill *were* all *built* alike.

Past participle The third principal part of a verb, the form of a verb used with the auxiliaries *have* and *had*. It usually ends in *-ed*, but irregular verbs have different endings. The past participle finds common use as an adjective:

The hymn, *sung* by the mighty choir, rolled out into the night.

Their *worn* faces showed the futility of their effort.

The past participle, used with some form of the verb *to be*, is necessary to the passive voice:

Jefferson Davis *was captured* while trying to escape to South America.

Gloss gram

Person   The form of a pronoun that tells whether someone or something speaks (I, me, we, our), is spoken to (you, your), or is spoken about (he, she, it, their, them). Verbs also change to show person in some tenses, especially in the third person singular.

First person: *I cry* (or *we cry*) at sad movies.
Second person: *You cry* at sad movies.
Third person: *He cries* (or *they cry*) at sad movies.

Personal pronoun   A pronoun that refers to a person, such as *I, you, he, she, who, whom,* or *they*. (See **Pronoun**.)

Phrase   A group of related words. It has neither subject nor predicate, and it serves as a part of speech in a sentence.

VERB PHRASE: We *are toiling* in the vineyard.
PREPOSITIONAL PHRASE: We must work *until sunset.*
PARTICIPIAL PHRASE: *Leaping the fence,* the horse carried me swiftly to safety in the woods.
INFINITIVE PHRASE: Lyndon Johnson yearned *to be somebody important.*
GERUND PHRASE: *Walking the dog* was his only exercise. [noun]
ABSOLUTE PHRASE: The car crashed through the house, *the front wheels coming to rest on the living room sofa.*

Positive degree   See **Comparison**.

Possessive case   The form of a noun or pronoun that indicates possession or a special relation. Some pronouns can only indicate possession — *my, mine, our, ours, your, yours, their.* The possessive of nouns (singular or plural) and some pronouns is formed by an apostrophe (') and an *-s* added at the end — *anybody's, everyone's, Getrude's, Hubert's, women's* bank, *children's* toys. The possessive of nouns ending in *-s* (singular or plural) is generally formed by the addition of an apostrophe alone — *James', Erasumus',* the *class'* responsibility, the *states'* governors. Some writers prefer to add *'s* even to those nouns that end in *-s* in the singular — *James's, Erasmus's.* (See **Case**.)

Predicate   Everything in a clause or sentence besides the subject and its immediate adjectives. The predicate declares something about the subject. The *complete predicate* includes everything in the sentence but the subject cluster; the *simple predicate* includes only the verb or verb phrase. In this example *the complete predicate, including the simple predicate, is in italics.*

The art of the late twentieth century *has departed from all the rules that supposedly guided both painting and sculpture for centuries.*

Predicate adjective   An adjective that comes after a verb and modifies the subject. (See **Complement**.)

She was *dignified.*

Predicate noun   A noun that comes after the verb and helps to identify the subject of the sentence. (See **Complement**.)

Ms. Smythe was an *architect.*

Prefix A letter or a group of letters, often derived from Latin or Greek, added to the beginning of a word to form another word. Common prefixes are *dis, ir-, un-,* and *a-,* implying some kind of negation, as in *disbelief, irreplaceable, unreliable,* and *asymmetrical; ad-* means something added or joined to something else, as in *admixture.*

Preposition A word that does not change its form and that, by joining with a noun object, brings the noun into the sentence to act as an adjective or adverb. Common prepositions are *about, above, across, after, against, outside, toward,* and *within.* A preposition and its object, the noun (or noun substitute), make a prepositional phrase, and the prepositional phrase almost always serves as an adjective or an adverb in the sentence where it is found.

Prepositional phrase See **Phrase.**

Present participle The form of a verb that ends with *-ing.* With the aid of auxiliary verbs, the present participle forms the progressive of the various verb tenses. Standing by itself, the present participle can be an adjective or an adverb.

 ADJECTIVES: *Staggering* and *shouting,* he protested his innocence.
 ADVERB: They went *singing* through the streets at Christmas.

Present perfect tense See **Tense.**

Present stem The present stem of every English verb except *to be* is the form used with the personal pronoun *I* in the present tense (I *go,* I *stop*). It is also the form of the infinitive (*to go, to stop*). The simple past of a regular verb is formed by the addition of *-ed* or *-d* to the present stem, and the present participle is formed by *-ing* added to the present stem. If the present stem ends in *-e,* that letter is almost always dropped before *-ing* is added. Dictionaries list words in alphabetical order according to the spelling of the present stem; so the present stem is sometimes called the *dictionary form* of the verb.

Gloss gram

Present tense See **Tense.**

Prewriting The first step in the writing process: preparation for writing. Thinking about your subject, learning about your topic, jotting down ideas, asking the journalist's questions, freewriting, clustering, and researching.

Principal parts of a verb The present stem, the simple past, and the past participle of a verb. The various tenses of verbs are formed from their principal parts. (See **Tense.**)

 Present stem: smile, do
 Simple past: smiled, did
 Past participle: smiled, done

Progressive tense See **Tense.**

Pronoun A word used in place of a noun. Many pronouns have an antecedent that comes before them either in the sentence where they are found or in an earlier sentence. But some pronouns such as *I, you, we, anybody*, and *everyone* may lack a formal antecedent, and sometimes the noun to which a pronoun refers may follow the pronoun in the text. Pronouns are generally classified in the following ways:

> PERSONAL: I, you, we, they, he, she, our
> RELATIVE: who, whom, which, that
> INTERROGATIVE: who? which? what?
> DEMONSTRATIVE: this, that, these, those
> INDEFINITE: anybody, anyone, everyone, everybody
> RECIPROCAL: each other, one another
> REFLEXIVE: myself, yourself, oneself
> INTENSIVE: myself, yourself, oneself

The difference between reflexive and intensive pronouns depends on how they are used in a sentence. Their forms are the same. If the subject is in the same person as the pronoun and acts on it, the pronoun is reflexive, as in the sentence *I did all the damage to myself.* But if the pronoun serves to make a statement much more emphatic than it would be without the pronoun, we say that it is intensive, as in this sentence: *I said it myself.*

Proper noun See **Noun.**

Reciprocal pronoun See **Pronoun.**

Reflexive pronoun See **Pronoun.**

Regular verb A verb whose simple past and past participle are both formed by the addition of -*ed* to the present stem: *play/played/played.* (See **Irregular verb.**)

Relative pronoun See **Pronoun.**

Restrictive element A modifying element that defines or restricts the element it modifies, so that its removal from a sentence would confuse the sense of the main assertion.

> The bicycle *that I rode to the coast* had eighteen speeds.
> The man *in the gray suit and white hat* held the gun.
> The woman *who spoke* allayed the fears of the crowd.

Rhetorical question A question asked so that the writer or speaker may provide an answer or may demonstrate to the audience that the answer is obvious. The rhetorical question is often a convenient device for getting into a subject or for shifting emphasis within an essay. It should not be overused.

> How long are we going to let a government of the people be the chief destroyer of the people's land?
> How can we explain the seeming shift between Thomas More's early humanism and his later fury toward the Protestants?

Run-on sentence Two independent clauses run together with no punctuation to separate them.

> Scientists, grammarians, and artists are all alike in one respect they depend on the work of others like themselves.

I rose to applaud the mayor's speech then I tripped over the woman's handbag.

Sentence A statement, question, or command made by a grammatical union between a subject and a predicate. The subject must be a noun or noun substitute, and the predicate must include a finite verb. The subject controls the verb, and the subject and the verb must agree with each other in number. In a sentence that is not a command, the predicate makes a statement about the subject. In a question, the statement is made in the form of an inquiry that asks to know if the statement is true.

The personal computer *will soon become as common in the American home as the sofa in the living room.*

Will the personal computer *soon become as common in the American home as the sofa in the living room?*

Sentence fragment A group of words that begins with a capital letter and ends with a closing mark of punctuation, but does not include a subject in grammatical union with a predicate. Correct a sentence fragment by giving it a subject or predicate (or both, when necessary) or by adding it to the sentence that comes directly before or after it.

The telephone dropped. *Onto the floor.*

Working at her desk. She suffered terribly.

Dr. Leyton introduced the visiting surgeon. *Who spoke formally without looking up from her notes.*

The telephone dropped. It fell to the floor.

Working at her desk, she suffered terribly.

Dr. Leyton introduced the visiting surgeon, who spoke formally without looking up from her notes.

Gloss gram

Simple predicate The word (or words) that reports or states a condition, with all the describing words removed; the verb.

Simple sentence A sentence with only one clause. Some simple sentences are not very simple.

Catherine arrived in England in 1501 and immediately encountered the English hatred of foreigners, a hatred shown in the scorn heaped on her retainers; in the bitter stinginess of her royal father-in-law, Henry VII; and in the indifference of those around her to her comfort and even to her dignity.

Simple subject The word(s) that serve as the focus of the sentence.

Subject The noun or noun substitute about which the predicate of a clause or sentence makes its statement. The *simple subject* is the noun or noun substitute; the *complete subject,* or the *subject cluster,* includes all the immediate modifiers of the subject.

The absurd and angry group that assembled in a beer hall in Munich that night in 1923 was to create, a decade later, the most bloody revolution in German history.

Subject complement See **Complement.**

Subjective case See **Case.**

Subjunctive mood The mood of the verb that indicates the writer's doubts about the truth of the statement made in the sentence.

> If we *were* in Athens now, we could see the sun shining on the Acropolis.
>
> I fear lest we *be* too optimistic about the outcome.

Subordinate clause See **Clause.**

Subordinating conjunction See **Conjunction.**

Subordination The act of placing some elements in sentences in a dependent relation with others so that readers will know what is important and what is not. So-called choppy sentences are usually sentences without adequate subordination.

> The hunters walked for miles.
> They did not know where they were going.
> They had never been in the woods before.
>
> Although the hunters walked for miles, they did not know where they were going, since they had never been in these woods before.

Suffix An ending that changes the meaning of the word to which it is attached. The suffixes in the following words are in italics:

> care/care*less,* delight/delight*ful,* boy/boy*ish,* visual/visual*ize*

Superlative degree See **Comparison.**

Syntax The part of grammar that considers the relations between sentences and between parts of sentences. In English syntax, the subject usually comes before the verb; prepositional phrases include a preposition and a noun or noun substitute that acts as the object of the preposition; and clauses serve as nouns, adjectives, or adverbs.

Tense The form of a verb that indicates time, whether present, past, or future. The *simple tenses* include the present, the past, and the future.

> PRESENT: I *speak,* she *laughs*
> PAST: I *spoke,* she *laughed*
> FUTURE: I *shall* (or *will*) *speak,* she *will laugh*

The *perfect tenses* indicate time previous to the simple tenses. Perfected tenses are formed with the past participle and an auxiliary verb, *have* or *had.*

> PRESENT PERFECT: I *have spoken,* she *has spoken*
> PAST PERFECT: I *had spoken,* she *had spoken*
> FUTURE PERFECT: I *shall have spoken,* she *will have spoken*

The *progressive tense* indicates continuing action. It is formed with the present participle and a form of the verb *to be* as auxiliary.

> I *am speaking.*
> She *was speaking.*
> They *had been speaking.*

Tone   The writer's attitude toward the subject—how the writer feels about characters and their actions, and how the writer makes the reader feel about them; the writer's perspective or point of view.

Transitive verb   A verb that conveys action from a subject to a direct object. (See **Verb.**)

>   He *walked* his dog late last night.
>   She *bought* a new tennis racket.

Verb   A word that reports an action or a condition; a word that makes an assertion. *Main verbs* combine with *auxiliary verbs* to form the various tenses. *Intransitive verbs* report that the subject acts or exists in a certain condition; these verbs do not take a direct object. *Transitive verbs* carry action from the subject to an object. A verb can be transitive or intransitive, depending on its use in the sentence. *Linking verbs* join a subject with a complement, either a noun or an adjective. (See **linking verb.**)

>   Jackson *smoked*. [intransitive]
>   Jackson *smoked* a pipe. [transitive; *pipe* is a direct object]

Verbal   A nonfinite form of a verb, that is, a form that does not express tense. Verbals are gerunds, participles, and infinitives. A verbal cannot make an assertion about a subject by itself. (See **Gerund; Infinitive; Past participle.**)

Verb complement   A direct or indirect object. (See **Object.**)

Verb phrase   A main verb and its helpers, or auxiliary verbs. A verb phrase gives a complete statement of tense.

>   I *am helping* with the project.
>   He *had been seen* in the vicinity.

Voice   The active or passive form of a verb. In the active voice, the subject acts through the verb; in the passive, the verb asserts that some action is done to the subject.

>   ACTIVE VOICE: Dwight Evans *hit* the ball out of the park.
>   PASSIVE VOICE: A ball *was hit* out of the park by Dwight Evans.

Word order   Most English sentences begin with the subject, or with an adverb or adverbial. The subject usually comes before the verb. The direct object usually comes after the verb. An indirect object always comes between the verb and the direct object. Most adjectives come immediately before or after the noun or noun substitute they modify. Predicate adjectives modify the subject of a clause but come after the verb. Adverbs may be separated from the word or phrase they modify.

Writing process   The various steps a writer takes from the moment he or she decides to write something until the moment the final draft is finished: thinking about a topic, gathering notes, making outlines, deciding on an introduction and conclusion, and preparing drafts and a final version.

**Gloss
gram**

INDEX

Numbers and letters in **boldface** refer to sections of the handbook (**A** and **B** refer to Appendix A and Appendix B, respectively; **GU** refers to the Glossary of Usage, and **GT** refers to the Glossary of Grammatical Terms).

CREDITS AND ACKNOWLEDGMENTS

Adler, Mortimer J., and Van Doren, Charles. Excerpt from *How to Read a Book*. Copyright © 1940, 1967 by Mortimer J. Adler. Copyright © 1972 by Mortimer J. Adler and Charles Van Doren. Reprinted by permission of Simon & Schuster, Inc.

American Heritage Dictionary, Second College Edition. Entries for "compare" and "include." Copyright © 1985 by Houghton Mifflin Company. Reprinted by permission.

Ardrey, Robert. Excerpts reprinted with permission of Atheneum Publishers, an imprint of Macmillan Publishing Company, from *The Territorial Imperative* by Robert Ardrey. Copyright © 1966 Robert Ardrey.

Baldwin, James. Excerpts from *Notes of a Native Son*. Reprinted by permission of the publishers, Beacon Press.

Baraka, Amiri. Excerpts from "City of Harlem" from *Home: Social Essays* by Amiri Baraka. Copyright © 1962, 1966 by the author. By permission of William Morrow & Co.

Bartoshuk, Linda. Excerpt from "Separate Worlds of Taste," *Psychology Today*, September 1980. Reprinted with permission from *Psychology Today*. Magazine. Copyright 1980 (APA).

Bate, Walter Jackson. Excerpt from *Samuel Johnson*, copyright © 1977, 1975 by Walter Jackson Bate, reprinted by permission of Harcourt Brace Jovanovich, Inc.

Bereiter, Carl. Excerpt from "Genetics and Educability: Education Implications of the Jensen Debate" reprinted with permission from *Disadvantaged Child, Compensatory Education: A National Debate*. Vol. 3, edited by Jerome Helmuth, Brunner-Mazel, publisher.

Bird, Caroline. Excerpt from *The Crowding Syndrome: Learning to Live with Too Much and Too Many*, David McKay, publisher. Copyright © 1972. Reprinted by permission of the author.

645

Gallo, Robert C. Excerpt from "The AIDS Virus," *Scientific American,* January 1987. Reprinted by permission of Dr. Robert C. Gallo, National Cancer Institute, Department of Health and Human Services.

Gerber, Philip. Excerpt from *Willa Cather* by Philip Gerber. Copyright 1975 and reprinted with the permission of Twayne Publishers, a division of G. K. Hall & Co., Boston.

Haley, Alex. Excerpt from *Roots.* Reprinted by permission of Doubleday & Company, Inc.

Horney, Karen. Excerpt reprinted from *The Neurotic Personality of Our Time* by Karen Horney, M. D., by permission of W. W. Norton & Company, Inc. Copyright 1937 by W. W. Norton & Company, Inc. Copyright renewed 1964 by Renate Mintz, Brigite Swarzenski, and Marianne von Eckardt.

Horton, Paul B. and Hunt, Chester C. Excerpt from *Sociology* by Paul B. Horton and Chester C. Hunt. Reprinted by permission of McGraw-Hill, Inc.

Horwitz, James. Excerpt from *They Went Thataway* by James Horwitz. Copyright © 1976 by James Horwitz. Reprinted by permission of Viking Penguin, a division of Penguin Books USA Inc.

Hughes, Langston. Excerpt from "Salvation" from *The Big Sea* by Langston Hughes. Copyright © 1940 by Langston Hughes. Renewal copyright © 1968 by Arna Bontemps and George Houston Bass. Reprinted by permission of Hill and Wang, a division of Farrar, Straus and Giroux, Inc.

Jolly, Alison. Excerpt from "Madagascar: A World Apart," *National Geographic,* February 1987. Copyright National Geographic Society, 1975, 1981.

Jong, Erica. Excerpt from *Fear of Flying* by Erica Jong. Copyright © 1973 by Erica Jong. Reprinted by permission of Henry Holt and Company, Inc.

Kidder, Tracy. Excerpt from *The Soul of a New Machine* by Tracy Kidder. Copyright © 1982 by John Tracy Kidder. By permission of Little, Brown and Company.

King, Martin Luther, Jr. Excerpt from "Letter from Birmingham Jail," from *Why We Can't Wait.* Copyright © 1963, 1964 by Martin Luther King, Jr. Reprinted by permission of Joan Daves.

Kingston, Maxine Hong. Excerpt from *The Woman Warrior: Memoirs of a Girlhood among Ghosts.* Reprinted by permission of Alfred A. Knopf, Inc.

Kohler, Dayton. Excerpt from "Willa Cather: 1876–1947," *College English.* Copyright © 1947 by the National Council of Teachers of English. Reprinted by permission of the publisher.

Kouts, Catherine. Excerpt from "Wilderness PinUps by Sierra Club," reprinted from the April 27, 1984 issue of *Publishers Weekly,* published by R. R. Bowker Company, A Xerox company. Copyright © 1984 by Xerox Corporation.